Empire City

*The Making and Meaning
of the New York City Landscape*

In the series

CRITICAL PERSPECTIVES ON THE PAST

edited by Susan Porter Benson, Stephen Brier, and Roy Rosenzweig

Empire City

The Making and Meaning of the New York City Landscape

David M. Scobey

TEMPLE UNIVERSITY PRESS

PHILADELPHIA

Temple University Press, Philadelphia 19122
Copyright © 2002 by Temple University
All rights reserved
Published 2002
Printed in the United States of America

♾ The paper used in this publication meets the requirements of the
American National Standard for Information Sciences—Permanence
of Paper for Printed Library Materials, ANSI Z39.48-1984

The publication of this book has been generously supported with an
illustration subvention from the Office of the Vice-President for Research,
University of Michigan.

Library of Congress Cataloging-in-Publication Data

Scobey, David M., 1954–
    Empire city : the making and meaning of the New York City landscape /
David M. Scobey.
        p. cm. — (Critical perspectives on the past)
    Includes bibliographical references and index.
    ISBN 1-56639-950-5 (cloth : alk. paper)
        1. City planning—New York (State)—New York.   2. New York (N.Y.)—
History—19th century.   I. Title.   II. Series.
    HT168.N5 S35 2002
    307.1'216'097471—dc21   2001054247

ISBN 13: 978-1-59213-235-5 (paper : alk. paper)

012908P

In gratitude to Joan Moisseiff Scobey

In memory of Raphael G. Scobey

The history of New York reads like a romance . . .

—Hermann H. Cammann, opening ceremony,
Real Estate Exchange and Auction Rooms (1885)

Contents

Acknowledgments

Writing *Empire City* has been an exhilarating, chastening, and at times costly experience. I want to thank many institutions and individuals who have helped me make this book and pay its costs.

The doctoral work on which *Empire City* is based was supported by graduate fellowships from the Danforth and Mrs. Giles Whiting Foundations, for which I am most grateful. I was fortunate to do that work in the Program in American Studies at Yale University, a stimulating and intellectually expansive place. I want to give thanks to my teachers there—especially Jean-Christophe Agnew, David Brion Davis, and Alan Trachtenberg, my dissertation adviser—for introducing me to the craft of historical and cultural studies.

In recasting and expanding *Empire City*, I was supported by fellowships from the Michigan Society of Fellows and the Institute for the Humanities at the University of Michigan. In addition to their material aid, both the society and the institute provided wonderful settings for intellectual dialogue and growth; along with the Program in the Comparative Study of Social Transformation, they have offered the sort of intense, interdisciplinary sustenance that is a hallmark of the University of Michigan.

Many librarians and archivists helped me research the history of city building, urbanism, culture, and politics in nineteenth-century New York. Let me express my appreciation to the staffs of the Sterling Library at Yale University; the Baker, Houghton, Langdell, Loeb, and Widener Libraries at Harvard University; the Harlan Hatcher Graduate Library at the University of Michigan; the Rare Book and Special Collections Division of the Library of Congress; the New-York Historical Society; the New York Public Library; the Museum of the City of New York; and the Municipal Archives of the City of New York. I am grateful too for Michelle Craig's indispensable aid in gathering the illustrations for publication and for the generosity of John Adler and his staff in enabling me to reproduce images from HarpWeek, LLC, the online archive of *Harper's Weekly*. David Schuyler thoughtfully lent me his personal copy of an illustration that eluded my research in the archives.

I have also been the beneficiary of a broad and generous community of scholars. Tom Bender, Iver Bernstein, Elizabeth Blackmar, Daniel Bluestone, David Hammack, Roy Rosenzweig, David Schuyler, and Christine Stansell have shared their expertise in the history of New York and in some cases important documentary finds. Elliot Gorn, Morton Keller, and Mike Wallace read an early version of the manuscript and offered helpful suggestions for revision. Versions of Chapters 5, 6, and 7 were presented at conferences on Calvert Vaux and the comparative history of New York and Budapest; I want to thank Gabor Gyani, John Kasson, Richard Oestreicher, Kathy Peiss, and others for their responses on those occasions. My first effort at recasting and expanding the manuscript was given a careful and affectionately critical read by Lauren Berlant, Fernando Coronil, Roger Rouse, and Julie Skurski. As I struggled to fulfill my ambitions for *Empire City*, Peter Agree, Sara Blair, George Chauncey, Geoff Eley, Julie Ellison, Jonathan Freedman, Valerie Kivelson, and Gina Morantz-Sanchez offered me the gift of their scholarly engagement, their insights into history and writing, and their support. Janet Francendese of Temple University Press has been heroically patient and encouraging with this manuscript; I have run out of words to say how grateful I am for that.

Other friends provided less scholarly aid but no less crucial emotional sustenance. Marc Margolius, Michele Reimer, Alex Aleinikoff, Rachel Cohen, Jill Medvedow, Rich Kazis, and Nan Fey have shared many conversations about *Empire City* on lakefronts, hiking trails, front porches, and New Year's Eves over the years; their questions, challenges, hopes, and care have contributed to the making and meaning of this book more than they can know.

Two other friends deserve special thanks. Since I came to Ann Arbor twelve years ago, June Howard and I have spent long hours talking about writing, teaching, interdisciplinarity, the future of American Studies, and our children's soccer careers; more than a fair share of those hours were devoted to *Empire City*. June's intellectual passion, personal loyalty, and insight have been a great blessing to me and this book. For a quarter-century now, Bill Cronon's friendship has been a source of intellectual adventure, endless conversation, energy, and joy. Bill has been especially important in helping me see this project to the end, offering a sympathetic ear, unflagging support, and an occasional nudge. We have shared many journeys, some of them unexpected; I am glad that this one is ending, and I am looking forward to the next.

Finally, I want to thank my families. I am grateful for the love, loyalty, and occasional electronic equipment that Bruce Thal, Ileane Thal, and the Thal and Siebert families have given me. Bruce Ragsdale and Rick Scobey have offered their wonderful mix of care, intellectual engagement, irony, and cheerleading. Early on in my life, my mother, Joan Scobey, gave me her love of language and her love of "the city," as we have always called New York; without these gifts, I could not have written *Empire City* or even known why I should want to. My father, Raphael Scobey, died before he could see my doctoral thesis grow into a book. But I trust that his intellectual curiosity, his humaneness, and his passion for the art of citizenship have found their way into my work here and elsewhere.

Most of all I want to thank the family I have made with Denise Thal. Isaac, Jake, and Rafe Scobey-Thal have lived with this book since before they can remember; they will be very happy that it is finished. Every day they remind me that the world is full of joys and challenges that have nothing to do with studying the past. But they remind me too why the past is worth studying in the first place: as a way of knowing how we got here and as a way of imagining our way out of here, into our own ideal city, a place good enough for our children to inhabit. I am grateful to them for all their reminders.

Denise Thal has helped me during the writing of *Empire City* in many ways. She taught me how to prepare the spreadsheets of land values and building records included in the text. She has done more than her share of taking care of our home and our children so that I could write. It is true that her uncommon sense, her grounded intelligence, and her mix of patience and impatience have made this a better book, and I am grateful for that. But it is even truer to say that her greatest gift was the sheer staying power of her support and love. This book is finished, but all our other journeys are unfinished.

Postscript: September 2001

It feels impossible to complete the preparations for a book subtitled *The Making and Meaning of the New York City Landscape* without acknowledging the horror of the attack on New York and the strength and beauty of the response to it. By the time this book is published, the meaning of the events of September 11 will surely have changed. In the early autumn of 2001, however, I am struck again by some of the lessons I learned in researching and writing *Empire City*: most of all by how deeply the energies and imagination of the city and the nation remain attached to New York's buildings and spaces. Twenty-first-century Americans do not use the same language to talk about the destruction of the World Trade Center as Victorian city builders might have. Yet, with all their bluster about "metropolitan destiny" and "the march of improvement," nineteenth-century boosters understood something essential about the New York landscape: it was meant as a bridge to the future, a form of hope. Along with the sheer horror of lives lost, the attacks of September 11 destroyed that bridge. By the time this book appears, I trust that the downtown landscape, the lives it holds, and the energy and hope it embodies will be making themselves anew.

INTRODUCTION

Can a City Be Planned?

Accident and then exigency seemed the forces at work to this extraordinary effect; the play of energies as free and planless as those that force the forest from the soil to the sky. . . . The whole at moments seemed to him lawless, Godless . . .

—William Dean Howells, *A Hazard of New Fortunes*

Bryant's Questions

One day, a decade ago, as I was browsing old volumes of the *Real Estate Record and Builders' Guide*, I came across a column that helped me see the focal question of this book. On March 21, 1868, the *Record* had reprinted an editorial from the New York *Evening Post* concerning New York's growth. The *Post*'s editor was the eminent poet William Cullen Bryant, a leading advocate of parks and public improvements for the city; it was not surprising that the local real-estate journal should have broadcast his views on the development of the metropolis.[1]

What Bryant wrote *was* a surprise. Entitled "CAN A CITY BE PLANNED?" the editorial represented nothing less than a call for a new science of urban growth and systematic landscape design. "We have always accepted without question the accidents of city growth as out of the control of scientific thought," he lamented. Now, however, "this reckless and idle policy is falling out of favor," and "thoughtful men are giving attention . . . to the important problem of how to plan and how to build a city so as best to accommodate business and promote health." The inquiry was still too new to have yielded firm conclusions, Bryant wrote, but he cataloged the questions that would-be planners would have to answer "with reference to New York":

Towards what limits must the city grow. . . .? How much and what portions . . . will be required for business purposes . . . ? . . . Where will the rich man's city palace stand? Where will the laborer's family rest? . . . What avenues of communication are needed between

the sections for business and those for residence? How shall the latter be connected with
the great park, and with other healthful and pleasant resorts? . . . Ought . . . the city have
. . . one great "Central Park"; or are a number of parks required in different sections . . . ?
Can any means be devised to make such places attractive to those who need them most;
. . . those who are suffering from the . . . close air of shops and factories?

Bryant praised "the recent report of the architects of Prospect Park" for "treat[ing]
some of the[se] questions . . . with an enlightened foresight." What inspired him to
comment was a proposal by Prospect Park's designers—Frederick Law Olmsted and
Calvert Vaux—to surround the Brooklyn pleasure ground with a planned network of
boulevards and suburbs. If Manhattan were also to adopt such thinking, the poet
urged, the city would "improve in plan still more rapidly than it grows in size" and
"hasten the natural work of those unmeasured . . . advantages which promise . . . to
make this the first city in Christendom."[2]

It is an interesting document. For one thing Bryant rehearsed every issue that pre-
occupied New York's city builders and urban reformers in the mid-nineteenth century. How to channel and contain metropolitan growth; how to array street plans,
residential geographies, and spaces of public leisure; how to order the city streets
physically and socially; how to design parks and other landscapes of sociability; how
to ameliorate and regulate class inequality in a capitalist metropolis—here were
nearly all the great themes of Victorian urbanism. Even more interestingly, Bryant
wrapped these issues in a question that would not have been asked in America
twenty years earlier. To be sure, intellectuals and builders had viewed American cities as plannable artifacts going back to L'Enfant's design for the District of Columbia
and even earlier. Yet the *Evening Post* editorial was imagining a different sort of project. It defined "planning" as a participle: not simply as the creation of a city ex nihilo,
a shape imprinted on empty ground, but as a process that "anticipate[d the] future
. . . and ma[de] provision for [its] coming wants." Such a conception treated cities as
dynamic spaces embedded in a world of dynamic growth, and it treated planning as
a social practice embedded in history: "It is not for one generation . . . to solve all
these questions and the many others which follow in their train," Bryant mused at
the end of his catalog of queries.[3]

What was it that enabled—and compelled—an influential editor to ask whether
a city could be planned, just then and there, in Manhattan in 1868? That is the question around which I came to construct the story of *Empire City*. Two fundamental facts
are essential to the answers that I have offered. First of all, the Manhattan landscape
underwent dynamic, systematic change in the third quarter of the century. In 1883,
the year the Brooklyn Bridge opened, New York was not merely a bigger city than it
had been at midcentury, but a fundamentally different one. It had changed from a
bustling but compact port to an expansive, internally segregated metropolitan area:
a landscape whose specialty districts, monumental architecture, and avant-garde
infrastructures mobilized capital, goods, and people with unprecedented efficacy.
Along with great achievements, this transformation had produced a nexus of spatial
and social frictions: sclerotic congestion, chaotic land use, dilapidated structures, and

a new-built landscape of tenements and workshops alien to the values and oversight of the urban bourgeoisie. Both the dynamism and the disorder of nineteenth-century capitalism were inscribed on the built environment of Manhattan and the city-building process that recast it.

Second, these changes spurred a novel response from New York city builders. Starting in the late 1850s, reform intellectuals, real-estate developers, and other urbanists pursued an innovative effort to regulate New York's environmental ills, redesign its landscape, and guide its growth. Their initiative took different forms in various parts of the cityscape: engineering triumphs like the Brooklyn Bridge, pioneering health and housing codes, the first campaign to systematically redevelop the Manhattan waterfront. Yet the most far-reaching effort involved the comprehensive planning of the metropolitan periphery. In upper Manhattan, outer Brooklyn, and other surrounding areas, genteel reformers and their allies sought to lay out a unified landscape of scenic parks, promenades, civic institutions, and planned residential districts: a civilizing otherworld that was designed to counter the commercial, class, and moral discontents of the urban center.

These interventions were not all of a piece. Yet they were nurtured by a common ideological and political milieu that linked changes in the real-estate economy, experiments in local state building, and new ideals of environmental uplift. The city builders most responsible for creating that milieu were precisely the groups whose connections we saw in the story of the *Evening Post* editorial: reform professionals like Prospect Park designers Frederick Law Olmsted and Calvert Vaux; civic-minded capitalists like the Brooklyn park commissioners to whom they reported; and property developers who would have reread Bryant's column in the pages of the *Real Estate Record*. This constellation of business leaders, growth boosters, and cultural arbiters articulated a complex vision of New York's place in national space and civilizational history; they elaborated a design program that specified what such an "Empire City" should look like; and they pursued the power to create that landscape on the ground. I call this nexus of cultural values, design ideals, and political action "bourgeois urbanism."

Empire City tries to solve the riddle of William Cullen Bryant's question by situating it in relation to these two stories of spatial and social change. On one hand, the book traces New York's growth and reconstruction in the third quarter of the nineteenth century, analyzing the market forces, institutions, and cultural values that organized city building in the new metropolis. On the other hand, it traces the rise of bourgeois urbanism, analyzing the ideological assumptions and political efforts with which Manhattan's would-be planners responded to the contradictory results of the city-building process.

In telling these stories, *Empire City* benefits from a wealth of existing research into the history of urban geography and planning. At the same time, it diverges from some long-standing paradigms in that research. Let me lay out the book's argument and sketch where it seeks to intervene in two sets of scholarly conversations: conversations about the history of city building and of urban planning in Victorian America.

City Building

For most of the nineteenth century, "New York" meant Manhattan Island (a usage to which *Empire City* conforms). Not until 1874, when the municipal government annexed portions of southern Westchester, did the city limits extend beyond Manhattan; not until 1898 was the five-borough "Greater New York" consolidated. Yet, as I shall argue, "lesser New York" was the scene of dramatic spatial change, change that laid the groundwork for metropolitan consolidation. Especially between the late 1840s and the panic of 1873, New York underwent a development boom that extended the urban fabric over most of Manhattan Island and recast the city's internal geography. "The march of improvement," as contemporaries called it, was fueled by a flood of capital into New York's property markets; it was organized by new real-estate institutions and infrastructures that knit Manhattan, Brooklyn, and the environs into an expansive metropolitan area. The midcentury boom reshaped both the island city and the larger region into a complex landscape differentiated according to economic function, social class, architectural type, and physical density.

In tracing New York's growth from a walking city to a segregated metropolis, *Empire City* builds on a valuable tradition of morphological analysis in American urban studies. Indeed the very category "walking city" comes from one of the masters of that tradition, Sam Bass Warner. Led by historians like Warner and geographers like David Ward, scholars in the 1970s and 1980s elaborated a sophisticated model of urban spatial change in American history. Their work reflected many of the assumptions of modernization theory, then so influential in U.S. social science; it tended to model city building in nineteenth- and early-twentieth-century America as a microcosm of modernization itself.[4] The model was organized largely around two sets of claims.

First of all, many researchers asserted, U.S. cities went through a systematic, phased process of spatial differentiation and metropolitan integration. The process was activated by the pressures of demographic growth and industrial complexity; and it seemed to mirror a larger imperative toward functional specialization and mass integration thought to characterize the social reorganization of turn-of-the-century America as a whole.[5] Second, it was widely argued, the key mechanism for this reshaping of urban space was changing technology, especially improvements in transportation and other infrastructures. Influential studies like Warner's *Streetcar Suburbs*, Melvin Holli's *Reform in Detroit*, and Kenneth T. Jackson's *Crabgrass Frontier* underscored the centrality of infrastructural change to land development and municipal politics; surveys of the "new urban history" tended to periodize the evolution of U.S. cities according to the transportation systems dominant in each phase of their growth.[6]

Together these claims offered a powerful model of urban spatial change. It attributed the dramatic reconfiguration of American cities in the late nineteenth and early twentieth centuries to the functional requirements of complexity and growth and the enabling effects of technological progress. Like other models grounded in a master narrative of modernization, such an analysis was vulnerable to criticism for being unilineal, automatic, and negligent of political conflict and contingency. Yet it stimulated a wealth of nuanced research into the evolution of such cities as Boston, Philadelphia, and Milwaukee, and it has proven very helpful in this analysis of New York.[7] As I describe in Chapters 2, 3, and 4, Manhattan and its environs *did* undergo a process of spatial and functional differentiation; indeed Victorian observers saw the bifurcation of the metropolis into a site-intensive, commercial "downtown" and an expansive, residential "uptown" as the defining mark of the midcentury boom. Moreover the boom culminated in a set of infrastructures—streetcar networks, the elevated railway system, and (most famously) the Brooklyn Bridge—whose construction accelerated New York's metropolitan integration.

Yet *Empire City* diverges from the classic modernization model in several ways. The most obvious is chronological: I situate New York's transformation in the third quarter of the nineteenth century, some thirty years earlier than the usual periodization of morphological change. In part this reflects the vanguard pace of New York's development compared with other cities in Victorian America; but it also marks my different sense of the *causes* of that development. Precisely because the classic model laid such stress on technological progress, it tended to privilege the late nineteenth and early twentieth centuries—the era of electric traction, structural-steel construction, and automobility—as the revolutionary epoch of American city building. By contrast, *Empire City* treats the development of the metropolitan real-estate economy as the key engine of spatial change. More than infrastructural determinism, I argue, it was the maturation of a dynamic, centralized market in space that drove the transformation of New York—a development that took place mainly in the middle decades of the nineteenth century.

Thus, much of the first half of *Empire City* is concerned with tracing the genesis and structure of New York's real-estate economy. As I argue, the rule of real estate may be said to begin with the famous street plan of 1811, which platted the unbuilt city as a uniform grid of blocks and lots. Yet the grid was only a groundwork. In the 1850s and 1860s, it was activated by a set of institutions and practices—a central real-estate salesroom, a weekly trade journal, regular auction and partition sales, institutional sources of mortgage credit—that made land and location into fungible, standardized, price-sensitive commodities in a relatively unified field of exchange. The commodification of space enabled (and compelled) propertied New Yorkers to treat the cityscape as a means of financial accumulation. They responded by pouring capital into it, fashioning a city that sorted land use and buildings according to the ability to pay for space. Within this market regime, new infrastructures like horse cars and rapid transit had important *proximate* effects on urban growth and specialization. Yet the introduction of public improvements was itself paced less by technological progress than by the dynamics of capital formation and land speculation.

In shifting my account of New York city building from technical modernization to the rule of real estate, I have found two bodies of research especially helpful. First I profited from a wide range of work on urban land markets, property relations, and the political aims of developers. Historians Michael Doucet, Elizabeth Blackmar, and Robin Einhorn, for instance, have explored the geographic and economic atomism of property markets in early-nineteenth-century cities and the patterns of political localism that often ensued.[8] By contrast, studies of late-nineteenth- and early-twentieth-century community developers stress the centralized planning aims of suburban "master builders."[9] *Empire City* draws on many questions posed by this scholarship, but it offers somewhat different answers. In contrast to accounts of earlier American cities, it portrays a New York whose real-estate economy has become spatially integrated and economically tied to other American capital markets (markets that were going through their own process of centralization on Wall Street). At the same time, unlike studies of later community planners, I describe a city where property ownership and city building remained piecemeal and dispersed. New York's metamorphosis, in sum, was fueled by a paradoxical mix of centralism and atomism characteristic of the midcentury era in which it took place. The cityscape that resulted from this volatile alchemy was a complex amalgam of rationality, dynamism, and disorder.

A second research literature helped me explore the economic logic and social effects of these changes. This was a tradition of spatial analysis, running from French historian Henri Lefebvre to contemporary geographers like Edward Soja and David Harvey, that has brought the resources of Marxist theory to bear on the study of urban environments.[10] Three key themes from this scholarship inform my account of New York. First of all, it argues that the urban landscape—indeed any landscape—needs to be understood not only as a *setting* for social and power relations but also as the *product* of those relations and a mediating *cause* in reshaping them. In Victorian New York, the "sociospatial dialectic," as Soja terms it, took the form of a complex, intimate interplay between local urban development and larger currents of capitalist growth. David Harvey's work on land markets and finance capital proved especially useful in analyzing this dynamic. Harvey helped me see the links between New York's physical transformation and its rise as a national finance center. Wall Street channeled vast resources into the midcentury boom, making city land into a more liquid asset and city land use more responsive to market cues. Conversely, the resulting landscape fostered the process of capitalist growth, circulating money, goods, information, and people at an unprecedented velocity and volume.[11]

The concept of a "sociospatial dialectic" underlies a second key theme of *Empire City*: the interplay between spatial change and *class formation*, especially bourgeois class formation, in Victorian New York. Given the mix of dynamism and market fragmentation that characterized city building in the midcentury boom, propertied New Yorkers were forced to come together in new ways to manage the juggernaut of change. Trade journals like the *Real Estate Record and Builders' Guide*, developers' coalitions like the West Side Association, reform groups like the Citizens' Association—such institutions cut across social networks, business sectors, and even political rivalries to cement city- and classwide collaborations. In so doing they fostered a sense of commonalty among a metropolitan bourgeoisie that drew its members from disparate parts of the nation. Class affiliation was thus both a precondition for the "march of improvement" and a consequence of the boulevards, parks, and neighbor-hoods that it laid out.

Finally, the Marxist tradition of urban studies helped me make sense of perhaps the most fundamental datum of New York's midcentury boom: its massively contradic-tory effects. If there was one truism that Victorian observers stressed again and again, it was that the new metropolis was divided against itself. New York was a vast melo-drama of "sunshine and shadow," as popular journalists put it, counterposing wealth and destitution, virtue and vice. These contrasts were inscribed in the built environ-ment itself, making the Manhattan grid a mosaic of grandeur, congestion, and decay. The human costs of living in such a city were moral and social as well as environ-mental and economic. Space was at once fractured and boundariless in Victorian New York, and the city streets became a theater of class distance, class friction, and persistent civil violence during the mid-nineteenth century.

As I argue in Chapter 5, the modernization model of city building tended to attrib-ute such ills to a lag model of change: rookeries, riots, and ramshackle piers were seen as the residua of a process of rationalization that had not yet fully run its course. In contrast, *Empire City* treats the frictions of Victorian Manhattan as part of an *emergent* pattern of uneven development. That pattern was grounded, I argue, in the peculiar qualities of urban land value as a commodity, its paradoxical melding of monopolis-tic power and fragile interdependence. New York's development boom reinforced both the inertia and the volatility of the market in space, generating a city-building process that careened between obsessive calculation and speculative excess. The re-sult was a "heteroscape" in which traffic was jammed alongside abandoned docks, palatial rail depots were surrounded by sweatshop lofts, and elegant townhouses went up a stone's throw from tenement speculations. The rule of real estate was a cat-alyst of contradiction.[12]

Urbanism

In response to these changes, as I have said, New York's city builders, reformers, real-estate promoters, and businessmen began to ask, "Can a city be planned?" during the middle decades of the nineteenth century. The second half of *Empire City* offers an ac-count of the assumptions, proposals, and political actions with which these urbanists answered Bryant's question. Chapter 5 unpacks the cultural discourses and urbanis-tic ideals that informed their view of what a rising capitalist metropolis like New York should look like. Chapter 6 analyzes which social constituencies took up the new urbanism, and it maps the political affiliations, models of state power, and ide-ologies of class authority that organized their (conflicting) efforts to guide the city-building process. Chapter 7 offers an interpretation of the initiatives that grew out of these efforts. It touches on efforts to regulate and coordinate land use, property de-velopment, and public works in the existing, downtown cityscape. Yet it argues that the centerpiece of the new urbanism was the campaign to lay out and oversee an "uptown utopia" of parks, boulevards, planned suburbs, and tutelary institutions on the metropolitan periphery.

As with the analysis of city building in the first half of *Empire City*, my reading of bourgeois urbanism both draws on and departs from established research in the history of American city planning. Let me clarify my dialogue with this rich body of work. Until the last decade, the dominant narrative of planning history fit squarely within what I have called the modernization paradigm in U.S. scholarship. As codified in Mel Scott's magisterial *American City Planning* (1969), an institutional history commissioned by the American Institute of Planners, and disseminated in the "new urban history" literature of the 1970s, that narrative was organized around three fundamental claims. It privileged the early twentieth century as the inaugural moment of city planning in the United States. It foregrounded the professional consolidation of physical master planning as the key achievement of that era, focusing on the maturation of Progressive environmental reform into an urban profession of design experts, civic managers, comprehensive planners, and applied social scientists. Finally it tended to treat the outcomes of twentieth-century planning reform—zoning codes, housing regulations, City Beautiful designs, and master plans—as fundamentally *technical* interventions against unregulated growth.[13]

This is not to say that planning scholarship was inattentive to the intellectual development of planning thought and design aesthetics; but it generally cast that evolution as a self-evidently rational response to the self-evidently disorderly side effects of urban modernization. The dominant narrative, in short, paralleled the historiography of city building not only in its periodization of change but also in its focus on the inexorable dynamics of growth and functional complexity. Planning emerged in Progressive-era America, this research argued, to manage the "organizational revolution" in urban space; and planning was required because nineteenth-century political institutions, property regimes, and infrastructural systems had proven plainly inadequate to the juggernaut of change. Within such a paradigm, it was less essential to explore the framing values or tacit ideological assumptions that planning advocates brought to their encounters with the cityscape. Planning did not need to have a cultural history.

New research on American planning and design has challenged these claims over the past ten to fifteen years. First of all, historians of Victorian America have reframed the periodization of the field, showing that by the middle decades of the nineteenth century, intellectuals, engineers, sanitarians, and design practitioners shared William Cullen Bryant's interest in the systematic shaping of urban space and urban growth. Moreover, scholars have traced this new planning impulse not merely to the proto-professional activities of environmental reformers but also to a wide array of social actors. David Hammack, for instance, has pointed to the role of urban business elites in nineteenth-century planning experiments; Jon Peterson and Clay McShane lay similar stress on civil engineers and other infrastructural innovators. Finally new research has made clear what is evident in Bryant's editorial: that the turn to planning was not simply a technical response to environmental disorder, but a self-consciously *cultural* project of social and moral improvement. Several scholars have underscored the centrality of "moral environmentalism" to Victorian urbanism, the notion that the natural and built environments exercised a profound tutelary influence on domestic and public life. Planning history on this view was inseparable from the history of American culture: not only because the new urbanists brought their moral values to the city-building process but also because they conceived city building as a culture-building project, an effort to embed virtue, taste, and civility in urban space.[14]

These revisionary claims—earlier periodization, less focus on the genesis of professional institutions, more attention to cultural context and aims—came together in the most influential strand of the new planning historiography: studies of Victorian landscape design, most notably the park and urban designs of Frederick Law Olmsted. As I elaborate in Chapter 1, recent scholarship has generated a veritable Olmsted cottage industry, marked by several biographies, nuanced research into Olmsted's landscape, reform, and intellectual work, and the publication of his personal papers. (Attention to Olmsted's collaborators, most of all his partner Calvert Vaux, has only just begun to catch up.) The result has been a narrative that situates the rise of American city planning in the settings and themes of Olmstedian design. David Schuyler's *New Urban Landscape*, for instance, incisively traces the extension of Olmsted's park work into a full-blown urban design program, one that sought to overcome the distempers of urban-industrial society by projecting the moral and functional distinctions of a well-ordered community into the spatial divisions of the planned metropolis. Schuyler argues that such a conception of the good city as a "house with many rooms," in Olmsted's phrase, constituted the first grand theory of the American planning tradition.[15]

Empire City owes much to this historiography. My periodization of bourgeois urbanism in New York echoes that of the new planning scholarship. Indeed New York was the setting for most of the experiments described in that scholarship; the country's first public-health board, tenement code, rapid transit system, and scenic park were all created in Manhattan in the third quarter of the nineteenth century. Moreover, *Empire City* shares the view that these environmental and political initiatives need to be seen as *cultural* interventions, not simply functional responses to the complexities of urban growth: as my subtitle suggests, the "making" of the New York cityscape was inseparable from the "meaning" with which Victorian city builders invested it. It is for this reason that the book begins its account of the new urbanism (in Chapter 5) with a reading of what New Yorkers imagined an "empire city" should look like. More generally, it is why I have borrowed the French usage *urbanism* to describe their efforts to direct the growth of the metropolis. Unlike the more technical "planning," "urbanism" seems to me to convey the cultural stakes of urban reconstruction, denoting both a program of physical interventions and the ideological and aesthetic discourses that inform them.

Finally *Empire City* joins with other recent research in stressing the centrality of Victorian park and landscape design, notably the work of Frederick Law Olmsted. A history of New York could not do otherwise: Olmsted's career began and flourished there in the midcentury boom, during which he collaborated on Central, Prospect, Morningside, and Riverside parks and engaged in pioneering efforts at parkway design, suburban development, and metropolitan land-use planning. I began this project many years ago out of curiosity about Olmsted's cultural politics. Although I have come to believe (with other scholars) that we need to decenter his contributions to Victorian urbanism in order to understand their full complexity, *Empire City* opens with a consideration of Olmsted's legacy and includes an extended reading of his politics and landscape design. As will be clear from my argument and my footnotes, that reading draws appreciatively on the insights of the scholarly Olmsted boom.

Nonetheless *Empire City* offers its own distinctive account of the values, social forces, and institutions that gave rise to bourgeois urbanism in New York. I would stress the significance of three themes vis-à-vis the historiography of American urban planning and design. The first concerns the nature of the cultural ideals that underlay the new urbanism; the second concerns the centrality of social class to its genesis and aims; and the third concerns its effect on American state building and politics. Let me sketch each of these themes in turn.

Along with other recent scholarship, *Empire City* stresses the importance of moral environmentalism to Victorian design. It argues that New York city builders (like many reformers, designers, and tastemakers) viewed the natural and built environment as an index and instrument of moral progress in American society. Yet their efforts entailed more than just a generic faith in the uplifting influence of planning and design. New York's urbanists infused moral environmentalism with a complex vision of what a great metropolis should look like, a vision that sought to link capitalist growth, civilizational order, and the city's rising power. Drawing on notions that historians have come to label booster discourse, bourgeois New Yorkers believed their city destined for greatness—or, to use the idiom of nineteenth-century boosters, for "empire." The midcentury boom reflected Manhattan's imperial power over space and history, they argued, and the cityscape should embody that imperium, confirming and enhancing New York's national dominion. Thus (more than scholars of Victorian design have tended to stress), the new urbanism melded genteel environmental reform with a booster erotics of growth. It envisioned a cityscape that could embody both commerce and civilization, market energy and moral uplift.

When New Yorkers looked at the actual city through these ideological bifocals, what they saw was a mixed record. The uneven effects of growth seemed simultaneously to affirm and to mock their ambitions. They turned to planning and design to project their divided loyalties across a complex metropolitan area. New York's city builders used opulent architectural style to celebrate commercial dynamism; park design to elevate public sociability; residential land-use planning to secure orderly home life; and public improvements to knit these spaces and values within a common cityscape. At the same time, they believed that such innovations could overcome the sociospatial disorders of the midcentury boom. Tenement codes would eradicate nests of disease and vice; planned suburbs would provide class-specific enclaves of domestic virtue; public parks would educate the masses from riotousness to refinement. Victorian city builders, in short, treated the cityscape as an ideological text, one that registered both their aspiration to oversee capitalism and civilization and the actualities that threatened it. They embraced the new urbanism as a way to simultaneously ratify and nullify the meaning of New York's growth.

These imperial ambitions grew out of a specific class milieu, the social world of the metropolitan bourgeoisie. *Empire City* argues that the new urbanism was a class-defined effort—a *bourgeois* urbanism—in several linked senses. First, its program of environmental regulation, public works, coordinated property development, and civilizing landscape design was shaped by the economic pursuits, social networks, and civic norms of propertied and refined New Yorkers. I do not mean by this *simply* that the new urbanism was an elite project—undeniably true—nor that all elite New Yorkers shared the same interests or values in pursuing it. Indeed, I do not believe that class identity can ever be reduced to a single socioeconomic position or a set of interests or values self-evidently grounded in that position. Yet, in a systematically unequal society like that of the nineteenth-century United States, socioeconomic hierarchies defined relatively distinct worlds within which people construed their interests and argued over their values.

Empire City devotes much effort to anatomizing the class world of New York's urbanists. It specifies three elites that sought most programmatically to guide the city's growth—genteel intellectuals and reformers, civic-minded business leaders, and real-estate developers and boosters—and it maps the political, associational, and moral commitments that bound and divided them. The book argues that the primary public to whom these groups addressed their efforts was the larger metropolitan gentry, "the moral and fortunate classes," as charity reformer Charles Loring Brace put it, who were assumed to have the highest stake in New York's commercial power and civic order.[16] Moreover I emphasize that the "content" of the new urbanism reflected class-based attitudes toward property, public civility, and domestic virtue.

At the same time, *Empire City* argues that the new urbanism helped to *shape* the class bonds of bourgeois New Yorkers, even as it was grounded in them. Spatial change and class formation were interactive processes. Through land development, civic associations, and leadership on public agencies, propertied and powerful New Yorkers did much to fashion themselves into an elite collectivity. The new landscape fostered this process of social consolidation, providing commercial, domestic, and public settings where bourgeois New Yorkers recognized one another as members of the city's "wealth and intelligence." *Empire City* thus treats the category of class as simultaneously material and cultural, constructed through patterns of sociability, moral convictions, symbolic practices, and political projects as much as through the tectonics of economic power. Urban space was at once a product of, and a medium for, this play of forces and discourses. In fashioning parks, rapid transit, and tenement codes, bourgeois New Yorkers remade themselves as well.[17]

Finally, *Empire City* stresses the hegemonic ambitions of New York's urbanists: it argues that they sought programmatically to embed their class authority in the fabric of the built environment. Such a linkage between spatial change and social stewardship would doubtless have characterized elite city building no matter what New York's stature; but the fact of the city's national dominance raised the stakes even further. The metropolitan bourgeoisie that was gathering itself in Manhattan was a self-consciously *national* class, drawn from every region of the country, drawn together by its control of national finance, trade, and commercial culture, defined by its hunger for national preeminence. Creating a sublime, civilizing metropolis seemed to elite New Yorkers proof of that preeminence, confirmation not only of the city's imperium but also of their own.[18]

The new urbanism thus invested the Manhattan landscape with enormous cultural and class ambitions. As a result, spatial change carried enormous *political* stakes as well—the third and final theme in my account of planning and design in Victorian New York. Innovative city building required innovative state building, and *Empire City* maps the political alliances, governmental institutions, and ideals of state power by which New Yorkers sought to construct a political regime capable of building an imperial metropolis. The book argues that bourgeois urbanism spurred a significant enlargement of public authority. Indeed, the two most innovative forms of state power in nineteenth-century America—the centralized party machine and the independent, appointive commission—were created in New York between the late 1850s and the early 1870s, in large part to oversee the infrastructure investments, landscape projects, and sanitary regulations of the midcentury boom. Park boards, health codes, and public-works departments thus represented pioneering experiments in the laboratory of American state formation.[19]

These new institutions of governance recast the terrain of political conflict in New York. They organized the city-building process as a struggle between two rival blocs, each with its own version of the imperial design ideal, its own vision of the purposes of state power, its own strategies for ensuring class order. On one side, a largely Democratic coalition of politicians and property speculators sought to cement cross-class electoral majorities around a booster program of patronage, public works, and an aesthetic of growth and grandeur. On the other hand, a largely Republican cadre of reformers and civic-minded capitalists turned to environmental reform and landscape design to civilize metropolitan life and induct the urban masses into its habits and virtues. For the Tammany machine, urbanism offered an arena of class oversight through clientelistic coalitions and market exchange. For genteel environmentalists, urbanism offered oversight by means of moral tutelage and uplifting discipline.

And yet, *Empire City* finally argues, we should not overdraw this division between bosses and reformers, politicos and "best men," that has structured the story of so much nineteenth-century urban historiography. For all their conflicts, New York's urbanists shared a common sense about the links between politics, landscape, and city building. Both camps agreed that the expansion of state power was an indispensable means of realizing New York's imperial destiny in space. Both agreed that the new urbanism was a way to protect that destiny from the corrosive threats of class and commercial disorder. And both agreed that the larger project of urban design was to secure both popular democracy and bourgeois "civilization" from—and for—

the explosive energies of capitalist growth. That common sense defined the common ground on which they pursued some very real conflicts and tactical skirmishing. It made for a city-building process in which unexpected agreements and alliances reached across the political fault lines.

City and Nation

I have given an overview of *Empire City* by situating its argument in relation to the historiography of spatial change and city planning in nineteenth-century America. There is one other important way in which the book diverges from the main tendencies of U.S. urban-historical research. It emphasizes the specifically *national* causes and consequences of city building in Victorian New York. The city's role as the headquarters of American capitalism and public culture, I argue, meant that its development was exceptional in both senses of the word. As a result, this book is not intended to be the sort of exemplary case study that has long been a strength of U.S. urban historiography. Rather it seeks to explain local city building and planning reform by reference to larger currents of economic and cultural change, class formation, and nation building—currents that made the reshaping of New York at once anomalous and uniquely significant. Chapter 1 frames this aspect of my argument with an overview of the interplay between national and metropolitan development; and subsequent chapters elaborate the significance of that interplay for such themes as the growth of the Manhattan real-estate economy, the process of local class formation, and the cultural stakes with which metropolitan space was invested. Let me briefly sketch my analysis here.

First of all, I argue, we cannot understand the transformation of Victorian New York without taking account of the forces that national power focused on the cityscape. Manhattan's economic dominance imposed complex functional demands on the urban environment, even as it flooded the local real-estate economy with investment capital. *Empire City* maps the circuits that channeled such resources into city building and the rise of a market regime capable of deploying them. At the same time, as I noted previously, it traces a concomitant process of class formation. New York drew capitalists, professionals, and intellectuals from across the United States, providing spaces, customs, and institutions by which they made themselves the "collective subject" of the city-building process and welded to it their ambitions for national stewardship. These ambitions were reinforced by New York's centrality to American electoral politics and genteel reform. Urbanists of all stripes were willing to lavish enormous public debt on public improvements, and the nation's leading architects, civil engineers, and public administrators—many recently settled in the metropolitan area—proved eager to make New York a laboratory of design innovation.

New York's preeminence shaped not only the making of the cityscape, but its meaning as well. As the emerging center of American publishing, taste-making, and commercial culture, the metropolis was scrutinized obsessively. Sketch writers, illustrators, editorialists, and reformers expounded the significance of the cityscape for a national public. Its grandeurs—Brooklyn Bridge, Grand Central Depot, Central Park —were read as tokens of American sublimity and civility; its disorders—traffic jams, tenements, tumbledown docks—as signs of corruption. This sense of the national stakes of local growth shaped debates over city building and environmental reform. Urbanists like Frederick Law Olmsted and the booster William Martin assumed that the eyes of the country were trained on their experiments in park design, public works, and planned growth, and that these efforts represented transformative experiments in democracy and civilization. Indeed, they linked the reconstruction of New York with other projects of nation building and cultural uplift: the reform of American politics, the consolidation of a national market, the settlement of the North American West, and Southern Reconstruction.

When William Cullen Bryant asked, "CAN A CITY BE PLANNED?" then, he was asking a loaded question. New York's urbanists loaded it with some of the most consequential issues in Victorian America: the reforming of culture, the stabilizing of class relations, the uniting of the nation, the oversight of a volatile economy, and of course the development of a booming, complex metropolis. As we shall see, their efforts produced many important changes in Manhattan and its environs. And yet, on its own ambitious terms, bourgeois urbanism proved a failure. Commercial palaces, rail depots, monumental bridges, and scenic parks were created; health codes and park commissions were founded; but the larger vision of bourgeois urbanism, the creation of an Empire City of civic order, capitalist dynamism, and civilized public and domestic life, was left unfulfilled. Behind that failure lay a larger crisis of authority and ambition for the bourgeoisie of New York and the nation. I discuss the contours and causes of that failure in Chapter 8.

CHAPTER 1

Metropolis and Nation

Here, starting from a definite origin in persons and principles, at the threshold of a broad continent, in bright ages, with a free development, with all the strength we require, we are working out our history in the future. The present supremacy of New York involves great intellectual and moral responsibility. In ancient times the provinces of the Roman empire erected temples and statues in honor of Rome. . . . New York must so fulfill her part as to merit the like recognition from a united country.

—William Martin, *The Growth of New York* (1865)

Saint Olmsted and Frederick the Great

Frederick Law Olmsted never lacked for audacity. In 1858, a year after his appointment as Superintendent of New York's new Central Park, six months after winning (with his collaborator, Calvert Vaux) the competition for its design, he lobbied his journalist friends for favorable notice in the press. "It is of great importance as the first real park made in this country," he wrote Parke Godwin, a leading Republican editor, imploring him to review the plan, "a democratic development of the highest significance & on the success of which, in my opinion, much of the progress of art & esthetic culture in this country is dependent." At a time when the park site was still largely rock, marsh, and shanty villages, this was an amazingly presumptuous claim—even more so coming from a novice engaged on his first landscape commission (Figure 1.1). Yet Olmsted's peers seconded his views, providing Central Park with the imprimatur on which he believed its success depended. Calvert Vaux, his collaborator on the "Greensward Plan" for the park, asserted its "vital importance to the progress of the Republic." The influential minister and reformer Henry W. Bellows called it "the first grand proof" that democracy and civility were commensurable with each other in America. "The actual existence of the Central Park," Bellows enthused in the *Atlantic Monthly*, offered "the best answer yet given to the doubts and

FIGURE 1.1   Rock clearing and grading along the Promenade in Central Park: this early lithograph illustrates the sheer amount of labor required to turn pastoral ideals into landscape. (*Valentine's Manual of the Corporation of the City of New York*, 1859; University Library, University of Michigan)

FIGURE 1.2   The Carriage Drive in Central Park, rounding the west side of the lake, is a portrait of the ideal of orderly, rustic leisure that defined the park design. (*Valentine's Manual of the Corporation of the City of New York*, 1861; University Library, University of Michigan)

fears which have frowned on the theory of self-government. . . . It is a royal work, undertaken . . . by the Democracy, . . . developing . . . new and almost incredible tastes, aptitudes, capacities, and powers in the people themselves."[1]

A century later, such praise may seem incontestable. In fact the creation of the park has become something of a civic myth of origins for New Yorkers, a heroic narrative of effective benevolence. Olmsted in particular has achieved near-apotheosis as a pioneer of the movement to humanize life in great cities. "During the great days of planning and building New York City—the Frederick Law Olmsted era in the 19th century, the Robert Moses era of the mid-20th—the park system was planned, built and maintained as an indispensable aspect of a livable city," a 1984 Op-Ed piece from the New York *Times* argued, pressing for reorganization of the Parks Department. Such invocations of the heroic past provide a powerful sanction for politics in the present. The Central Park Conservancy, for instance, has won stunning improvements in the park's funding, safety, and ecological stability in recent years through a self-conscious return to "Olmstedian" canons of planning, regulation, and use. The core of its program has been "the acceptance of the Park as its original creators saw it"—to quote the conservancy's master plan—"a scenic retreat, a peaceful space that would act as an antidote to urban stress." Park officials have pursued many of the policies first formulated by Superintendent Olmsted: protecting naturalistic effects, dispersing use, curbing social and ecological disruptions. Pastimes like team athletics and rock concerts have been curtailed, and a more pastoral treatment of the park grounds has been enhanced—all in the name of restoring the vision of "Saint Olmsted," as park administrator Elizabeth Barlow Rogers has called him.[2]

The pristine, restorative value of Central Park as originally laid out; the heroism and vision of its creators, most of all Olmsted; the triumph of the park as a humanizing "antidote" to the ills of city life—here are the elements of a civic hagiography. It has shaped not only current-day park policy but also the ways in which Central Park, Olmsted, and nineteenth-century New York are cast in public memory. When I have described this book to nonspecialists—as a history of the making and meaning of the Victorian cityscape—that memory is what frames their response. *So you are writing about New York?* they usually ask. *Will you discuss Central Park?* To begin a history of nineteenth-century spatial change and city design in Manhattan with the grandest achievement of Victorian urbanism seems natural—as natural as the parkscape itself.

Yet Central Park was not a natural development, and neither is the story of "Saint Olmsted." As historians Elizabeth Blackmar and Roy Rosenzweig have shown, the park was a massively made thing, produced out of the barrens of mid-Manhattan with dynamite, drainage machinery, tons of imported topsoil, nursery-bred plantations, and the efforts of several thousand laborers during the 1850s and 1860s.[3] Similarly the canonization of Olmsted was the result of a complex history of intellectual and political labor, mainly dating to the past thirty years. To be sure, since the founding of the park, journalists, intellectuals, and political activists have cast Olmsted as its presiding genius and taken his program of a disciplined space of rustic retreat to be its definitive ideal (Figure 1.2). Yet, far from seeming incontestable, Olmsted's role was challenged from the start: by administrative rivals like commissioner Andrew Haswell Green, urbanists with less pastoral conceptions of the park, and members of the public who sought more open use of it.[4]

Olmsted's friend and codesigner, Calvert Vaux, offered perhaps the most poignant and pointed of these challenges. Vaux resisted Olmsted's obsession with the hierarchical control of park construction and use, and he resented his own subordinate status in the public mind. In a series of bitter letters, he castigated Olmsted's "conversion of this many sided, fluent, thoroughly American high art work into a machine —over which as Frederick the Great, Prince of the Park Police you should preside, and with regal liberality dispense certificates of docility to the artists engaged in the work. All this side of the affair is nauseating and odious."[5] As I will discuss in Chapter 6, Vaux's painful words encoded fundamental political conflicts over the mission and shape of the new park—conflicts concerning the very meaning of freedom and discipline in a democratic public culture. These struggles ebbed and flowed throughout the first century of Central Park's existence. The cult of Olmsted received renewed impetus during the 1920s and 1930s, when regionalist, conservationist, and design intellectuals like Lewis Mumford and Frederick Law Olmsted, Jr., enlisted him as a forebear for their own endeavors. Yet the "idolatry of Olmsted," as one disgruntled park goer called it, was more honored in the breach when it came to actual policy. The early twentieth century saw many recreational and consumer additions to the parkscape: ball fields, playgrounds, the skating rink, the elegant Casino restaurant, Robert Moses's zoo. It was against these "encroachments" that preservationists celebrated Olmsted's status as a founding father and sought to defend his scenic and disciplinary ideals.[6]

Only in the past two decades has "Saint Olmsted" held unchallenged sway over the critics of "Frederick the Great." In part his canonization was a response to ecological and social problems that beset Central Park in the 1950s and 1960s: problems of overuse, underfunding, crime, and vandalism, in a city fractured by ethnicity, class, and neighborhood. At a time when muggings and graffiti in the park had come to emblematize the national "urban crisis," scholars, archivists, designers, and activists began to revisit Olmsted's writings, landscapes, social thought, and career. The result was an extraordinary outpouring of research materials, including several fine biographies, anthologies of Olmsted's reports and lectures, and museum exhibits on his design work. Scholars produced nuanced treatments of his landscape practices, contribution to Victorian social theory, and place in the evolution of nineteenth-century urban design. A multivolume edition of Olmsted's papers published records of his landscape, reform, journalistic, and commercial pursuits. It is not surprising that park advocates found in Olmsted's career a usable past for their own efforts to reverse Central Park's neglect.[7]

Like most narratives of restoration, then, the canonization of Olmsted and "his" park had more to do with the dreams and needs of the narrators than with the times to which they looked back. To say this is not to diminish the value of reclaiming Central Park and its creators. The recent physical and fiscal renewal of the park represents an extraordinary civic achievement in its own right—one which does not require the warrant of a myth of origins. Similarly, the intellectual work of the "Olmsted boom" has been immensely important. It is no longer possible to narrate the development of environmental reform, landscape design, and city planning, in the United States and elsewhere, without giving Central Park and Olmsted (and increasingly Vaux) pride of place. Thus, one historian describes Olmsted as a "taproot" of the City Beautiful movement during the Progressive Era; another stresses his influence on the pioneering English planner Ebenezer Howard.[8] Certainly my own exploration of urbanism in Victorian New York has been vastly enriched by the scholarly reconstruction of the park and its most celebrated makers.

Why, then, begin this book by putting "Saint Olmsted" in his place? My point is not to debunk his achievements; rather it is precisely to put him *in* his place. As an icon in the hagiography of reform, a founder of the lineage of planners, "Saint Olmsted" does not have much to tell us about the world in which Frederick Law Olmsted and others made Central Park. The very brightness of his image tends to bleach out much of the complexity, contingency, and significance of urbanism in Victorian New York. It cannot help us understand what Olmsted meant, and what he did, in laying claim to the park as "a democratic development of the highest significance," a key to "the progress of art & esthetic culture in this country." Understanding such words means placing them in a different narrative, narrower in time and broader in context: a history of the New York cityscape as it was built, used, and interpreted in the third quarter of the nineteenth century. It is a history in which the shape and meaning of spaces like Central Park were still up for grabs: a history in which the utopian aspirations of "Saint Olmsted" were inseparable from the power politics of "Frederick the Great."

Within that frame, Central Park was not some generically benevolent "'public good." Its proponents were more self-consciously ideological than that, more aggressive and pointed in their aims. They conceived of landscape design and environmental reform not as local, ameliorative ends in themselves, but as elements in a regime of political, social, and moral governance. They linked the improvement of urban landscapes—of New York's landscape in particular—to the most ambitious projects of the Victorian bourgeoisie: the military and ideological consolidation of the nation, the extension of state power and class discipline over an unruly democratic polity, the creation of tutelary institutions to inculcate "civilized" values across a fractured social order. It is the echo of these ambitions that we hear in Olmsted's and Bellows's words.

Allegories of the National Cityscape

Let us start over, then, with these reformers' claims for Central Park. What can they tell us about the making and meaning of urban space in Victorian New York? "My dear Godwin, I have been wishing for some time . . . to see you again," went Olmsted's 1858 appeal to Parke Godwin, "& now [comes] a scheme which I hope will have that result":

> There has not yet been a single . . . honest criticism of the plan of the park. . . . The Tribune has had some articles written by Mr. Dillon . . . based on . . . misrepresentation of the design. . . . It is of great importance as the first real park made in the country—a democratic development of the highest significance & on the success of which, in my opinion, much of the progress of art & esthetic culture in this country is dependent.
>
> . . . It is important to me that the public should have more interest, confidence & pride in it than they yet have. It is important especially that the misrepresentations . . . should be corrected. As a matter of business therefore, I would be glad to get you to write about it & to pay you fairly for the time & study . . . to obtain a complete . . . understanding of it.
>
> I think you could . . . write a general article . . . for the Atlantic, & a thorough review & criticism for the Tribune.

The first thing to note about the letter—and the reason I have quoted it at length—is the contentiousness that surrounds Olmsted's boast. This is a supremely practical document, part of a broad battle for control of Central Park in its early years. In the depression winter of 1857, Olmsted had been pressured by city politicians and working-class crowds to expand the patronage hiring of construction labor; the following spring, as the letter intimates, several Democratic park commissioners led by attorney Robert Dillon sought to amend the Greensward Plan to make it more economical and less rustic. Olmsted's letter was a response to these challenges. Parke Godwin was a trusted friend and a former partner of Olmsted's, a powerful voice in Republican Party circles and, as political editor of the New York *Evening Post*, a leading spokesmen for genteel values. No one was better placed to oppose these patronage and design incursions.[9]

Godwin never did write the "general article . . . for the Atlantic" for which he had been recruited, but two years later the Reverend Henry Bellows did. Bellows's paean to the park for justifying "the theory of self-government" displays the same mix of lofty assertion and political maneuvering. His essay was the result of a new round of publicity tactics. Olmsted was again under challenge in 1860, this time from Albany legislators investigating Democratic charges of cost overruns in the construction of the park. Once again he solicited aid from the journalistic gentry; in a letter to James Fields, the powerful Boston publisher and editor of the *Atlantic Monthly*, Olmsted proposed "Dr. Bellows" and several other possible authors for "an article on the park." Once more his choice was shrewd; the minister was an influential public intellectual who had worked with Olmsted on several publishing and reform projects. His essay for the *Atlantic* was everything Olmsted could have wanted. Not only did it rebut "the leading objections . . . to the plan," but it also boosted Olmsted personally as the sole American with the training and temperament to "appreciate and embody . . . a people's pleasure-ground."[10] Such praise was curious, given the ragged condition of the park in 1860. Yet Bellows's essay was not meant as a report of established fact. It was a performative utterance, designed to call into existence the spatial, social, and political order that it named. It asserted the prerogatives of Superintendent Olmsted against rival interests—politicians, landowners, labor, the visiting public—with whom he was negotiating the layout, construction, use, and governance of the park.

Ironically, then, the very boldness of these claims underscored the open and conflictual nature of city building in New York. Given that contentiousness, it is striking how expansive were the meanings that urbanists attached to the New York landscape. To Olmsted and Bellows, the shaping of Manhattan seemed bound up with the most consequential issues of politics, culture, class order, and nationhood in Victorian America. "[The park] is a matter of very public interest," Olmsted asserted in his letter to Godwin, "as is evident from the fact that already visitors come here from distant parts of the country to study it."[11]

Why did urban design seem so charged to Victorian intellectuals? As Thomas Bender has argued, many social critics were coming to stress the newly urban condition of American society. The "townward tendency," as Bellows called it, posed a complex challenge to Victorian social thought. Cities had long been feared as threats to a free, self-governing society, "plague spots" of class division, idleness, and political corruption. At the same time, bourgeois Americans looked to them as centers of civility and taste without which the republic would remain mired in backwardness—and as a home base for their own claims to political and cultural stewardship. Urbanization rendered visible the tensions within the genteel vision of the nation, its commitment to contradictory ideals that depended on each other for legitimacy. Spaces like Central Park represented the possibility of reconciling these divided loyalties: the possibility of a public sphere that was at once popular and refined, disciplined and open. "[It is] the first grand proof that the people do not mean to give up the advantages and victories of aristocratic governments, in maintaining a popular one," Bellows enthused, "but to engraft the energy, foresight, and liberality of concentrated powers upon democratic ideas." Defending the park was a way of accommodating democracy and civility—democracy and class authority—under the sign of "culture."[12]

This link between urbanism and nationality, between local skirmishes in the city-building process and the moral establishment of "American civilization," was not forged solely in grand public landscapes like Central Park. Nor was it articulated only by genteel reformers like Olmsted and Bellows. It formed part of the common sense with which property developers, politicians, design professionals, and journalists viewed the New York landscape. Beginning in the early 1850s, the city and its environment were invested with meaning as a figure or microcosm for the nation—"a symbol, an intensification of the country," as one popular journalist put it. Such notions were part of a larger discourse of urban portraiture with which Victorian writers, illustrators, editors, and reformers scrutinized the Manhattan landscape. Middle-class magazines and parlors throughout the United States were filled with sketches of the city's streets, exposés of its tenement districts, lithographs of its architectural monuments, commentary on the progress of its public improvements—all at a time when New York was undergoing unprecedented change in scale and geography.

"New York is essentially national in interests, position, and pursuits," James Fenimore Cooper wrote. "No one thinks of the place as belonging to a particular State, but to the United States."[13]

As the descriptions of Central Park make clear, the notion of New York as a national landscape was inseparable from the practicalities of city building. It provided an ideological yardstick by which bourgeois New Yorkers judged the landscape and justified its reconstruction. "New York is as vigorously engaged in doing the work of a nation as either London or Paris," a sketch in the monthly *Hours at Home* lamented, "yet as compared with those cities it is raw and unfinished and . . . wholly unconstructed." John Roebling solicited support for his Brooklyn Bridge design with the claim that its "great towers . . . will be entitled to be ranked as national monuments." Indeed New York's status as "the American metropolis" (to quote the title of an *Atlantic* sketch) was used to buttress a wide range of experiments in landscape design, planned growth, and public works during the third quarter of the nineteenth century. "A grand plan and purpose must . . . control [the] details" of New York's growth, argued Fernando Wood, former mayor, Democratic congressman, and uptown property owner, in an 1871 plea for massive, coordinated public improvements on Manhattan's northern periphery:

> What . . . ought to be the great plan and purpose of this city? The answer must be, that it shall be the Metropolis of the country . . . [and] the commanding, commercial, and financial centre of the civilized world. All great nations have, through history, had . . . but one national capital, exercising its power and influence over all other localities. . . . This is seen in the homogeneous and well-knit nationalities of Europe. If we are to have a great and united country, the Union must be . . . regulated from one great centre or national heart.[14]

Of course the figure of the national metropolis did not always mean the same thing. The assumptions of a Democratic politico and developer like Fernando Wood were different from those of a genteel reformer like Olmsted. For the latter, urbanism was part of a *mission civilisatrice* to the nation. He envisioned a civilized republic overseen by a strong, tutelary state, an America in which "the progress of art & esthetic culture" depended on the influence of men like himself. Wood's ideal of a vigorous commercial empire headquartered in Manhattan underwrote a somewhat different urbanism. He advocated an activist program of public works, party patronage, and speculative growth, but one whose booster policies were tempered by Democratic suspicions of centralized state power and elite moral regulation. It should not surprise us that Superintendent Olmsted resisted Mayor Wood's patronage demands during the 1850s; nor that, as a staunch propagandist for the Union, he detested Wood's leadership of Northern Peace Democrats during the Civil War. Yet in spite of these clashes over local space and national politics—or because of them—both men turned to the allegory of the national cityscape to pursue ambitious (and sometimes convergent) programs of planned city building in New York. Both the genteel planner and the booster politician assumed that national progress, however defined, depended on the way Manhattan was designed and built. That assumption defined the terrain on which they fought.[15]

The American Metropolis

What was it that made the shape of Victorian New York so important? Three factors in particular raised the stakes of city building. First there was New York's dominance over a national economic and cultural order. The city's role in consolidating American markets and publics—and the profits that flowed into it as a result—meant that urban and national development were mutually reinforcing processes. They were in turn linked with a second factor: changes in bourgeois class formation. New York was the scene of a great ingathering of wealth and refinement during the third quarter of the nineteenth century. Metropolitan city building was of special concern to these elites. They invested heavily in city real estate; they used the built environment as a theater of class sociability; and it was largely within their social world that the ideals and institutions of Victorian urbanism were elaborated. Bourgeois New Yorkers portrayed the city as an imperial metropolis whose built fabric ought to embody its destiny as a center of capitalist dynamism and civilizational order. This discourse of empire set the terms of public debate over urban growth and reconstruction. It was the third key factor that raised the stakes of the city-building process.

Let me start with the first of these themes: New York's role in the economic and cultural consolidation of the nation. It would be only a slight exaggeration to say that the city's dominance of capitalism, information flow, and public cultural discourse reconstructed American nationhood in the middle decades of the nineteenth century. Of course republican politics and the cult of patriotism had long served to ground a fervently shared national identity among white Americans. Yet as Eric Hobsbawm, Benedict Anderson, and other scholars have illuminated, nations are not natural facts or perpetual motion machines; they are produced through enormous social and ideological labor, constantly up for grabs and constantly made anew. Between the mid-1840s and the mid-1880s, nationhood in the United States was remade by linked processes of capitalist, cultural, territorial, and political-military expansion and unification. New York presided over key elements of that transformation: most notably, the consolidation of financial and trade markets and a bourgeois public sphere. In the process, the city grew from a leading port to the organizing center of American capitalism. City and nation were changing simultaneously and interdependently in the mid-nineteenth century; the reconstruction of Manhattan served as an instrument and emblem of that dialectic.[16]

This interdependence between city building and nation building was of course one of the great epics of mid-nineteenth-century history. Paris was rebuilt under Louis Napoleon to reinforce and reaffirm the Bonapartist regime. The Viennese Ringstrasse was designed to announce the turn to liberal constitutionalism by the Habsburg empire.[17] Yet the case of "the American metropolis" was conditioned by a great paradox. New York had gained its economic and cultural ascendance *without* holding the seat of government. Some commentators argued that the process of nation building would require New York's eventual assumption of formal state authority. "We believe that New York is destined to be the permanent emporium not only of this country, but of the entire world—and likewise the political capital of the nation," the journalist Fitz-Hugh Ludlow wrote in an 1865 *Atlantic* essay. "Had the White House . . . stood on Washington Heights . . . , there would never have been a Proslavery Rebellion." There are many reasons to doubt this assertion, not least Manhattan's role as a center of antidraft violence and antiwar politics during the Civil War; yet Ludlow's sense of New York's *de facto* political leadership is correct. New York played a linchpin role in national party competition, political culture, and state formation.[18]

Its centrality stemmed partly from the electoral value of New York State, the most populous in the Union and site of the country's most lucrative source of federal patronage and revenue, the New York Customs House. From the election of Lincoln to that of McKinley, the victorious party carried the Empire State in all but two contests—as good a record as the legendary predictor Maine—and New Yorkers were placed on one or the other national ticket in every presidential year between 1868 and 1892 (indeed with two exceptions, between 1868 and 1944). In the Democratic Party especially, local dominance conferred national power. City organizations like Tammany Hall and business leaders like investment banker August Belmont, iron manufacturer Abram Hewitt, and railroad lawyer Samuel Tilden held disproportionate weight in the party's factional struggles and fund-raising. Conversely, national leaders played important roles in local politics, especially the politics of city building. Belmont was a Central Park commissioner; Hewitt's mills supplied cable for the Brooklyn Bridge; Tilden's law partner and political field marshal, Andrew Haswell Green, was the single most powerful administrator in the planning of Central Park and upper Manhattan.[19]

Such linkages made Victorian New York a political incubator for the nation, a place where new modes of organization and governance were developed. As scholar Amy Bridges has argued, two of the most effective modes of community mobilization in nineteenth-century U.S. politics—the local party machine and the reform citizens' association—first developed in Manhattan. So did an array of administrative innovations crucial to the development of American urbanism. During the 1860s, municipal and state legislators passed the country's first comprehensive building, health, and housing codes. At the same time, Albany Republicans and Tammany Democrats created new (and rival) public agencies designed to institute centralized control of policing, parks, and other public works and municipal services. New York's dominance ensured that its city-building experiments played a key role in American state building.[20]

Clearly, however, the foundation of the city's national importance lay in business and communications. "New York stands in relation with the whole country as its commercial and financial capital," real-estate booster William Martin asserted in 1865. "The metropolis will ere long stand in as close business relations with every town of the United States, as, fifty years ago, it did with its own up-town wards."[21] Starting just before midcentury, the city grew from a leading commercial entrepôt to the metropolitan hub of a national market and the country's chief threshold to world markets. By the late 1860s, the port of New York transacted more than half of U.S. foreign trade; its waterfronts were the principal terminus for three of the five key trade routes into the North American interior (the Erie Canal, Erie Railroad, and New York Central system).[22] Wall Street had emerged as the sole center capable of organizing and financing the projects that bound this national market together: the construction of a rail infrastructure, the circulation of commodity credit, the Union military effort. By the end of the Civil War, city banks functioned as a "central reserve" with what one historian calls "virtual control of the [U.S.] credit structure." Downtown bond and commercial-paper traders underwrote the fall movement of farm commodities to market. The Stock Exchange supplied the capital for western land and mineral development and the expansion of the national rail and telegraph networks. "Every new mine opened, every town built up, comes into relation with New York," Martin boasted, "and every railroad, no matter how short, has one terminus here."[23]

At the same time, the circulation of trade information and cultural discourse was coordinated from New York. Firms like Harper Brothers, Western Union, and the New York *Tribune*, housed in some of the grandest edifices in downtown Manhattan, organized a new kind of public sphere in the mid-nineteenth century. Through journals, telegraph offices, stock tickers, and lithographs, middle- and upper-class Americans of all regions consumed increasingly standardized business data, translocal news, and visual and narrative representations of themselves as a public. Unlike Wall Street—with whose growth it was deeply entwined—the history of this public sphere has yet to be fully studied. Yet it is possible to offer some markers of New York's growing power over it.

First of all, Manhattan was home to the country's leading firms in commercial communications: credit agencies like Bradstreet's and R. G. Dun, business periodicals like the *Commercial and Financial Chronicle* and *Bradstreet's Weekly*, and an amazing variety of trade journals.[24] By the late 1860s, two downtown monopolies controlled the flow of news and business information throughout the United States: the Associated Press (a consortium of New York dailies) and the Western Union Company, formed in 1866 from six regional telegraph networks. AP and Western Union transmitted perhaps 90 percent of American telegram traffic, price quotations, and nonlocal reportage during the Gilded Age.[25] Their control was contested by reformers, populist politicians, and western rivals, but with limited success. The radical journalist Henry George tried and failed to sustain a San Francisco daily without the imprimatur of the AP moguls; it was on an 1869 trip to New York, seeking contraband sources of wire news, that George had the epiphany of class inequality that pushed him into his crusade against private land ownership. "The power of associated capital," he said in a bitter aside to *Progress and Poverty*, "deprives the people of the United States of the full benefits of [the telegraph], tamper[s] with correspondence and crush[es] out newspapers which offend it."[26]

George's rhetoric protested more than just corporate control *over* public information; it testified to a new regime *of* information, in which the proliferation of "news" —an atomized and transient, but easily massed and reproducible commodity—transformed "the people" into a national market and little more. Benedict Anderson argues that the daily consumption of newspapers has served historically as a key template of national consciousness, "creating that remarkable confidence of community in anonymity which is the hallmark of modern nations." Credit ratings, ticker tape, wire news, and trade reportage had a similar effect in mid-nineteenth century America, addressing readers and businessmen as communicants in a triumphant commercial order subordinated to the metropolis.[27]

The consumer trades of the Victorian culture industry remained more dispersed, but New York was their largest, most innovative center. The city was "the great pillar of lithography," with as much as 50 percent of the country's business. Dozens of publishing houses gave it a similar preeminence in the book and magazine trades; the city controlled one-third of U.S. periodical circulation in 1860, twice that of second-place Philadelphia.[28] More significant than sheer market share was New York's vanguard role in the transformation of the industry. American publishing was swept by an economic revolution in the mid-nineteenth century. Innovations in printing, illustration, and book production; the growth of mass marketing and rail distribution; the emergence of omnibus houses that linked the book, journal, and primer markets; the creation of a star system of best-selling novels and celebrity (primarily female) authors—together these factors worked to enlarge and consolidate the American reading public, promoting what one scholar has called a "shift from a local to a national print culture." Reading materials became cheaper, more varied, and more widely consumed: the issuance of new titles grew an estimated ten times faster than U.S. population in the 1840s and 1850s, and sales figures for best-sellers like *Ruth Hall* or *Uncle Tom's Cabin* were in the hundreds of thousands. "Literature has gone in pursuit of the million," boasted *Harper's Magazine*, "press[ing] its way into cottages, factories, omnibuses, and railroad cars."[29]

The publishing boom did not create or cater to a homogeneous reading public. To the contrary, it proceeded unevenly across regional lines—southern readers seem to have been incorporated more slowly than westerners—and differentially across those of class and gender. Where working-class families may have subscribed to cheap story papers, elite households were certain to carry genteel monthlies like *Harper's* or the *Atlantic*. Middle-class women, by all accounts the largest constituency of literary consumers, made "domestic" writers like E.D.E.N. Southworth and Harriet Beecher Stowe the era's biggest sellers; the smaller male reading public seems to have preferred political, sporting, or adventure writers. In short, the new print culture constituted the "imagined community" of Victorian America as a field of distinct readerships and markets, each with its preferred genres, cultural commodities, and ideological preoccupations.[30]

Both the common trends and the divisions in nineteenth-century publishing enhanced New York's dominance. It was Manhattan story papers that supplied the most popular serial fiction: Robert Bonner's *New York Ledger* held the exclusive rights to such female best-selling authors as E.D.E.N. Southworth and Fanny Fern; Street and Smith's *New York Weekly* published Ned Buntline and other favorites of the masculine adventure and mystery market. After the Civil War, these and most other serials were distributed nationally by the American News Company—the Western Union of popular serial publishing—from its sumptuous office building across the street from City Hall.[31] A block away, on Franklin Square, was Harper and Brothers, the country's largest purveyor of genteel reading matter. As Frank Luther Mott has argued, it was the founding of *Harper's Magazine* in 1850, more than any other event, that inaugurated the new epoch in American publishing. Melding refined but lively commentary, pirated English fiction, engaging illustration, and efficient distribution, the monthly built a national readership of nearly 200,000. By the late 1860s, Harper's had added two more periodicals—the political *Harper's Weekly* (1857) and the fashionable *Harper's Bazaar* (1867)—aimed at satisfying the gender-specific tastes of the American middle-class home. Harper's formula was widely imitated by other New York houses like Leslie's, Appleton's, and Scribner's. During the Gilded Age, some two-thirds of American mass-circulation journals were published in Manhattan.[32]

Between about 1840 and 1880, in sum, New York presided over the consolidation of a national market and a predominantly middle-class public sphere. The mutual development of the metropolis and "its" nation was a complex interaction, one that it is useful to imagine as a kind of dialectic of projection and appropriation. On one hand, New York spread its power centrifugally throughout the country. The clearest instances of this projective dominance were financial: the extension of Wall Street capital along the national rail and telegraph networks, the proliferation of partnerships, brokerage agreements, and credit obligations that bound hinterland businesses to Manhattan merchants. "Lowest *New York jobbing prices*," advertised one Chicago dry-goods firm, whose inventory was "constantly replenished by one of the partners permanently residing in New York." Yet the city's power was equally evident in other media. Observers of women's fashions claimed that "all other cities accept the *cue* from the dealers in Broadway"; the English writer Anthony Trollope reported finding "Harper's everlasting magazine" in even the most rudimentary Western settlements.[33]

Indeed, for cultural entrepreneurs like the Harpers or Currier and Ives, the work of reaching out to and colonizing a national middle-class public composed one of the central themes of their "product." Books, essays, engravings, and lithographs addressed western, southern, and other nonmetropolitan consumers as cultural dependents; these audiences were given sketches of their own (now provincial) social worlds and glimpses of the cosmopolitan center from which the new, civilizing commodities were delivered (Figure 1.3). Especially after the Civil War, lithographers' inventories and magazine indexes offer a précis of the process by which regional lives were simultaneously marginalized, celebrated *as* marginal, and civilized through national incorporation. To take only one example: volume 43 of *Harper's Monthly* (1871) included visits to Maryland's Eastern Shore, the Florida coast, Stockbridge Village,

FIGURE 1.3   Many engravings, lithographs, and stereographs portrayed New York's economic and cultural influence. This *Harper's Weekly* cover shows a postmaster's daughter from a western hamlet waiting for the mail train—which will no doubt deliver her latest magazines. (*Harper's Weekly*, September 4, 1875; image courtesy of HarpWeek, LLC)

Montauk Point, and Watkins Glen, New York; educative reports on the climate of the Great Lakes, O. C. Marsh's dinosaur expedition to Montana, and the social policies of Mormon Utah; and patriotic tours of Monticello, the Naval Academy, and an 1812 battle site—all in six issues. Conversely, the same volume published several examples of what could be labeled sketches from the metropole: feuilletons on elite travel settings in Europe and the Caribbean and essays on two New York City landmarks, the Customs House and the new, monumental Manhattan Post Office.[34] Such a table of contents *represented* the nation in both senses of the word. It composed a common "American" landscape from an array of local settings, one knit together by the process of serial consumption. And through that process, it composed a middle-class public for whom *Harper's* itself represented a privileged source of national cultural access. Small wonder that Gilded Age tourists made the publisher's offices "one of the regulation metropolitan sights"; in an early-twentieth-century memoir, J. Henry Harper recalls the scene in Franklin Square:

FIGURE 1.4 The South Street waterfront is shown here littered with the world's freight —some of the resources that flowed back into the city as a result of its economic and cultural influence. The stereograph is by Charles Bierstadt, brother of western landscape painter Albert Bierstadt and himself a purveyor of popular western images. (*South from Fulton Ferry*, stereograph, circa 1876; Museum of the City of New York; gift of George T. Bagol, Esq.)

Visitors were always welcome, and never a day passed that parties of countrymen were not on tour through the establishment. . . . Each yokel [left] firmly clutching an illustrated pamphlet entitled, "My Visit to Harper & Brothers" . . . , a diploma of romantic adventure to be carried back in triumph . . . to Lonelyville . . . [and] chewed over again and again during the long evenings of a North American winter. A visit to the House of Harper . . . was equivalent to a pious Mohammedan's journey to Mecca . . .[35]

This reminiscence points to the other, "centripetal" aspect of New York's power. As with Mecca or (to use the more frequent comparison) Rome, all roads led *into* Manhattan. The city was not just a point of departure for national movements of money and meaning; it was also a point of convergence, drawing the country's resources, talents, and ambition into itself, appropriating them as its own. "All the social, political, intellectual and moral tendencies of the Republic show accretion and centralization here," one monthly magazine asserted, "as unerringly as gravitation working downward." New York's force of gravity was first of all commercial, and its clearest expression was the waterfront. Visual and narrative sketches of the docks portray a congeries of merchandise: southern cotton, midwestern flour, Great Plains meat and hides, cloth from Massachusetts and Manchester, sugar from Louisiana and Cuba, fruits from Latin America, household luxuries from Europe, Persia, China, and Japan, and much more (Figure 1.4). Such scenes dramatized the profuse energies of the national and international market and New York's role in concentrating and channeling them. William Martin described the city's dominance precisely as a power to concentrate a continental geography of trade into a local appropriation of capital: "The products of the wheat fields of the prairies, the gold mines of the Pacific coast, the coal fields and oil wells of Pennsylvania, the factories of New England, and the plantations of the South, will heap up a portion of their accumulations here, just as accurately as if all these fields of labor were within the city limits."[36]

What is most striking here is the rhetorical deftness with which Martin analogizes capital accumulation to metropolitan dominance. He composes (New York into) a neatly miniaturized tableau of the national market, listing among the city's hinterlands all the component regions of the United States in 1865, replete with their signature commodities. At the same time, Martin portrays the metropolis as separate from and transformative of that market: a place where the horizontal geography of regions and resources is condensed into a vertical landscape of "accumulations," "heap[ed] up . . . within the city limits." Such tropes of microcosm and appropriation cast New York as more than just a repository of capital. The city became the very *embodiment* of national productive energy: capital in the form of locality. The economic history of the Gilded Age would confirm such a view; by 1876, more than 90 percent of urban banks in the United States kept reserves with correspondent institutions in Manhattan.[37]

New York's power to "heap up" was not limited to trade and finance; the city accumulated stocks of cultural capital too. Here was the other implication of the *Harper's* volume that I discussed above; it offered a catalogue of provincial life for the consumption of the metropolis. Like merchandise on the New York waterfront, the magazine's table of contents represented a sort of concentrated heterogeneity; it aggregated disparate locales together *as* the nation, making New York the privileged center at which those fragments could be brought to critical mass. The emblematic site of this massing and condensation was not the publishing house or the docks; it was the downtown street. Cultural observers portrayed Broadway in particular as a "kaleidoscope" where all the social and moral extremes of America were gathered together. "Broadway represents the national life,—the energy, the anxiety, the bustle, the life of the republic at large," wrote the popular *Tribune* reporter Junius Browne. "Take your stand there, and Maine, and Louisiana . . . and California, Boston, and Chicago, pass before you."[38] Like William Martin's regional tableau, such language used techniques of stereotype and catalog to present New York as a microcosm, the point of concentration where all constituents of the Union could be grasped in a representative (or representable) whole.

Of course, such claims of centrality were necessarily overblown. Broadway did *not* "represent the national life," except insofar as any representation works by effacing aspects of the social reality it purports to express. Junius Browne's image of the Broadway crowd as a national procession took certain constituencies as standing for "the republic at large"; it foregrounded a respectable public that was wholly white, largely native-born and Protestant, disproportionately northeastern, sometimes (not always) exclusively male, and predominantly bourgeois. A similar critique can be made of my own account of New York's role in nineteenth-century nation building. Like Browne, I have foregrounded the upper reaches of U.S. capitalism and culture. A fuller presentation would have to attend to what Eric Hobsbawm calls the "dual phenomena" of nation building: the unpredictable interplay between elite nationalist projects and "the assumptions, hopes, needs, longings and interests of ordinary people." Such an account would complicate the narrative of New York's ascendance. Yet I believe that recent innovative scholarship on such topics as popular fiction, blackface performance, and vaudeville would confirm and enrich the story of metropolitan dominance and nation building that I have been telling here.[39]

Even within the social world of the Victorian bourgeoisie, New York's ascendance was never total. Throughout the latter nineteenth century, there were always rival investment and publishing centers and regional circuits of information and credit. As Robert Wiebe and Morton Keller have argued, we ought not to underestimate the persistent localism of American society in this period. The great majority of firms did not look to Manhattan for capital, but to family property or local partners; the great majority of towns had their own photographic parlors. We still do not know how fully and rapidly metropolitan finance, public opinion, and commodity culture penetrated the "island communities" of the Gilded Age, nor what effects differences of party, region, religion, or economic sector had within bourgeois culture.[40] Thus, a history of nation building narrated from Manhattan Island is bound to be distorted—especially if it relies on city boosters like William Martin and city journalists like Junius Browne. These voices can be expected to have exaggerated the hegemony of the metropolis, treating their own (economic and ideological) investments in New York's growth as done deals. The historian of nineteenth-century city building—who traffics with speculators, utopians, and hucksters—must take care to distinguish facts on the ground from castles in the air.

These cautions notwithstanding, I believe that the dialectic of metropolis and nation sketched here is largely and usefully accurate. It provides a starting place for the story with which I am most concerned: the making and meaning of urban space in New York. For if we cannot grasp all the complexities of American nation building from the vantage point of Victorian Manhattan, it is equally true that we cannot understand city building in Manhattan *without* the vantage point of the nation. Even when journalists and urbanists exaggerated the supremacy of the metropolis—especially when they did—they made clear the national frame through which the New York landscape was scrutinized. They made clear the national stakes of the city-building process.

Those stakes were first of all economic. As I describe in the next three chapters, the New York landscape underwent a fundamental change in the third quarter of the century, shaped by the city's centrality to American capitalist development. The growth of the national market imposed complex demands on local land use and circulation, and these informed the actions of New York city builders. "In a few months the great chain [of the transcontinental railroad] will be completed which shall bind the Atlantic to the Pacific, and bring the traffic of the Indies to the warehouses of New York," one group wrote, lobbying for a franchise to redevelop the waterfront. "Shall we not accept our destiny, and make our port accommodations equal to our growing needs?"[41] At the same time, New York's prosperity underwrote lavish private and public improvements. Commercial palaces like the Western Union Building, infrastructures like Brooklyn Bridge, public spaces like Riverside Drive, Fifth Avenue mansions: all of these projects were undertaken in the 1860s and early 1870s, and none would have been possible—or seen as necessary—but for the fact of New York's metropolitan dominance.

The stakes of city building were ideological as well. Quite apart from any economic resources, "America" served as a moral and political referent for New York; it invested the reconstruction of the cityscape with meaning and purpose. Consider this passage from John Dix's 1853 address on "The Growth of New York" to the New-York Historical Society. A leading Democratic politician, civil servant, and western railroad investor, Dix praised such recent improvements as the Croton Aqueduct by invoking national topography and destiny:

> The great features of this continent seem to mark it out for . . . labors and destinies of corresponding magnitude,—the Mississippi pouring into the ocean . . . ,—the Niagara, collecting the waters of an inland sea . . . ,—the Rocky-Mountain chain, pushing up its snowy summits to the heavens. . . . A country thus strongly marked in its physical lineaments is a fit theatre for the great experiment we are making of the competency of mankind to self-government, and for the social developments which are in progress here on so vast a scale.
>
> This city, as the metropolis of such a country, should correspond with it in the magnitude of its improvements. Though yet in its infancy, it has proved itself . . . not unworthy of the distinction.[42]

Dix weaves a complex web of correspondences: between landscape and destiny, the flow of great rivers and the dynamics of progress, the sublimity of national space and the civility of metropolitan space. He embeds his praise for New York in an expansive paean to Young America, identifying "the magnitude of [the city's] improvements" with the "corresponding magnitude" of the continent and the "great experiment" it stages. Such language puts the cityscape under the lens of nationality, so to speak, at once enlarging its stature and intensifying the scrutiny to which it is subjected.

Not everyone elaborated the links among city, nation, and landscape so obsessively. More often the national implications of city building were invoked to justify or attack some concrete proposal; but the logic of magnification and ideological investment remained the same. Thus, William Martin agitated for costly uptown improvements on the grounds that "the wisest and truest economy" was "to make [New York] beautiful and magnificent for the metropolis of a free and rich people." Merchant A. A. Low, the head of the city's Chamber of Commerce during the mid-1860s, called for a new headquarters "commensurate with the growth in wealth of the chief commercial city of the New World; the heart-centre of a commerce which promises to exceed in magnitude that of any country hitherto known to history!" Such appeals were not limited to business promoters. Republican gentry shared the view that the built environment of New York ought to reflect and improve the life of the nation. The patrician litterateur Charles Astor Bristed, for instance, a scion of the city's wealthiest landowning family, used such arguments in an 1863 pamphlet opposing streetcar lines on Broadway and Fifth Avenue:

> The question . . . concern[s] . . . every man who is interested in the beauty, glory, and pros-
> perity of New York. . . . It is for every man's interest, whether he call himself Republican,
> war Democrat, peace Democrat, or what not, that this metropolitan city should not de-
> generate into a vast squalid suburb, with every available thoroughfare disfigured and en-
> cumbered by tramways. . . . New York is virtually our metropolis, and the appearance of
> a metropolis will always be accepted (and not without reason) as an index of the national
> character.[43]

*The appearance of a metropolis will always be accepted as an index of the national charac-
ter*: here was a touchstone of Victorian urbanism, offered in the confident tones and passive voice of a ruling assumption. Of course Bristed's dictum was not invoked every time a street was opened or a row house built on Manhattan. Yet it should not surprise us that Charles Astor Bristed thought it appropriate, in the most uncertain days of the Civil War, to issue a pamphlet claiming the question of Fifth Avenue horse cars as integral to American national character. Nor that he viewed this as an issue on which even wartime adversaries could unite. For he was right: however bitter their other antagonisms, prowar Democrats like William Martin or John Dix, peace Democrats like Fernando Wood, and Republicans like Olmsted or Bristed himself were agreed on the national significance of the metropolitan landscape. That consensus did much to set the terms within which they pursued (and contested) the experiments in capitalist development, public planning, and landscape design that made Victorian New York an innovative center of American urbanism.

The Class World of Bourgeois Urbanism

In another sense, however, Bristed was quite wrong. For the notion that "the appear-
ance of [the] metropolis" was "an index of the national character" was *not* universally accepted. It expressed the common sense of a small, class-defined metropolitan pub-
lic. The mid-nineteenth century witnessed the formation of a new bourgeoisie in New York, one that was wealthier, more numerous, more socially heterogeneous, and more expansive in its ambitions. Bourgeois New Yorkers were by no means unified in their beliefs and actions, but they did share a class world of social networks, marital and business alliances, voluntary associations, and cultural rites. It was among the men of that world that the material and ideological stakes of city building were defined.

Bourgeois New Yorkers were not, of course, the sole makers of the built environ-
ment. They bought land, put up buildings, laid out parks, opened streets, and lent and borrowed capital in concert with and struggle against other class constituencies. Developers, for instance, took careful measure of the availability, housing needs, and collective demands of city labor in deciding where, what, how much, and how fast

to build. Party politicians used public contracts and patronage jobs to cement electoral majorities. Riots, strikes, and other popular disorders fueled shifts in residential geography and campaigns for environmental uplift aimed at "improving" working-class life. We cannot understand the making of the New York landscape, then, if we do not see it as a site of class negotiation and class struggle.[44]

Nonetheless the story of New York's transformation needs to begin from above. It was propertied, professional, and genteel New Yorkers who amassed the capital, expertise, state power, and cultural authority necessary for the real-estate and public-works boom of the third quarter of the century. And it was they who defined the meaning of the landscape that resulted. When John Dix or Charles Astor Bristed cast New York as the American metropolis, the condensed, local scene of the nation, they invoked assumptions and ambitions to which only bourgeois New Yorkers had the capacity, or the need, to lay claim. *Class* was thus the third term in the dialectic of city building and nation building: the term that specified *for whom* New York's dominance and its physical design were inseparable projects.[45]

It is almost tautological to say that the development of the midcentury city was led by men of property. The entry costs of the real-estate market saw to that. During the third quarter of the nineteenth century, only about one in nine Manhattan households held real property, and two-thirds of these owned no more than their own place of residence.[46] Population growth, commercial expansion, and the constricted topography of Manhattan Island all worked to increase land pressure and bid up the price of property. During the late 1860s, when $750 constituted a good annual income for a wage-earning household—and $3,000 an ample white-collar salary—both individual real-estate transactions and new construction projects averaged more than $15,000. The structure of credit made these levels even more restrictive than they seem today: buyers were expected to pay 40–50 percent of the price in cash and to repay a mortgage loan for the rest within three years.[47]

The salience of social class is even clearer in qualitative markers of participation in the city-building process. The institutions and networks that most powerfully shaped the Manhattan cityscape were led almost exclusively by capitalists, elite cultural arbiters, and professional gentry. Thus, the Board of Commissioners of Central Park (1856–70) was primarily composed of lawyers, bankers, manufacturers, and merchants; its staff was led by professional and reform intellectuals like Olmsted, architect Calvert Vaux, and engineer George Waring.[48] Even after 1870, when Tammany leader William Tweed replaced such elite, state-appointed commissions with a "home rule" regime of party-dominated municipal departments, parks and public works officials were drawn mainly from the upper ranks of commerce and the law.[49] (Tweed himself, who headed the Department of Public Works until 1872, was a key exception.) Similar demographics characterized the leading landowners' lobby in the Victorian city, the West Side Association. Organized by William Martin in 1866 and open to owners of all real estate north and west of Central Park, the Association was governed by an executive committee that included every large commercial interest in New York: real-estate professionals like Martin, old-guard landowners like Benjamin

Beekman, entrepreneurial developers like James Ruggles, wholesale merchants like Marshall Roberts, Wall Street financiers like Russell Sage, politician-speculators like (ex-mayors and electoral adversaries) Fernando Wood and Daniel Tiemann.[50] Such a parliament of capital testified to the energy with which the various sectors of New York's bourgeoisie sought to consolidate their influence on the city-building process.

Of course, belonging to the same boards did not make these urbanists clones of one another. It would be more accurate to say that they lived in a class world that was internally divided, socially heterogeneous, and yet thickly interwoven. They came to the city-building process with different, often conflicting economic interests, political ideals, party loyalties, social ties, and cultural styles. At the same time, they shared a common ground of assumptions and institutional arrangements on which divergent interests and ideals could be negotiated. It was this mix of commonalty and division among New York's urbanists that made groups like the West Side Association possible and necessary.

We can start to map the class world of bourgeois urbanism by looking at biographical sketches of the three men whose national claims for the New York landscape I quoted above: Charles Astor Bristed, William Martin, and John A. Dix. Bristed was a patrician Republican, a rentier without commercial pursuits, a Cambridge-trained classicist and genteel man of letters. His old-guard wealth and fastidious temperament made him both respected and somewhat feared as a social critic and satirist of New York's nouveaux-riches. For Bristed, the sine qua non of metropolitan life was refined sociability, especially the elite sociability of the boulevards. He agitated against horse cars on Broadway and Fifth Avenue to protect these "show streets" from the instrumentalities of traffic and political profiteering.[51]

William Martin, by contrast, was the sort of upstart promoter whom Bristed would probably have "cut." A real-estate lawyer and Democratic insider, he founded the West Side Association and served as a Tammany-appointed commissioner of public parks after the fall of the Tweed ring. Yet Martin was less a politician than a booster ideologue. He believed that the transcendent value of a metropolis consisted in its capacity for monumental growth. More particularly, as an uptown property owner and developer, he agitated for bold public works—parks, promenades, street extensions, rapid transit, planned suburban districts—that would open the New York periphery to lavish improvement. While Martin shared the ideal of New York as a landscape of civility articulated by Charles Astor Bristed, he sought to embody that ideal differently: not by protecting enclaves of refinement, but by laying out a landscape of expansive grandeur. Unlike Bristed, Martin not only supported the enfranchisement of horse-car railways on Broadway, but called for the construction of a steam-driven subway underneath it as well.[52]

As for John Adams Dix, he fell somewhere between Bristed's patrician flaneur and Martin's visionary boomer. A trained soldier, railroad attorney, and high-ranking public servant, he belonged to a cohort of politician-capitalists—including August Belmont, Samuel Tilden, and Andrew Haswell Green—who rose to power in the Democratic Party and Wall Street of the mid-nineteenth century. As his talk at the

New-York Historical Society suggests, Dix's politics melded an expansive sense of American historic destiny, support for national commercial development, and a conservative belief in gentility and deference. He envisioned New York as a center of both capitalist dynamism and cultural discipline.[53]

We can array these figures on a spectrum aligning their urban ideals with their political affiliations, socioeconomic status, and generation. On one end would be patrician figures like Bristed or Olmsted: men of established (but not necessarily excessive) wealth and prestige, likely to be Republican, and committed to a program of political stewardship, commercial discipline, and cultural uplift for New York.[54] On the other end were growth-minded boosters like William Martin or Fernando Wood: often men of nouveau-riche or petit bourgeois backgrounds, likely to be Democrats (indeed political deal makers in one of the party's "halls"), and committed to a vision of New York as a center of dynamism and display. In the middle were figures like John Dix or Andrew Haswell Green: men of respectable Protestant stock, neither "old-guard" nor "shoddy," who acquired wealth before the boom times of the Civil War and the Gilded Age. Conservative and class-conscious in their politics, they tended to build elite alliances across party lines, often seeking to curb populist politicians and patronage bosses in their own organizations. (During the 1870s, Green was made city comptroller in the reform regime that toppled the Tweed ring; Dix was elected governor on the Republican ticket, although he never formally switched parties.) Just as they straddled political and status divides, such figures often played a mediating or regulatory role in the city-building process. Green veered between policies of imperial development and fiscal retrenchment, first as treasurer of the Central Park Commission in the 1860s boom, then as city comptroller during the fiscal crises of the 1870s.[55]

Such differences in political affiliation, socioeconomic milieu, and urban ideal sorted New York city builders loosely into camps. It is possible to understand much of the story of Victorian urbanism as a tale of struggle between rival blocs situated at either end of this spectrum—patrician Republicans versus machine Democrats, metropolitan civilizers versus public-works boosters. As I discuss in Chapter 6, each bloc had its own program of planned growth and landscape design, its own vision of the class and political regimes required to undertake such a program. We have already seen some traces of this conflict, in Frederick Law Olmsted's publicity skirmishes to "save" Central Park from the patronage and design interventions of Democratic leaders like Fernando Wood and John Dillon. Indeed no one is more useful than Olmsted for mapping the alliances and divisions that organized the politics of city building in New York. His influence was grounded in a set of social and political connections clustered at one end of the spectrum sketched earlier: a network of patrician capitalists, Republican publicists, and genteel intellectuals who viewed New York as the headquarters for linked projects of nation building, cultural uplift, and urban design.

Olmsted entered this network in the late 1840s as a Staten Island farmer influenced by the Hudson Valley architect and reformer Andrew Jackson Downing. It was at Downing's Newburgh home that he first met Calvert Vaux—then the architect's partner—as well as such rising New York literati as journalist George Curtis and art critic Clarence Cook.[56] In the mid-1850s, these friendships gave Olmsted entry into literary and intellectual circles associated with the nascent Republican Party. With Curtis, Parke Godwin, and others, he launched a (short-lived) genteel monthly; he won notoriety for a series of southern travel writings, free-labor critiques of the slave system, commissioned by editor Henry Raymond of the New York *Times*.[57] By the Civil War, Olmsted had established himself as a leading voice of genteel reform and Republican nationalism in New York. He was at the center of a nexus of cultural projects, all centered in Manhattan, that were central to the Union war effort. He served as executive secretary of the U.S. Sanitary Commission, a novel effort at battlefront medical aid and "scientific" philanthropy (whose president was Henry W. Bellows). He helped found the Union League Club to mobilize business and civic leaders behind Republican policies of loyalism, centralized government, racial equality, liberal political economy, and moral uplift. Finally, with his friend Edwin L. Godkin, he drafted the plan for the (aptly named) *Nation*, the influential journal of opinion that began publication in 1865 under Godkin's editorship.[58]

Olmsted's wanderings during the 1850s and 1860s were symptoms of a painful vocational crisis. Although widely respected as an intellectual and reformer, Olmsted felt thwarted in his quest for a career that could combine personal ambition, financial security, professional authority, and benevolent influence. As he wrote one lifelong friend, the charity reformer Charles Loring Brace, his work seemed "constantly & everywhere arrested, wrecked, mangled and misused."[59] Yet the sheer energy of Olmsted's psychodrama makes him an ideal guide to genteel networks and institutional projects in New York. And paradoxically, his itinerancy made him all the more effective when he *did* turn to urbanism as a vocation, first in the making of Central Park (1857–61), and then as a professional landscape architect whom Vaux coaxed into full-time partnership after 1865. For, as we have seen, Olmsted brought all his social capital to bear on the city-building process. When he applied to be superintendent of Central Park—at the urging of park commissioner Charles Elliott, a friend from the Downing circle—his supporters included such eminences as the poet-editor William Cullen Bryant (Parke Godwin's father-in-law), Republican jurist David Dudley Field (E. L. Godkin's first employer), and investment bankers James Brown and Morris Jesup. In 1878 the same networks mobilized—this time unsuccessfully—to protect Olmsted from dismissal by Tammany adversaries. For two decades, then, his influence as an urbanist was inseparable from and dependent on the social fabric of "patrician-Republican" New York.[60]

And yet this sort of social-positional mapping is much too simple and reductionist. All historical actors are complex and surprising; and more than most, bourgeois New Yorkers lived in a world of divided loyalties, unexpected sympathies and enmities, fluid alliances, and multiple commitments. On one hand, the spectrum that I have sketched here tends to *understate* the political and cultural heterogeneity of the city-building process. On the other hand, it tends to *overstate* the fixity of the divisions among bourgeois urbanists. Here again Olmsted is a useful guide: at both his hiring in 1857 and his firing twenty-one years later—times of intense interparty turmoil—he drew support not only from "patrician-Republicans" but also from elite Democrats like manufacturer Peter Cooper and banker August Belmont.[61] Even the most disparate members of the metropolitan bourgeoisie were bound by a complex fabric of economic, social, and cultural solidarities: the integuments of a shared class world.

One place to begin understanding the heterogeneity and unity of that world is at a small Gramercy Park dinner party held on November 18, 1865, in honor of the visiting war hero Ulysses S. Grant—a dinner, as it happens, to which the conservative-Democrat Dix and patrician-Republican Bristed were both invited. Dix's presence is no mystery. Commissioned as a Union general at the start of the Civil War, he was himself a local hero to propertied New Yorkers, having overseen enforcement of the draft after the bloody riots of July 1863. Charles Astor Bristed had no special credentials other than his old-guard status; but he was, like Dix, a friend and coparishioner of the host, Republican attorney George Templeton Strong. (All three belonged to Trinity Church, the city's most elite congregation and one of its largest landlords; Strong and Dix each served as treasurer of Trinity's vast holdings, and Dix's son occupied its pulpit.) Among the dinner guests were other prestigious Unionists: Senator Edwin Morgan of New York, editor Henry Raymond of the New York *Times*, and Samuel Ruggles, the developer of the fashionable square where the party took place (and George Templeton Strong's father-in-law). "It was a brilliant, distinguished, and 'nobby' assemblage," the host noted with relish in his now-famous diary, "and they all seemed to have a pleasant time." After dinner, as was customary, "the ladies withdrew," and the men indulged in cigars, liquor, and conversation: "The Lieutenant General thinks black regiments trustworthy if they have good officers, but not otherwise," Strong reported. "He holds General Lee in high respect." Toward the end of the evening, the ladies and gentlemen reconvened for an impromptu musicale, and one guest "sang Mrs. Julia Ward Howe's version of the John Brown song with immense spirit and effect."[62]

Grant, his family, and his staff in fact spent a whole week in New York; throughout the triumphal visit, we see the same mix of class sociability, cultural refinement, and bipartisan patriotism. Bourgeois New Yorkers feted the war hero with testimonials at the Union League and other elite clubs, carriage drives in Central Park and upper Manhattan, special performances of opera and Shakespeare, gifts of trotting horses—honoraria which were at the same time insignia of New York's metropolitan rank. The climax of the visit was a "public" reception at the Fifth Avenue Hotel, two days after the Strongs' dinner, hosted (and bankrolled) by one hundred fifty civic leaders. The organizing committee included Unionist politicians, editors, businessmen, military officers, and cultural gentry of every stripe: Republicans like Senator Morgan and editor Raymond, conservative Democrats like Judge Charles Daly and dry-goods retailer A. T. Stewart, even Tammany leaders William Tweed and Oakey Hall. While the three thousand invited guests enjoyed oysters, ices, wines, and fireworks over Madison Square—and George Templeton Strong's wife, Ellie, chaperoned a nervous Julia Grant—the general received greetings from New York's civic, business, cultural, and "society" leaders until "his right hand was . . . swollen and shapeless." Already positioning himself for a presidential bid in 1868, Grant needed the good will of Manhattan's power elites, and he reciprocated in words that showed his mastery of the native idiom: "It affords me great pleasure to accept this invitation . . . from the citizens of the metropolis of our country, and, twenty years hence, of the world."[63]

The details of Grant's visit afford us a wonderful glimpse of the alliances and attitudes that bound bourgeois New Yorkers together across the spectrum. They welcomed the general into a class world delineated by rituals of mutuality and cultivation, assertions of racial and class hierarchy, choreographies of gender mixing and segregation. The overt agenda of the celebration, of course, was to identify this complex drama of "civilization" and class unity with a bipartisan politics of loyalism and national unity—and, as Grant understood, to identify New York's stature with the Union victory. What was less explicit is how much these social bonds, cultural assumptions, and nationalist ambitions shaped the city-building process. Within a few weeks, Grant's praise of New York as "the metropolis of our country" had found its way into local debates over the urban landscape; William Martin published it as the epigram of his manifesto for uptown development, *The Growth of New York*. This was not simply a case of rhetorical opportunism, although it was that too. Despite his own less than "nobby" credentials, Martin's agitations were not so distant from the social world of George Templeton Strong's parlor and the reception at the Fifth Avenue Hotel. When he headed the West Side Association, the group's secretary was James Ruggles, son of the Gramercy Park developer and Strong's brother-in-law; the executive committee included Knickerbocker proprietors like Benjamin Beekman, who delivered the Grant testimonial on behalf of the Union League Club.[64]

But William Martin's most important ally in the Republican gentry was Frederick Law Olmsted. His brother Howard was a clerk and dear friend of the reformer, a trusted assistant who followed Olmsted from Central Park to the U.S. Sanitary Commission, to the management of a gold-mining venture in central California in the mid-1860s, and back to New York and landscape design after the war. Yet William Martin's ties to Olmsted were not just personal. In his tenure as a parks commissioner (1875–78), the two were New York's strongest advocates for metropolitan planning, working together on expansive proposals to lay out the northern periphery as a region of parks, boulevards, and landscaped suburbs. Despite their differences in party, status, and (to some degree) aesthetics, they collaborated in a series of bitter fights against the retrenchment policies of Comptroller Andrew Green. It was the aftermath of these struggles that led to Olmsted's 1878 dismissal and the defeat of the comprehensive program that he and Martin envisioned.[65]

In short, bourgeois urbanism took shape in a social milieu that was heterogeneous, diverse, and yet surprisingly interfiliated. Both city-building discourse and real-estate capital circulated through that world; programs of property investment, public works, and environmental reform were debated and worked out within it. Its members created an array of new institutions—park commissions, real-estate associations, trade journals, reform groups—that made New York a national center of experimentation in architecture, planning, and urban design. And, as we have seen, they linked these innovations to the dialectic of metropolis and nation. For elite New Yorkers, debates about the urban landscape—about the desirability of horse cars on Broadway or the need for uptown boulevards—naturally engaged issues of American character and destiny, appeals to the sublimity of the continent, invocations of Union war heroes. Why did the link between city building and nation building seem so central, so self-evident, to them?

Put simply, New York's rise as "the American metropolis" coincided with the emergence of the city's bourgeoisie as a national class. As many observers noted, Victorian Manhattan was the scene of a vast ingathering of propertied, cultivated, and socially ambitious Americans. "New York attracts all the brains, and all the cash of the nation," reported *Leslie's Illustrated* in 1875. "It is the heart, whence flows the all the blood required to keep the meanest railroad in the most distant State in running order." Here was the demographic reality behind Junius Browne's tableau of Broadway as a national procession; in the latter half of the nineteenth century, more than three-fifths of the wealthiest New Yorkers had been born elsewhere. Before the Civil War, city-born merchants and rentiers were supplemented mainly by northeastern migrants like Cornelius Vanderbilt or Levi Morton and European immigrants who channeled international capital into Wall Street (most famously, the Rothschild agent August Belmont). These financiers grew rich in early rail development, government bonds, and war contracting, and they in turn drew a cadre of midwestern and western capitalists who sought financing for the new infrastructural, industrial, and extractive projects of the Gilded Age. Collis Huntington came east in 1862 to fund the Central Pacific Railroad on behalf of California's "Big Four" and never left. Andrew Carnegie arrived five years later, directing the consolidation of his steel empire from a suite at the Saint Nicholas Hotel. By 1890, an estimated half of the country's three to four thousand millionaires lived in the metropolitan area. As the city's real-estate trade paper reported, New York was "the great concourse, not only for the new rich men of Denver, Chicago, and Cincinnati but also for the Bonanza kings of . . . the Pacific."[66]

The confluence of what *Leslie's* called "the brains . . . of the nation" was a more complex story. Through much of the nineteenth century, New York's cultural stature remained inferior to that of Boston, home of Harvard, *Atlantic Monthly*, and other genteel bastions. Yet from 1850 to 1890, the aegis of cultural authority did shift to Manhattan. The shift began with an impressive cohort of reformers, journalists, and intellectuals who arrived or came of age in New York in the 1850s: Charles Loring Brace, the creator of the Children's Aid Society in 1853; George Curtis and E. L. Godkin of *Harper's Weekly* and *The Nation*, the foremost political editors of the Gilded Age; religious intellectuals Henry Bellows and Henry Ward Beecher; women's rights activists Susan B. Anthony and Elizabeth Cady Stanton, who launched *The Revolution* in Brooklyn in 1868; literary professionals Jane Croly and Sarah Parton, who founded the pioneering women's club Sorosis in the same year; artists and design experts like Frederic Church, Clarence Cook, Olmsted, and Vaux. This generation was responsible for much of the leading journalistic, reform, and artistic work in Victorian America.[67]

What underlay all of these itineraries was a process of collective self-identification. Just as Wall Street incorporated the economies of the continent into a single capital market, so regional elites coalesced into a *metropolitan* class whose business, social, marital, and moral solidarities with one another outweighed their bonds to the communities from which they came. The resulting class world was characterized by a sort of cosmopolitan localism, a mix of heterogeneity and concentration distinctive to the metropolis. "New York is cosmopolitan in feeling," William Martin observed. "It has received its accessions . . . from the middle states, the proud-spirited South, the true grit of New England; and these accessions have included the very best elements. All feelings and all opinions are represented here. We are all closely in contact. . . . How rapidly these conflicting opinions have their points rubbed off; and, day by day, truth appears. . . ." Notwithstanding Martin's breezy tone, elite solidarity did not come easily. Rivalries like the concert-house war between the (Knickerbocker) Academy of Music and the (new wealthy) Metropolitan Opera House made New York infamous for snobbism and status mongering. Indeed, along with the city's commercial ascendance came a series of social arbiters—most notoriously, Ward McAllister, the Astor's gatekeeper—to guard the portals and ballrooms of established "society" against arrivistes.[68]

Yet, as historian Fredric Cople Jaher has shown in rich detail, New York "society" in the long run made a virtue of its volatility. Unlike Boston and Charleston, the Manhattan bourgeoisie was marked by multiple, overlapping elites and intergenerational alliances, patterns that undermined its cohesion as a "Brahmin"-like caste, but enhanced its capacity to regenerate wealth and power.[69] The money market and the marriage market were perhaps the most important mechanisms of elite integration, venues where old guard and newcomers, merchants and financiers could come together. Yet the construction and use of the urban landscape also furthered the process of class consolidation.

First of all, city building offered business opportunities. As property owners and mortgage creditors, old- and new-moneyed New Yorkers transferred the profits of national growth into local space. John Jacob Astor was the first celebrated case of this practice, parlaying his fur-trading fortune into New York's largest real-estate portfolio in the early nineteenth century, but he was not the last. James Slevin, a dry-goods merchant based in Manhattan and Cincinnati, turned to city real estate after an initial push into Ohio Valley town booming; by his death in 1870, Slevin owned a dozen commercial and residential properties throughout Manhattan, worth some three-quarters of a million dollars. Californian William Belden bought into the cast-iron wholesale district, while Chicago land and railroad mogul William B. Ogden invested in uptown rapid-transit development. Such strategies were not limited to merchants and robber barons: Frederick Law Olmsted invested in several California ventures with Howard Martin and in Brooklyn real estate with E. L. Godkin and others.[70]

In Chapter 4, I analyze more fully the structure of the capital market in New York's real-estate economy. Here I want to stress the social, sectoral, and geographic fluidity of these patterns of investment and accumulation. It is almost impossible to lay down hard and fast distinctions between "local" and "cosmopolitan" investors, merchants and industrialists and landowners. Rather it makes more sense to see city building in New York as a permeable, connective process, one that tended to breach the barriers among regional and sectoral markets, linking various constituencies in circuits of partnership and debt. The result was a complex network of solidarities and interdependencies, integrative of both class and nation, that was embedded in the property, credit, and spatial structure of the built environment.[71]

Urban space also mediated the process of national class formation in another, less instrumental way. It served as the stage for a complex dramaturgy of politeness with which bourgeois New Yorkers acknowledged each other as peers. The city's pleasure grounds, parlors, promenades, and places of amusement were "properties" in a theatrical as well as an economic sense, apparatuses of sociability for a diverse and far-flung class. The *Real Estate Record and Builders' Guide*, for instance, praised "the attractions of our metropolis, its parks, drives, opera houses, club houses, and general vivacity" for "drawing moneyed men from other states to our city." The *Times* echoed such assertions, noting that Central Park in particular "increas[ed] the wealth of New York, by helping to draw to it people of fortune from all parts of the Union." Moreover the idea that urban space was a medium of class integration fed back into the city-building process itself. Urbanists touted their proposals by presenting them as lodestones for a national bourgeoisie; as William Martin wrote in *The Growth of New York*:

> There are beginning to appear here in large numbers . . . men of acquired and invested fortunes . . . who occupy themselves in developing the resources of the country, . . . men who have acquired wealth in other places and come here to enjoy it. Such as these, with more feeling for the elegancies of life . . . are irresistibly attracted to the great centres, and . . . [they] will call upon the taste and skill of the architect for his ablest productions. When the borders of the [Central] park come to be lined with houses, with churches, hotels and other public buildings . . . , they must be worthy of the metropolis of the western world.[72]

The mutual development of metropolis and nation was thus inseparable from a second dialectic, one of class and space. Local city building and national class formation were interdependent processes in New York. The reconstruction of the city offered a means by which propertied and refined Americans came together as a collectivity. At the same time, their material and cultural investments in the cityscape were framed by their claims to national leadership. Bourgeois New Yorkers viewed the built environment not just as a site of capital accumulation or genteel performance, but as a medium for projecting their power; this was what made Fifth Avenue horse cars and uptown parks so consequential. The allegory of the national cityscape was finally an allegory of their own ambitions.

The Meanings of Empire

What, then, did bourgeois New Yorkers mean when they spoke of "the American metropolis"? How did their vision of national power—both the city's and their own—shape the discourse of Victorian urbanism? To answer these questions, we need to turn from mapping class networks to analyzing the rhetoric that circulated through them. As often occurs with ideological discourses that are widely used yet taken for granted, discussions of New York's metropolitan dominance were profuse and revealing in their metaphors.

When boosters, journalists, reformers, and officials sought to describe the relation between New York and the nation, they resorted to richly figurative language. Sometimes the metaphors were kinetic or mechanical ("the lever that moves the American world"); sometimes military ("the commanding . . . centre of the civilized world"); often geometric ("an immovable, magnificent centre," "the one great centre or national heart"); and often hydraulic and vascular ("the great heart of the country," "the heart, whence flows all the blood required to keep the meanest railroad in the most distant State in running order").[73] Several patterns typify these images. They tend to inflate or monumentalize New York's stature, as the recurrence of words like "great" or "magnificent" suggests. They tend to naturalize the city's power, often drawing on the lexicon of flows and forces with which market circulation was naturalized in Victorian social thought. Most interestingly, they tend to link dynamic or kinetic relationships with topographical or geometric ones. The effect is to endow New York with both agency and centrality, to stress the city's power over both national history and national space.

One figure especially shaped nineteenth-century conceptions of New York's "metropolitan" relationship with the nation. This was the figure of *empire*—one of the most important and, for us, opaque keywords in the politics and culture of Victorian America. Like images of New York as a beating heart or an Archimedean point, the trope of "the Empire City" implied a double power over time and space, the linked possession of a world-historical destiny and a tributary expanse of territory. New York seems to have first won the epithet in the 1820s, when the completion of the Erie Canal secured its commercial dominion over rival ports and a western resource hinterland. By 1850—the year that journalist George Foster used it as the title of a popular book of urban sketches—the name figured in many city firms and voluntary associations and was a commonplace means of invoking New York's growing influence.[74]

The trope had a surprisingly broad range of meanings and contexts. Most often, of course, it referred to mercantile power, an imperium based in New York's growth as an emporium. "London became the commercial metropolis of the world by controlling the commerce of the Indies," wrote a group of waterfront developers in the mid-1860s. "Yet in less than five years, the Empire City of the Western Hemisphere will have diverted that trade to herself." At other times, the significance of empire was moral and political, entailing not just market power, but civilizational responsibility.

"Great cities have always wielded a moral sovereignty in human affairs," argued the Citizens' Association, a good-government reform coalition of the 1860s. "This Empire City, thus grandly enthroned on the point where all the great interests of the world meet . . . , this great Metropolis, with its magnificent capabilities and exalted destiny, ought . . . to enjoy the wisest and best government that man can bestow." Not surprisingly, such talk saturated the city-building process, setting an ideological standard with which the progress and problems of the built environment were debated. "In view of the imperial destiny of the metropolis," the *Real Estate Record* editorialized in an 1868 plea for comprehensive planning, "is it not a shame that its building and streets should be left to chance?"[75]

Empire thus had a rich and varied field of signification. Equally important, it had a *different* field of signification from twentieth-century usage. The word had not acquired the meaning or moral stigma that it has today: that of a predatory, militarized, antidemocratic state power, expanding over borders—often overseas—to subjugate other peoples and regions, while at the same time enforcing their juridical and racial inferiority and their unincorporable difference. This sense of empire accurately describes core elements of nineteenth-century U.S. expansion: its land hunger, its reliance on armed power to gain territory, its racist rationales for Mexican conquest and Indian removal.[76] Yet when Americans of the period used "empire" to describe the nation-building process, the modern meaning of the word is not generally what they had in mind. That usage was codified (by both advocates and detractors) in the era of Euro-American adventurism and mass nationalist insurgency between the 1880s and World War I. Especially after the defeat of fascist aggression and the spread of anti-colonial movements in the post-1945 Third World, its connotations became almost wholly negative. No one today would seriously propose a project of political, economic, or cultural development under the sign of "empire." Yet that is exactly what civic boosters, builders, and urban observers did in speaking of Victorian New York.

There were, to be sure, "anti-imperial" utterances, even in the Empire City. Here, for instance, is Benjamin Beekman's testimonial for U. S. Grant at the Union League Club in 1865: "The rebellion you have crushed had for its object the establishment of an empire. It was the foe of republican institutions, though disguised in republican form." Such language drew on a republican intellectual tradition that, not unlike modern anti-imperialism, drew a sharp moral contrast between imperial and democratic regimes; the autocracy, inherited privilege, and professional armies of the former were juxtaposed to the citizen rule and civic equality of "republics." Again like twentieth-century usage, the republican critique tended to brand the European great powers as the exemplars of empire, enemies of New World liberty; Beekman links the Confederacy to French efforts to install Maximilian as emperor of Mexico: "European ambition has striven to establish another empire over a sister Republic. . . . A Mexican GRANT will yet restore his country, as you have saved your own."[77] Unlike modern anti-imperialists, however, nineteenth-century critics did not construe empires as historically dominant or secure. Quite the contrary: as the fate of the Confederacy and (a few years later) Napoleon III made clear, the moral of imperial history was mutability; overreaching and decadence inevitably corroded empires from within and defeated them from without.

The fall of Rome was the proof text for this lesson, but in nineteenth-century American culture, its locus classicus was Thomas Cole's monumental cycle of paintings *The Course of Empire*. Exhibited in New York in 1836, it portrayed a (fictive) city's arc from savagery to civilized grandeur to defeat and ruin in a series of five allegorical landscapes. The cycle was widely construed as a fable of decline from which the American republic would remain exempt, but, as Angela Miller has illuminated, such an exceptionalist reading mistook the artist's aims. Cole was using republican iconography to offer a conservative jeremiad against the self-seeking and jingoism that he saw in Jacksonian society. It was a critique shared by many American Whigs: "[Do not] convert the Republic which our fathers created for us into an Empire," wrote an opponent of the annexation of northern Mexico, "a great Power bearing imperial sway over distant provinces and dependencies."[78]

Between the Mexican-American and Civil Wars, however, such warnings gave way to a rival sense of empire: the portrayal of America precisely *as* an imperial republic. The celebratory nationalism of this rhetoric is familiar to us from the history of Western expansion, with its appeals to "the empire of our *continental* geography."[79] Landscape art of the era gave powerful expression to similar dreams. In contrast to Thomas Cole's iconography of ruin, artists like Asher Durand, Frederick Church, and Emanuel Leutze created expansive, iconic scenes that invited the "magisterial gaze" of both figures within the composition and the viewing public. Perhaps the most emblematic of these nationscapes was Leutze's "Westward the Course of Empire Takes Its Way," a mural composed for the west wall of the U.S. Capitol in 1861 (Figure 1.5). Like Cole, Leutze took his title from Berkeley's famous "Verses on the Prospect of Planting Arts and Learning in America," but he invested *the course of empire* with quite a different meaning. The mural depicts a party of heroic pioneers, centered around a Daniel Boone–like figure and family, who have attained the crest of a mountain divide and look out upon the light-suffused plain they are about to occupy. Below the main panel, a vignette of San Francisco Bay tacitly invokes the conquests and mining boom of the late 1840s, the *anni mirabiles* of U.S. continental expansion. Indeed the mural can almost be read as a visual pun on "gold rush," with its jubilant pioneers shouting "Eureka" over the vision of a golden West that itself overlooks the Golden Gate. At once a tableau of national space and an allegory of U.S. history as westering progress, the work comprises a sort of pictorial précis of the Turner thesis.[80]

Clearly *empire* has been morally and ideologically transvalued here. The term retained a sense of acquisitive power, but not one of despotic, corrupt, or transient rule. Rather it named a progressive, world-making dynamism, the possession of which endowed America with both a civilizing mission—an "imperial destiny"—and a set of territorial claims that the mission required and justified. This version of empire did not connote political subjection or violation of borders. How could it? Empire was what constituted the nation within its "natural" boundaries and unities to begin with, channeling popular energies into an organic, ordained process of growth: "I do

FIGURE 1.5   Painted in the U.S. Capitol in 1861, Emanuel Leutze's mural "Westward the
Course of Empire Takes Its Way" gave official, visual sanction to the mythologies of American expansionism. It portrays a party of pioneering families pausing atop a mountain divide
to gaze westward on its future: a vacant, golden land. (Courtesy of the Architect of the Capitol)

not care whether you like it or not," Stephen Douglas proclaimed in defense of U.S.
continental expansion, "you cannot help it! It is the decree of Providence!" Nor did
this rhetoric equate imperial expansion with armed force; it often represented the
course of American empire as uniquely *peaceful* because based on commerce rather
than conquest. In the words of one Cincinnati booster, "A commercial people, using
only pacific means, have gained an empire whose breadth and wealth might satisfy
the ambition of even a Napoleon."[81]

In the face of this sort of rhetoric, of course, we need to remind ourselves that the
actual effect of imperial nationalism was to foster policies of race war and territorial
conquest from the annexation of Texas (1845) to the Wounded Knee massacre (1892).
Yet it is striking that, in contrast to turn-of-the-century U.S. imperialism, this discourse did not typically foreground the *ideal* of racial or military supremacy.[82] Its
racism and coerciveness were often more effaced than asserted. Imperial nationalism
tended to portray the continent like Leutze's golden plain: as a space luminous with
possibility but lacking internal marks and boundaries, emptied of rival states and
racial "others"—or so sparsely peopled that these were fated to vanish away—await-
ing only occupation by white Americans for its fulfillment. I would argue that this ca-

pacity to *erase* the marks of domination and conflict is what made landscape so important a medium of nationalist ideology in the mid-nineteenth century. Landscape transmuted nation into nature, human agency into providential destiny; it rendered the course of empire as if this were prescribed in the topography and scenery of North America itself.

By the Civil War, then, "empire" had become a key trope of American nationhood. Walt Whitman invokes it, for instance, in "A Broadway Pageant," composed on the occasion of the Japanese legation's arrival in New York in 1860. First published in the *Times* as "The Errand Bearers," the poem is organized around the juxtaposition of two antipodal "errands": on one hand, the diplomatic mission of "Niphon's" envoys parading up Broadway; on the other, the millennial errand of republican America—"Libertad of the world"—as it disseminates its energies abroad:

> I chant the new empire grander than any before, as in a vision it comes to me,
> I chant America the mistress, I chant a greater supremacy,
> I chant projected a thousand blooming cities yet in time on those groups of sea-islands,
> My sail-ships and steam-ships threading the archipelagos,
> My stars and stripes fluttering in the wind . . .

Whitman's bardic patriotism reflects his roots in the Democratic Party, the wellspring for so much antebellum expansionism; the poet's work often invests the party's celebration of commercial dynamism, global mission, and boundless national space with transcendental meaning. All the more telling, then, to find similar language in *Harper's Weekly* eight years later. In a column likely written by Republican political editor George Curtis, the genteel weekly sounded the strains of imperial nationalism to link completion of the transcontinental railroad with diplomatic and trade openings to Asia: "The United States have become the great highway between Western Europe and Eastern Asia; and New York is rapidly becoming the 'world's greatest mart'—the centre of the commercial world. Our own vast empire is rapidly increasing in population and developing in wealth, natural commerce, manufactures, and agriculture; indeed, it is becoming apparent that the whole Pacific coast must soon become ours, thus extending our actual territory."[83]

The surprising commonalty of these texts measures the ideological sway that imperial nationalism had attained by the 1860s. Three aspects of the discourse are especially notable. First of all, the ideals of continentalism and imperial expansion pervade the whole political spectrum. Indeed, even as they opposed the conquest of Mexico, Whig leaders like John Quincy Adams and Henry Clay had always set forth their own version of American empire, grounded in the peaceable acquisition and settlement of a continental territory, the prosecution of internal improvements, and overseas trade. Such views gained a foothold in the Republican Party through New Yorker William Seward. As secretary of state under Lincoln and Johnson, Seward advocated the completion of the transcontinental railroad, the acquisition of Alaska, proposals for the annexation of Hawaii, and trade openings to Asia. ("Abroad our empire shall no limits know,/ But like the sea in boundless circles flow," he versified in an 1867 letter.) It was this nexus of initiatives that spurred *Harper's Weekly* to publish the breathless column just quoted.[84]

Second, both Whitman and Curtis elide geographic expansionism with rhetorical expansiveness. On one hand, each uses the trope of empire to link American national destiny with the growth of an *inter*national capitalist order. This linkage of nation building and global market building is characteristic of much nineteenth-century bourgeois thought; we see it, for instance, in the spatial classifications of world's fairs or the ideal of free trade as a system of nationally defined competitive advantages. Here the geography of expansion focuses particularly on the opening of the Asia market—the legendary "passage to India"—as the telos of American empire, the end point of its westering course. For both Whitman and Curtis, processes of national consolidation and Pacific expansion imply one another: the projection of American energies overseas is driven by, and in turn reinforces, the compactness of American energies "at home." On the other hand, each text articulates this claim in a semantics of repetition, dilation, and possession. Whitman make this explicit: "I chant . . . I chant . . . My sail-ships . . . My stars and stripes . . ." Yet with its repeated "becoming" and "ours," the *Weekly* has something of the same, self-intoxicated expansiveness.[85]

Finally, and most important for our purposes, there is the way both texts *place* themselves. For they each mark New York City as the spot where the imperial nation and the world market are joined. The force of Curtis's editorial turns on its confusion of metropolis and nation: we cannot tell which *ours* is meant by "our own vast empire." Whitman makes equally ambiguous the "us" to whom his poem is addressed: "Superb-faced Manhattan!/ Comrade Americanos! to us, then at last the Orient comes." Whether intended or not, the significance of these confusions is clear: New York was the seat of national empire. "As Rome, in olden times, was the mistress of millions in remotest provinces," argued the Citizens' Association, "so must imperial New-York fulfil a like destiny to the teeming States and territories which commerce, science and other interests shall attract towards her bosom."[86]

We should not be surprised that New York held a privileged place in the nationalist imagination of the mid-nineteenth century. This was just when the city was establishing its sway over American markets and middle-class publics; "empire" offered New Yorkers a powerful image for the dialectic of metropolis and nation. Yet to note this fact is to underscore an aspect of the trope that is sometimes scanted in discussions of frontier myths and manifest destiny: its fundamentally urban frame of reference. To mid-nineteenth century American ears, the word *imperial* went with *city* as naturally as it did *nation*. The energies that it named were thought to be lodged in urban centers, and those energies circulated according to developmental laws that made cities the engines of commercial and civilizational history. Or so argued the great theorists of urbanization in Victorian America: the cadre of economists, commercial promoters, and speculators whom we have come to label civic boosters.[87]

It is easy today to deride the booster writers as mystical idiots and confidence men, figures akin to the mesmerists and phrenologists of nineteenth-century pseudoscience. Yet in their day, such men as Toledo's Jesup Scott, Chicago's John Wright, the western administrator William Gilpin, and New Yorker William Martin codified a set of claims about the links between urban growth, commercial geography, and cultural progress that were widely believed and quite sophisticated. Scholars like Charles Glaab and William Cronon have analyzed their ideas mainly in connection with townsite speculations and intercity rivalries in the West. With good reason: booster theories were central to the region's urban and economic development. Taking them seriously enables us to grasp the extent to which the American West was city made. Yet booster discourse had an eastern variant as well, one whose history remains largely to be written. New York has a prominent place in that story. Boosterism pervaded elite commentary about the growth of the metropolis and did much to shape how bourgeois urbanists sought to reconstruct the cityscape.

The booster writers collectively formulated the dominant model by which nineteenth-century elites explained, and sought to direct, urban growth. It was a curious mix of economic theory and entrepreneurial practice: in part, a nuanced analysis of the role of urban centers in catalyzing capitalist development; in part, a huckster jargon aimed at capturing the energies of that development on behalf of particular communities. Like modern regional economists, Scott, Gilpin, and their peers argued that commercial growth depended on the capacity of leading cities to organize markets, resource fields, investment flows, and rival trade centers into subordinate hinterlands. The historical career of a city was shaped by its success in wresting this "imperial" role from its competitors and consolidating as broad a "tributary" domain as possible. Boosters elaborated complex theories concerning the natural and economic factors—access to raw materials, local topography, transport facilities, even climatic patterns—that would determine the ascendance of particular cities or settings. William Gilpin argued with near mystical fervor that thermal and ecological patterns ordained the rise of a new "Centropolis" in the Kansas prairies. Jesup Scott, in contrast, viewed trade and transport routes as paramount; these would orient the country's vast internal market to one of the Great Lakes gateway ports, he argued, nominating Chicago and his native Toledo as the likeliest contenders for greatness.[88]

More often than not, some sort of special pleading lay at the heart of booster theories. They were designed in large part to make the claim for a city's imperial destiny into a self-fulfilling prophecy, by calling forth the private and public enterprise that would confirm it. In fact booster rhetoric forms an important subgenre of the literature of boasts and propaganda so central to commercial and real-estate investment in the nineteenth century. Western boomers used it to promote their chosen hamlet as the "Paris of the prairies"; Chicago elites invoked it to encourage rail investments that would ensure the city's control of the midwestern grain and lumber trades. Boosterism, in short, served the moral and material needs of local capitalists and promoters. It offered a fable of destiny that invested entrepreneurial will with inevitability.[89]

All of which made it supremely useful to Victorian New Yorkers. Manhattan's boosters tended to be a bit less nakedly opportunistic than their western cousins;

they were concerned with elevating the stature of the metropolis, not with fashioning it out of whole cloth. Yet business, real-estate, editorial, and political elites avidly used booster discourse to assert the natural basis, historic certainty, and geographic reach of New York's imperium. "THE NATURAL SITE FOR A GREAT CITY," William Martin opened one chapter of *The Growth of New York*: "There is no spot in Christendom where Nature has been more lavish of her gifts or promises for a great city than the site where New York stands." The *Real Estate Record* celebrated the frantic growth of the late 1860s with similar confidence: "This whole country is bound to be the great commercial centre of the world, and the city of New York the world's metropolis. . . . Be not afraid, this is the veritable land of promise, and New York will be the New Jerusalem." Martin and the *Record* were among the most sophisticated exponents of booster ideology in the metropolis. Like their western counterparts, they melded a subtle analysis of New York's economic prospects with the strategic touting of local development interests, and they clothed both in a triumphalist rhetoric of destiny. Yet we see similar notions coming from the sort of reform voices whom scholars often assume to have been at odds with urban commercialism. The executive council of the Citizens' Association opened one report with a paean to Manhattan's mercantile vitality that would have done the most overheated promoter proud: "New York is just bursting into giant life. Its location is on a point where all the continents meet. The Atlantic washes its feet, the tropics pour their riches into its lap, the Arctic brings its products, the vast interior of our own country fills its warehouses, while by the [Union] Pacific Railroad the regions of China and Japan and the East Indies are brought to its doors."[90]

As the sheer excess of this rhetoric suggests, something more was at stake than the analysis of economic incubators and land values. Civic boosterism offered Victorian New Yorkers a heroic narrative of urban power, investing Manhattan with the energies that Whitman and Leutze saw in national expansion. For the *Real Estate Record*, the Empire City became a promised land of millennial profits; for the Citizens' Association, it was a figure of "Oriental" fable, a giant potentate to whose feet and lap the world brought tribute. Boosterism amplified the facts of metropolitan dominance into a magical narrative of mastery over time and space: a metahistory of destiny, a metageography of centrality.

This narrative of mastery framed the ways in which elite New Yorkers imagined the Empire City. It offered them a city-centered model of human history, an epic of contest and succession among the great world capitals. The idea of a lineage of metropolitan centers, ordained by the laws of time, was what American boosters read in Berkeley's famous verse about the course of empire. For them the reference was not to hardy pioneers, but to the westering journey of civilization from one imperial city to the next: Ur to Tyre to Athens to Rome to Paris to London . . . to New York. Of course the same forces of destiny that enthroned a metropolis could also propel it into decline. By the turn of the century, Manhattan elites began to worry that the course of empire was westering its way to Chicago; such fears fueled the consolidation of five-borough Greater New York in 1898. During the 1850s and 1860s, however, commercial, political, and editorial leaders were confident that the arc of history pointed straight at them. To the east, their dependence on European centers—especially the world financial center of London—was being overturned: "New York will . . . [become] the harbor of ten thousand marts," State Senator Cheney Ames exulted at the end of the Civil War, "and advance . . . to a successful rivalry with London, with London, with whom it will dispute the title of the commercial metropolis of the world." To the west, the formation of a continental hinterland promised an incomparable future of wealth and dominion: "What, with the Atlantic and Pacific coasts united with ropes of iron," the *Real Estate Record* prophesied, "our resources will be increased . . . faster than we have ever yet dreamed of. When we consider that New York is the nucleus and national centre to which this vast wealth will flow, we may well pause to consider the glorious future which awaits us." The *Record* did not pause long, as any reader of its weekly effusions can testify.[91]

At the same time, boosterism offered New Yorkers a *spatial* vision of empire, a geography of urban power. At its heart was the fantasy that William Gilpin called "Centropolis": the great city that had composed the regional, national, or world market around itself. Manhattan's elites believed that New York was that central place. "If commerce ever finds an immovable, magnificent centre, it will be here on this small island of Manhattan," asserted the Citizens' Association. *Harper's Weekly* went even further. In an 1868 column—the one about "our own vast empire" discussed earlier—it published a two-page engraving of new developments in the "COMMERCIAL RELATIONS OF NEW YORK": the transcontinental railroad, trade openings to Honolulu and Central America, the expansion of consular ties with China (Figure 1.6). At the center of the image, a world map stretched from Shanghai to Paris, and in the center of the center was New York. "[We] show at a glance the relation which New York bears . . . with the great commercial cities of *our* East, Europe and West, Asia," the *Weekly* commented. "By it the reader will perceive that we are really in the centre of the universe."[92]

As we shall see, being "in the centre of the universe" mandated an *internal* geography as well. Urbanists debated what sort of cityscape would best embody and extend New York's power over time and space. Such concerns shaped the ways in which the city was imagined even in the midst of civic and national crisis. In the spring of 1864, for instance, the Manhattan gentry held a Metropolitan Fair to raise medical aid for the Union army. On the last day, in a column in the fair's newspaper, one "M." sought to imagine how New York would look one hundred years hence—an epoch, it was clear, when all the booster prophecies would be fulfilled. "First, it will be the heart of the world," the author wrote, in language much like that of *Harper's Weekly*. "Midway between Asia and Europe, it will be to both their market, bank, mine, granary, and library." Such dominion would be inscribed in the texture of the cityscape: new bridges, "marble and granite piers," and teeming crowds in Broadway and Central Park would testify to New York's centrality and power. At Union Square (the site of the current fair), "the spot we now stand on will be . . . covered with marble arcades,

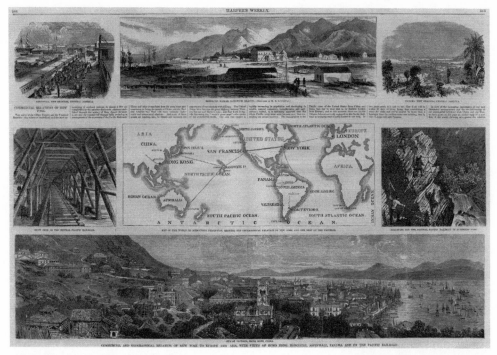

FIGURE 1.6   This striking two-page spread from *Harper's Weekly* (1868) dramatizes the scale of New York's booster ambitions. Like the format of the magazine itself, the illustration links multiple events at varying geographic scales—rail expansion, diplomatic agreements, transoceanic trade openings—to present a tableau of New York's reach and centrality. (*Harper's Weekly*, May 30, 1868; image courtesy of HarpWeek, LLC)

where the Japanese and Abyssinian will lounge away a shopping hour, and order their purchases sent home to the other continents by evening."

It is a remarkable vision: New York as the heart of a global, transracial capitalist civilization. And it is all the more remarkable for coming in the midst of civil war, nine months after the city's bloody, racist draft riots. Of course the author was indulging a narcissistic fantasy as well: the column ends with a twentieth-century reader coming upon an old copy of the paper in "some tranquil library alcove, far in the depths of the present Yonkers" and "sighing to recall . . . the living inspiration of our cause in this second great era of American history." Precisely because it *was* a wish fulfillment, the piece makes clear what it was that bourgeois New Yorkers wished for: a future in which they presided over the vast metropolis of a still-united nation and a newly united world.[93]

Olmsted's Return

Almost exactly a year later, Frederick Law Olmsted was in the midst of another crisis of vocation. He had quit Central Park at the start of the Civil War to serve as executive secretary of the U.S. Sanitary Commission. In 1863, he resigned in turn from the commission, mired in conflict with several members of its board; he spent the rest of the war managing the Mariposa Estate, a gold-mining venture near Yosemite Valley, for a group of Wall Street moneymen. Olmsted went to California mainly to win his fortune, and he did make profitable investments there; but Mariposa never struck it big, and by mid-1865 the estate was near bankruptcy. Meanwhile the North had won its war; it was a time of hope and confidence for the Republican gentry; and Olmsted was weighing new opportunities, each linked to his core concern with cultural uplift and nation building. A group of philanthropists had asked him to direct a national society to aid the freed slaves; E. L. Godkin invited him to be associate editor of the newly launched *Nation* magazine.[94]

It was at this juncture that he received from Calvert Vaux the angry correspondence about "Frederick the Great" with which this chapter began. Their bitter tone notwithstanding, the letters had a straightforward goal: to lure Olmsted back to New York and the profession of landscape design. Throughout the spring and summer of 1865, Vaux had been lobbying to regain a guiding hand in the development of Central Park and win the design commission for Prospect Park, then being planned across the river in Brooklyn. He felt he could do neither without his old collaborator, and he sought to cajole and hector Olmsted into renouncing his other prospects: "There can be no doubt that together we are better fitted to take up these matters than anyone else, and that this . . . is of vital importance to the progress of the Republic," he wrote in early July. "There are plenty of people to write for 'The Nation.' . . . There are plenty of Gold mines to superintend but who is going to be the better for the Gold[?]"[95]

Fortunately for our story, Vaux prevailed. In June, the Brooklyn park commission asked him to prepare a design for Prospect Park; a month later, he and Olmsted were officially reappointed landscape architects for Central Park. In mid-October, the latter sailed from San Francisco via the Central American isthmus, arriving in New York after a tiring six-week journey. Within a few days—having settled his family in a boardinghouse near Union Square—he and Vaux plunged into the Brooklyn project, presenting their preliminary plan to the Prospect Park board in late January. By midsummer, the partners were at work on park, campus, and residential projects throughout the country. Over the next decade, they would play defining roles not only in greater New York but also in the development of landscape architecture nationally. Olmsted himself became the most influential American writer on park and city planning in these years. Even after the partnership broke up, he never revisited the issue of his vocation; indeed much of Olmsted's most innovative work—for instance, his plans for New York's Annexed District and the Boston park system—followed the firm's dissolution in 1874. Ironically, Calvert Vaux had badgered Frederick Law Olmsted through his final identity crisis.[96]

I hope that it is clear by now why, for someone like Frederick Law Olmsted, a career of urban design centered in New York could match the claims of racial philanthropy or political journalism. Even on the eve of national Reconstruction—especially then—the making and meaning of the metropolitan landscape were matters of the greatest consequence to Victorian Americans. New York's economic and cultural ascendance meant that the Manhattan cityscape was an instrument of national progress and an emblem of national identity. Bourgeois New Yorkers treated it as a site of capital accumulation, a stage on which to enact their solidarity as a class, a means of asserting their political and moral stewardship. These links among nation building, class formation, and urban development helped to define an ambitious ideal of what "the American metropolis" should look like. Organized around the trope of empire, it envisioned a built environment that would be commensurate with New York's destiny as a center of capitalist energy and civilizational order. It was this nexus of assumptions and ambitions, I think, that lay behind Olmsted's bold claims for Central Park in 1858—"a democratic development of the highest significance"—and that informed his decision to return to New York and landscape design seven years later.

As it happens, he and his family arrived in New York on November 22, the very day that Ulysses Grant and *his* family were returning to Washington after their week in the metropolis. It is tantalizing to imagine a meeting of the two parties on the Hudson River docks; Olmsted would no doubt have wanted to pay his respects to the savior of the Union. Indeed, had the trip been shorter, we can imagine him turning up at George Templeton Strong's dinner party for the general, for Strong was treasurer of the U.S. Sanitary Commission and a supporter of Olmsted. Two days later, at a meeting of the Sanitary Commission, the diarist did run into the reformer. "Olmsted with us, returned from California day before yesterday by the Nicaragua route," he noted that night. "He has given up Mariposa . . . [and] had much to tell us. He looks well and is as bright as ever."[97]

Strong had good reason to pay attention to news of Mariposa: along with his work for Trinity Church and the Sanitary Commission, he was a trustee of Columbia College with an interest in its School of Mines. A few days after, he had Nevada's silverite Senator William Stewart for supper, and again the conversation turned to western mines, national politics, and New York. Stewart argued that the recent surge in prices was "permanent and progressive," caused by western gold and silver strikes rather than a debased paper currency. "That's very bad for me, a holder of mortgages and a receiver of fixed income," Strong commented in his diary. "I shall probably die a pauper. But inflation is a great fact for Trinity Church and Columbia College. . . . Both are rent[ing lots] at rates that would have seemed fabulous ten years ago. There is much consolation in that fact."[98]

Frederick Law Olmsted returned to a city where the links between national and local development, western mines and downtown rents, were daily concerns of bourgeois New Yorkers. Those links had begun to shape a new landscape in Manhattan, to change the city faster and more massively than ever before. The results, as George Templeton Strong understood, inspired both hope and worry.

CHAPTER 2

The Midcentury Boom

New York is a series of experiments, and every thing which has lived its life and played its part is held to be dead, and is buried, and over it grows a new world.
—*Harper's Weekly* (August 14, 1869)

The American Museum

On July 13, 1865, calamity struck P. T. Barnum and New York. One of the great landmarks of lower Manhattan, Barnum's American Museum, located at Broadway, Fulton, and City Hall Park, burned to the ground. The fire began just past noon in the furnace of a nearby restaurant. It spread throughout the museum quickly, from the menagerie in the basement to the upstairs theater, where "moral dramas" were presented to middle-class audiences, to the famed "Happy Family" of animals displayed on the fifth floor. Not all was lost to the flames. Human exhibits like the Fat Lady were able, fortunately, to escape from their quarters, and many treasured objects were carried off by onlookers. In a bizarre rite of post-Appomattox patriotism, crowds seized the effigy of Jefferson Davis and hanged it from a Fulton Street lamppost. And one policeman, perhaps emulating a hero of Victorian melodrama, plunged into the conflagration and reemerged with the *Greek Slave*, Hiram Power's celebrated female sculptural nude, in his arms. The fire, in short, testified to Barnum's genius for turning curiosities into popular fetishes, for making artifice so fascinating that it became indistinguishable from actuality.

Despite the thefts, seizures, and rescues, the blaze consumed most of the impresario's vast miscellany of historical relics, natural wonders, and humbuggery. The collection was worth some $400,000, although insured at only a tenth of its value. Many other establishments on the block were destroyed too: Knox's hat store, Rogers's haberdashery, several restaurants, and some two dozen shops, mainly in the print trades —lithographers, bookbinders, stationers—that catered to nearby publishers and government agencies. Yet the American Museum was the greatest loss, not only to its owner's ledger but also to the public culture of the city. "Probably no building in New-York was better known, inside and out," lamented the New York *Times*. "For many years, [it] has been a landmark of the city, afford[ing] us in childhood [the] fullest vision of the wonderful and miraculous . . . and reveal[ing] to us the mysteries of the past." George Templeton Strong, usually so sardonic, struck a similarly elegaic note: "Alas, for the 'Happy Family,'" he wrote that night in his diary, "and the inmates of scores of Aquaria, and for the stuffed monkey riding on the stuffed yellow dog, which my childhood venerated."[1]

The burning of Barnum's museum presents us with a poignant vignette of a cityscape that was undergoing—and seen by observers *as* undergoing—dramatic change. It is striking that both Strong and the *Times* portrayed the fire as the end of a simpler, more enchanted era, a loss of childhood itself. For the museum was rooted in, and emblematic of, the cultural and spatial logic of an earlier New York (Figure 2.1). Barnum had bought it in 1842, and its patriotic mementos, exotica, and entrepreneurial verve reflected the values and energies of the antebellum city, a provincial center just attaining its majority as a national and global emporium. The museum did not concern itself with the refinements and civilizational hierarchies so sacred to the Gilded Age bourgeoisie. Rather, like much antebellum public culture, it was a jumbled mélange of hucksterism and respectability, popular entertainment and public edification. Lyceum lectures and "moral dramas" appeared cheek-by-jowl with Tom Thumb and the Fat Lady; fraudulent wonders like the "Feejee Mermaid" were displayed in the midst of a natural-history collection that was the envy of the nation's scientists. Moreover the museum was situated at the commercial heart of a city—literally, the focal intersection of Broadway, Fulton, and City Hall Park—in which the processes of geographic differentiation and functional segregation remained underdeveloped. For all its wealth and complexity, lower Manhattan in the 1840s and 1850s was still a place where theaters, retail shops, wholesale merchants, and craft workshops were crowded together, like the Feejee Mermaid and the Greek Slave. The culture of Barnum's museum found its counterpart in the geography of the walking city that surrounded it.[2]

By the time of the 1865 fire, these cultural and spatial logics had begun to change, and the changes would accelerate over the next decade. From the mid-1850s on, and especially after the Civil War, the mixed landscape of lower Manhattan gave way to a more rationalized, corporate, and hierarchical regime of urban space and public culture. Nowhere was this process more visible than at Broadway, Fulton, and City Hall Park. Barnum's Museum was not rebuilt there, but replaced by two newfangled business palaces: the *Herald* Building and the National Park Bank (Figure 2.2). Across Park Row, at the lower end of the Park, the federal government erected a huge Post Office building a few years later. Headquarters to the city's most widely read newspaper, its richest bank, and (along with the Customs House) its most important government agency, these buildings composed an American museum of a different sort.

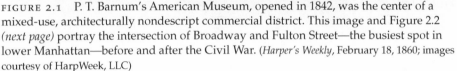

FIGURE 2.1   P. T. Barnum's American Museum, opened in 1842, was the center of a
mixed-use, architecturally nondescript commercial district. This image and Figure 2.2
(*next page*) portray the intersection of Broadway and Fulton Street—the busiest spot in
lower Manhattan—before and after the Civil War. (*Harper's Weekly*, February 18, 1860; images
courtesy of HarpWeek, LLC)

They were icons of New York's power over national finance, communications, and
print culture. And they were landmarks of the district from which that power was
deployed: a new kind of business district, intensively built and used, geographically
specialized and integrated, organized to foster the efficient circulation of capital,
goods, and information.[3]

Graphic depictions of Broadway, Fulton, and Park Row make clear the new visual
and architectural regime that accompanied these spatial and economic changes. Barnum's Museum had been a large but nondescript building, most remembered for
"the horrible little brass band that was always tooting in its balcony." By contrast, the
Herald, Park Bank, and Post Office (as well as many other commercial palaces going
up in lower Manhattan) were self-consciously monumental, opulent, and spectacular; massive and ornamental, they announced the prosperity and grandeur of their
tenants and their city. The Park Bank seemed to exude a special authority. One of the
wealthiest of the national banks founded by Congress in the Civil War, its headquarters was a pretentious hash of neoclassical and Second Empire quotations, fronted by
huge statues of Justice, Abundance, and the Genius of Finance "holding a horn of

FIGURE 2.2   After Barnum's museum (Figure 2.1) burned down in 1865, the intersection became the site of the New York *Herald* and the National Park Bank *(left and right, respectively)* as lower Broadway developed into a specialized area of grandiose financial, press, and governmental offices. (*Broadway and Ann Street*, photograph, 1870–80; Museum of the City of New York; gift of Essex Institute)

plenty in her [left] hand, [while] from her [right] she is scattering coin." Evidently the results dazzled observers: "It has been erected at immense expense," one guidebook reported, "and is one of the most attractive features of Broadway."[4]

The rebuilding of the commercial district formed part of a larger story of growth and reconstruction that transformed New York in the third quarter of the nineteenth century. In the process, the amusements that Barnum had mixed together came to be supplied by an array of specialized institutions distributed across a complex metropolitan area. Natural and ethnological curiosities were displayed at the American Museum of Natural History, opened in 1878 west of Central Park. Wild beasts could be viewed at the Central Park menagerie (1859), the Bronx Zoo (after 1895), and Barnum's own famous circus in Madison Square. "Moral drama" migrated uptown to the "legitimate" theaters that began to proliferate on Broadway north of Union Square. The heterogeneous pleasures of the American Museum, in short, were disaggregated and dispersed. In tracking them, we glimpse the differentiation of the older walking city into an expansive, functionally segregated metropolis—and the differentiation of an older popular culture into the hierarchies of Victorian public life.[5]

It would be misleading, however, to view the spatial processes at play in Barnum's fire purely as rational, hierarchical, and efficient. For these were matched by contradictory tendencies toward spatial *dis*organization. Here again, Broadway and Fulton is a good place to find our bearings. During the third quarter of the nineteenth century, this was quite simply the most congested spot in Manhattan (if not the country), the intersection of New York's busiest uptown avenue and its most heavily trafficked commercial cross street. "For several hours in each day," one trade journal reported, "that section . . . below the City Hall is so crowded that passengers on the sidewalk find it embarrassing to get forward, and the blockade of vehicles is complete." So difficult was it to cross Broadway that in 1866 several store owners financed their own pedestrian bridge at Fulton Street.[6]

The fire at Barnum's Museum thus offers a microcosm of city-building processes that were recasting New York in dramatic but contradictory ways. My aim in this chapter is to describe three aspects of this transformation. First, I want to offer a bird's-eye view of the changing landscape itself, to sketch New York's evolution from a walking city to a metropolitan area and the mixture of order and disruption that resulted. (The next two chapters will elaborate on this sketch, analyzing in some detail the contradictory effects of New York's growth.) Second, I want to situate and periodize these changes within the larger story of nineteenth-century capitalist development. The third quarter of the century in particular saw the consolidation of a global economic regime; New York's development boom coincided precisely with this "age of capital," as Eric Hobsbawm calls it, and reflected the city's nodal role in the new world order. Finally, I want to sketch some of the ways in which New Yorkers experienced these turbulent changes. As the story of Broadway and Fulton suggests, their responses were as conflicted as the landscape itself. Sometimes the dynamism of New York's development provoked lament for the older city being razed; sometimes, booster praise for the metropolitan order that replaced it. Often the Manhattan landscape seemed to augur a brave new imperium of palatial architecture, broad streets, unfettered development, and heroic public works; and yet it could be a nightmare of traffic jams, construction sites, speculative binges, and transience.

New Yorkers were right on both counts. The same forces that set the city's streets and real-estate markets into frantic motion could also, without warning, stalemate them in blockades and panics. The drive to accumulate that produced the Park Bank also spurred a vast landscape of built-to-order tenements. New York's almost unearthly dynamism seemed to invest the city with power over time and space; but at the same time it created a volatile, unstable geography that uprooted people from their accustomed locales and corroded any sense of community or continuity. Its conflicting, unruly energies represented both a promise and a problem for bourgeois city builders.

Overview of a Boom

Concerning one matter, all observers of mid-nineteenth century New York were agreed. Whatever they thought about the actual or desired shape of the cityscape, they knew that it was undergoing an unprecedented process of growth and reconstruction. Ten months after the conflagration in the American Museum, for instance, George Templeton Strong recurred to the fire in his diary: "Much pulling down and building up in progress on Broadway," he wrote. "A costly white marble edifice is fast rising on [Barnum's] site, destined to be the printing office of the New York *Herald*, a conspicuous monument." Strong noted other antebellum landmarks falling just then to the wrecker's ball: St. Thomas's Church, the Stuyvesant Institute, and the Apollo Building, "where I first heard Beethoven's symphonies and much good music besides, 1842–48." A few years later, after another of his evening strolls, he cataloged all the grand public works being built around Manhattan: the elevated railway, a massive seawall on the waterfront, the East River Bridge. "These changes, all now under way," Strong mused, "will make this a new city within ten years."[7]

It was a response shared by many middle- and upper-class observers. Beginning around midcentury, journalists, travelers, real-estate experts, and other commentators stressed New York's ceaseless "pulling down and building up," as Strong put it, the razing and reconstruction of the urban fabric. "Every day sees some old tenement leave its ancient bed and some new cloud-kissing structure of freestone or marble proudly take its place," the *Times* noted in 1852. "Down come the venerable walls to be supplanted by new and loftier inclosures. . . . Consecrated as they are . . . they cannot stand in the pathway of Improvement." Architect Samuel Sloan echoed the substance of this comment, but not its wistful tone, in an 1869 essay: "Progress in New York seems disposed to turn everything into something else; and all for the sake of change, untiring change," he exulted. "We cannot dream visions of future greatness fast enough; for, the fastness of the times will wake us up to their realization." Whether one greeted the city's transmutations with the ambivalence of a genteel editor or the booster exuberance of a builder, the message was clear. New York seemed swept up in changes of almost seismic proportions.[8]

Looking back from the early twenty-first century, it may be hard to grasp the feelings of disorientation or exhilaration that pervade these accounts. The Manhattan of 1870 would not possess for another three decades those elements that tend to emblematize modern, metropolitan New York for us: the jagged skyline, the subway, Beaux Arts monuments like Penn Station, the electric-lit phantasm of Times Square at night. Moreover, well *before* the 1850s, New Yorkers were already expressing amazement at the pace and scale of spatial change. "The spirit of pulling down and building up is abroad," the elite diarist Philip Hone noted in 1839, in words uncannily like those of George Templeton Strong a generation later. "The whole of New York is rebuilt about once in ten years." Thus, it may be tempting to conclude, as one eminent urban historian does, that New York's midcentury development "left no discernible mark on the physical appearance of the city. . . . [It] looked in the decade of the 70s much as it had when . . . its first horsecar [opened]"—that is, in 1832.[9]

To New Yorkers of the period, however, such a view would have seemed nonsensical. They were emphatic that the city had entered a threshold moment in its physical development. "HOW WE GROW AND SPREAD," the *Real Estate Record* proclaimed in 1869, detailing "the immense, nay, marvelous improvements that have daily appeared to our astonished gaze." In upper Manhattan, "costly residences" were replacing the "vacant lots" and "unsightly wooden huts," while "splendid buildings . . . testif[y] forcibly to the advance of commerce" farther downtown. "Go where one will," the *Record* exulted, "one sees improvements on all sides, and new and more beautiful structures take the place of the old." Fifteen years later, the president of the Real Estate Exchange surveyed recent city building with satisfaction: "The history of New York reads like a romance," Hermann H. Cammann told his membership. "If we merely consider the changes that have taken place within [thirty] years, the wonderful growth of the city, its broad thoroughfares and stately buildings . . . , the progress of New York in earlier days appears slight enough in comparison with its recent rapid strides. . . . The financial centre of the country, . . . the port of entry for ships from every clime . . . , [New York] is gradually but surely assuming the position she is destined to occupy as the great metropolis of the world." Such New Yorkers were sure that they were living through epochal, almost magical changes in the urban fabric. And, as President Cammann's words suggest, they framed those changes within the larger "romance" of New York's commercial ascendance and imperial destiny.[10]

What was it that so captivated the "astonished gaze" of midcentury New Yorkers? Why did the "pulling down and building up" of Strong's era seem so different from Philip Hone's? We can begin to answer these questions by examining some of the visual records of spatial change most commonly looked at by Victorian urbanites themselves: lithographic bird's-eye views.

Such views, according to their leading historian, John Reps, "may have been the single most popular category . . . of printed images in 19th-century America." Certainly they were the era's most influential medium for portraying urban geography and growth. Hardly a town existed across the continent that did not have its bird's-eye portrait drawn sometime. Indeed many views were published of places that did not exist at all outside of a speculator's fantasy: lithography was a primary means of townsite promotion. Spurred by technological improvements in color lithography, steam-powered printing, and rail transport during the 1840s and 1850s, these images composed a key element in the national public sphere whose consolidation I sketched in the previous chapter.[11] Their pictorial conventions evolved at the same time; an older tradition of naturalistic perspectives and painterly landscape depiction gave way to a new emphasis on cartographic realism and frankly fictitious points of view, high above the built environment. Such "bird's-eye" views, displayed on the walls of parlors, hotel lobbies, realty and law offices, clubs, reading rooms, and retail shops, testified to bourgeois America's fascination with its increasingly urban milieu. Especially between 1850 and 1890, they also composed a rich archive of the progress of American city building.[12]

Nowhere more than in New York. As I noted in Chapter 1, the national metropolis was an object of special fascination for viewers and readers. Accounts of the Manhattan scene abounded throughout the Victorian culture industry: in guidebooks, magazine sketches, stereoscopic photographs, genteel fiction, exposés of the city's "nether side." Lithographs had a central place in this discourse of metropolitan portraiture. Isaac Newton Phelps Stokes, the pioneering archivist of the iconography of Manhattan, estimates that the Victorian "mania" for urban prints led to the production of "hundreds of views" of the city; recent research confirms that it was the most lithographed community in America. Urban historians have usually linked bird's-eye views, like other booster genres, with the boomtowns and "instant cities" of the western frontier. Yet they also provide a unique look at Victorian New York, a sketchbook of the city's transformation from antebellum port to Gilded Age metropolis.[13]

We can glimpse the overall lines of that transformation by comparing lithographs of Manhattan from the late 1840s and the mid-1870s.[14] Earlier prints tend to show a cityscape defined and constrained by its maritime, mercantile setting. In one characteristic view from 1848,[15] for instance, we look northeast from a point above Bedloe's Island, the future site of the Statue of Liberty (Figure 2.3). A seascape of harbor, rivers, and shipping surrounds and visually diminishes Manhattan Island; the city itself appears compact, huddled, and low, bounded along West and South streets by thickets of masts seemingly taller than the buildings they enclose. There is an aura of prosperity and enterprise here, in the city's crowded wharves, the strollers on the Battery, and the commercial facades of Broadway. Yet the "spirit of pulling down and building up" that was so striking to Philip Hone seems muted here, more contained by the built environment than expressed in it. Rather we are given a view whose most impressive visual elements—Castle Garden, the Customs House, Trinity Church, the Merchants' Exchange, City Hall—represent the older communal, commercial, and religious landmarks of an established maritime center, yoked to its port.

This was not, to be sure, the classic preindustrial city described by historians of urban form, with its jumble of mixed-trade neighborhoods and unspecialized land uses. Twenty years earlier New York's business elite had begun to segregate itself into residential enclaves like Union Square and Gramercy Park on the urban periphery. By 1850 the downtown and riverfront had developed a matrix of specialized trade districts; Manhattan even boasted a single, rather ineffective horse car line. Yet, taken as a whole, the New York portrayed here was still the sort of landscape that historian Sam Bass Warner has labeled a "walking city": a place defined by its compact scale, unsystematic geography, rudimentary infrastructure, and relatively homogeneous physical fabric. Indeed, with its visual focus on City Hall, a scant mile north of the Battery, the lithograph seems to underscore this sense of New York's limits. The rendering of Manhattan Island breaks into formless confusion just above Twentieth Street, the uptown edge of development, as if to mark in the composition itself a structural limit on the city's growth.

A quarter century later, lithographic views show us a cityscape transformed. In one 1876 print, published by the leading firm of Currier and Ives,[16] the built environment seems to have exploded outward, encompassing a crowded Brooklyn waterfront to one side, the Jersey City railroad complex to the other, and a Manhattan uptown that stretches north to Central Park and beyond (Figure 2.4). What had been the

FIGURE 2.3   This 1848 lithograph depicts a bustling port organized around the harbor and characterized by the traditional landmarks of church steeples and ship masts. Combined with Figure 2.4, it offers a rich overview of the transformation of Manhattan during the third quarter of the nineteenth century. (*New-York et Brooklyn,* 1848; courtesy of Yale University Art Museum)

FIGURE 2.4   Twenty-eight years later than the scene in Figure 2.3, this 1876 view emphasizes new commercial buildings and outsize infrastructures such as the Brooklyn Bridge. The cityscape has exploded northward, and Manhattan Island itself seems to have replaced the harbor as the emblem of New York's power. The island seems almost like a vector pointing uptown—the direction of the city's future. (*The City of New York,* 1876; courtesy of Yale University Art Museum)

visual terminus of growth in 1848—the convergence of Broadway and the Bowery at Union Square—now defines the pictorial center of the scene; and uptown sites like the new Grand Central Depot and St. Patrick's Cathedral appear as distinct compositional landmarks. Indeed the sheer expansion of the built environment has forced the artist to take a point of view that is at once higher and more aligned with the topography of Manhattan Island. The result is an image that diminishes the visual importance of the harbor, foreshortens the downtown waterfront, and heightens our sense of the reach of the cityscape as a whole. I do not mean that the port seems less busy than in earlier views—it visibly teems with craft—but it no longer dominates the representation of the New York scene. The primary visual marker of the city's prosperity and enterprise is not the port, but the island itself. Instead of the attenuated landmass of the 1848 lithograph, we see an arrowlike Manhattan pointing northward to its next frontier of city building. Instead of the structural compactness of the walking city, we see a *metropolitan* area, extending across topographical divisions and unifying them, stretching to the horizon with no apparent constraint on development.

Underlying the expansiveness and grandeur of this view is a dynamism that seems inscribed in the cityscape itself. From the oversized steamships to the traffic jam on Broadway, from the S-curve of the elevated line to the streetcars of Brooklyn, from the constellation of railway depots to the multitude of river craft, this is the portrait of a city in motion. Moreover, it is a city whose incessant circulation through space mirrors its headlong development over time; the landscape itself seems to be in transit here. The lithograph's overscaled or underscored elements, for instance, tend to mark the most *recent* developments in metropolitan architecture, engineering, and urban form. The landmarks and labeled structures include high-rise office buildings like the Western Union headquarters, transport infrastructures like the elevated railway, and grand public works like Central Park—none of which had existed twenty years earlier. The print's most conspicuous symbol of New York's "futurism" was of course Brooklyn Bridge, which is presented here, in gargantuan scale, seven years before its actual completion. (In 1876, only the towers had been built.)[17] The point of the anachronism seems clear: New York was a city so dynamic, so monumentally audacious in its development, that its present fabric could not be separated from its future prospects. The cityscape was, in its very incompleteness, a prophecy.

Most important for our purposes, all this dynamism and growth have produced a scene with a dramatically new geography and physical fabric. Antebellum prints had shown a crowded but rather homogeneous Manhattan. The Currier and Ives view depicts a more expansive and differentiated built environment, one that seems both a product and a conduit of the dynamism on display here. Three types of change are especially legible. First of all, the downtown landscape possesses an internal complexity and a monumentality of design absent from earlier views. The lithograph uses whitewash and overscaling to portray lower Manhattan as a grand business district, not just an aggregate of commercial structures; its labels cue us to the emergence of specialized locales for finance, port commerce, government, and publishing. Second, and conversely, this New York has developed an extensive periphery dedicated to manufacturing, transport, and domestic life. The lithograph shows us the smokestacks of "gashouse" and nuisance-industry districts along the riverfronts; Jersey-side rail terminals that connected New York port with its western hinterland; and a new uptown realm of genteel home life, served by churches, parks, boulevards, commuter railroads, and speculative suburban developments. Finally, downtown and uptown are bound into a common metropolitan area by a technically advanced system of circulation. The elevated, Brooklyn Bridge, railway depots, steam ferries, horse car lines: together these constitute the portrait of an "infrastructure," a dense and interconnected engine of movement, not evident in images of antebellum Manhattan.

The Currier and Ives view, in short, shows us a sea change in New York's urban fabric. It depicts a cityscape that is larger, faster, and higher than that of antebellum prints; more voracious in its expansion; more complex in its geography; more avant-garde in its technologies; more monumental in design. Something like this vision of ordered dynamism was what Hermann Cammann had in mind, I think, when he told his fellow real-estate operators that the history of the New York cityscape "reads like a romance." With its iconography of a complex, modern, growing metropolis marching into the future, the 1876 view reads like a romance of empire.

Of course, romance is the mode of fantasy, of magical shape-shifting and desire fulfilled, and Victorian city views were often romances in this generic sense. We cannot treat them as strictly accurate renditions of urban space, for they reflected the interests, longings, and blind spots of the bourgeois urbanites who circulated and displayed them. The bird's-eye perspective in particular worked to exaggerate the order, wealth, and grandeur of the community on display; it tended to efface evidence of disorder, squalor, or conflict. This power to mystify was central to the popularity and significance of urban views, and I will return to it at the end of the chapter. Yet it is important here not to *over*stress the problems of falsity or fantasy. The ideological authority of bird's-eye views rested on their claim to verisimilitude, a claim underwritten by formal conventions of territorial inclusiveness and meticulous detail. Thus, it makes sense to read an image like the 1876 lithograph not *simply* as a booster fantasy, but (in Reps's words) as a "flattering, carefully posed, and retouched portrait" that was "substantially accurate . . . as a whole." The print enables us to see New York's development from the vantage point of those who sought to oversee it.[18]

What it shows us is the portrait of a boom. Between the late 1840s and mid-1870s, New York went through an unprecedented surge of growth, construction, and reorganization. Manhattan property values appreciated more than fourfold in those years; construction rates doubled, reaching two thousand new buildings per year in the frenzied markets of the late 1860s and early 1870s.[19] The development boom transformed the landscape of New York and its environs into an expansive, complex metropolitan area: the landscape that we glimpse in the Currier and Ives image. It was marked by three sets of changes: in scale, in physical and functional integration, and in the differentiation of land use and social geography.

First of all, as the lithograph suggests, the midcentury boom extended the built environment far uptown, converting the older villages, farms, and wastes of northern Manhattan into urban real estate. Nearly all the island, of course, had been platted by

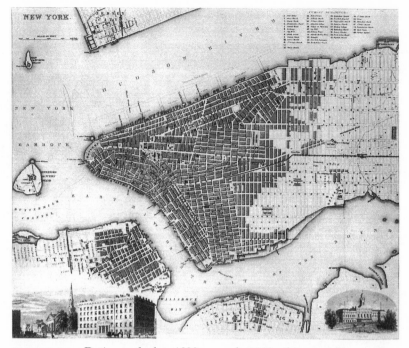

FIGURE 2.5 Dating to the late 1830s or early 1840s, this map shows a port city where "the march of improvement" is still organized around the river-front. (Map Collection, University Library, University of Michigan)

the street plan of 1811. Yet for the first half of the century, the grid remained some-thing of a legal and cartographic fiction. In the late 1830s, the built edge of New York lay just north of Union Square, three miles above the Battery (Figure 2.5); by the mid-1850s, it had migrated only another mile and a half, to about Forty-second Street. Over the next quarter-century, however, the pace of urban expansion accelerated. The frontier of city building advanced four miles farther, incorporating the established villages of Yorkville, Bloomingdale, and Harlem. By the late 1870s, maps show nearly continuous (though incomplete) property development up to 125th Street east and north of Central Park and Fifty-ninth Street west of it (Figure 2.6).[20] Of course this crude index ignores variations in building density from ward to ward and block to block. Yet if anything, it understates the expansiveness of the midcentury boom. Growth rates were even higher in peripheral districts being urbanized for the first time: Brooklyn grew at two to three times the pace of New York, and Jersey City even faster.[21]

"THE MARCH OF IMPROVEMENT," as New York's booster press called this surging outward growth, entailed a cognitive transformation as well. It enlarged the *concep-tual* city limits of New York, extending the imaginable terrain of development to the municipal borders of Manhattan and beyond. "Nothing is more clearly written in the book of Fate," the *Real Estate Record* proclaimed in its inaugural issue in 1868, than

FIGURE 2.6   By the time this extraordinary Galt-Hoy map was published in 1879, development activity had largely built up the East Side all the way to Harlem (compare Figure 2.5), but—to the puzzlement of many boosters and the chagrin of many speculators—the upper West Side remained stagnant and unoccupied. (Courtesy of the Library of Congress, control no. 75694818)

that "we *must* go on building . . . until we have not only covered every square foot of Manhattan Island, but laid tribute to the opposite shores of the East and Hudson Rivers for our overflowing numbers." As the 1876 bird's-eye view suggests, this expansionism was not only a booster dream but also a growing reality. That same year, the German geographer Friedrich Ratzel noted the regional consolidation taking place in and around Manhattan: "Today, New York proper . . . can no longer be separated from the [surrounding] areas. . . . If one speaks of the . . . future of New York, one does not think of the city of one million inhabitants which actually carries that name, but of the entire urban complex around the Hudson estuary, which . . . will one of these days probably unite to form the political unit that the nature of things already seems to have predestined." Native New Yorkers seconded Ratzel's view that the de facto integration of the metropolitan area made the administrative creation of a "greater" New York all but inevitable. "A consolidation of the Cities of New York and Brooklyn into one municipality is but a question of time," Mayor William Wickham asserted in 1875. "When [Brooklyn] bridge is completed, that union may become a fact."[22]

The midcentury boom, in short, had the effect of "metropolitanizing" space in New York. It impelled New Yorkers and visitors to construe the cityscape as a unified, complex, and theoretically limitless artifact, subject to systematic processes of development and, potentially, to unified governance. Of course—as Mayor Wickham made clear in his nod to Brooklyn Bridge—this "construction" of the metropolitan area was not just a discursive act; it required the physical construction of new facilities for integrating urban circulation and land use. Here, too, the third quarter of the nineteenth century proved decisive. The Currier and Ives view highlights the most monumental instances of infrastructural modernization undertaken in New York from the mid-1850s to the mid-1870s. Upper Manhattan and southern Westchester were opened to development and settlement by the steam-driven elevated railway, the city's first rapid-transit system (1869–78). The port and downtown were linked to national markets and suburban hinterlands by new freight and passenger terminals in Jersey City and Manhattan—most famously, the "Grand Central Depot" built by the Vanderbilt interests at Fourth Avenue and Forty-second Street (1869) (Figure 2.7). Finally, lower Manhattan and Brooklyn were joined by the crowning engineering work of the age, the East River Bridge (1867–83).[23]

Yet these were only the most conspicuous achievements in a broader process of infrastructural development. In 1850, Manhattan had a single horse car line, the "city line" of the New York and Harlem railroad; twenty-five years later, eighteen streetcar franchises occupied nearly all major thoroughfares in the city besides Broadway and Fifth Avenue. A complex telegraph system, headquartered in the grandiose Western Union building at Broadway and Dey (completed 1875), linked New York with national markets and Wall Street with business offices across Manhattan. The waterfront underwent a more uneven but still impressive process of improvement. Before the Civil War, Brooklyn land companies developed the Erie and Atlantic Docks, vast enclosed basins that integrated pier, wharf, and storage facilities. The Manhattan waterfront remained more hampered by disorganization and underinvestment, as I will discuss in Chapter 4, but it too began to modernize. Steamship and ferry lines built new cast-iron passenger terminals in the 1860 and 1870s, and the New York Central developed a huge complex of railroad shops, grain elevators, stockyards, and storage facilities along the upper Hudson riverfront.[24]

These public and corporate improvements constituted the rudiments of a metropolitan infrastructure. It was not fully "modern" by our lights, for it antedated the electric power grid and the internal combustion engine, the touchstones of twentieth-century mass urbanism. Like the nineteenth-century industrial economy as a whole, it synthesized older technologies—especially steam and animal power—with new methods of iron construction, telegraphy, and structural engineering. Yet it enabled people, goods, capital, and information to mass and flow in much greater volume and complexity than before. Annual ridership on Manhattan's streetcars grew more than fourfold, from 36 million to 160 million, between 1860 and 1875. Freight tonnage

FIGURE 2.7   Erected by the Vanderbilt railroad interests at Forty-second Street and Fourth Avenue, Grand Central Depot introduced palatial, European railway design to the United States. The Second Empire station house was expanded and rebuilt in 1889 and replaced by the Beaux Arts Grand Central Terminal in 1913. (*Harper's Weekly*, February 3, 1872; image courtesy of HarpWeek, LLC)

on New York's two largest rail systems, the Erie and the New York Central, increased five- and sixfold, respectively, in the same years. Telegraph traffic tripled in the decade following the consolidation of the Western Union monopoly in 1866.[25]

Metropolitan growth and infrastructural modernization also made the possible a third transformation: the emergence of a social geography marked by functional specialization of land use and class segregation of residence. As I will argue in Chapter 3, this process of spatial change had complex and sometimes unexpected results. At its core, however, was a growing bifurcation of "downtown" and "uptown." "The wants of business are . . . causing [downtown] dwellings to be torn down and replaced by handsome stores," John Kennion reported in an 1868 guide to New York's architecture, "while the people thus crowded out are constrained to emigrate northward and settle in the upper wards." On one hand, as we saw at Broadway and Fulton, the commercial district of lower Manhattan grew larger, more site intensive, more geographically specialized, and more monumental in design. Dozens of office buildings went up at Wall Street and lower Broadway, employing the new passenger lift to break the old five-story limit on rentable space; around Canal and Houston, cast-iron design was used to build warehouses and wholesale lofts; a retail and amusement district between Union and Madison Squares served as the stage for a new bourgeois ethos of urbane consumerism and display.[26]

On the other hand, the "MARCH OF IMPROVEMENT" created a new kind of uptown landscape: extensive, space hungry, devoted primarily to residence and large industry. The most active site of development was the East Side, especially the Nineteenth Ward, where one-fifth of the city's rise in land values and one-third of all new construction took place in the late 1860s and early 1870s. The ward's signature improvements were the mansions and civic institutions around Fifth Avenue. Yet, as I shall show in the next chapter, these were only the tip of the iceberg: Ward Nineteen also contained more than half of *all* the nontenement housing erected in the postwar boom and—more surprisingly—nearly 30 percent of the tenements.[27] The building activity was accompanied by a huge uptown resettlement, a "horse car migration" that was as significant to the demographic history of New York as the trans-Atlantic movement. "The late registry of voters shows that there will shortly be as many persons living above Forty-second street as below," the *Real Estate Record* reported in 1882. By then some four hundred thousand New Yorkers inhabited a landscape of townhouses and tenements that had hardly existed on the eve of the Civil War.[28]

Terminals and Tenements

Why was it that the Manhattan landscape began to grow and change so dramatically in the third quarter of the nineteenth century? To answer that question, we need to move from a local bird's-eye view to a more global perspective. New York's development boom was driven by a long swing of growth that reshaped international capitalism between the late 1840s and the mid-1870s. As Eric Hobsbawm has argued, this era saw the consolidation of a new macroeconomic regime, replete with international credit markets, mass migratory labor, transoceanic communications and shipping, continental rail and telegraph networks, and interlinked national business cycles. The "great boom," as Hobsbawm calls it, was unique in economic history, for it was the founding boom of the modern world market; it instituted the rapid, predictable, fluid circulation of capital, labor, information, and goods.[29]

In so doing, it also transformed the function, shape, and scale of urban space. Great cities were nerve centers of the new world economy and showcases for the consumption of its surplus. Thus, it is not surprising that the "age of capital" was also an era of heroic urbanism. Especially in the latter half of the period, as population and wealth flowed into metropolitan centers, European and American city builders undertook massive programs of reconstruction. The refashioning of central Paris, the laying out of Vienna's Ringstrasse, the building of the Thames embankments by London's Metropolitan Board of Works, the rebuilding of Chicago after the great fire—all were initiated between the late 1850s and the mid-1870s. So were Central and Prospect parks, Brooklyn Bridge, Grand Central Depot, and Manhattan's elevated railway system.[30]

Two sets of processes unleashed by the "great boom" had particular impact on New York; each left its characteristic traces on the new urban landscape. The first was demographic. As is well known, the growth of commercialized agriculture and in-

dustrial development in Europe fueled processes of proletarianization and displacement that made New York a world port and immigrant metropolis. At the peak of the
"first wave" of immigration (1845–54 and 1866–73), 200,000–300,000 persons each
year arrived at New York harbor. (Castle Garden, an old fort at the tip of Manhattan,
was converted from a concert hall to a federal station in the mid-1850s to process the
flood of newcomers.) New York's population went from 370,000 in 1845 to more than
a million three decades later; Brooklyn grew sixfold in the same period.[31]

The human consequences of this huge movement were manifold. As Richard Stott
has shown, immigrants often secured a better living in New York than they had enjoyed in Germany, Ireland, England, and elsewhere. Good food was more plentiful,
social pleasures more available, rents often less burdensome.[32] Yet, despite their access to fresh meat and melodramas, immigrants also faced new vulnerability in New
York. The occupational and geographic structure of the metropolitan economy
tended to foster seasonal and irregular patterns of employment and (therefore) residential congestion near glutted labor markets. These conditions were especially severe in dock, transport, and outdoor construction work, sectors that required great
numbers of casualized day laborers. Yet they also afflicted industrial workers, most
notably in the consumer and commodity-processing trades—garment-making, cigar
rolling, printing—that led the manufacturing sector in New York. These sectors were
structured around small firms, competitive subcontracting, a highly divided work
process, and low piece rates. They often needed to locate near sources of credit, supplies, and market information—that is, in expensive downtown sites—and were
forced to use labor-intensive or sweated production in order to compensate for scarce
space and high rents.[33]

For landowners and builders, these demographic and land pressures offered unprecedented opportunities. Many responded by producing what was essentially a
new architectural form: the built-to-purpose tenement. For the first time in New
York's history—and perhaps modern urban history as a whole—the mass provision
of working-class housing became a profitable proposition. "All our real-estate dealers know that as business [grows], the first result upon the population it crowds out,
is to increase it," the *Real Estate Record* reported. "The added value of the land com-
pels the erection of immense tenement houses." Landlords and speculators put up
thousands of such houses during the midcentury boom. Some investments were
small-scale, like the eight-unit building that Peter Seebald erected at 211 Delancy on
the lower East Side in 1870. Other developers pursued wide-ranging operations: the
clan of Nathaniel, Jonathan, and Henry Burchell built fifty-seven tenements that
same year, nearly all of them north of Madison Square and east of Third or west of
Seventh Avenue. Between 1862 and 1872, New York's Superintendent of Buildings
estimated, the number of houses classified as tenements went from twelve thousand
to twenty thousand; tenement dwellers increased from 380,000 to 600,000, nearly
two-thirds of the city's total population.[34]

Given the immiseration with which the new tenements are (rightly) associated, it is
hard for us to grasp what an achievement of capitalist city building they represented.
Yet they transformed New York. For one thing, they were not confined to the lower

wards that had long housed the mass of city workers; as the Burchell investments suggest, the uptown march included a procession of tenements. Out of more than a thousand tenement houses built in 1870, for instance, half went up north of Forty-second Street. Here was the beginning of a new class geography, one that Jacob Riis would find full-blown a generation later: "Where are the tenements of to-day?" the housing reformer wrote in 1890. "Say rather: where are they not? In fifty years they have crept . . . the whole length of the island." Before the Civil War, the line between "uptown" and "downtown," conventionally placed at Fourteenth Street, seemed to mark a class divide. By the 1880s, that line was effaced, and new tenements were, in Riis's words, "strung along both rivers, like a ball and chain tied to the foot of every street."[35]

The new tenements also recast the architectural fabric of working-class life. In the slums of early nineteenth-century New York, "tenant-houses" were ad hoc and aggregated in form. Usually older structures that had been recycled for rental income, they were a congeries of cellars, garrets, outbuildings, rear additions, subdivided rooms, and other leftover spaces (Figure 2.8). The images with which antebellum reformers and journalists described this housing evoked the residual, the crooked, the subterranean, and the creaturely: they were "dens of sin," "nests of contagion," "burrows," "rookeries." By contrast, the new tenements were economically and architecturally "rational": large, symmetrical, bare, brick structures that maximized ground coverage and rents. The infamous Gotham Court housed seven hundred souls on a 20-foot-by-200-foot lot near the East River. Another rent barracks on the lower West Side—"an immense brick block, seven stories high," reported the *Times*—was said to contain three thousand tenants, their sanitary needs met by a hundred privies dug in the fifteen-foot-wide inner court. Of course these were the horror stories, fodder for reform tracts and sketch journalism. More often, especially after the building-code reforms of the 1860s, new tenements were four to six stories high, with a single or double stack of apartments. The Burchell projects of 1870, for instance, averaged 7.25 units and probably no more than fifty tenants per building. There were no Gotham Courts in the group, but enough new rental space to shelter a small mill town.[36]

Such buildings constituted a new type of cityscape, familiar to us from Riis and other Gilded Age observers: a world of congestion and confinement, of massive street walls punctuated by endless fire escapes. For this slum, the appropriate metaphors were not animal lairs, but spaces of regimentation and enclosure: the prison, the factory, the beehive. Hence one journalist's comment after the 1863 draft riots: "The high brick blocks and closely-packed houses where the mobs originated seemed to be literally *hives of sickness and vice*." This shift in the portraiture of the tenements—from wood to brick, from "rookery" to "hive"—registered an ironic truth. Many bourgeois New Yorkers had hoped that the new houses would have a renovative effect on working-class life, "rescuing the poor people," as Riis put it, "from the dreadful rookeries they were then living in." Instead, they merely served as mills for the mass production of rent. Population densities in New York rose steadily throughout the latter half of the century. By 1880, the lower East Side averaged more than 200,000 persons per square mile, and by 1900, 300,000, making it the most crowded human commu-

FIGURE 2.8   The older downtown "rookery" depicted here, with its ramshackle additions and recycled outbuildings, testifies to the horrified fascination with which the tenement landscape was scrutinized in middle-class visual culture. (*Harper's Weekly*, April 5, 1879; image courtesy of HarpWeek, LLC)

nity on earth. The main effect of the new tenements, in short, was to rationalize congestion instead of ameliorating it.[37]

The second engine of change unleashed by the "great boom" was New York's rise to commercial and financial primacy. Metropolitan dominance positioned the city on the threshold—or rather *as* the threshold—between global and national markets. New York's share of U.S. overseas trade doubled between 1840 and 1870, from less than a quarter to nearly half the national tonnage. Journalistic sketches give a dazzling sense of the array of goods that was swept into Manhattan on the crest of this trade: "Here are tier upon tier of hogsheads of sugar, perspiring molasses with the memory of the Cuban sun," one visitor to a riverfront warehouse wrote, "dusty white barrels of China clay," "huge heaps of 'allspice' pepper from Jamaica," "sticky dates from Arabia," "hemp from the Philippines," "rags from London," and "cotton from all over the world." New York's role in the domestic market was a bit less kaleidoscopic, but more voluminous and economically important. Canal and trunk-rail traffic to the port tripled between the mid-1850s and the Panic of 1873; by 1880 an estimated half of the goods shipped between the eastern seaboard and the West passed through docks and depots in the metropolitan area.[38] Even more impressive was the city's financial dominance. By the late 1860s, the value of stock traded on the New York Exchange—$3 billion per annum—was more than twice that of *all U.S. securities* circulating twelve years earlier. Much of the new capital flowed into Wall Street from abroad; European and other overseas investors channeled as much as $1.5 billion per year into rail, telegraph, mining, and land ventures after the Civil War, the lion's share of it through lower Manhattan.[39]

These shifts in trade, transportation, and finance had a twofold effect on the New York landscape. They placed complex demands on urban circulation and land use, while at the same time making available a huge capital fund for public works and property development. In Chapter 3, I analyze how these factors interacted to transform lower Manhattan. Here let me offer an overview of the urbanistic effects of New York's economic power by looking at the issue of metropolitan rail modernization.

Manhattan boasted railway service as early as the 1830s, but the first facilities were rudimentary and scattered. Beginning in the late 1850s, the city's leading railroads undertook ambitious programs of local development. The New Haven line built a depot at Madison Square in 1857; four years later, the Erie completed a unified freight, passenger, and ferry terminal at Jersey City. The Pennsylvania road won a right-of-way to the Jersey riverfront in 1871 and broke ground for its own complex.[40] Yet the most important city-building efforts were pursued by the Vanderbilt family. In the late 1860s, "Commodore" Cornelius and his son William won control of the New York Central, an upstate line linking Albany with the Great Lakes. Merging it with three downstate roads—the Hudson River, the Harlem, and the New Haven— the commodore consolidated a trunk-line system that, for the first time, ran from the agricultural heartland into the heart of Manhattan Island. "His ambition is a great one," the reformer Charles Francis Adams, Jr., wrote in a brilliant essay on the Wall Street rail wars, "to make himself master . . . of the great channels of communication which connect the city of New York with the interior of the continent, and to control them as his private property."[41]

Over the next decade, the Vanderbilts set about building an urban infrastructure with which to realize that ambition. They developed an extensive district of stockyards, grain elevators, lumber stores, and petroleum tanks on the upper Hudson west of Central Park (Figure 2.9). They lobbied, without success, for state franchises to build the elevated transit system and a freight railway around the waterfront.[42] Most importantly (or at least most visibly) they erected the first modern terminals in Manhattan. In 1871, Cornelius Vanderbilt consolidated passenger traffic from the Hudson, Harlem, and New Haven roads into a "Grand Central Depot" at Fourth Avenue and Forty-second Street. Ridership on the three lines had doubled in the 1860s, partly from the growth of uptown commuting, partly from such long-haul improvements as through ticketing and sleeper cars. Vanderbilt responded with a terminal that cost $3 million and covered five acres of ground. Its Second Empire station house contained the most up-to-date baggage, waiting, and consumer facilities (see Figure 2.7); its train shed, spanning a dozen tracks with a vault two hundred feet wide, was reputedly the largest permanent interior space in the world (Figure 2.10). It was, one

FIGURE 2.9 The New York Central grain elevator along the upper Hudson riverfront exemplifies the corporation as city builder. Like Figures 2.7 (the station house of Grand Central Depot), 2.10 *(below)*, and 2.11 (the freight terminal at St. John's Park), this structure testifies to the role of the Vanderbilt rail interests in New York's growth. (*Harper's Weekly*, December 22, 1877; image courtesy of HarpWeek, LLC)

FIGURE 2.10 The train shed for Grand Central Depot was a feat of avant-garde engineering. (*Grand Central Station, Interior, Shed*, stereograph; Museum of the City of New York; gift of Dr. Herman S. Riederer)

paper commented, "by far the . . . stateliest, most costly, most commodious edifice devoted to like purposes on this Continent."[43]

Like the great European depots built in the same era, Grand Central was an instrument of and a monument to the centralism of the "great boom." Cornelius Vanderbilt was among the first American capitalists to grasp the integrative possibilities of the boom, and the station gave physical form to his concentration of money, machinery, movement, and corporate authority. At the same time, Grand Central was also a monument to New York as the metropolitan seat of such power. With its great glass shed, high cupolas, and neo-Renaissance lines, the depot rang all the changes of imperial urbanism, staging the railway journey as a triumphal entry into a grand, central city. Or so the city's boosters thought: "The stranger who visits us for business or pleasure should be impressed by the magnificence of the great city upon his very entrance within its limits," the *Real Estate Record* wrote when plans for the terminal were announced. "So we endorse Mr. Vanderbilt's proposed depot on 41st street."[44]

The linkages between the "great city" and the "great boom" were even more apparent in the second of the Vanderbilt terminals. In 1867 the commodore paid Trinity Church $1 million for its St. John's Park property, a once-genteel residential square near the Hudson River on the lower West Side. He replaced the shady, if by then seedy, park with a massive, three-story freight depot (Figure 2.11). The impact was immediate. The tonnage hauled by the New York Central grew by a third in its first year of operation (1870), and it doubled again over the next five, surpassing that of the archrival Erie Railway.[45]

The Hudson Square freight depot was razed early in the twentieth century, and it is far less famous today than Grand Central. To many Victorian New Yorkers, however, it seemed an awesome civic and industrial achievement. As it was nearing completion, a "committee of leading citizens" commissioned a monument to honor the edifice and its owner. Quietly backed by Vanderbilt himself, they subscribed $250,000 for a bronze memorial "illustrat[ing] the career and achievements of the Commodore," "the marvelous inventions of the nineteenth century," and "the growth and prosperity of the great American Republic." The result was a 150-foot pediment, mounted over the main gate, that celebrated the great man's exploits on sea and land. On one side was a bas-relief of marine scenes: steamships, tropical fruit on a wharf, the commodore's first ferry plying the Hudson, and Neptune on a half shell. On the other were American railroad scenes: locomotive machinery, farm produce, a New York Central train passing a homestead, and Liberty grasping the national shield. Between them stood a statuary niche with a figure twelve feet high, "a colossal Cornelius Vanderbilt looming up in the midst of the chaos," as George Templeton Strong described it, "beaming benignantly down on Hudson Street, like a *Pater Patriae. . . .* As a work of art, it is bestial."[46]

Reading such accounts today, we may find it hard to see the making of the "Vanderbilt Bronzes" as anything more than a monumental act of egotism and sycophancy. They were certainly brazen in every sense of the word. Yet despite their naked grandiosity—or because of it—the bronzes were a fitting memorial to the "great boom." With a frankness that is almost refreshing, they paid tribute to the

FIGURE 2.11   The freight terminal at St. John's Park: this image, along with Figures 2.7, 2.9, and 2.10, illustrates the ideological ambition with which New York's infrastructures were associated. It depicts the ceremonial unveiling of the "Vanderbilt Bronzes," a frieze atop the depot that celebrated Cornelius Vanderbilt as a hero of American initiative and progress. Although the frieze itself has been lost, the statue of Vanderbilt at its center now overlooks the Park Avenue facade of Grand Central Terminal. (*Frank Leslie's Illustrated Newspaper*, November 22, 1869; negative no. 74689; © Collection of the New-York Historical Society)

fetishism of commodities: they implied that freight should get as triumphal an entry into the metropolis as human beings. Their iconography and placement reinforced this sacralizing of market exchange. They presented Cornelius Vanderbilt literally as a gateway figure, central yet liminal, poised between sea and land, depot and dock, domestic and global markets. To some observers, the result was barbaric. It is an "act of Idolatry and Mammon Worship," Strong fumed in his diary: "We bow down before [Vanderbilt], and worship him, with a hideous group of molten images, with himself for a central figure. . . . These be thy Gods, O Israel!" For the most part, however, elite commentators found the work "magnificent in execution" and "admirable in design," a tableau of progress, national abundance, and commercial expansiveness. And, as the opening ceremony made clear, they identified the sublimity of its hero with the grandeur of New York. "How appropriate to unveil them at the threshold of this immense commercial temple!" the featured orator, Mayor Oakey Hall, told the assembled notables. "How equally appropriate is your presence to honor . . . [one who] by manifold public enterprises . . . of national importance, has honored all of us and our beloved City."[47]

The depot and its memorial, in short, told a booster's tale. Yet it was a story marred by a grim irony. For, in the course of the midcentury boom, the district over which the colossal figure of Vanderbilt presided had devolved from a genteel square to an industrial slum. "One of the curious features about New York is the constant changes which are going on in different parts of the city," the *Real Estate Record* mused. "At one time a location is pleasant and even fashionable, and in a few years, presto! change—it has become degraded and almost unusable by decent people. . . . Less than twenty years since, the neighborhood of St. John's Park was full of charming residences, but look at it now,—the noble Park itself is a huge freight-house, and the surroundings tenement houses and rumshops!" The *Record* strikes a disingenuous note here—"presto! change"—but its editor understood perfectly that there was nothing mysterious about the link between "decent people" fleeing St. John's Park and the development of the terminal and tenements. These were elements in a single, complex pattern of spatial change.[48]

Of course, the "decline" of the park did not begin with the freight depot. Its initial cause was the growth of commercial and transport activities up the lower West Side in the early years of the boom. That expansion in turn provided the enabling conditions for the Vanderbilts' efforts; it eroded the residential land values of the local gentry, while fostering the complex ecology of workshops, warehouses, factories, and transshipment sites that rail terminals both serviced and required. The building of the Hudson Square depot thus culminated a longer process in which "improvement" and "decline" were inseparable and interdependent. Land-use maps of the Fifth Ward show the results of these changes. Clustered around the depot were stables for the American Express delivery company, bonded warehouses, wholesale grocers, storage yards for barrels and lumber, iron works, a lard refinery, a tin can factory, and many of the "tenement houses and rumshops" noted by the *Real Estate Record*. As for the gentry who first made St. John's Park a center of fashion—the peers of those who assembled to celebrate the Vanderbilt Bronze—most had moved uptown by the mid-1850s.[49]

A freight palace surrounded by tenements: we could not have a better emblem of the paradoxes of New York's growth in the age of capital. The scene testifies to the emergence of a new spatial order in the midcentury city—monumental in scale, intensive in land use, complex in its capacity to mass capital and labor—and to the macroeconomic regime that underlay and underwrote it. At the same time, it underscores the contradictory effects of the great boom. The boom produced an uneven landscape of expansiveness and confinement, bronze grandiosity and brick squalor, the mobilization of things and the warehousing of people. Moreover it made the *temporality* of city building equally uneven: a broken rhythm of dynamism, volatility, and stalemate.

The Eternal Building Up and Pulling Down

The march of improvement: even today we can hear the progressivist, triumphalist resonances in that cliché of Victorian city building. The words conjure up an organized, almost military mobilization of energies: serried ranks of new buildings extending along freshly paved avenues, modern infrastructures converging on monumental edifices. To nineteenth-century urbanists, the phrase connoted a temporality in which a city's physical development embodied the booster dream of boundless expansion and predestined ascent. Bourgeois New Yorkers had good reason to use it when discussing Manhattan's growth. Yet their actual descriptions of the cityscape tend to belie the image of a singular, purposive movement in time and over space. Rather they portray a city-building process whose rhythm often seemed propulsive and unpredictable: the "idiosyncracy of our city's growth . . . is unaccountable and inexplicable," mused the *Real Estate Record*, "but nevertheless an irresistable [*sic*] law of our development."[50] For this sort of process, the defining image was not a civic or military procession. It was a construction site.

New York was full of open building sites. Observers of the urban scene recurred to them constantly, fascinated and sometimes disquieted by their mix of order and entropy, focus and fragmentation (Figure 2.12). When the newlyweds Basil and Isabel March arrive in Manhattan at the start of William Dean Howells's 1872 novel *Their Wedding Journey*, for instance, their dawn walk from the railway depot brings them a veritable epiphany of the "forces of demolition and construction" reshaping the city: ". . . in many places the eternal building up and pulling down was already going on . . . ; here stood the half-demolished walls of a house, with a sad variety of wallpaper showing in the different rooms; there clinked the trowel upon the brick, yonder the hammer on the stone; overhead swung and threatened the marble block that the derrick was lifting to its place." It is a profoundly ambiguous vision to give newlyweds on the first day of their honeymoon—literally, a broken home. The novelist underscores the heterogeneous, unfinished quality of the scene, its dialectic of creative and destructive energies, prosperity ("marble block") and pathos ("a sad variety of wall-paper"). The result is a moment in which spatial change is more a matter of rupture than of progress. Such intimations of mortality were not limited to fiction. "Vast spaces in the air, which had remained open and free from the morn of time . . . are every day enclosed with walls of masonry," a *Times* editorialist mused concerning construction work in the 1850s. "No richness of association can stay the hand of the mason. . . . So, too, profound abysses yawn under your feet. . . . Frightful are the abrupt precipices on the crumbling edges of which you find yourself suddenly walking."[51]

These accounts of "the eternal building up and pulling down" provided the occasion for a deeply felt ambivalence to which I will return at the end of the chapter. My point here is that the iconography of the building site also registers an important truth about the city-building process: its fundamental volatility. New York was changing dramatically in the mid-nineteenth century, but not stably or seamlessly. Consider, for instance, the periodization of the midcentury boom. Its temporal structure did not take the form of a single, ascendant arc. Rather New York went through three distinct phases: a "prewar prosperity" that lasted from the late 1840s to the Panic of 1857, a "postwar prosperity" from Appomattox to the Panic of 1873, and a period of economic depression and Civil War in between. This uneven rhythm—a roller

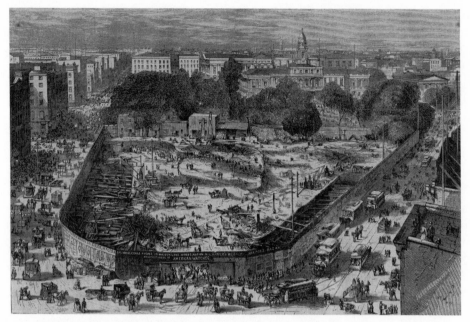

FIGURE 2.12   The city as building site: this illustration of the construction of the Federal Post Office at City Hall Park suggests both the dynamism and the chaos that typified New York's boom. Figure 5.5 shows the Second Empire building as completed. (*Harper's Weekly*, October 23, 1869; image courtesy of HarpWeek, LLC)

coaster, so to speak, with a dip in the middle—had important effects on the making of the New York cityscape. Each of the three periods fostered different processes of change, with differential effects on the built environment.

The prewar years were most importantly a population boom, the heyday of the first wave of immigration. Demographic pressure fueled impressive increases in land values and construction; the site for Central Park was chosen and assembled, and, in New York's first intensive burst of transit development, horse car companies received franchises to build railways on Second, Third, Sixth, Eight, and Ninth avenues. Yet in its physical effects, the first phase of the development boom was more modest than that of the postwar period. As Elizabeth Blackmar has shown, the pace of real-estate development lagged behind population growth, and the city faced a mounting housing crisis in the 1850s.[52] The middle period of depression and war was even flatter; new construction rates averaged one thousand buildings per year during the Civil War, only 50–60 percent of the early years of the boom. Yet this was not merely an era of stagnation. Hard times are always useful to some forms of urban development (as to capitalist development generally), especially those that benefit from low wages, surplus labor, and property consolidation. Large public and corporate infrastructures in particular get financed during good times but often finished in bad. Thus, much of Central Park was laid out in the late 1850s to give work to unemployed laborers; without the Panic of 1857, its progress would have been slower. Similarly the war had a paradoxically vibrant effect on New York's trade and financial power. Government bonds, military contracts, the nationalization of the banking system, railroad expansion, and the blockade of Confederate ports all fostered the flow of resources into Manhattan. The middle "dip" in city building was thus at the same time a boom in capital formation.[53]

Paradoxically the very unevenness of New York's roller-coaster ride during the first two periods accelerated its physical transformation in the third. After the Civil War, property developers and public officials responded to the city's pent-up land pressures and burgeoning capital supplies with an unprecedented surge in construction. "New buildings are everywhere in the course of erection," architectural critic John Kennion reported in 1868. "Capital has at last been turned into a channel by which the city will be improved and the wants of the public relieved so far as the insufficiency of house-room is concerned. The excessive prices that are now obtained for rents . . . [have] convinced capitalists that there is no better investment than house building, and the consequence is seen in the piles of brick and lumber that one encounters at every turn." Here were the "forces of demolition and construction" witnessed by Isabel and Basil March. The results were impressive: no matter what factor we track, the graph of city building takes a sharp turn upward. Assessed land values doubled to nearly $900 million between 1865 and 1874 (and quadrupled in the wards north of Fortieth Street). Building levels not only surpassed, but averaged, two thousand structures per year for the first time.[54] The pace and scale of public works received a similar boost. Manhattan and Brooklyn officials built on the success of Central Park by planning a network of pleasure grounds and parkways throughout the metropolitan area. Transport capitalists modernized New York's circulatory "plant." In 1860, the city boasted six franchised streetcar lines; by 1875, there were eighteen, carrying four and a half times more people.[55] Moreover a series of avant-garde infrastructures—the Vanderbilt depots, the first elevated line, and Brooklyn Bridge—were starting to render the old system of horse cars and ferries obsolete; all were undertaken between 1867 and 1869.

The late 1860s and early 1870s, in short, produced an astonishing compression of change; territorial growth, infrastructural modernization, and uptown and downtown development all came to a boil at once. Indeed, it is hard to describe New York in the last phase of the development boom without lapsing into the rhetorical excesses of its boosters. Yet we would do well to resist such triumphalism. For the very intensity of the postwar surge produced a frantic, erratic, often irrational rhythm of growth. Nowhere is this more apparent than in the cycle of land speculation and market collapse that climaxed the boom.

It is not surprising that the New York property market went through a speculative binge after the Civil War. Speculation flourishes precisely at times of mushrooming growth, when rapid, unstable inflation makes possible a kind of effortless profiteering. Under such conditions, speculators bet that the upward play of prices will magnify the exchange value of land without the need of improving its use value; they flood the real-estate market, often investing on credit, without clear information about the pace, stability, or direction of growth. The resulting market behavior is simultaneously "rational" and "irrational": an obsessive but fickle sensitivity to price cues, staccato shifts of attention from place to place, the rapid turnover of unimproved land, or conversely its overimprovement in the absence of specific demand.

This description was especially accurate in postwar Manhattan. Lured by an inflated postwar currency and booster visions of boundless prosperity, operators engaged in what one turn-of-the-century history called "the greatest speculative craze that has so far affected New York real estate." In auctions at the Real Estate Exchange Salesroom, privately brokered deals, and improvised gatherings at uptown intersections, thousands of New Yorkers entered the market, often speculating on ninety-day contracts secured by as little as 5 percent of purchase price. The most fevered activity took place in upper Manhattan. Vacant land north of Fifty-ninth Street appreciated by 200 percent between 1868 and 1873; many lots quadrupled in value without being built on, drained, or improved in any way. Uptown speculation was fueled by an ambitious program of public works aimed at opening the northern periphery to investment and settlement. Especially at the height of the Tweed regime's power (1868–71), municipal officials pursued park, boulevard, transit, and street improvements that would add to New York's tax base, reward party allies, expand patronage employment, and enrich themselves. "Streets and imposing boulevards . . . were opened, graded, curbed, sewered and paved with a celerity . . . which rivalled the Arabian tales," the *Real Estate Record* sardonically recalled in the mid-1870s depression, and "these very public benefactors . . . [were] ready and generous buyers of the new-made lots . . . under the profound conviction that their investments would double in a few months."[56]

The land rush both accelerated and deranged the development process. By the early 1870s, real-estate transactions in Manhattan averaged $20,000, the highest prices of the nineteenth century. Six dollars were spent on property conveyances for every one of new construction, a "speculation ratio" two-thirds higher than that of the Gilded Age as a whole. Such activism and profit taking, however, tended to distort the flow of market information; as one insider recalled, "Purchasers scarcely took any thought of prices, and many never saw the lots to which they took title. Nothing . . . approaching to business judgment controlled the market. No one had any real idea of value. Property changed hands quickly and many of these turn-overs . . . resulted in such dazzling profits that it is little wonder that the rational business instincts of the community were confounded." The mystification of market conditions was only sometimes accidental. Mock auctions, bogus sales, falsified deeds, and insider trading were endemic in the postwar surge—useful deceits for "booming" a locality to drive its prices up or disguising its value in order to buy into it more cheaply.[57]

Not surprisingly, the effects of the "speculative craze" were contradictory and erratic. Many operators won huge windfalls, earning profits of 25 percent or more on a few months' turnover. Yet the frantic rhythm of postwar city building also made the location of choice real estate unpredictable and fluid. "[The] peculiarly enigmatical character of our best property . . . [is] a difficult and even a dangerous [problem]," the

Real Estate Record warned. "Ownership of property becomes a veritable lottery in which the . . . prizes are greatly outnumbered . . . by the possible blanks." Postwar Manhattan was dotted with tales of such "blanks": wrong guesses, unsellable lots, overdone edifices. The Knickerbocker landowner James Beekman developed part of his family estate at Forty-ninth Street and the East River into first-class townhouses, although they were too near the riverfront to attract a bourgeois clientele; not until the 1920s did "Beekman Place" gain an upscale character. Similarly financier Samuel Pike built a sumptuous opera house at Twenty-third Street and Eighth Avenue—too far west of Ladies' Mile to supplant the Academy of Music as the city's premier concert stage. When the art speculation failed, Pike sold the Grand Opera House to rail barons James Fisk and Jay Gould, who made it their headquarters in the war for control of the Erie Railway. (Its location was a plus when they needed to flee across the Hudson to avoid New York State court injunctions and vigilante violence.) They backed productions of opéra bouffe there, featuring "ballet-girls" with whom Fisk was enamored. By the 1890s, the Grand Opera House had found its niche as a popular musical comedy and vaudeville venue.[58]

The most important case of postwar speculation gone awry was not a single building or block; it was the upper West Side as a whole. Real-estate experts had predicted great things for the district west of the Central Park after the Civil War. Endowed with magnificent, rolling terrain, high vistas of the Hudson valley, proximity to the new Central and Riverside parks, and a network of planned boulevards and rail links, the region seemed fated to be "the crowning glory of the Metropolis," as William Martin put it, with "residences . . . much in advance of the upper Fifth Avenue region" and "greater value, lot for lot, than . . . any other district in the Island." It was these expectations that made Martin's West Side Association the most broad-based and intellectually visionary of New York's property lobbies. "Upon this narrow strip, bounded easterly by the Park, westerly by the river . . . nature has bestowed its chiefest handiwork," Fernando Wood assured his fellow landowners at an association meeting. "and . . . man . . . shall establish what will be known hereafter as the most healthy, the most enchanting and most desirable section of this emporium." In the booster map of the Empire City, this was the center. What America was to the world and New York was to the nation, the upper West Side would be to the metropolis: the place of destiny, the seat of wealth and civilization.[59]

All the more striking, then, that the upper West Side proved a bust in the postwar years. Speculators bid up property values by more than 300 percent between 1865 and 1875, but even at the height of the land rush, the West Side remained as empty as its boosters' rhetoric. There are "hardly ten new and permanent buildings on the whole area," William Martin lamented in 1871, "and the region [is] the most inaccessible of any within thirty miles of the City Hall." Photographs and maps confirm that the district from Sixtieth to 110th Street was almost wholly vacant until the mid-1880s (see Figure 2.6). Indeed when the Dakota was built at Seventy-second Street and Eighth Avenue in 1883—partly to renew interest in the area—bourgeois folklore attributed the name of the huge apartment house to its location in an unsettled wilderness.[60]

The reasons for the West Side's stagnation were complex. Transit, utility, and street extensions lagged behind those on the flatter, more accessible East Side. "Not a single avenue or main thoroughfare [is] open for travel," complained the West Side Association's Martin, "not one street in ten ready for building; the sewerage system devised, but all unexecuted . . ." High carrying costs—mortgage debt, property taxes, and special assessments for the unfinished public works—tended paradoxically to inhibit development, especially when speculating on unimproved land was so lucrative: "The only object seems to be to spend money, and put expenses on owners," one uptown proprietor wrote bitterly against paving assessments. "Nine-tenths of this property will have to be sold for the payment of expenses . . ." Finally, as builders noted with grim puzzlement, even after improvements *were* completed, bourgeois New Yorkers continued to settle between Fourth and Sixth avenues, unwilling to adjust the "march of improvement" toward the northwest. "The West Side, instead of entering as a factor into the . . . city's growth, has become a separate problem," the *Real Estate Record* concluded in 1877. "A visitor . . . cannot help being impressed with the contrast between the predictions once so recklessly uttered with regard to it, and the condition in which it now stands. . . . [Despite] every possible street improvement that can be desired, and an unstinted measure of artificial adornment laid upon it, . . . the building improvements . . . are too insignificant and few in number to be worth recounting." Precisely because it witnessed so much speculation and public investment, the upper West Side served as a crucible for the design ideals of the new urbanism; as I discuss in Chapter 6, its landowners were key activists in the politics of city building. Thus, its halting progress underscores the volatility and unevenness of New York's growth, even—or especially—under conditions of booster confidence and booming investment.[61]

The flux of city building was most apparent when Manhattan's real-estate market collapsed in the mid-1870s. The crisis began on Wall Street, where the failure of banker Jay Cooke in the autumn of 1873 set off a chain reaction of insolvencies and a massive contraction of assets. The Panic of 1873 ushered in five years of national depression that—among other effects—brought New York's development boom to a close. The shrinkage of capital and confidence worked its way through the local real-estate economy, closing off access to credit and sending property values downward. By 1877, the rate of new buildings and real-estate conveyances had declined by half from "the dizzy heights of '71." Mortgage defaults grew threefold in the same years; lenders conducted nearly twelve thousand foreclosure sales between 1874 and 1879. Needless to say, uptown real-estate entrepreneurs were the hardest hit; as many as half the speculative builders in New York were thought to have failed in the panic. "The inflation of values north of 59th street was pricked in an instant," one expert recalled. "The equities of thousands of property owners were wiped out as with a sponge. . . . Everything that was sold was slaughtered, and, in a multitude of cases, selling was merely the process by which the mortgagee gathered up the remnants of what was left."[62]

For those who went under, the Panic of 1873 must have seemed like a horrible deus ex machina or a natural catastrophe, sweeping down on them from without. Yet the collapse of the Manhattan real-estate market was anything but arbitrary. It was built into the logic of city building, and its severity was enforced by the same factors that fueled the postwar surge in the first place. Geographer David Harvey argues that a rhythm of frantic speculation and real-estate crisis typifies the endgame of the business cycle; as other investment sectors become saturated, state and private investors turn to land and public works in "a last-ditch hope for finding productive uses for rapidly overaccumulating capital." The resulting activity hastens the financial crisis rather than averting it, promoting overconstruction and debt to the point where any perturbation induces a cascade of failures across the real-estate economy. Whether or not Harvey's analysis offers a *general* model of the links between urban and capitalist development, it surely fits New York's roller-coaster ride in the 1860s and 1870s. Postwar growth fueled levels of building and borrowing that strained capital markets to the breaking point. When the panic came, every factor that had first set the city-building process into motion—generous public spending, speculative risk taking, easy credit—now weighed it down like a beached ship. The depression of the 1870s thus represented the "end" of the midcentury boom in a double sense: its termination and its culmination. It brought to a climax a quarter-century of growth in which "improvement," irrationality, and inertia had gone hand in hand.[63]

May Day

Victorian New Yorkers would not have been shocked to hear either the Manhattan landscape or the temporality of city building described as uneven and contradictory. They experienced the new landscape as more of a crazy quilt than an integrated circuit; and they knew that it was a crazy quilt in permanent flux, a fractal landscape, constantly disrupted and reconfigured by the energies of capitalist development. "Progress in New York seems disposed to turn everything into something else; and all for the sake of change, untiring change," architect Samuel Sloan wrote in 1869. "Nor is this perpetual *May movement* at all likely to abate. . . . The Harlem river may yet be the centre of the ambitious city, and the Central Park be the Southern Park." Sloan invokes an image here that would have been familiar to any New Yorker: May Day, when, by custom, annual leases expired and Gothamites pursued an anarchic game of musical chairs in quest of better rents. From the early 1800s, moving on May 1 was a study in contradictions, a mix of market discipline and chaos on the streets (Figure 2.13). By the midcentury boom, that contradiction seemed embedded in the spatial fabric of Manhattan itself. City building had become a "perpetual *May movement*" of dynamism and disorder.[64]

This sense of New York's tireless, tiring shape-shifting pervades Victorian commentary on the midcentury boom. Even the city's gentry portray themselves adrift

MAY-DAY IN THE CITY.

FIGURE 2.13   The day when New Yorkers' annual leases were terminated, May 1 was notorious for traffic jams and domestic chaos. For many observers, May Day epitomized the
city's inhospitality to home and family life. (*Harper's Weekly*, April 30, 1859; image courtesy of
HarpWeek, LLC)

and homeless in a landscape of change. "When I was a boy, the aristocracy lived
around the Battery, on the Bowling Green," George Templeton Strong recalled.
"Greenwich Street, now a hissing and a desolation, a place of lager beer saloons, em-
igrant boarding houses, and vilest dens, was what Madison Avenue is now. . . . We
are a nomadic people, and our finest brownstone houses are merely tents of new pattern and material." *A nomadic people living in brownstone tents*—it is an amazingly
melodramatic way for a Gramercy Park lawyer to portray bourgeois life in the Empire City. Yet William Dean Howells confronts Basil and Isabel March with much the
same experience in *Their Wedding Journey*. "The hand of change had fallen," Howells
writes, depicting the newlyweds' walk through a midtown neighborhood. "It was no
longer a street solely devoted to the domestic gods, but had been invaded . . . by the
bustling deities of business: in such streets the irregular, inspired doctors and doc-
tresses come first . . . ; then a milliner filling the parlor window with new bonnets;
here even a publisher had hung his sign beside a door, through which the feet of little children . . . [used] to patter."[65]

Such scenes of domestic shabbiness and dislocation were resonant, I think, because
they dramatized the disruptive energies of New York's transformation. They brought
home—quite literally—the derangements of a city-building process that made New
York seem like a permanent construction site, a perpetual moving day. They regis-

tered the moral and emotional costs of that process for elite New Yorkers, evoking a current of anxiety that was central to the bourgeois experience of capitalist growth. For Victorian observers responded to the boom with deeply mixed feelings. Their accounts of "the eternal building up and pulling down" were shot through with ambivalence, veering between exhilaration and regret, triumphalism and nostalgia. "If we glance prospectively, how shall we venture to limit [New York's] progressive march in opulence and greatness," an 1866 guidebook proclaimed in the cadences of boosterism. Yet only a few pages away, Manhattan's "progressive march in opulence" drew more somber comment: "The denizens of New York are such utilitarians that they have sacrificed to the shrine of Mammon almost every relic of the olden time. The feeling of veneration for the past, so characteristic of the cities of the Old World, is lamentably deficient among the people of the New."[66]

Elite ambivalence entailed something more than a wistful acknowledgment of the price of "improvement." It put into question the legitimacy of the booster narrative under whose banner "the march of improvement" was thought to take place. Civic boosterism offered bourgeois New Yorkers the promise of mastery over time and space. It cast Manhattan as a capital of commerce and civilization from which the course of world history and the geography of the world market would be reordered. Within that heroic narrative, the remaking of the urban landscape was both a prophecy and a means of dominion. *That* was the theme of the 1876 Currier and Ives lithograph: the image transformed Manhattan Island into an icon of imperial power, a massed vector all of whose energies converged on the future.

As I have tried to show in this chapter, such a bird's-eye view was not false so much as ideological: it overlooked much of what it meant to oversee. On the ground, the workings of the midcentury boom told a more ambiguous story. New York's growth was indeed magnificent, but it was ruled by a volatile logic that left disparate and sometimes irrational effects on the Manhattan landscape. The city-building process uprooted preexisting geographies of property value and land use, even the most cherished forms of bourgeois "civilization." Instead of mastery over time and space, the built environment embodied a propulsive drama of rupture and displacement. Karl Marx famously noted that the capitalist revolution of the mid-nineteenth century "annihilated space with time," collapsing the earth into a world economy driven by accelerating, centripetal circuits of capital, commodities, and information. The story of the midcentury boom suggests that we extend his insight. In New York, capitalist city building annihilated *both* space and time, dissolving all traces of locality and legacy in a sublime flux, creating a landscape that was at once monumental and provisional, centralized but endlessly dislocated. "In London or Paris you may see some relics of past centuries; these are reverenced and preserved as long as they endure," an 1869 sketch from *Harper's Weekly* commented. "But New York is a series of experiments, and every thing which has lived its life and played its part is held to be dead, and is buried, and over it grows a new world."[67]

As the *Harper's* essayist understood, New York's corrosive dynamism posed a threat to its destiny as the new world metropolis, the great heir to civilization. The very success of the development boom raised doubts about the city's capacity to discipline capitalist energy with civic form. Metropolitan elites sought to allay those doubts, and urban and architectural design represented a crucial means of doing so. "But there is one edifice in New York that, if not swallowed up by an earthquake, will stand as long as the city remains," continued the *Harper's Weekly* essay. "There is not anything like it in the world, not even among the palaces of the European nobility." The essay was describing the enormous mansion that dry-goods baron Alexander Stewart had just completed at Fifth Avenue and Thirty-fourth Street. Stewart was among Manhattan's most celebrated millionaires: the founder of the city's most fashionable department store, owner of its most impressive art collection (displayed in the new mansion), sponsor of many charitable projects. To *Harper's*, his home offered lasting proof of New York's metropolitan stature, a bulwark against the flux of space and time: "[It] will ever be pointed to as a monument of individual enterprise, of far-seeing judgment, and of disinterested philanthropy." Yet the prophecy proved false. Thirty-five years later, Stewart's palace of capital and culture was razed; in its place arose the offices of the Knickerbocker Trust Company.[68]

CHAPTER 3

The Rule of Real Estate

Business . . . has been New York's real Napoleon III, from whose decree there was no appeal.
—Jacob Riis, *How the Other Half Lives* (1890)

Myth of Origins

On Tuesday, April 14, 1885, the leadership of New York's real-estate elite gathered together to pat themselves on the back. The occasion was the opening of the new Real Estate Exchange and Auction Room, organized to replace the old Exchange Salesroom that had been the center of Manhattan property markets since the 1860s. The assembled owners, developers, auctioneers, builders, and brokers—"represent[ing]," it was claimed, "nearly one-third in value of the landed wealth in the city"—had good reason to celebrate. Over the previous thirty years, they had presided over an extraordinary development boom, during which New York had become the nation's commercial and cultural metropolis and the point of integration between North American markets and a new global economic order. Such dominance made possible—indeed necessary—a sea change in the city's physical fabric. New York grew from a port to a metropolitan area whose complexity and scale seemed to embody its imperial destiny. Property values had skyrocketed. At the same time, however, the new urban landscape was plagued by less happy effects. Tenement districts proliferated across Manhattan. A business depression had stalemated improvements and bankrupted many investors during the 1870s. And the return of prosperity brought its own troubles: only a month earlier, the streets of Manhattan and Brooklyn had been convulsed by a wave of bitter horse car strikes.[1]

Needless to say, the ceremony at the Real Estate Exchange kept the focus on New York's prosperity and power. Speakers limned the city's progress with the familiar grandiosity of booster discourse, exulting in New York's future as "the great metropolis of America." At the same time, they invoked the city's past, hearkening back to a legendary event that often served as the starting point for New Yorkers' booster tales. "It is a curious and noteworthy fact that the first authenticated real estate transfer on Manhattan Island took place in May, 1626," realtor James Varnum told his listeners, "when Peter Minuit, then Director-General of the province, purchased from the Indians the whole island of Manhattan . . . for the sum of sixty Dutch guilders, equal to about $22 in our money. Is it not difficult to realize . . . that this beautiful island, now covered by this enormous city, the value of whose real estate is to-day estimated at more than $2,000,000,000, should have been sold . . . for the paltry sum of $22?"[2]

It was a story that every schoolchild knew, then as now. In the beginning was the purchase: Indians sold Manhattan to the Dutch for twenty-two (or as it was usually told, twenty-four) dollars. It is one of those tales that is closer to the facts than the truth. The facts are these: in 1626, Peter Minuit, appointed by the Dutch West India Company to oversee the fur-trading colony of New Netherlands, gave a sum of trade goods to a local group of Delaware Indians for control of the island. "Our people there are of good courage, and live peaceably," reported one of the company's directors to the Dutch parliament toward the end of that year. "They have bought the Island Manhattes from the wild men for the value of sixty guilders . . ." Secondhand and laconic, this one surviving record conveys little of what the sixty guilders of goods meant to the parties involved. For the Dutch, buying "the island Manhattes" was less a project of colonial town building than a minor warehousing venture. They needed an entrepôt for the backcountry fur trade; indeed the letter goes on to offer a detailed inventory of the pelts brought back from New Netherlands. For the Delawares, even to use the word "purchase" may be to miss the mark. We do not know how their views of possession, exchange, or territory differed from Dutch notions or our own. Nor can we be sure of the importance of the activities that they gave up in forgoing the use of the island. Their villages were concentrated in what is now Yonkers and the Bronx; they kept only a few up-island settlements in the Washington Heights area and some summer encampments by the streams of lower Manhattan. What does seem clear is that their actions involved systems of land use and property relations more fluid than the ledger-book rhetoric of the Dutch could convey.[3]

Knowing what the "purchase" of Manhattan Island meant to those involved, however, would not tell us what it meant to James Varnum and his listeners at the Real Estate Exchange. For the story has more to do with the age that recounted it than with the age that it recalled. Its signature detail signaled as much: sixty Dutch guilders amounted to twenty-four dollars under late-nineteenth-century exchange rates. It was in the late nineteenth century, in fact, that Peter Minuit's purchase became something more than a Knickerbocker legend. Victorian New Yorkers retold the story constantly, not only in real-estate circles, where one might expect it but also in popular journalism, local histories, guidebooks, and even moral reform tracts. They transformed the incident into something like a myth of origins. For it narrated New York's entry into history, the moment when the city's career as a great metropolis properly commenced. "It was, in itself, a commonplace event," declared one local history in 1877, "but in its relation to what has since taken place, it . . . stands out in immortal characters as the chief starting-point of the great commercial capital of the west."[4]

We should not be surprised that the episode had so much resonance to nineteenth-century New Yorkers; it embodied two ideas that were central to booster visions of the Empire City. First of all, it made an act of trade the constitutive event of New York's public life, prefiguring the city's commercial ascendance: "The first act of the colonial government," one civic chronicler boasted, "was an honest, honorable trans-action, worthily inaugurating the trade and traffic of America's mercantile and finan-cial capital." Even more important, it specified that primal scene of exchange as a transaction in *land*: the first great killing in a long tradition of New York real-estate speculation. Even the famous pittance paid by Peter Minuit seemed ironically to con-firm Manhattan's telos as the most valuable space on earth. "A little more than two centuries since, the entire site of this noble city was purchased of the Indians for . . . the nominal sum of twenty-four dollars," wrote one midcentury tour guide. "Now the total amount of its assessed property is ten and a half millions of dollars. If such vast accessions of wealth have characterized the history of the past, who shall com-pute the constantly augmenting resources of its onward course?" The moral of the story was clear: capital accumulation and commodity exchange were aboriginally in-scribed on Manhattan Island. The landscape had been real estate from the start.[5]

For Victorian New Yorkers, then, the tale of the twenty-four dollar deal portrayed an almost primordial bond between global commerce, local space, and civic identity. It projected backward the promise of their imperium, adumbrating New York's rise to power within a nineteenth-century capitalist world where international exchange rates and local land speculations were fatally bound together. Most important, it made the commodification of space—the constituting of land as real estate—not only the originary moment of New York's history, but the very engine of its progress. In that sense, the tale was closer to the truth than the facts: it offered the perfect founda-tional narrative for an imperial metropolis in the age of capital.

Such narratives tend to serve, in Michael Denning's elegant phrase, as "the dream-work of the social." They symbolize in occulted form "the wishes, anxieties, and in-tractable antinomies" of the social world in which they are produced; and we can use them in turn to decipher the conditions and conflicts underlying that world.[6] This seems especially true of Peter Minuit's purchase. For the episode—so brief and folk-loric—gives us an important clue to the historical issue that I want to explore in this chapter: the mechanisms that governed New York's physical transformation from a coastal port to a capitalist metropolis, from walking city to Empire City. The first two chapters offered an overview of the city's pivotal role in national and global markets and its development of an expansive and specialized—but also divided and volatile—landscape. This chapter explores the processes that linked those changes together. What factors translated the macro forces of national and global consolidation into a new regime of local space? What institutions shaped patterns of building and land use in the Victorian cityscape? What was it that drove and directed the city-building process?

Although the answer to these questions will ultimately include important changes in municipal politics and bourgeois culture, it must start with the theme of Peter Mi-nuit's story: the transmutation of land into real estate. For it was, first of all, the institution of the real-estate economy that organized city building in Victorian New York. "Institution" is meant here in two ways: not only the usual sense of a compact social agency with its own members, resources, projects, rules, and field of interests but also the process by which that agency was brought into being, was "instituted." For even a seemingly neutral mechanism like the New York property market was a historical artifact. It had to be made, and its making was intimately bound up with the city's dramatic ascendance in the age of capital. The maturation of the real-estate economy was at once a primary effect of New York's midcentury growth and the precondition for embedding that growth in urban space.

Of course, Manhattan real estate has a history that stretches back to Peter Minuit's day. Indeed, my argument draws on the work of scholars—especially Elizabeth Blackmar and Hendrik Hartog—who have illuminated the effect of property relations on the New York landscape prior to the midcentury boom.[7] Yet the boom coincided with, and reinforced, changes in New York's development economy that made real-estate transactions more efficient, land use more systematic, and property investment more profitable. At the heart of these changes were two complementary processes of economic rationalization.

First of all, space was transformed into a standardized, alienable commodity. That transformation had begun in 1811, when New York's famous street plan, with its uniform block and lot lines, inscribed the principle of calculable exchange on the uneven terrain of Manhattan. Yet the laying out of the grid merely inaugurated a longer process by which farms, estates, and municipal landholdings were disaggregated into city lots and brought to market, a process that climaxed during the midcentury boom. At the same time, the commodification of space was matched by a "liquefaction" of property capital. The emergence of lower Manhattan as the nation's financial center brought vast resources into the local development economy, fostering credit and investment arrangements that enlarged and accelerated the flow of capital between the money and property markets. In the process, real estate became an efficient medium of capital accumulation, and the New York cityscape served as a "savings bank" for national capitalist growth.

These two changes required new means of coordination and control. The sheer complexity of the real-estate, building, and credit markets—with thousands of landowners and hundreds of lenders and developers—kept any constituency from dominating them. Rather, propertied New Yorkers created a series of institutions to organize information, capital flows, and market contacts. In 1862 they established the Exchange Salesroom at 111 Broadway as a specialized, centralized mart for property transactions. Six years later, the *Real Estate Record and Builders' Guide* commenced publication, offering weekly records of land, mortgage, and building transactions. Owners organized *themselves* as well, creating a network of property associations that lobbied for tax policies and public services amenable to their interests. Thus, when New York's real-estate leaders convened to open the new exchange in the spring of 1885—the occasion on which James Varnum regaled them with the story of Peter Minuit's deal—they were culminating and celebrating thirty years of economic and class consolidation.

It was these market and institutional innovations that underlay the astonishing transformations of the midcentury boom. By streamlining the circulation of capital and land, the real estate economy fueled New York's "march of improvement." By subjecting investment and land use to the discipline of market cues, it sorted the cityscape into the mosaic of specialized districts that typified the new metropolitan area. At the same time, market discipline reinforced New York's spatial disorders, contributing to the flux of the building cycle, the congestion of the new tenement districts, and the arterial sclerosis of the downtown streets.

This chapter examines the rule of real estate in New York's boom. It offers a *genealogy* of the development economy and a *geography* of some of its key effects on the Manhattan landscape. It is organized around the spatial change that Victorian observers thought most fundamental to New York's emergence as an imperial metropolis: the division of Manhattan into an intensively built commercial center and an extensively built residential periphery. The boom transformed "downtown" and "uptown" into two divergent, interdependent landscapes, each of which embodied distinct aspects of the city-building process and a distinctive built environment. The chapter starts with the remaking of lower Manhattan into a complex mosaic of specialized enclaves and commercial building types, the first modern business center in urban America. The new downtown served as a vast "plant" for the circulation of goods, information, and money; it concentrated the profits of national growth in local space and channeled massive flows of capital into the cityscape as a whole. Upper Manhattan, in contrast, took quite a different form. The busiest site of land speculation and construction, it grew into an expansive corridor of genteel residence bounded on each side by industry, tenements, and infrastructures. Where lower Manhattan shows the workings of the capital and rent markets in shaping the new metropolis, uptown underscores the role of the land market itself, especially as it was embodied in the street grid that organized "the march of improvement."

Together downtown and uptown tell a story of fiscal discipline and physical rationalization. It is not the only story that needs to be told. In the next chapter, I will analyze the physical, geographic, and social disorders that constituted the "nether side" of the midcentury boom. Yet the contradictions of the boom can only be grasped if they are seen against the real effectivity of the real-estate economy. The rule of real estate transformed Victorian New York, reconfiguring buildings and land uses according to their ability to pay for space as a commodity. It transformed bourgeois New Yorkers as well, habituating them to obey market cues that overwrote all other local attachments. It was the triumph of this economic, spatial, and cognitive regime that the story of Peter Minuit's purchase commemorated.

The Landscape of Accumulation

Imagine a Victorian Rip Van Winkle, returning to lower Manhattan after a generation's absence. Say: a young clerk in a dry-goods store, who ventured north for an outing one summer afternoon in the late 1840s and fell mysteriously asleep by

Spuyten Duyvil Creek. When he awoke a quarter-century later—let us say, in the summer of 1873—and went back downtown to find his employer, what would look different? For the hero of Washington Irving's fable, awakening offered a lesson in political revolution and generational continuity. To our white-collar Van Winkle, it would reveal the effects of economic and architectural transformation. How would he find the familiar landscape of lower Manhattan different?

Three changes would strike him most of all. The first would be the sheer growth of the space devoted to business. As we saw, the built-up area of New York extended perhaps half a mile above Fourteenth Street in the late 1840s. Returning down Broadway twenty-five years later, the clerk would enter a succession of commercial districts from almost the same point: a shopping and amusement area around Union Square, publishers and printers at Astor Place, wholesalers and cast-iron warehouses from Houston to Canal, news and communications agencies around City Hall, and the financial district at Wall Street. It would be an exaggeration to claim, as the *Real Estate Record* did, that "population [had been] driven off the lower end of the island by the pressure of . . . trade." Immigrant workers were teeming into the wards east of the Bowery at just the same time, making the lower East Side the most congested neighborhood in New York. Yet commercial growth did force a massive residential shift during the midcentury boom. When our Van Winkle left on his ill-fated outing, 85 percent of New Yorkers lived below Fourteenth Street, and more than half lived west of the Bowery. When he returned, about 45 percent lived south of Union Square; only one-fifth of the city's residents were on the lower West Side; and the area south of Canal Street and west of the Bowery was losing population. Business had claimed much of lower Manhattan and forced the vast majority of the remaining residents to crowd into the East Side.[8]

Second, our clerk would have been astonished by the variety, scale, and style of the built forms in the new downtown. The earlier business district—between City Hall, the Battery, and the riverfronts—had been a largely horizontal, homogeneous streetscape, organized around the ground-level meeting of entrepreneurs, customers, and suppliers in sales rooms, showrooms, counting rooms, and warehouses. Interiors were street bound as well: the inconvenience of climbing stairs kept elite business on the first two stories, with upper floors used for storage, workshops, or lower-rent trades. Such constraints were not unduly limiting: antebellum firms were generally small and unspecialized, often containing wholesale space, retail sales rooms, offices, and workshops within the confines of the row house form (Figure 3.1). Not surprisingly, there were few examples of monumental commercial design. The landmarks that broke the line of the downtown streetscape tended to be ecclesiastical edifices such as Trinity Church, public institutions like the City Hall, and a handful of elite hotels and theaters. Perhaps the grandest spot in lower Manhattan was the corner of Fulton, Broadway, and Park Row, where a stroller of the 1840s would be able to gaze on Barnum's American Museum and St. Paul's Chapel opposite each other, and the Astor Hotel, Park Theater, and City Hall just uptown (see Figure 2.1). It was a landscape, in short, that accorded with republican visions of New York as a commercial port of citizen-entrepreneurs and "horizontal" market relations.[9]

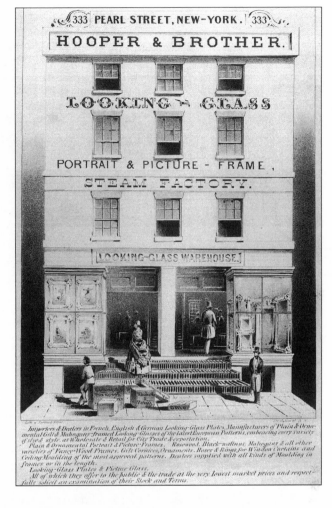

FIGURE 3.1 Nineteenth-century business advertising often featured the firm's works or headquarters. This 1840s circular for Hooper and Brothers of Pearl Street, dealers and manufacturers of frames and mirrors, portrays a typical establishment of the antebellum business district. Note the store's relatively small scale, orientation to the streetscape, and mixing of wholesale, retail, import, and manufacturing functions. (*Hooper & Brothers, 333 Pearl Street,* trade card, circa 1849; Museum of the City of New York; Print Archives, 29.100.2481)

By the end of the boom, however, downtown architecture had grown diverse in its forms and functions and unabashedly monumental in design and scale. "Every year builders are engaged in pulling down old edifices," reported New York's super-intendent of buildings in 1869, "and erecting new and improved buildings, larger, more commodious, and better adapted to the business requirements of a flourishing metropolis." Our clerk would be struck by four new building types in particular. North of Houston Street, along Broadway and Union Square, he would notice lux-ury-goods emporia such as A. T. Stewart's new store on Tenth Street (built in 1862) or Lord and Taylor on Twentieth (1869). These retailing palaces made "Ladies' Mile," as the midtown shopping and entertainment district was coming to be called, a scene of elite consumer spectacle. Using plate glass and cast-iron girders—technologies of the facade—they promoted a culture of class distinction and fashionable display that abandoned older norms of republican modesty and restraint.[10] Farther downtown, and west of Broadway, he would notice wholesale and warehousing establishments, many of them suppliers to the bazaars of Ladies' Mile. In the Fifth Ward alone, over

FIGURE 3.2   Steam-driven, floating grain elevators transferred midwestern grain from Erie Canal boats to freight cars and steamers. In contrast to Chicago's vast dockside elevators (and the New York Central facility depicted in Figure 2.9), these vessels exemplify New York's penchant for spatial improvisation and compromise. (*Harper's Weekly*, November 15, 1873; image courtesy of HarpWeek, LLC)

two hundred such lofts were built after the Civil War, "buildings of magnificent proportions," as one booster wrote, "modelled after the sumptuous palaces of Italy."[11] Heading toward the riverfronts, the clerk would see a new infrastructure of port and transport facilities. I discuss elsewhere some of the most famous instances of Victorian infrastructural modernization: the East River Bridge, the freight terminal at St. John's Park (next to the new wholesaling district), and Grand Central Depot uptown. A clerk in a mercantile house might also note the new abattoirs on both shores of the Hudson River; cast-iron terminals for local ferries and transoceanic steamship lines; and steam-driven floating elevators that transshipped grain from Erie Canal barges to Atlantic steamers or dock basins in Brooklyn (Figure 3.2).[12]

Finally, he would be struck by another group of structures, farther downtown: huge office buildings, some as high as eight or ten stories, that dotted the district around City Hall, Printing-House Square, lower Broadway, and Wall Street. Precursors to the skyscraper, these "business palaces" housed the most powerful actors in the downtown economy: banks, insurance firms, newspaper and book publishers, telegraph and railroad companies, and a host of related services. From such buildings New York's capitalists and communications barons oversaw their rise to power; not surprisingly, the structures themselves came to symbolize the city's imperium. "The old policy of conducting business in a rookery is dying out, and New York is building up a series of business palaces which will be without a rival in any city on the

FIGURE 3.3 The antebellum downtown: Park Row, alongside City Hall Park, is shown here with its five-story, horizontal streetscape of diverse, relatively small firms, including stationers, publishers, clothiers, and dry-goods stores. (*Park Row Stores*, lithograph; Museum of the City of New York; gift of John A. Kouwenhoven)

FIGURE 3.4 By 1870 the midcentury boom had transformed the lower Manhattan business district. Park Row evolved into Newspaper Row, a publishing and printing district, with a growing number of high-rise edifices such as Richard Hunt's *Tribune* building. (*Park Row, City Hall Park*, photograph, circa 1876; Museum of the City of New York; Print Archives)

globe," one paper commented. "Our business men are building up to the clouds." Nowhere was this metamorphosis clearer than at the corner of Fulton and Broadway. There the clerk would no longer find Barnum's museum—whose destruction by fire would probably be the biggest shock of all—but rather the Park Bank and *Herald* offices. On Park Row, in place of the old mix of stores and theaters, he would see a phalanx of newspaper buildings (Figures 3.3 and 3.4). Down Broadway, the unfinished, ten-story Western Union headquarters, soon to be the tallest building in the city, would dominate the scene (Figure 3.8). And in place of the old uptown vista across City Hall Park, the clerk's view would be blocked by the massive, Second Empire U.S. Post Office, begun in 1869, for which half the land in the park had been taken.[13]

These buildings composed an impressive tableau of design innovation. Instead of the homogeneous fabric of the antebellum downtown, lower Manhattan was more site intensive, internally complex, and differentiated in function, form, and location. It was also more self-consciously "aesthetic" and monumental. Downtown property owners hired prestigious architects like Richard Upjohn, Griffith Thomas, and Leopold Eidlitz to design commercial projects; historicist styles and lavish ornament were used to adorn not only office blocks and retailing palaces, but even ferry terminals and wholesale lofts. Architectural ambition in the new downtown, in short, highlighted precisely the *emergent* institutions and spaces of a capitalist metropolis, not the residual landmarks of the republican port.[14]

Yet these buildings would not be the strangest aspect of the new downtown to our clerk. He would be even more bemused by a third change: the spatial reorganization of the business district. In fact he would be hopelessly lost. In all likelihood, his employer had been located along the lower East River waterfront; dry-goods importers, jobbers, and commission houses clustered on Pearl, Water, and Front streets in the 1840s. By the early 1870s, most of the trade had relocated at least twice: west of Broadway to the Third Ward in the 1850s and then uptown to the side streets of the Fifth Ward near St. John's Park after the Civil War. (About the time our Van Winkle was awakening, some firms were moving north again, across Canal Street, to the Eighth Ward.) His firm—if it existed at all—was probably now in one of the cast-iron lofts that he had passed a half-hour earlier on Duane, Thomas, or White streets.[15]

Yet even that image of the geographic changes that his work had undergone is too simple. The activities of the dry-goods house would probably be distributed to more than one site: a financial office near Wall Street, a wholesale-warehouse operation in the lofts of the Fifth or Eighth Ward, perhaps cheaper storage for bulk commodities near the Hudson riverfront or a retail storefront on Ladies' Mile. In the early 1870s, for instance, the silk importer Horace Claflin built a lavish warehouse in the Fifth Ward while maintaining his old quarters on Church Street. Ellen and William Demorest, the owners of the largest mail-order dress pattern business in the country, also divided their facilities as they moved uptown. In 1874 they relocated their pattern-cutting workshops and retail store to Fourteenth Street and Union Square; they shipped inventory from warehouses on the west side and were partners in a new eight-story print works on Astor Place, where *Demorest's Monthly*, their fashion magazine and catalog, was printed. At the same time, William Demorest became one of the most active real-estate operators on Ladies' Mile, buying up much of Fourteenth Street from Union Square to Sixth Avenue.[16]

In short, as our clerk wandered about the new downtown, he would experience two of the most powerful tendencies of the midcentury boom. First of all, there was the extraordinary dynamism of New York's spatial change. The rhythm of building up and pulling down was especially intense in lower Manhattan; as the *Real Estate Record* marveled, "ceaseless unrest" and "the constant overturning of business centres" typified downtown development. At the same time, there was a method to this madness: the economic geography of lower Manhattan grew more specialized, complex, and functionally integrated. The *Record* summarized the change in the grand rhetoric of Victorian social science: "The growth of a city like New York [accords] with the law of development drawn by Herbert Spencer, that is, . . . from the simple to the complex. . . . The wholesaler occupies a different quarter from the retailer. . . . The brokers congregate in one locality, the dry goods dealers in another, and so the differentiation goes on through every branch of business. It is these changes that lead to repeated rebuildings of certain districts in New York." The clerk was returning to a landscape that, like New York as a whole, had emerged from the chrysalis of the walking city.[17]

Of course, the antebellum downtown already showed a tendency to functional differentiation. Yet such specialization remained small-scale and spatially compact, organized more by street than by district; and it tended to reflect the diversity of mercantile niches rather than a full-blown logic of sectoral segregation. We can see the pattern by mapping a cross section of downtown trades: dry-goods houses, wholesale grocers, packing-box manufactories, commercial banks, and daily newspapers. In the 1840s and early 1850s, dry-goods merchants still hug the older East River waterfront. The jobbers (merchants who take title to merchandise and resell it at a profit) dominate Pearl Street, while commission merchants (who simply charge a commission for moving others' goods) cluster in Front and Water streets a block away. Many wholesale grocers occupy Front Street too, especially near the produce, flour, fish, and meat docks at Coenties Slip and Fulton Market, but they also congregate at Washington Market on the western riverfront. A scattering of packing-box makers service these warehousing businesses a block or two inland. Commercial banks and daily newspapers maintain offices around lower Broadway from Wall Street to City Hall Park. In short, we see a pattern of rudimentary sorting within a compact landscape that lacked the infrastructural capacity—and the need—to extend far from the lower port. The downtown economy contained an elaborate fabric of production and service linkages; but these were dispersed amid, and subordinate to, the "extensive warehouse district" that geographers like Alan Pred and David Ward find to be "the dominant central land use" of antebellum port cities.[18]

A generation later, the geography of lower Manhattan has changed dramatically. Commercial banks (nearly twice as many) have maintained their place on Wall Street but also proliferated up Broadway into the Third Ward. Daily newspapers have concentrated east of City Hall Park in an area that, around 1860, comes to be called Printing-House Square. Dry-goods firms and other mercantile establishments have left the East River front for the new lofts of the West Side. Commission merchants now cluster between St. John's Park and the commercial hotels of Broadway; more than 130, nearly 90 percent of the city's total, are located in a five-block stretch between Thomas and White streets. Packing-box makers, along with other workshops, have also moved to the fringes of this new wholesaling district.

Such locational patterns represent little more than "stills" from an elaborate moving picture of spatial change, but they offer a sketch of New York's emerging commercial geography. Economic growth has enlarged the downtown landscape, appropriating most of the land west of the Bowery and south of Houston Street and displacing all but the most profitable land uses uptown or over to the "sweated" East Side. On the perimeter of this metropolitan core, extending along rail and water corridors, a zone of transport and processing infrastructures has been developed: freight and passenger terminals, dock basins, grain elevators, abattoirs. The mercantile district that dominated the antebellum downtown has shifted north and west toward this infrastructural belt, forming a wholesaling, warehouse, and workshop district that finishes, stores, and merchandises goods moving through the port. In the old downtown, a "tertiary sector" has sprung up, subdivided into financial, news, government, and other centers; and a new midtown district of luxury retailing, commercialized amusements, and the national publishing industry has coalesced from Astor to Madison squares.

Such an overview is oversimplified of course. For one thing, the specialty districts of the new downtown were themselves heterogeneous: Printing-House Square housed not only the daily press but also magazine publishers, news agencies, job printers, type founders, stationers, paper manufacturers, and other related trades. Moreover, lower Manhattan was shaped as much by linkages *among* districts as by the concentrations of activities *within* them: at a time when newspapers and printers depended on party and government patronage, for instance, Printing-House Square could not have been far from City Hall and the county courthouse. Finally it is important to remember that every locale had its own quirks; specialization was a *tendency* of capitalist development, not a law of the land. Thus, Knox's hat manufactory—which had burnt down with Barnum's Museum in 1865—hung on at Broadway and Fulton as late as 1890, even as some of the city's biggest office buildings went up around it.[19]

Yet it is fair to say that lower Manhattan gained a new morphology in the midcentury boom. The compact center of the walking city gave way to a mosaic—or an integrated circuit—of expansive specialty districts. Such changes were not unique to New York; as much research has shown, "internal spatial differentiation and selective outward expansion" were typical of nineteenth-century downtown development in ports like Boston and manufacturing centers like Chicago. Indeed the growth of concentrated, segregated business districts is seen as one key index of the evolution from "mercantile" to "urban-industrial" form in American cities, a shift that is generally dated around 1870.[20] New York, however, represents a somewhat idiosyncratic example of the paradigm. The city's economic power and the sheer complexity of its trade placed demands on circulation and land use that were uniquely intensive; conversely, it provided developers with resources that were uniquely abundant. Moreover, the topography of New York defined advantages and constraints unlike those of any other American city. Manhattan's narrow, insular setting offered unrivaled possibilities for commercial development, but at the same time it made commercial space scarce, high priced, and inaccessible to overland transport.

Thus, what is most significant about the geography of lower Manhattan is not its representativeness, but its particularity. Two complementary mechanisms were especially salient in translating the energies of American (and international) capitalist development into a new kind of downtown landscape. On one hand, the commercial division of labor overturned established *use values* in downtown locations, impelling land users to reorganize their activities in order to enhance the movement of commodities through the metropolitan core. On the other hand, commercial growth bid up the *exchange value* of those locations, impelling landowners, landlords, and land users to treat space itself more systematically as a commodity. The result was a fabric of building, rental, and siting decisions that tended to conform commercial property to what locational economists call its "best and highest"—its most remunerative—use. Such market discipline worked to maximize land values across the downtown as a whole, sorting activities according to their ability to pay rent for space.[21]

To see how New York's ascendance affected the downtown division of labor, we need only look at business directories and trade statistics. Between 1855 and 1870, for instance—a period in which the population of Manhattan grew by 49.6 percent—the number of trade and technical publications doubled; lawyers increased by two and a half times; commission merchants tripled; and the amount of clearances by New York banks grew fivefold. As might be expected, Wall Street showed the most stunning growth: with railroads and governments seeking capital on the securities markets, the number of brokers and private bankers in Manhattan skyrocketed from 170 to 1,800 in just the five years following the Civil War.[22] Such changes pressured commercial land use in myriad ways. Different sectors and actors each had their own needs for access to supplies, services, credit, transport facilities, customer markets, or simply more or cheaper space. Their locational decisions melded these requirements into spatial strategies that produced differential patterns of clustering, specialization, contiguity, and circulation.

Consider, for instance, the sector in which our imaginary clerk was employed: dry goods. As we saw, the trade underwent several changes in geography and architecture during the midcentury boom: it moved uptown, it divided into distinct retail and wholesale sectors, and it developed new building types for each specialty. What shaped these changes?

As early as the 1850s, the expansion and wealth of the Manhattan bourgeoisie encouraged a specialized class of retail merchants. Dry-goods entrepreneurs like A. T. Stewart and R. H. Macy broke with their old habit of staying close to the downtown wholesale district and built palatial stores on Ladies' Mile. They did so to take advantage of two related economies of scale. First, they "tr[o]d in the tracks of their customers," as the New York *Times* wrote, following the uptown migration of genteel New Yorkers and settling along midtown avenues, squares, and transit routes where women could be respectably massed into a consumer market. They sought to attract this clientele by concentrating an unprecedented array of luxury goods under a single roof. What made their emporia profitable was an innovative business strategy of fixed prices, low mark-ups, and rapid turnover of inventory; like the factories that produced much of their merchandise, retailers sought to speed up the "throughput" of goods and people in their stores. The design of the retailing palace was meant to do just that. Commodious and ornate, its typical appointments—a central court often

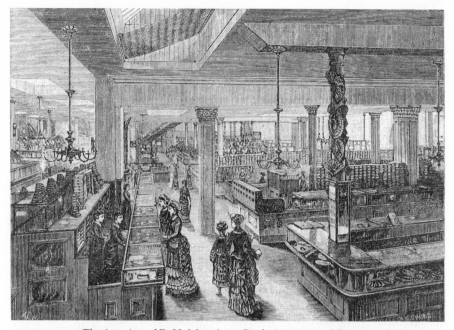

FIGURE 3.5   The interior of R. H. Macy's, at Sixth Avenue and Fourteenth Street, suggests the design strategies by which retailers sought to attract elite consumers to Ladies' Mile: lavish displays of goods, opulent architectural detail, and liberal use of glass, mirrors, and dark woods. (*Macy's Interior, View from 14th Street, Staircase Through to 13th Street*, reproduction; Museum of the City of New York; Print Archives)

framed by a glass rotunda and grand staircase, open floor spaces created by cast-iron columns, merchandise displays framed by mirrors, plate glass, and polished woods —created a setting that was both efficient and seductive. The resulting mix of centralism and spectacle drew praise even from New York feminists: "In such an establishment, the idea of an Eastern Bazaar is completely carried out," *Woodhull and Claflin's Weekly* wrote of B. Altman and Company. "A lady . . . finds herself in the midst of a lavish display of everything that could be thought of in the way of fancy goods. No need of running over ten or twelve blocks and into fifteen or twenty shops when making varied purchases" (Figure 3.5).[23]

The wholesale district was similarly specialized in geography and architecture, but it was shaped by different factors. A nineteenth-century warehouse was a nexus of multiple business and market relationships. Its textiles might come from Lowell or Manchester; its rugs from Yonkers or the Levant; its silks from Limoges or Paterson. Inventory might be destined for a midtown emporium or an inland merchant; if the latter, the wholesaler might have to absorb the costs of owning and moving goods until he was repaid. Thus, dry-goods merchants needed access to shifting networks of suppliers, shippers, customers, and creditors. They clustered together not to gain economies of scale, but to take advantage of what geographers call *agglomeration economies*: efficiencies caused by the proximity of heterogeneous but functionally linked activities.[24]

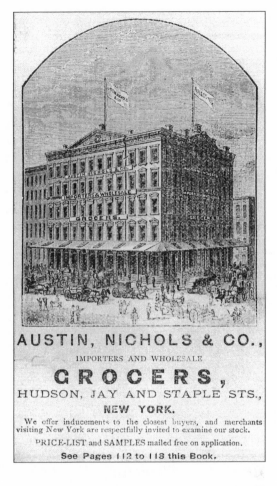

FIGURE 3.6   This ad for the grocery firm of Austin, Nichols and Company shows one of the many lofts built in the West Side wholesale district during the midcentury boom. Promotional materials like this were aimed at merchants who frequented nearby commercial hotels. (*Austin, Nichols & Company, Grocers*, trade card; Museum of the City of New York; Print Archives)

The commercial West Side offered an apt solution to these needs. It was accessible to uptown retail shops, enabling wholesalers to "follow, albeit at a respectful distance, the upward growth of the city." It was close to Broadway hotels where commercial travelers came to display or examine samples. It was near the freight depot at St. John's Park: dry goods, like most low-bulk, high-value merchandise, were usually moved to interior markets by rail rather than water. Finally, it was relatively near downtown credit markets—the commercial paper market in particular—that enabled merchants to carry their inventory. The architecture of the loft district also helped to meet the merchants' requirements. With its prefabricated structural elements, light frames, myriad windows, and widespread use of hoists and elevators, the cast-iron loft was comparatively economical to build and efficient in its use of some of the most expensive land on Manhattan (Figure 3.6). It supplied light, room, and equipment without pricing merchants away from sources of inventory, services, customers, and credit. Moreover it offered rental space for workshops that "finished" consumer goods—garments, cigars, artificial flowers, boxes—as outwork extensions of the wholesale trade.[25]

Along with these changes in the downtown division of labor, a second sorting mechanism was even more salient in reshaping lower Manhattan: the location markets. To a great extent, the play of "exchange values" in the land, building, and rental markets mirrored the shifting geography of "use values" that I have just described. Yet market discipline worked autonomously (and not always "functionally") to distribute land uses and buildings in space. Its importance was intensified by the rise in land values that accompanied New York's development boom. Manhattan property appreciated more than fourfold during the third quarter of the nineteenth century. Although the sharpest increases took place uptown, where land was being incorporated into urban markets for the first time, older real estate also rose impressively. Between the end of the Civil War and the Panic of 1873—the most active phase of downtown redevelopment—property assessments west of the Bowery and south of Fourteenth Street grew by 56.7 percent.[26] Such increases subjected landowners and users to rigorous price discipline. Commercial space was simply too expensive not to be put to its "highest" uses; other activities were displaced to cheaper locales.

The growth of the new office district in the First, Second, and Third wards—the most expensive land in Manhattan—offers a particularly visible example of the invisible hand at work. The needs met by the district are clear. New York's oversight of national communications and finance required a huge massing of capital- and information-processing institutions: banks, brokerages, insurers, law firms, telegraph networks, trade journals, newspapers, and government bureaus. Such institutions needed little horizontal expanse, but depended on access to each other. During the 1860s and 1870s, they crowded into the high-priced lots and narrow streets between City Hall and Wall Street. The Turner Building at Nassau and Cedar, for instance, housed the Fourth National Bank, several insurance companies, a half-dozen investment banks (including the building's owners), many lawyers, and the New York offices of the Union Pacific railroad. Such lucrative tenants bid rents up to unheard-of levels. Trinity Church, one of the largest landholders in lower Manhattan, recorded a doubling of income on its lower Broadway properties in the early 1870s—and a *tenfold* increase from the Guardian Mutual Life Insurance Company and several other tenants near City Hall.[27]

Property owners responded to this market pressure with a new kind of architecture: the office building. "The demand for first-class offices is so great," a city almanac noted in 1872, that "millions [are being] lavished . . . on imposing business edifices." What made the new buildings feasible was a set of technical innovations that enabled more intensive use of downtown space: internal pneumatic and telegraphic communications, better fireproofing, improved load-bearing design, and, most of all, reliable elevators. The steam-powered passenger lift revolutionized office design, perhaps even more decisively than the celebrated invention of skeleton-frame construction in Chicago fifteen years later. The lift enabled commercial developers to add a third dimension to the location market.[28]

Steam-powered elevation had been mastered in the 1850s, and freight elevators were widespread in downtown New York before the Civil War. Yet the full commercial potential of the lift was not demonstrated until its installation in the new Equitable Life Insurance building at Broadway and Cedar in 1868. The pioneering role of the insurance industry is not surprising here. Life insurance was one of the most profitable and bureaucratized sectors of the downtown economy in the 1860s. The assets of New York companies, which controlled 85 percent of the national market, multiplied elevenfold during the decade, to nearly a quarter of a billion dollars. The Equitable was particularly successful; led by president Henry Hyde, it used innovative (some said fraudulent) actuarial and promotional schemes to mass-market policies to Civil War soldiers and white-collar urbanites. Hyde proved an equally visionary land developer, convincing his directors to have a lift installed in the company's Second Empire home office as a rental speculation. The venture paid off handsomely: the Equitable's staff of two hundred clerks, agents, and administrators occupied the middle floors, and within two months, the building leased fifty upper-story offices to financial and legal tenants. For the first time, height was money.[29]

The Equitable's success provoked a rash of "elevator buildings" from some of the most powerful interests in the downtown economy (Figure 3.7): bankers (the Drexel Building), publishers (the American News Building), transport capitalists (the Delaware and Hudson Building), and rival insurance firms (the New York Life Building). Five of the city's daily newspapers—whose workforce, equipment, inventory, and record keeping made them among the heaviest users of downtown space—bought or built new offices in Printing-House Square, most notably Richard Hunt's *Tribune* building (Figure 3.4).[30] Yet it was the ten-and-a-half-story Western Union Building, designed by George Post and erected two blocks south of City Hall Park, that gave the new architecture its fullest expression (Figure 3.8). Here site-intensive design embodied the national dominance of a key Gilded Age corporation. After its consolidation in 1866, Western Union had a virtual monopoly of American telegraphic communications. Its message volume tripled by 1875, the year the headquarters was completed, and the building reflected that growth, vertically projecting the company's integration of resources and specialization of labor. Separate stories were apportioned for the street-level message business, administrative offices, electromagnetic equipment, and rental space. On the eighth floor, the company's nerve center, dozens of exterior wires converged on a vast, open workroom where an army of telegraphers tapped out intelligence between lower Manhattan, the rest of the nation, and overseas commercial centers.[31]

Edifices like the Western Union home office constituted an unusually direct instance of the location markets at work. The effect of price discipline on downtown space was not always so straightforward. Property owners and land users possessed a wide range of strategies, from the monumental to the incremental, for enhancing land values; indeed land in lower Manhattan was so expensive that "Monopoly-game" transactions—one buyer, one seller, one building—were comparatively rare. Owners might improve their property more fractionally by adding to existing buildings or exploiting their lots more intensively. The dockets of the Department of Buildings record dozens of such alterations: an extra story added at 7 Depeyster Street, the

FIGURE 3.7   This mid-1870s view down Broadway from the Post Office records the spread of "elevator buildings" in lower Manhattan. In the foreground is the *Herald* building (see Figure 2.2); the Western Union building, still under construction, dominates the middle distance; and the New York Life headquarters can be made out across from Trinity Church. (*"View down Broadway from the New Post Office,"* *Broadway & Vesey Street*, stereoscopic view; Museum of the City of New York; Print Archives)

FIGURE 3.8   Depicting the same stretch of Broadway as Figure 3.7, but from the opposite direction, this drawing shows the completed Western Union office, with its grandiose Second Empire tower and its tangle of telegraph connections to Wall Street and the North American interior. (*Western Union Building, Broadway and Cortlandt Street*, drawing; Museum of the City of New York; Print Archives)

division of the upper floors of 5 Dey Street into offices, the replacement of walls with iron girders at 62 Barclay Street. Long-term leases offered another means to "incrementalize" growth, dispersing the costs and risks of development between lot holders and builder-landlords.[32]

For their part, land users who were not owners themselves confronted different choices and constraints. They had to weigh the utility of remaining in central locations against the cost of paying for them. The results of this balancing act were calibrated each year in the degree of gridlock caused by the city's moving drays on May

Day. Indeed, springtime in New York, the season of construction projects and rent negotiations, was like an annual plebiscite on the geography of the built environment. In 1870, for instance, the *Times* reported that downtown tenants were voting with their feet: "Many people find it impossible to pay the large rentals that have been heretofore demanded; . . . [they] are determined to take up with smaller stores . . . than they now occupy."[33]

Yet commercial tenants had other options besides staying and paying or moving uptown; they could also deploy their activities into multiple local markets. D. Appleton and Company offers an illuminating case. One of New York's leading publishers, the firm combined several key sectors of the downtown economy: journalism, consumer-goods manufacturing, long-haul wholesaling, and local retailing. Its complex needs required a variety of spatial strategies, and it moved seven times between 1850 and 1880. After leapfrogging up Broadway, the Appletons built a cast-iron palazzo at Astor Place for their main office and retail bookstore; they leased less pricey warehouse space on the West Side; and like many large manufacturers, they abandoned production in lower Manhattan altogether, erecting a print works and bindery for six hundred workers on cheap land near the Brooklyn Navy Yard. The firm thus pursued strategies of buying, building, renting, and moving all at the same time, dispersing its business into several localities, each with its own "gravitational field" of use and exchange values. The resulting pattern of specialization, displacement, and growth mimicked the reshaping of lower Manhattan as a whole.[34]

Most downtown land users did not engage in such complex migrations. Yet whether we look at a singular, massive improvement like the Western Union tower, at a Mansard roof added for rental space, or at multiple interventions like the Appletons', commercial landowners, leaseholders, and tenants were responding to the same set of cues, the same regime of city building. The market in space sifted out all but the most remunerative or site-efficient activities, arranging lower Manhattan into ever more profitable configurations of rent.

The Discipline of Land Values

One rule above all shaped the reconstruction of downtown New York: the idea that commercial space was a commodity, or more precisely, a *financial* commodity. Urban geographer David Harvey argues such a "liquefaction" of space represents the defining precondition for all city building under capitalism. When landowners treat their property as a calculable, fungible asset, he argues—one that can be exchanged not only *for* money but also *into* other financial forms—"the land market shapes the allocation of capital to land and . . . the geographical structure of production, consumption, and exchange." This theoretical claim provides a helpful tool for making sense of the empirical changes I have sketched. The reshaping of lower Manhattan was driven precisely by the willingness—and the necessity—of propertied New Yorkers like Henry Hyde or the Appletons to "treat land as a pure financial asset." Without that habitus, the location markets could not have been so relentless an arbiter of land use, and the business district would not have changed so dramatically.[35]

I use the word *habitus* because this orientation was not automatic or natural to New York's property owners; they had to be habituated to it, schooled in the discipline of the location markets. Even in the age of capital—and in entrepreneurial America—real estate was circumscribed by precapitalist norms that distinguished it legally and morally from other forms of property. Land and inheritance law was designed to make the transfer of real estate slow, careful, and cumbersome. Political economy, republican thought, and patrician culture vested land with moral significance, celebrating it as a repository of wealth, a guarantor of generational continuity, or a source of yeoman independence and artisanal use value. These worldviews were often in conflict with each other, but they all treated stable proprietorship of land as a bulwark of moral virtue and social order. Of course, as much research has made clear, northern farmers, artisans, and rentiers aggressively used real property as an economic resource, but such remunerative activity was held in check by a deep suspicion of land speculation and rent gouging. The idea that property owners should treat real estate as a commodity or liquid asset had to overcome a burden of legitimacy in antebellum America. It had to be instilled in new ways of thinking and instituted in new legal and market arrangements.[36]

In New York, as Elizabeth Blackmar has shown, the process of turning land into capital, and proprietorship into investment, began early in the nineteenth century. Blackmar traces the formation of "a new entrepreneurial class of landowners" who used leaseholds, a freer credit market, and other devices to provision the antebellum city with speculative improvements and rental housing. Such market-driven development was largely decentralized and localistic, however. Mortgage and building networks were "more personal than institutional," and the cityscape remained a congeries of activities that did not systematically conform land use to land value. Not until the midcentury boom was the habitus of the market fully developed.[37] By 1870, property markets were coordinated not through local networks, but through central institutions that gathered price data and investors from the whole metropolitan area; the circulation of investment capital and mortgage credit was permeable to other financial sectors; and land values exerted a systematic pressure on land use. Landowners had begun listening to the market early in the century; by the end of the boom, they had no other cues to hear.

We can track this process of market regimentation among a group of landowners that might have been expected to resist it: benevolent and civic institutions. Several of Manhattan's most important charitable and educational foundations—including the New York Hospital, Columbia College, and Trinity Church—possessed large downtown landholdings, with grants dating back to colonial times. The prosperity and inflation of the midcentury boom forced them to jettison conservative and patrimonial policies of proprietorship in favor of aggressive property development and rent maximization. For Columbia and New York Hospital, this change meant leaving lower Manhattan and exploiting their downtown property for income. The hospital, for instance, was land wealthy but cash poor, relying on city and private donations to fund its operating budget until the mid-1860s. In 1865 the municipality refused to contribute further, seeking to force the hospital to commercialize its valuable Broadway site a few blocks north of City Hall. The board of governors voted to "relieve this charitable corporation from . . . pecuniary embarrassment" by moving to Union Square and leasing its property for commercial purposes. Rental income jumped from $61 in 1866 to $150,000 twenty years later—about a third of the hospital's annual budget.[38]

Trinity Church went through a more subtle schooling. As the owner of fifty-seven blocks between west Fulton Street and Greenwich Village—the result of a 1705 patent from Queen Anne and other acquisitions—the church was one of the largest proprietors in New York, rivaled only by the Astors and the City Corporation itself. Trinity had early on learned the rewards of street and land development; St. John's Park represented one of the most successful residential projects of the early nineteenth century. By the 1850s, the church relied on a steady income from its leaseholds, collecting annual rents of seventy to eighty thousand dollars. After the Civil War, however, it faced a debt crisis that forced an even more entrepreneurial stance toward its landholdings and tenants. Trinity met its immediate needs through massive land sales, earning $750,000 from the divestment of St. John's Park and other properties in the late 1860s. At the same time, it drove hard bargains as its leases came up for renegotiation; rental income reached $325,000 in 1865 and half a million dollars a decade later. The days were gone when peppercorns and nominal payments sufficed to purchase a lease on its lands; now, as a trustee of the Bank for Savings informed George Templeton Strong, "The comptroller of Trinity Church was ex officio a financial magnate of the first order . . ."[39]

The effect of market discipline on these civic institutions was evident in the landscape of lower Manhattan. With New York Hospital and Columbia moving uptown, St. John's Park becoming a freight depot, and half of City Hall Park taken for the U.S. Post Office, the space devoted to any "nonprofit" land use grew more and more constricted. Both public "disinterestedness" and greenery were disappearing from the downtown in a process that might be likened to the rural enclosures of eighteenth-century England. The physical sealing of the street wall was at the same time a reflection of the institutional "enclosure" of the city-building process itself. The logic of land values had become total, crowding out any other regime of land use or spatial change.

What was it that enforced the habitus of the land market so fully in Victorian New York? In the 1860s and 1870s, as I have said, Manhattan's real-estate economy underwent a series of changes that completed the transformation of urban land and location into commodities. These changes compelled city builders to act like Harvey's ideal-typical land developers, treating their property as a financial asset with which, and for which, to accumulate capital. Three changes were especially crucial.

First, the real-estate markets became centrally coordinated through the formation of two key institutions: the Exchange Salesroom and the *Real Estate Record and*

Builders' Guide. Prior to the founding of the salesroom, land auctions and real-estate transactions had taken place through personal networks or (along with dealings in many other goods) at the Merchants Exchange on Wall Street. In 1862 the latter Exchange was bought by the U.S. government to house the New York Customs House, and a new salesroom dedicated wholly to real estate was opened at 111 Broadway. (The landlord, by a priceless coincidence, was Trinity Church.) The salesroom provided the first specialized, comprehensive gathering place for auctioneers, brokers, builders, lenders, proprietors, and speculators from the whole metropolitan area. It served as a means of professional specialization and self-regulation, founding the Board of Real-Estate Brokers to police misinformation and insider dealing. Such efforts did not eradicate the fraudulent activities that were endemic to land speculation. Yet, as the *Real Estate Record* boasted in 1869, the salesroom did transform "the fluctuating activity of former years" into "a permanent body of transactions quite as regular and settled as [those] of the Stock or Produce Exchange."[40]

The *Record* itself was crucial to this establishment of regularity. Founded in 1868 and published a block north of the Exchange Salesroom at 137 Broadway, the weekly contained a vast fund of market information: the cost and location of every land, mortgage, and construction contract in the metropolitan area; price quotations for building supplies; mortgage rates; reports on land auctions, building projects, speculative hot spots, Exchange Salesroom gossip, and market conditions in other cities; and shrewd editorials on spatial change and urbanism in the metropolitan area.[41] The journal was matched by a second medium of urban landscape description, one that was equally innovative in its expansive coverage and granular detail: real-estate and fire-insurance maps. These bound, multiplate atlases had their origins in late eighteenth-century London, but their modern format and labeling conventions were codified in New York in the 1850s. Manhattan-based cartographers like D. A. Sanborn provided insurance underwriters, real-estate brokers, and others with fine-grained maps of American cities that displayed not only street plans, natural features, and public landmarks but also lot boundaries, building heights and materials, street and sidewalk dimensions, sewerage lines, public transit routes, and other utilities. Sanborn's firm, established a few doors up from the Exchange Salesroom in 1867, controlled the lion's share of insurance cartography in Gilded Age America, but the Perris and Bromley atlases were the most widely circulated maps of Victorian New York (Figure 3.9).[42]

It will be clear from the footnotes of this study how exhaustively the *Real Estate Record* and property atlases cataloged the cityscape of nineteenth-century New York. What may be less clear is the transformative role that these media played in the city-building process. They not only recorded the built environment but also reconstituted it into a notational field that was at once atomized, standardized, and potentially limitless. The journal and atlases in effect established the cognitive regime within which urban space could be treated as a commodity: a discrete, mobile good whose value was measurable in the play of real-estate bids, lease offerings, and mortgage rates. "Few people can tell . . . whether a piece of Appalachian land will spout

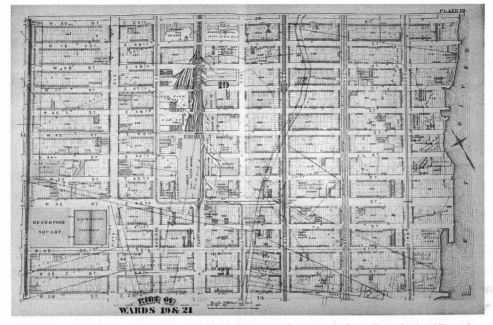

FIGURE 3.9   This plate of the Nineteenth and Twenty-first wards from Bromley's 1879 real-estate atlas illustrates the systematic, detailed records about lots, buildings, and infrastructures that the atlases provided. Such cartographic information was essential in rationalizing the real-estate economy. (Courtesy of the William L. Clements Library, University of Michigan)

with petroleum when a hole is bored through it or not," the *Commercial and Financial Chronicle* noted wryly, "but every one knows what a house and lot is worth in New York, and how much rent it will bring to the owner."[43]

Implicit in the *Chronicle's* comparison of city lots and oil wells was a second key change in the real-estate economy. Paradoxically, the formation of specialized institutions to coordinate property markets made those markets more open to other financial sectors. As urban development came to depend less on personal networks and local sources of information, it became easier for investors from other capital markets—and, given New York's national centrality, other regions—to direct their resources at metropolitan real estate. Of course Manhattan landowners had drawn capital from other enterprises long before the midcentury boom; the Astors and Lorillards, to take two of the largest proprietors of the early nineteenth century, financed their initial operations with profits from the North American fur trade and tobacco wholesaling, respectively. Yet during the 1860s, the paths between different sectors became broader and better traveled. "New York City real estate [took] on a mercantile quality rarely found . . . before," one turn-of-the-century chronicle writes, "and [it] bec[a]me a favorite medium of investment for persons of surplus means."[44]

Much evidence confirms this claim. When "all the large property holders on the east and west side of Central Park" petitioned the park commission to open a crosstown drive at Ninety-sixth Street, for instance, the remonstrators included not only land speculators like Edward Clark and rentiers like Henry Beekman but also banker John Gray, retailer C. L. Tiffany, hotelier Amos Eno, editor David Croly, California railway magnate Collis Huntington, wholesaler (and ex-Senator) Edwin Morgan, and many others. Both the integration of the land market and the sheer rise of land values encouraged collective, multisector investment after the Civil War. When New York Hospital auctioned leaseholds on its Broadway site in 1869, the lots were developed en masse by a pool of merchants and speculators who had incorporated as the New York Real Estate Association. Two years later, a group of realtors, bankers, transit capitalists, and other entrepreneurs—including Tammany leader William Tweed—chartered the Real Estate Trust Company, a joint-stock corporation to manage properties, perform surveys and title searches, and issue (and resell) mortgages.[45]

Such corporate experiments were infrequent, but they underscored a larger pattern of class and financial integration. The "collective subject" of real-estate development was not a particular sector or set of interests, but the (male) metropolitan bourgeoisie as a whole. Certainly the *Real Estate Record* thought so, addressing itself to a pan-capitalist public that was assumed to be diversified, peripatetic, and interested in the best rate of return: "No security offers so many advantages for profit and safety as real estate," it urged during the 1870s depression. "Railway and other shares are no longer the class of securities in which funds should be placed for safe keeping . . . [and] bonds are so high and unremunerative that real estate alone . . . must very soon attract the abundance of money in this market." Notwithstanding the *Record*'s tone, what was most important about these patterns of investment was not the competition, but the permeability, between capital markets. New York investors moved freely among them, integrating local real estate into the national financial market; in the process, they brought the resources of American economic development to bear on the remaking of the cityscape. "Our market . . . is a savings bank, or rather a safe deposit company," the *Record* wrote, "wherein are gathered the fruits and profits of the general trade and business of the country."[46]

The third key area of change in the city-building economy involved access not to equity capital, but to debt. Like the land market itself, mortgage finance became more coordinated and institutionalized in the 1860s, distributing credit more liberally to developers and making urban growth more dependent on debt. Of course, compared with the post–World War II era, the "liberality" of the Victorian credit market should not be oversold. At no time in the nineteenth century were mortgages widely available to nonwealthy New Yorkers. Although the terms varied according to the business cycle, local real-estate conditions, and the resources of the borrower, information from land sales and loan tenders conveys a fairly constant picture throughout the century. Mortgages were offered by the seller as an ordinary part of a real-estate transaction, usually for 50–60 percent of the purchase price of a parcel—the balance being due immediately or on delivery of the deed—with full repayment in one to five years at 5–7 percent interest. These terms eased during the third quarter of the nineteenth century, however, as New York's growth and rising land values encouraged less stringent lending policies. By the end of the midcentury boom, property sellers often agreed to lend 70 percent of a purchase on mortgage at 5 percent.[47]

Such tendencies reflected larger changes in the structure of the credit market itself. In the early nineteenth century, debt circulated—like real estate itself—mainly through family, personal, and local networks; an 1831 survey by the developer Samuel Ruggles estimated that only one-third of the mortgaged funds in New York City came from "incorporated companies." By the 1860s, in contrast, most real-estate loans were from institutional sources. The institutionalization of mortgage finance had several important consequences. It tended to standardize credit terms across the whole metropolitan area, freeing them from local variations in business conditions. It detached the circulation of debt from that of land itself, promoting competition among third-party lenders, diffusing risk across the whole credit market, and exerting some pressure for easier money. Most importantly, the institutionalization of debt finance worked to integrate real-estate investment into the national money market. The largest providers of mortgage credit were two of the most dynamic sectors of the downtown economy: savings banks and life-insurance companies. Savings banks proliferated during the second half of the postwar boom—two-fifths of those chartered at any time in the United States were founded then—and they aggressively used mortgages as a means of capital formation, usually lending close to the legal limit of 50 percent of their assets. Between 1857 and 1873, for instance, New York State savings banks increased their lending by 500 percent. Life insurance companies were even more active, multiplying their level of lending tenfold between 1865 and 1875.[48]

Given the unevenness of nineteenth-century financial data, it is difficult to calculate precisely how much capital these institutions channeled from their depositors and policyholders into the New York built environment. It is certain, however, that the institutional credit market provided the majority of resources for the reconstruction of Victorian New York. In 1873, for instance, when approximately $170 million was spent on real estate and new construction in Manhattan—$85 million to $100 million of it borrowed—the money lent on mortgage by city savings banks alone totaled nearly $50 million. The extent of this activism was painfully clear in the ensuing depression. In early 1879 (when a five-year grace period extended to defaulting borrowers reached its statutory limit), New York savings and insurance institutions were compelled to foreclose on about $4.5 million of mortgages. Henry Hyde's Equitable Life, for instance, took title to properties in a tenement district at Eleventh Street and Avenue D, the middle-class neighborhood of Yorkville on the upper East Side, an upscale townhouse area at Madison Avenue and Seventy-sixth Street, the speculative barrens west of Central Park at Ninety-sixth Street, and the office district at Liberty Street and Trinity Place. The Dry Dock Savings Bank foreclosed on lots on Avenue D, East Tenth Street, and Elizabeth Street (as its roots on the lower East Side would have predicted) but also on a Madison Avenue residential property. Such data vividly illustrate how much New York had become a unified field of commodity exchange by the 1870s—and how much that unity depended on a risky system of speculative growth.[49]

During the midcentury boom, in sum, New York's real-estate economy grew more centralized and predictable. New institutions and coordinating mechanisms—the Exchange Salesroom, the *Real Estate Record*, land atlases, investment consortia, corporate lenders—mobilized information, capital, and credit on a metropolitan scale and linked local city building with national finance. In the process, proprietors like Henry Hyde, the Appletons, and Trinity Church learned the habitus of treating space as a commodity and land as a liquid asset with which (and for which) to amass profit. Manhattan had become fully "enclosed," so to speak, within the discipline of land values.

The landscape of lower Manhattan was simultaneously a cause and an effect of that discipline. Following the cues of the location markets, downtown property owners and land users created geographies, buildings, and technologies that accelerated the movement of capital, information, and goods through the commercial district. The landscape that they made fostered commodification *in* space even as it embodied the commodification *of* space. These two changes were mutually reinforcing, of course. Lower Manhattan could not have been rebuilt—at least not so rapidly—without the regimen imposed by the real-estate markets. Conversely, those markets depended on resources accumulated from a (geographically specialized, high-rising) Wall Street. And that same dialectic of process and product characterized the links between lower Manhattan and the rest of the city. The new central business district was not only a microcosm of New York's transformation, but its engine as well. The resources and energies that it amassed reshaped the metropolis as a whole.

The March of Improvement

Which brings us to upper Manhattan. For it was on the city's uptown periphery that the midcentury boom achieved its most impressive results. Between 1860 and 1875, two-thirds of the total rise in Manhattan land values took place above Fourteenth Street; four-fifths of the new construction in New York between 1863 and 1871 was built there.[50] This activity was grounded in the development of the commercial center: downtown expansion made the "march of improvement" necessary, and downtown capital made it possible. Yet uptown embodied a different spatial logic from the business district. If the development of lower Manhattan underscored the "liquefaction" of real estate—its transmutation into a financial asset—uptown development dramatized the standardization of land itself.

To many observers, the differentiation of uptown and downtown seemed the defining feature of the midcentury boom. "New York advances towards its northern boundary for a residence, while the lower portion of the city is to be devoted exclusively to commerce," the *Real Estate Record* proclaimed. Frederick Law Olmsted mapped the cityscape similarly: "If we look at . . . New York as divided, say, at Fourteenth street, we shall see that one side is mainly occupied for commercial purposes, the other for domestic." As such comments make clear, Victorian urbanists saw "uptown" above all as a landscape devoted to residence rather than trade. Its spatial order was extensive rather than intensive, horizontal rather than vertical; it was governed by "a dispersing and colonizing tendency," as Olmsted put it, rather than the "increasing motive to compactness" evident in the commercial district. And such functional differentiation entailed class segregation too: "The form of [Manhattan] is such . . . that space near the business-portion of the city becomes of great value," the reformer Charles Loring Brace noted. "These districts are necessarily sought for by the laboring classes and mechanic classes, as they are near the place of employment. They are avoided by the wealthy on account of the population which has already occupied so much of them. The result is, that the poor must live in certain wards; and as space is costly, the landlords supply them with . . . very high and large houses, in which great numbers of people rent only rooms . . ." In the mental map of Victorian urbanism, in short, "uptown" was a place of genteel domesticity, marked by the absence of both commercial densities and tenement crowds.[51]

To a great extent, this mental map was accurate. The new uptown landscape *was* geographically expansive and primarily residential. More than 7,200 residential structures were built north of Fourteenth Street between 1863 and 1871; this amounted to two-thirds of all uptown construction during those years, five-sixths of the new housing in Manhattan, and 55 percent of all the building activity in the city as a whole. The burst of housing development provisioned the great residential resettlement of the 1860s and 1870s, and it was in fact disproportionately weighted toward the middle and upper classes. Three-quarters of the residences built above Fourteenth Street were first- or second-class buildings—flats, single-occupant row houses, mansions, villas—and 96 percent of all such residences were built uptown. Property owning was similarly distributed: seven out of ten owners of Manhattan real estate lived in the upper wards. The majority of New York's wage earners, by contrast, lived south of Fourteenth Street, and the tenement districts of the lower East Side were the most populous and congested neighborhoods of the city. There were good reasons, in short, for bourgeois New Yorkers to associate their class status with uptown space.[52]

Yet such a map presents a simplified view of a much more variegated landscape. For one thing, upper Manhattan was part a larger "peripheral boom" that included Brooklyn, Long Island, New Jersey, and Westchester County. All of these areas were characterized by rapid population growth and active property development. Passenger improvements on the Harlem, New Jersey, Long Island, and other railroads spurred a wave of commuter suburbanization during the 1860s and 1870s; Hackensack, New Jersey, for instance, doubled to six thousand residents from 1864 to 1868, mainly due to the out-migration of New York businessmen's households. "All the country surrounding [Manhattan] for forty miles . . . will be filled with the homes of its merchants and its thrifty mechanics," one journalist predicted in 1868. "Thousands . . . daily crowd the trains leading out into the towns . . . that are springing up like magic along the iron highways in all directions." Many of those "magical" towns

FIGURE 3.10   The mansion of retail baron Alexander T. Stewart at Fifth Avenue and Thirty-fourth Street, built in 1869, was one of the most famous landmarks of upper Manhattan. (*Harper's Weekly*, August 14, 1869; image courtesy of HarpWeek, LLC)

were land speculations begun just after the Civil War; retail baron A. T. Stewart founded Garden City on Long Island's Hempstead Plains in 1869, for instance, with its own railway to the East River. By the early 1870s, some three to four hundred local trains served Manhattan or riverfront connections, carrying perhaps 300,000 commuters each workday.[53]

Moreover, upper Manhattan was itself quite heterogeneous. William Martin offers us a glimpse of its diversity in his 1865 pamphlet, *The Growth of New York*: "The river borders are taken up for business purposes, for brick, stone, and lumber yards, factories and machine shops. In the streets and avenues next to them congregate the . . . laboring classes, next . . . the great marts for retail business[,] the Eighth and Third avenues. . . . In the centre of the island, and following the line of Broadway and Fifth avenue are found the residences of the wealthier classes . . ." As Martin makes clear, the uptown stereotype was most accurate along the central axis of Manhattan Island. There, between Lexington and Seventh avenues, and symbolically associated with Fifth, the boom produced an elite residential enclave. Beginning in the late 1850s, genteel New Yorkers quit older centers of fashion like Union Square and settled between Madison Square and the borders of Central Park; in the Nineteenth Ward alone, nearly 2,500 first-class residences went up from 1863 to 1871. A procession of palatial residences—most famously, the Astor homes at Thirty-third Street and Fifth Avenue (1856, 1859) and A. T. Stewart's mansion a block to the north (1869)—served as landmarks of this elite migration (Figure 3.10).[54] Yet its primary architectural ex-

FIGURE 3.11   More typical of the elite residential district than the Stewart mansion (Figure 3.10) were these row houses a few blocks to its north. Such homes crammed luxury into the narrow dimensions of city lots. At the same time, their horizontal uniformity expressed the class bonds of the metropolitan bourgeoisie. (*Fifth Avenue Row Houses, 42nd–49th Streets*, photograph; Museum of the City of New York; gift of Public Library, Montclair, N.J.)

pression was the (slightly) more modest row house (Figure 3.11). Hundreds of these went up on East Side lots after the Civil War, their narrow spaces stuffed with state-of-the-art comforts and opulent appointments: central heating, modern plumbing, pneumatic bells, parquetry floors, bronze fittings, parlors with carved mantels and beveled mirrors, bathrooms graced by "Basin Slabs of Statuary Marble." Here was the destined scene for much of the materiel purchased on Ladies' Mile.[55]

Yet "Fifth Avenue" represented more than just an aggregate of luxury commodities. Its parlors, dining rooms, libraries, and promenades served as settings for class rituals of solidarity and display. It contained an archipelago of public institutions and spaces, most of them begun in the midcentury boom, in which bourgeois New Yorkers pursued the practices of "civilization": religious congregations like St. Patrick's Cathedral (Fifth Avenue and Fiftieth Street, 1858–79) and Temple Emanuel-El (Fifth and Forty-first, 1868); clubs like the Union League (Madison Square, 1868); civic and tutelary institutions like Columbia College (Fifth and Fiftieth, 1857), the Lenox Library (Fifth and Seventieth, 1870–77), and the Metropolitan Museum of Art (Fifth and Eightieth, 1879); and pleasure grounds like Central Park (begun in 1857). Such spaces constituted a social world in which the metropolitan bourgeoisie composed itself as the "national class" that I described in Chapter 1 and gave expression to its ideals of sociability and culture.[56]

A few blocks east or west, however, uptown was neither exclusively bourgeois nor purely residential; class status and land values declined as one approached the rivers. As Martin noted, Third and Eighth avenues represented dividers in that gradient of value. These avenues contained the most heavily trafficked horse cars in the city and functioned as both gateways to the upper island and retail strips for the new East and West sides. (It is largely for this reason that the first elevated lines were routed over them in the mid-1870s.) The result was a social and architectural boundary between fashionable and plebeian corridors of development. Building records show the pattern clearly. In 1870 the city government received plans for 238 residential projects in the Nineteenth Ward (Fortieth to Eighty-sixth streets, Sixth Avenue to the East River). Four-fifths of the first-class houses (91 of 115) were west of Third Avenue, but only one-third of the second-class flats (13 of 38); most of the flats were on or near Third Avenue itself. Of the third-class (tenement) houses, more than 80 percent (62 of 75) were located between Third and the river.[57]

The building of upper Manhattan thus formed a kind of class sandwich where riverfront tenement neighborhoods enclosed the fashionable district on either side. There were exceptions, of course—the Beekmans' upscale speculation on the East River at Forty-ninth Street, for instance—but these stood against the general line of uptown development. "Beekman Place . . . is unlike any other part of the city," George Templeton Strong noted after an evening stroll in 1871. "Its brownstone houses look very reputable but are separated from civilization by a vast tract of tenement rookeries and whiskey mills." This class geography meant that middle- and upper-class New Yorkers were a bounded minority even in the toniest regions of Manhattan; one 1864 survey of the Eighteenth Ward (including Madison Square and Gramercy Park) found that 62 percent of the residents lived in tenements or cellars. As I discuss in the next chapter, the mix of spatial proximity and class distance fueled popular disorder and genteel anxiety in an era when both ran high.[58]

The *functional* geography of uptown was equally heterogeneous. New York's wage earners did not have the time, money, or job security to live far from the labor markets on which they subsisted. Working-class homes tended to cluster near sources of income, and upper Manhattan was no exception. Heading toward the rivers thus meant going from a sequestered district of genteel domesticity—the "uptown" of stereotype—to mixed-use neighborhoods of industry and tenements. Tracing a finger eastward along Forty-fourth Street on the 1880 Bromley *Atlas of the 19th and 22nd Wards*, for instance, we note a Fifth Avenue bank and the Church of the Disciples on Madison, machine shops behind Grand Central Depot, a marble works at Third, a brewery between Second and First, and an abattoir and chemical works on the East River. Moving west along Forty-second Street, we see brick and stone townhouses near Fifth and Sixth avenues; hotels, churches, and a riding academy near Seventh and Eighth; and tenements, a wagon-making workshop, a wallpaper manufactory, a slaughterhouse, the Metropolitan Gas Light Works, and E. S. Higgins's carpet mill between Ninth Avenue and the Hudson.[59]

FIGURE 3.12   "Give Us This Day Our Daily Bread" (1868), by the little-known New Jersey painter Alessandro Mario, offers a vivid portrayal of New York in the midcentury boom. In the foreground, looking west along Forty-sixth Street from Third Avenue, we see a Brueghelian depiction of the city-building process: a chaos of mired carts, spewing hoses, explosions, and laborers in motion. The background shows the strange mosaic that resulted: a respectable church surrounded by vacant lots, a half-block of speculative row houses, a townhouse in scaffolding, and a matrix of tilted telegraph poles. The painting captures wonderfully the mix of progress and incoherence that marked New York's growth. (Accession no. 1939.586; © Collection of the New-York Historical Society)

"Uptown," in short, contained a social-geographic complexity at odds with its reputation as an expanse of genteel homes. This complexity was the result of an astonishingly rapid development process: every datum of architecture or geography cited in this section comes from the period between 1855 and 1880, most from the decade after the Civil War. If we were walking in upper Manhattan during those years, what would strike us most forcibly is not any particular building, but the sheer, ragged energy of building itself: tenement rows broken off in midblock, villas rising up amid vacant lots with the apparent randomness of chess pieces in an endgame (Figure 3.12).[60] What was it that shaped this heterogeneous and dynamic landscape?

George Curtis offers us a clue to the riddle of upper Manhattan in an editorial sketch for *Harper's Monthly*. Recounting a spring stroll on New York's suburban periphery, the genteel editor describes "the pathetic forlornness of the municipal frontier" that marked "the advance of a great city": "Pleasant country-houses, spacious, rambling, with broad piazzas and gardens and lawns, had been apparently suddenly overtaken by streets and stone sidewalks and lamps. There were the rattle and shriek of the incessant railway trains near by. . . . The quiet old houses . . . had a helpless air, as if nothing remained but submission to division into regular building lots and the absolute extinction of rural seclusion and charm." By now we are all too familiar with the genteel pathos evoked here, the nostalgia for simpler days and places that was the grace note of booster discourse in New York. What is more interesting is the sketch's precise rendering of the "submission" of uptown land, like livestock in an abattoir, to "division into regular building lots." Curtis captures wonderfully the abruptness with which one landscape regime—a patchwork of farms, estates, commons, and squatters' settlements—was giving way to an urban grid of streets, blocks, and lots. This spatial transmutation laid the groundwork for New York's "march of improvement," making possible the pace and complexity of uptown growth. It began well before the midcentury boom, in an event that, even more than Peter Minuit's legendary deal, founded the rule of real estate in New York: the adoption of the Manhattan street plan in 1811.[61]

The Logic of the Grid

In 1807, at the behest of New York's Common Council, the New York State legislature commissioned Simeon DeWitt, Gouverneur Morris, and John Rutherford to develop a street plan for the northern, rural territory of the city. The commissioners' plan, submitted four years later, was radical in its simplicity (Figure 3.13). From Greenwich Village north to Washington Heights (whose rugged uplands were left unplatted), Manhattan Island would be laid out as a grid of twelve north-south avenues and 155 east-west streets. The 2,028 blocks, nearly identical in dimension, were themselves subdivided into standard lots one hundred feet deep by twenty-five feet wide. Land was set aside for a municipal market, a parade ground, and four uptown squares, but the plan overwhelmingly privileged private and especially residential development above the securing of public space or landscaped adornments. "A city is . . . composed principally of the habitations of men, and . . . right-angled houses are the most cheap to build, and the most convenient to live in," the commissioners concluded. They avoided "circles, ovals, and stars, which . . . embellish a plan" at the expense of "convenience and utility"; and they decided that New York's ample harbor precluded the need for more than a "few vacant spaces . . . for the benefit of fresh air."[62]

It is difficult today to grasp the audacity of the 1811 street plan. In part this is because the grid has come to seem like second nature, New York's aboriginal geometry; in part, because it has provoked so much criticism in the intervening years. As I discuss in Chapter 7, the plan was derided by nearly every leading urbanist in Victorian New York, from boosters like William Martin to genteel reformers like Frederick Law Olmsted. Bourgeois urbanists attacked it for several reasons. They saw the grid as a makeshift whose relentless linearity erased topographic and local variety even while—or rather by—requiring costly land preparation; they excoriated it for fueling

FIGURE 3.13   The 1811 map of the state commission that laid out the Manhattan street grid: so accustomed have we become to the grid—as if its geometry were a fact of nature— that it may be hard to grasp the audacity of the commissioners' map. It visually equated the landscape of Manhattan with the cityscape of New York, appropriating the rocky, rolling countryside for urban growth. It offered a blueprint for the rationalization of the real-estate economy. At the same time, the map conveys a feeling for the expansive, almost magical power with which New York real estate would become invested. (Negative no. 2081; © Collection of the New-York Historical Society)

a speculative ethos that made city building volatile and morally corrosive; and they argued that monotony rendered the cityscape unsuitable for monumental architecture or grand urban design. As we shall see, much of the program that Victorian city builders pursued in the 1860s and 1870s was designed to overrule the grid. For Olmsted, Martin, and their comrades were right: by enclosing New York in a nearly featureless field of blocks and lots, subordinating specific use values to fungible exchange values, and refusing to fix any configuration for the cityscape to be, the 1811 street plan undermined the imperial design ideal. The atomism, abstraction, and fluidity of the grid were inimical to the creation of a metropolis that counterpoised commercial dynamism, public refinement, and domestic virtue within a well-bounded, well-administered landscape.[63]

The critics were wrong, however, to attribute these qualities to a failure of imagination. The grid was no speculator's makeshift. As its shrewdest modern observer, architect Rem Koolhaas, has argued, it was a peculiarly visionary effort to prescribe a process of growth that would be at once dynamic and controlled, concerted and dispersed—to make New York, in Koolhaas's apt phrase, "a metropolis of rigid chaos." We can see this mix of contraries in the formal dimensions of the plan itself. On one hand, it projected a landscape four or five times larger than the New York of 1811, indeed vaster than any municipality of its day. On the other, it disaggregated the unbuilt city so minutely as to ensure that urban growth would remain fluid and decentered. "It is the most courageous act of prediction in Western civilization," Koolhaas proclaims in his manifesto, *Delirious New York*, but "with its imposition, Manhattan is forever immunized against any (further) totalitarian intervention. In the single block . . . it develops a maximum unit of urbanistic Ego." The legal and economic effects of the 1811 plan reflected a similar mix of expansiveness and confinement. As legal historian Hendrik Hartog has argued, the plan was an aggressive exercise of public power; its lot and street lines erased the privileges of the past, forcing rentiers and farmers to close private roads, reorient their houses, and conform their plans to a single, totalizing regime of spatial change (Figure 3.14). Yet that act of enclosure opened a process of market-driven growth that was more inclusive in scale and competitiveness.[64]

The 1811 plan did not found the Manhattan real-estate market, but it did make that market more systematic and predictable. It did for land what the *Real Estate Record* did for land values: it instituted a unified, disaggregated, citywide field of commodity exchange. Or, more precisely, it instituted the *possibility* for such a field. For on April 2, 1811 (the day after the commissioners filed their map), very little was actually changed on Manhattan. Rather the grid initiated (and stood for) a longer process by which the uptown periphery was reconstituted into 25-foot-by-100-foot lots, a process that reached its culmination during the midcentury boom.

Turning rural land into urban real estate entailed a complex series of transformations. First of all—as George Curtis noted in his *Harper's* sketch—street and transit extensions were required to create a public matrix within which uptown property could be brought to market (Figure 3.15). Streets had to be opened in accord with the 1811 plan and subsequent revisions to it. "Opening" a street did not mean physically improving it. It was a legal and fiscal procedure by which property was taken through eminent domain and reserved for a public thoroughfare; it had to precede the actual work of grading, paving, and curbing, but might do so by many years. The municipality of New York tended to take such action with a mixture of confidence and caution in the midcentury boom, opening long stretches of the avenues early, but reserving the side streets until the actual frontier of city building drew near. Thus, in 1850, most north-south thoroughfares from Second to Tenth Avenue were opened to Harlem or beyond, but only about two dozen streets between Fifty-ninth and 155th. By the end of the boom, however, nearly every uptown street was opened, and a network of scenic boulevards, avenues, and promenades had been added to the 1811 plan.[65]

New streets made no difference if prospective owners had no means of reaching the property that abutted them. Since only the wealthiest New Yorkers could keep private carriages, uptown development depended on public transit. Here again the midcentury years were crucial. As I have noted, New York's boom was a period of intensive transit improvement. The number of franchised horse railways rose from one to eighteen in the third quarter of the century, and ridership grew even more steeply, from about 5 million to 165 million annual fares. Uptown riders, traveling to and from new residential blocks in northern Manhattan, composed the bulk of this increase. The Second, Third, Sixth, and Eighth avenue lines were the first streetcars enfranchised during the midcentury boom (1851–53), and by the late 1860s, they carried nearly 55 percent of the city's riders. The Third Avenue line drew the heaviest traffic; with some 25 million passengers annually after the Civil War, it formed the backbone of the upper East Side's frenzied growth.[66]

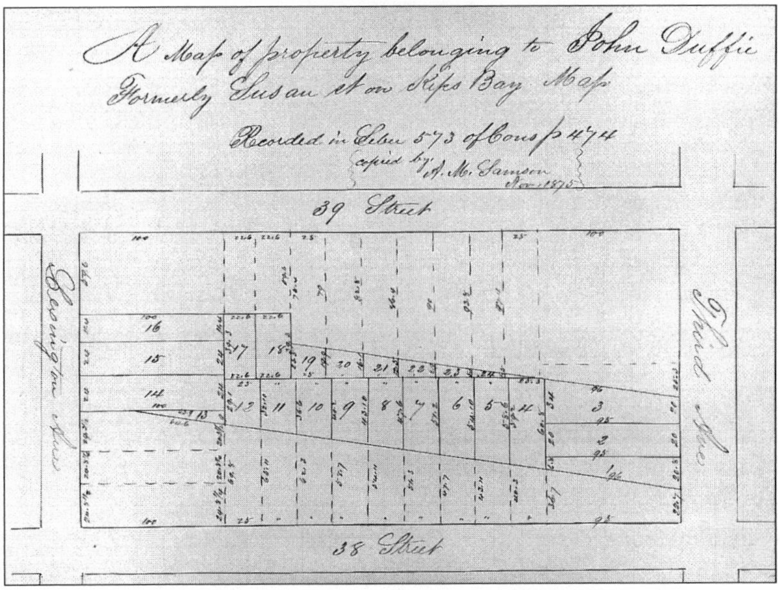

FIGURE 3.14 This 1875 property survey of John Duffie's holdings at Thirty-ninth Street and Lexington Avenue illustrates the process of re-alignment by which rural land was turned into urban real estate. (*Map of Property of John Duffie*, document; Museum of the City of New York, 29.100.3190)

FIGURE 3.15 In this 1861 lithograph of Second Avenue a few blocks away from Duffie's property (Figure 3.14), we see the results of the incremental process required to translate the abstract street grid into an actual cityscape: a raw mix of old villas and new row houses where streetcar tracks and strolling families extend middle-class urbanity into the countryside. (*Valentine's Manual of the Corporation of the City of New York*, 1861; University Library, University of Michigan)

To a certain degree, then, the growth of upper Manhattan conformed to a familiar paradigm in American urban history: that of infrastructural determinism. Scholars like Sam Bass Warner and Clay McShane have long stressed the importance of street and transportation improvements in spurring urban growth and shaping urban form in nineteenth-century America; among historians of New York, Eugene Moehring and Carl Condit have shown the salience of infrastructural innovations to metropolitan development.[67] Yet New York's growth, and especially that of upper Manhattan, tell that story with a difference. For although new streets and streetcars were preconditions to uptown development, they served more often as proximate causes than as prime movers. They were themselves paced by the rhythms of the real-estate economy.

The primacy of real-estate interests is especially clear in the case of street openings. For most of the nineteenth century, local land values dictated who was to pay for street improvements, and local landowners exercised a veto over all projects. State law built such control into the legal process: when the New York Common Council sought to open a street, it asked the state Supreme Court to appoint an ad hoc "commission of estimate and assessment" that surveyed the land and calculated the costs and benefits to affected landowners. The commission covered the costs of reimbursing owners whose property was taken under eminent domain by levying "special assessments" on adjacent owners who stood to benefit from the new or upgraded street. It was an elegant system, one that normally paid the full expense of street work with a local transfer of money that compensated for local shifts in land value. Moreover, as Robin Einhorn argues in her incisive study of special assessments in Chicago, it vested control over urban growth and public works in the hands of the "private" interests who paid for it. New York law required street work to be endorsed by the owners of three-fourths of the abutting frontage—a mere majority was needed in Chicago—and proprietors were not shy to oppose projects that they judged too expensive or unremunerative.[68] As we shall see, the system eroded somewhat during the midcentury boom; massive projects like Riverside Drive were undertaken by central planning agencies and partly financed through long-term municipal borrowing. Yet uptown public works remained a target of intense lobbying by real-estate groups like the West Side Association.[69]

The case of transit extension is somewhat more equivocal, but here again the interests and dynamics of real-estate development seem to play the leading role. What *is* clear is that the growth of New York's streetcar system was not driven by technical innovations in the cars themselves. Until the introduction of nonsurface, steam-driven rapid transit (the elevated railway) in the mid-1870s, and of cable cars and electric trolleys fifteen years later, the technology of intraurban rail transit changed very little from the 1830s: horses pulled cars on tracks laid in the city streets.[70] What *did* change were the demographic, financial, and political pressures that surrounded the technology. On the "demand" side, population growth and uptown resettlement increased the pressure for public conveyances, especially from middle-class New Yorkers who sought domestic seclusion from the "promiscuity" of urban life, but lacked the means to own private transport. On the "supply" side, the growth of the downtown financial sector amassed the capital required to maintain a citywide plant of railways, cars, horses, stations, stables, and repair facilities.

Yet despite these pressures, streetcars were only a secondary cause of Manhattan's uptown growth. What kept them so was the political milieu in which riders and investors pursued their interests. Nineteenth-century horse railways, it should be remembered, were neither "public" services, owned and run by the municipal or state governments, nor fully "private" businesses. They were corporations that had been given special franchises by local or state governments (in this case, the New York Common Council and, after 1860, the Albany legislature). Each franchise imposed specific (and varying) conditions concerning routes, lease payments, tenure, and fares, in exchange for the exclusive privilege of selling public mobility along particular streets. The system was based on the long American "commonwealth" tradition of commissioning corporate monopolies to provide public goods; but it proved ill suited to promoting transit in New York.[71] Streetcar franchises were notorious objects of legislative corruption, partisan bickering, civil litigation, and fractious lobbying during the midcentury boom. The grants of the early 1850s, for instance—the uptown avenue lines already noted—were won by massive bribery of the Common Council. So great was the outcry against "the Forty Thieves," as the aldermen were called, that New York voters swept a reform administration into power in 1854, halting further transit improvements. At the same time, the state legislature required new franchises to be endorsed by half the owners along the proposed route; a coalition of Broadway proprietors, including the Astors and A. T. Stewart, used the new law to block rail transit along the city's busiest thoroughfare. The city's ability to promote uptown transit was further hobbled in 1860, when the state legislature, led by a new Republican majority, reclaimed the power to grant franchises for itself, setting off a new round of bribe taking and legislative standoffs in Albany.[72]

Thus, instead of the government-corporate alliance envisioned by the "commonwealth" ideal, transit development tended to promote political and commercial stalemate. Indeed, it is clear from the complaints of Victorian observers that transportation facilities lagged far behind population growth and property investment in Manhattan. "[New York's] stupid, dilatory, inconvenient system of locomotion . . . would disgrace a village in Turkey," grumbled the daily press, "*it would not be decent to carry live hogs thus.*" Crowding, delays, and poor service were especially acute on the uptown lines. "It is now quite common for [Third Avenue horse cars] to carry . . . *sixty fares* . . . to Harlem, although each car can seat but twenty-two persons," the *Real Estate Record* lamented in 1872. "The heavy additions which are being made to the population along this road will cause [a] . . . demand for more accommodation than the 3rd Avenue line can possibly afford." Uptown landowners seconded such concerns, lobbying the Albany legislature for improvements—most of all, steam rapid transit—that would open their property to building and settlement: "The necessity of improved means of city transit, is a question needing no longer to be argued," Simeon Church pleaded at a West Side Association meeting. "Our whole population,

men, women and children cry out for it, with one voice . . ." Finally, toward the end
of the midcentury boom, Albany *did* take concerted action, approving franchises for
seven horse cars between 1860 and 1874 and establishing an elevated system in the
mid-1870s. Yet this was less a stimulus than a *consequence* of growth, driven by the
pressures of uptown resettlement and the agitation of uptown landowners.[73]

Upper Manhattan was not, in short, a showcase for infrastructural determinism;
the real-estate economy did more to create the technical matrix for uptown growth
than transit technologies did to organize the land market. This is not to say that the
uptown landscape was the work of big, centralized developers, acting as "private-
sector planners" over expansive stretches of property and space. Nineteenth-century
urban history is full of examples of such large-scale land development, from suburban "estates" undertaken by elite developers to townsite speculations in the American West. In the New York area, such projects were pursued only beyond the city limits, where land was comparatively open and cheap. Thus, in the early 1850s,
merchant Llewellyn Haskell developed a five-hundred-acre tract in West Orange,
New Jersey, hiring architect Alexander Jackson Davis to plan "Llewellyn Park" as a
romantic suburb. Fifteen years later the Van Cortlandts, a venerable Knickerbocker
clan, laid out 105 acres of their Westchester estate as "Oloff Park," a rustic community
of curving roads, scenic circles, and "admirable Villa sites."[74]

In New York City proper, however, the development process was never so centralized. The largest residential project in upper Manhattan was Gramercy Park, which
Samuel Ruggles assembled from some two hundred city lots in the early 1830s. Although dwarfed by suburban ventures like Llewellyn Park or Garden City, Ruggles's
private square was bigger than any real-estate project undertaken during the midcentury boom, apart from corporate or public works like the Vanderbilt rail facilities
and Central Park. The boom produced no new villa "parks" or residential squares in
upper Manhattan. Rather the rule of real estate took the form of a highly active but
fragmented land market: the form of the grid itself.[75]

Such decentralization is clear in patterns of landownership and investment. Some
twenty thousand New Yorkers owned real property on Manhattan at the end of the
midcentury boom, about 2.1 percent of the island's population and one-tenth of its
households. An estimated two-thirds of propertied families owned only the plot on
which they lived. Yet even the largest estates controlled no more than a small share of
the New York real-estate market; in 1868, celebrated rentier families like the Astors,
Rhinelanders, and Goelets held 2.9 percent, 1.4 percent, and .8 percent, respectively,
of New York's assessed land value. Ownership was especially dispersed north of
Fourteenth Street, home to nearly three-quarters of propertied New Yorkers. Even on
the upper West Side, where lagging construction might have been linked to more
concentrated patterns of landholding, ambitious developers tended to assemble
parcels no larger than forty or fifty lots; 84 percent of the area's blocks had multiple
proprietors, and 54 percent more than five separate owners. Construction patterns
tell a similar story. In 1870 the Department of Buildings recorded more than two
thousand plans for new buildings and alterations, undertaken by several hundred

different owners. The largest plan comprised twenty-two lots; the largest developer—the family of Nathaniel, John, and Henry Burchell—owned a total of sixty-two lots, spread among twenty-one separate projects. The "march of improvement" thus advanced rapidly, but in small, multiple, and uncoordinated increments.[76]

How did the uptown landscape become fragmented into this jigsaw map of interests and projects? Before the mid-nineteenth century, upper Manhattan was a rural quilt of estates, market farms, and municipal landholdings.[77] The street plan might have produced a "gridded" version of the same pattern—like a digitized photograph—with old landowners retaining their property and serving as new developers. For several reasons, it did not. The rapid rise of real-estate prices, the risk of investing in a volatile land market, the heterogeneity of the uses to which uptown property was put, and (as I discuss later) the cautiousness of large rentiers—all of these factors worked to downscale the development process. The shift from quilt to grid was accompanied by a disaggregation of property and decisional power.

The key mechanism by which this dispersal occurred was the partition sale, especially the real-estate auction. As residents, buildings, and transit moved uptown, landholdings in upper Manhattan were placed under the hammer and divided up. Such sales were of two types, each of which predominated in distinct periods of the boom. From the mid-1840s to the mid-1860s, municipal land auctions represented the single most important "feeder" into the New York real estate market. The city corporation had been given title to all "waste and common land" on Manhattan in its 1730 charter, a grant estimated at over one-seventh of the island's acreage. Although the city sold off some holdings early in the nineteenth century, it began to divest in earnest in 1844, primarily to pay down the debt on the new Croton Aqueduct. On seven other occasions between the mid-1840s and 1866, municipal authorities held public auctions that "converted . . . the [city's] estate . . . into current funds, and applied them to reduce the debt" on public works. Such auctions had a twofold effect on the city-building process. On one hand, as Hendrik Hartog has argued, they helped recast the Corporation of the City of New York from a proprietary to an administrative agency: a state power that employed taxes and bonds, instead of rents and leases, to pursue distinctively *public* goods like waterworks and parks. On the other hand, local state building gave an impetus to metropolitan city building; public land sales invigorated the real-estate economy. The 1866 auction, for instance, offered hundreds of lots on the upper East Side, just as the improvement of that district was shifting into high gear.[78]

By the close of the Civil War, New York City had sold off the bulk of its estate. At just the same time, a second mode of land partition gained importance: private sales of homesteads and farms in rural Manhattan (Figure 3.16). The postwar decade saw the division of many up-island estates (most famously, the Dyckman homestead, comprising several hundred acres on the northern tip of Manhattan, which was auctioned in several sales during 1869–71). "One by one the old landmarks of New York pass away," the *Record* lamented with crocodile's tears, when the Bradhurst estate (Tenth Avenue and 147th to 149th streets) was divided in 1873. "Those who take an

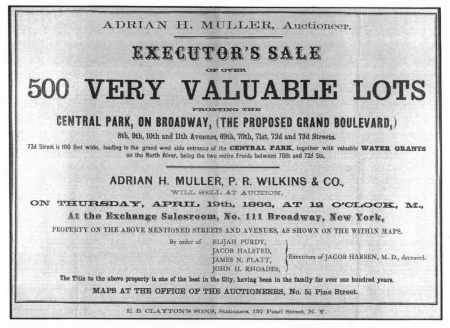

FIGURE 3.16   This 1866 circular announces an executor's sale of 500 lots west of Central Park. Land auctions were a key mechanism by which uptown estates were divided and incorporated into the real-estate market. (*Executor's Sale Advertisement*, document; Museum of the City of New York, 50.358.55)

interest in the old mansions of the city can gratify their tastes . . . before roads, streets, avenues, fences, brick and brown-stone fronts, with the auctioneer's hammer, cut them into 25-feet lots."[79] Auctions were not the only means of partition. Working with "Mr. Zittel, of Third Avenue," the Beekmans sold small parcels of their East Side estate directly to builder-developers. Moreover, as real-estate operators accumulated their own (smaller) aggregations, bankruptcy or death became the occasion for new sales. After wholesale merchant James Slevin died in 1872, his executor offered several lots on upper Broadway, a loft on Church Street, a brownstone on Thirty-fourth Street, and other properties. In 1880, Mutual Life liquidated all the property on which it had foreclosed during the 1870s depression. Partition sales, in short, functioned as a sort of gizzard for the city-building process, digesting and redigesting property into pieces small enough for the grid work of improvement.[80]

Moreover, even when large proprietors like Trinity Church or the Astors sought to maintain or expand their real estate portfolio, they did not undertake large development projects; they did not typically develop their own property at all. Rather, estate holders dispersed the risks and costs of improvement by leasing small parcels to small builders. As Elizabeth Blackmar has shown, such long-term leases were a common feature of New York's real-estate economy from the early eighteenth century. Usually twenty-one years in duration, but often as long as ninety-nine, they suited a city that combined large landed estates, a complex economic geography, and a fluid property market. Leases opened the city-building process to smaller entrepreneurs— master carpenters, speculators, neighborhood artisans—who lacked the resources to acquire or carry real estate on their own. Conversely they offered estate owners a kind of effortless profiteering, displacing risk into a secondary market of leaseholds and development rights.[81]

By the midcentury boom, New York's large proprietors were notorious for their timidity in the face of spatial change and speculative opportunity: "Representatives of all the old real estate interests are very conservative, and rarely take up novelties in the way of building," the *Real Estate Record* commented. "The Astors, Rhinelanders, Goelets, Gilseys, Roosevelts, and Lenoxes have so far avoided the responsibilities of . . . new and immense structures." Such rentier passivity could sometimes include daring land speculations; the Astors were famous for engrossing large tracts of New York real estate just ahead of the frontier of development—and leasing it to builders for lucrative ground rents. In 1880, for instance, William Backhouse Astor bought twelve hundred lots in the city's Annexed District (now the southern Bronx) for $500 million. "Let any one desirous of going to work on these lots . . . apply to [Astor's] office in Prince street," the *Record* noted, "and he will readily ascertain that the owner is perfectly willing to grant a lease for any series of years for any number of lots." Similarly (as the activities of Trinity Church made clear) large rentiers assiduously sought to maximize their rental income. Yet they were surprisingly marginal to the city-building process itself. The result was a paradox: the property owners who profited most famously from the city's growth were rarely those who shaped it most decisively.[82]

New York's real-estate economy was characterized, in short, by a dispersion of property and power. The logic of the grid—and of the partition sale, the local assessment system, and the leasehold market— was one of atomization. New York moved uptown under the rule of markets that were centrally coordinated and supremely powerful, yet highly decentralized. It must be stressed that these markets excluded nearly all but the wealthiest New Yorkers. Yet for those who could afford to play, the real-estate economy diffused the rights, powers, and rewards of city building across a grid of small projects and divided interests.

Here was a primary cause of the complexity and dynamism of uptown development. The grid encouraged active, fluid, price-sensitive choices about land use and construction, providing a "substrate," so to speak, for the interplay of use values and land values. Consider, for example, the riverfront industrial districts that we saw to be an unexpected result of the march of improvement. They grew out of the downtown rental boom: large manufacturers were priced off lower Manhattan by their need for cheap, expansive sites. As a result, metropolitan industry was bifurcated into an inner-city sector of labor-intensive workshops, small contractors, and fluid markets, and a peripheral sector of capital-intensive factory production. In 1865 fewer than a quarter of New York's tailors—the classic case of a sweated workshop trade—resided uptown. Although garments were cut and sewn in every ward of the city, most tailors lived east of the Bowery and south of Fourteenth Street; and they used strategies of outwork, subcontracting, and sheer crowding to absorb or displace the high overhead costs of their location. By contrast, half of the city's piano makers lived uptown, mostly in East Side districts near factories like Steinway and Sons at Fourth Avenue and Fifty-second Street.[83]

This rent-based bifurcation of industry was reinforced by divergent *functional* needs among New York's manufacturers. On one hand, downtown trades like garment making or job printing depended on proximity to shifting networks of customers, contractors, and creditors. Many large industries, on the other hand, were pulled north by the cheap transport, storage, or waste-disposal facilities that the uptown waterfront afforded. The New York Central, for instance, developed the upper Hudson into a complex of train sheds, stables, stockyards, lumber yards, grain elevators, and oil refineries, aimed at streamlining the transfer of commodities among rail, ship, and wagon. Nuisance industries like gas works and abattoirs were also drawn to the outer waterfront: they were space hungry, dependent on bulk transport, prone to use the rivers as sewers, and increasingly restricted from populous areas by public-health legislation. Such siting decisions produced their own spin-off effects: clustered near the slaughterhouses were tanneries, bone-boiling shops, glue factories, and chemical works—enterprises that processed animal carcasses into still more commodities.[84]

The same play of land values and use values ordered the *residential* mosaic of upper Manhattan. Here, however, the grid of prices did not reflect functional needs for cheap space so much as cultural ideals about privacy and class separation. As Robert Fishman has shown, the desire for expansive residential segregation that drove the Victorian middle and upper classes to the periphery of Anglo-American cities was shaped by powerful, nationally specific values. (Bourgeois urbanites created quite different residential geographies in the cities of continental Europe.) Fishman argues that evangelical reform and moral environmentalism schooled genteel Americans to link domestic privacy, moral virtue, and greenery, and to shun the inner cityscape as a scene of promiscuity and vice. Such notions shaped not only genteel planning reform—as I discuss in Chapter 7—but also the market activity of Manhattan real-estate developers. Auction notices and advertisements touted the benefits of "residences beyond the turmoil and foul atmosphere of city life," where "[urban] refinements . . . will be united with rural freedom." Speculators linked images of domestic seclusion with appeals to uptown class segregation: "It has no tenement-house neighborhood nor can have any," one speculator claimed of his upper West Side property, "the character of the buildings and the value of the land absolutely preclude the tenement house."[85]

Of course, high land values could not "absolutely preclude" low land uses; owners often resorted to deed restrictions and other controls to protect property from unwanted uses and classes. Yet the location market *did* exert a determining influence on the residential geography of upper Manhattan. As much as any moral appeal, it was often price discipline pure and simple that drove homeowners uptown. "We are tempted with prices so exorbitantly high that none can resist," Philip Hone noted, wistful but well paid, when he sold his Broadway home to a commercial developer, "and the old downtown burgomasters . . . [march] reluctantly north to pitch their tents in . . . orchards, cornfields, and morasses . . ."[86]

Moreover, as we have seen, market forces differentiated the uptown landscape into class-based corridors of residence. Bourgeois households, seeking locational prestige, class exclusiveness, and proximity to elite shopping and amusements, bid up the cost of residential construction on the spine of Manhattan to $15,000 to $30,000 per lot after the Civil War. Middling and working-class New Yorkers, who needed access to horse car transit or riverfront labor markets, were pushed east of Third Avenue and west of Seventh, where new (multiunit) housing cost only $8,000 to $12,000 per lot. Uptown was thus marked by "sharp gradations of locality and choice of position," as the *Real Estate Record* put it, from "the elaborate and costly mansions" of Fifth avenue to "plain dwellings" nearer the rivers. This heterogeneous, highly compressed class geography was reinforced by perhaps the most ironic effect of the uptown boom: the growth of industrial and waged work organized precisely to surround and serve the metropolitan bourgeoisie. The world of "Fifth Avenue" depended on a complex support economy of household labor, luxury production, and transit facilities. Not only did the majority of New York's 33,000 servants live north of Fourteenth Street in the mid-1860s; so did 60 percent of the stable keepers, 61 percent of the drivers and coachmen, and 70 percent of the hostlers. Indeed provisioning horses for carriage owners, commercial stables, and street railways represented one of the most active sectors of uptown development; nearly one thousand stables were built in New York from 1863 to 1871, four-fifths of them above Fourteenth Street.[87]

The midcentury boom, in short, transformed upper Manhattan from a patchwork quilt of estates, farms, and squatters' villages to an expansive, bounded, but surprisingly heterogeneous grid. If "uptown" was a refuge of genteel domesticity, it was also a complex field of class differences; indeed, it succeeded as a genteel refuge *because* it was a field of class differences. It served as a residential catchment for internal migrants in the new, functionally segregated metropolis, but it also contained some of the most important industrial and wage work in the metropolitan area—from the dirtiest nuisance industry to the "backstage" labor of bourgeois civility. As in lower Manhattan, the logic of spatial markets created a landscape of contradictions.

Dreamland

To its partisans and profiteers, the rule of real estate represented more than an engine of spatial change; it was an emblem of social order, proof of the beneficence of capitalist city building. They took it for granted that the real-estate market constituted not only an economic but also an ideological regime; they invested even the most mundane aspects of the development process with heroic significance. "The growth of New York in wealth and population is unparalleled," opened an advertisement for the Dyckman estate partition sale. "It is so rapid, and so great, that those of us who live and move in it, and are a part of it, . . . are left so far behind in our calculations that we seem to have been in dreamland." Such rhetoric helps to explain why stories of Peter Minuit's deal or booster prophecies held so much appeal to New York's real-estate leaders. The message was clear: to buy and sell land on Manhattan Island was to participate in transformations that had the power of myth or magic. It was to awaken, Rip Van Winkle–like, into a "dreamland" of destiny where calculating men might attain incalculable ends.[88]

As I have tried to show in this chapter, propertied New Yorkers had good reason to talk like this. During the midcentury boom, they recast the city-building process and made the real-estate economy the most powerful arbiter of spatial change in the Victorian metropolis. Landowning and financial elites pursued a broad campaign of institutional modernization, creating a network of agencies—the Exchange Salesroom, the *Real Estate Record*, property atlases, partition sales, lending corporations—that mobilized spatial information, market contacts, and capital with new efficiency. These institutions consolidated citywide markets in land, rents, building rights, and mortgage credit; opened local development to national capital formation; habituated landowners, land users, and builders to treat space as a standardized, fungible commodity; and subjected New York's growth to the discipline of price competition. The result was a metropolitan area organized around two novel, complementary landscapes: a site-intensive, internally differentiated commercial downtown and an expansive uptown of residential and industrial districts.

The new metropolis corresponded in many ways to the "dreamland" of booster desire. Its very antinomies—uptown and downtown, centralism and atomism, extensive and intensive growth—integrated the twin commitments of the metropolitan bourgeoisie to kinetic progress and cultural order. On one hand, the midcentury boom "overcame the frictions of space," in the useful phrase of the modern land economist Robert Haig: it created a vast geographic "engine" for massing and moving money, information, goods, and people. On the other, these flows were channeled in a landscape of systematic, bounded complexity, one whose physical, functional, and social demarcations were thought to ensure civic order: "It is no small consideration in the future harmony of the city's growth that these several types of dwelling house may be constructed . . . without intermixture or confusion," the *Real Estate Record* concluded in the uptown housing survey quoted previously. "The natural tastes of citizens are thus likely to find their easy gratification and ideals, with no impassable barrier dividing them." The location market was a benevolent despot, in short, and the landscape that it summoned into being embodied the ideal of a capitalist civilization: the dream of ordered energy, at once monumental and moral in its local effects.[89]

Such claims, however, told only part of the story. For, far from "overcoming the frictions of space," friction was the byword of New York in the third quarter of the nineteenth century. Spatial and social disorder were endemic to the city's growth and transformation; the boom produced dysfunctional patterns of land use, physical underdevelopment, unstable property markets, and recurrent sociospatial conflict. The next chapter explores these environmental ills. As I shall argue, they reflected the unevenness of the city-building process itself—and, more fundamentally, the contradictory nature of urban space as a commodity. Even as real estate markets spurred grand, systematic improvements in the New York cityscape, they also enforced effects of vexing irrationality. Faced with spatial and social disorders from which the marketplace could not, unaided, rescue itself, bourgeois city builders turned to urban design and the politics of planning with the same utopian brashness that shaped their booster dreams.

CHAPTER 4

The Frictions of Space

Bad roads meant bad morals.
—Henry Adams, *The Education of Henry Adams* (1918)

Uneven Development

"New York is the most inconveniently arranged commercial city in the world," complained William Cullen Bryant in the *Evening Post* in 1867. The editor went on to catalog the environmental ills that afflicted Manhattan: "wharfs [that] are badly built, unsafe, and without shelter"; "streets [that] are badly paved, dirty, and necessarily overcrowded"; shipping, storage, and rail facilities without "labor-saving machinery" or "proper relation" to one another. The costs of such disorder were human as well as technical: "[The city's] laborers are badly lodged," the editorial warned, and its transit arrangements "so badly contrived that a considerable part of the working population spend a sixth part of their working days on the street cars or omnibuses." Such jeremiads were not limited to genteel voices like the *Post*. Trade journals decried "the clogging of the great arteries of commerce" that had accompanied downtown growth, doing "great injury to the business of the city." Public officials criticized the lack of "any systematic arrangement . . . of the different branches of trade" on the waterfront. Real-estate elites deplored similar irrationalities in upper Manhattan—most notably west of Central Park, where feverish land speculation kept "the most picturesque portion of the whole island" in "as bleak, barren and unattractive an appearance as it [had had] twenty years ago."[1]

Precisely at a time of epochal growth and reconstruction, New York was marked by vexing disorders. Large stretches of the city were at once overcrowded and underdeveloped, too improvised, obstructive, and expensive to function efficiently; the built environment exhibited a mix of rigidity and volatility at odds with the monetary and cultural investments that bourgeois New Yorkers made in it. What caused these problems? How do we square them with the grand, modernizing improvements that—

just as surely—characterized the metropolitan landscape during the midcentury boom? How did real-estate activists and other city builders respond to the patterns of uneven development? The present chapter seeks to answer these questions.

At one level, of course, it is easy to reconcile the booster account of New York's progress with the discourse of environmental complaint: they concern different parts of the cityscape. Much (but not all) of the last chapter foregrounded the central spine of Victorian Manhattan, the high-priced corridor from Wall Street and lower Broadway through Ladies' Mile to Fifth Avenue. That was where space proved most responsive to price discipline, where the rule of real estate imposed its grandest improvements. By contrast, much (but not all) of this chapter will focus on the margins of Manhattan. Thus, it was on the downtown waterfront that the *dys*functional effects of commercial development were most visible; it was on the boundaries of the uptown tenement and industrial districts that riots, labor conflict, epidemics, and other class-related disorders most often encroached on "the march of improvement."

Yet this is not the whole story. The congestion, underinvestment, senseless land use, and sociospatial conflict in the Manhattan landscape were not mere accidents of the midcentury boom; they were constitutive effects, quite as much as Grand Central Depot or the Western Union headquarters. Nor were these disorders simply residua of growth, the unfinished business of modernization. Rather they were to a great extent *emergent* results of capitalist city building, produced and reinforced by the same factors that spurred New York's "march of improvement." The real-estate economy was essentially contradictory: it created a "heteroscape" of dynamism and stagnation, boundaries and boundarilessness. These contradictions reflected something paradoxical in the city-building process itself: the strange mixture of power and fragility, sluggishness and mercuriality, that characterized land value as a commodity.

This chapter begins by sketching some of the environmental problems that beset Victorian New York, concentrating first on the downtown docks and streets, where the technical and economic costs of disorder were most evident. It goes on to analyze the causes of these frictions, comparing lag models by which many scholars have explained nineteenth-century urban disorder with an account that stresses the uneven effects of city building in the age of capital. The next section foregrounds the *social* disorders of uneven development, focusing on the crowd violence and class conflict that attended the midcentury boom. The geography of riot made clear to bourgeois New Yorkers not only the permeability of social borders in the metropolitan landscape but also the fragility of their dream of a bounded and disciplined civic order. The frictions of space thus posed a challenge to the very legitimacy of the imperial ideal. Beginning in the 1860s and 1870s, bourgeois city builders sought to meet that challenge. A coalition of civic capitalists, real-estate boosters, and genteel reformers, embracing a surprisingly robust vision of state activism, articulated a novel program of environmental regulation, urban design, and planned growth. In seeking to overcome the disorders of the Manhattan cityscape, they ended up recasting the city-building process as a whole. In seeking to secure their dream of empire, they helped to invent city planning.

Arterial Sclerosis

The frictions of space were especially visible in lower Manhattan, on the downtown docks and streets. The disorganization and blight of the waterfront, for instance, stood in stark contrast to New York's economic power and the natural endowments of its port. Ships commonly experienced delays of up to a week in landing their cargoes; the growth of trade, combined with an ad hoc method of assigning berth space, made it nearly impossible to obtain dockage without patience or bribery. Berths were distributed with little regard for New York's commercial geography: thus long-standing custom sent Atlantic steamers to Hudson River piers, while Erie Canal boats rounded the Battery for East River slips. The canal boat fleet represented the port's grandest irrationality. During the delivery of western grain—arguably the city's most important line of trade—they crowded Coenties Slip, exceeding its capacity four times over; then from the harvest to the spring thaw, they squatted along the Slip, dozens abreast, occupying valuable East River frontage like so many gigantic waterfowl (Figure 4.1). Such scenes, fulminated the *Times*, "produce[d] a crowding, confusion, and inconvenience to the public and to commerce, such as no civilized city ever endured so long and so patiently."[2]

Even after they obtained space, however, shippers did not obtain satisfaction. Widespread dumping of sewage and refuse made Manhattan's slips "little better than so many receptacles for garbage"; if they were not constantly dredged, they posed a threat to both commerce and public health. "In summer, at low tide," one official reported, "this filth lies frothing like yeast, setting free . . . offensive and pernicious gases and insupportable odors . . . which every breeze . . . spreads over the island." The structures themselves met with universal scorn. Thrown up for the most part in the expansionary burst of the 1840s and 1850s, usually built of unprotected wood, the wharves and piers were "mere temporary structures in all stages of dilapidation and decay, very few of them fit for occupation and use." An 1864 survey found less than 10 percent in good or fair repair; docks periodically broke up in the river currents or collapsed from the weight of the merchandise on their rotting timbers. "Instead of a line of wharves and piers of approved model and substantial material," complained the daily press, "the City presents a front of wretched, tumble-down wooden structures that lack even the merit of cheapness to palliate their ugliness and inutility" (Figure 4.2).[3]

Even stable structures were often ill designed and ill equipped. Piers were too short, and wharves too narrow, to accommodate the larger vessels and volume of the midcentury boom. For the most part, they lacked state-of-the-art expedients like steam-powered hoists, rail connections, or dockside stores (Figure 4.3). The absence of nearby warehouses and terminal facilities meant that riverside streets were "constant[ly] blockade[d] from the pressure of drays carrying goods backward and forward," with teamsters "detained sometimes over a day, waiting their turn to get down the dock." Such inefficiencies increased cartage costs, delays, and property

FIGURE 4.1 Along with Figures 4.2 and 4.3, this illustration from *Harper's Weekly* offers a glimpse at the disorders that bedeviled the Manhattan waterfront. Erie Canal boats are camped along prime wharfage at Coenties Slip, one of the port's many locational irrationalities. (*Harper's Weekly*, February 16, 1884; image courtesy of HarpWeek, LLC)

FIGURE 4.2 The Manhattan docks were often ramshackle and in disrepair. (*Harper's Weekly*, May 28, 1881; image courtesy of HarpWeek, LLC)

FIGURE 4.3   Although Brooklyn and Jersey City boasted modern infrastructures for transferring freight, the Manhattan waterfront largely depended on the age-old means of human and animal muscle. (*Harper's Weekly*, July 14, 1877; image courtesy of HarpWeek, LLC)

loss. At night, carts were simply abandoned—beds for street children—and freight was left on unsheltered and unsecured wharves, exposed to weather and theft. It was estimated that a million dollars worth of merchandise was stolen from the docks each year. In part the losses came from "an organized system of plunder by river-thieves," working in gangs from the water; in part, from the informal labor of poor women and children, for whom scavenging food, fuel, and tradable bric-a-brac contributed to a hardscrabble living.[4]

Not every quarter of the port was poorly equipped, of course. The Hudson waterfront was less squalid than the East River. Much of the West Side frontage was controlled by large transportation corporations—steamship, ferry, and railroad lines—whose growing traffic and capital in the 1860s led to "the lengthening, widening and strengthening of their wharves, [and the] erecting [of] substantial . . . houses upon them." Yet modern facilities remained the exception in Manhattan. The city could not match the vanguard improvements on the opposite riverfronts—the dock basins in Brooklyn and rail depots of Jersey City—or the superior facilities of other Atlantic ports, which had to make up for the natural advantages of New York harbor. Indeed Manhattan's merchants feared that the frustrations of the waterfront were driving shipping away: "A tax of $5 is put on every ton of commercial wares that is landed on our piers," one businessman warned the dock commissioners in 1870. "If something

FIGURE 4.4 City magazines delighted in publishing tableaux of Manhattan traffic jams. This 1883 engraving shows a "block-ade" at Broadway and Fulton, in front of the *Herald* and Post Office buildings. Note the overturned dray in the left foreground. (*Harper's Weekly*, December 29, 1883; image courtesy of HarpWeek, LLC)

were not done forthwith . . . , the commerce of New-York will have passed from it . . . [to] Philadelphia, Baltimore and other cities."[5]

The problems did not stop on the shoreline, however. A network of cramped, crowded streets led into the heart of the business district, producing that other invention of modern downtown life, the traffic jam (Figure 4.4). Part of Manhattan's problem was topographical: the long riverfronts and narrow landmass fed a huge volume of traffic into constricted, irregular streets. The city inherited from colonial times a "tortuous labyrinth" of crooked lanes and unrelated grids, inadequate to its growing trade. Besides Fulton Street, there was no direct connection between the rivers; besides Broadway, no unimpeded route from downtown Manhattan to the uptown wards. As a result of "this bungling arrangement of streets," the *Real Estate Record* argued, the main arteries of commerce were "so overcrowded . . . as to make it all but impossible for people to move about their business," while other routes "are given over to . . . perennial inertia and silence."[6]

These topographical shortcomings were compounded by the physical condition of the streets themselves. Not until the turn of the century did advances in petrochemicals and civil engineering produce a cheap, durable, smooth, quiet surface in Trinidad asphalt. Before then, the city's efforts to replace the cobblestones on streets like Broadway, the Bowery, and South Street yielded a series of frustrating trials. Public works officials experimented with wood, concrete, and stone pavements during the 1860s and 1870s before settling on the "Belgian" method of embedding granite blocks in sand. This was the most durable surface for heavy commercial traffic, but its problems were great. The stone shifted in its foundations, trapped water and filth between paving blocks, and, under the action of horseshoes and wheel rims, grew rounded, slick, and noisy. Combined with the horse car tracks that were laid along all major roads, the result was a slow, jolting, clamorous ride. "[New York's] streets are horribly paved," a French visitor reported. "The carriages appear to rise and fall as if on a troubled sea."[7]

Moreover the "pavement question" was almost moot in a city dependent on the labor of forty thousand horses (Figure 4.5). Every working day generated some four hundred tons of manure, twenty thousand gallons of urine, and almost two hundred carcasses of dead animals. Along with human wastes, leftover food, and commercial refuse, these were dumped onto the streets, creating piles of "reeking, disgusting filth, which in some places is . . . almost impassable by vehicles." During the thaw, this "odious mixture" became a filthy muck in which "pedestrians [had to] wade nearly to the knees at times." By late spring, it dried into a gritty, nauseous dust that attacked the eyes and blew contagion through the city. Only in winter did street filth cease to plague Victorian New Yorkers—and only then because it was blanketed by snow and slush that made cartage and commuting even more difficult.[8] Although City Hall had ostensible charge of sanitation and snow removal, these services were notorious sources of patronage and insider contracts. Not until 1894, when reform mayor William Strong and sanitarian George Waring created the uniformed Department of Street Cleaning, could any but the most elite residential and commercial streets count on regular, reliable service.[9]

Finally New York's economic geography exacerbated the physical inadequacies of the city streets. On one hand, the midcentury boom increased the need for freight transport; the number of licensed carts in Manhattan doubled between 1867 and 1871. On the other, the separation of wharves, depots, and warehouses required merchants to send those carts through the busiest streets of lower Manhattan—just as the streets were becoming more and more obstructed. Abutting landowners, shopkeepers, building crews, and peddlers treated public thoroughfares as rent-free space for retailing, parking, publicity, deliveries, and storage. At Fulton and Washington markets, the roads were "literally blocked every day and all day by boxes, barrels, stands, and every other receptacle for produce." Apple sellers, musicians, hawkers, newsboys, and bootblacks—the street entrepreneurs memorialized in Horatio Alger books and popular melodrama—blockaded City Hall Park and Printing-House Square. In the wholesale district, merchandise and refuse spilled out from storefronts; around

FIGURE 4.5   As the humorous portrait of "The City Horse" in *Harper's Weekly* suggests, dependence on horsepower was another source of discontent about the New York streets. Besides the health and environmental ills caused by animal waste, the inefficiency of downtown cartage along ill-paved streets led to endemic abuse of the animals themselves. (*Harper's Weekly*, July 24, 1858; image courtesy of HarpWeek, LLC)

construction sites, piles of lumber, brick, and other materiel littered the rights of way. During the late 1860s, municipal officials tried to limit encumbrances by licensing and vagrancy ordinances, but with little success. The downtown streets were clogged with the flotsam of growth.[10]

Modernization and Its Discontents

Lower Manhattan, in short, was a paradox: a perpetual motion machine that perpetually threatened to fall motionless. Its frictions exacted a heavy toll on New York, undermining growth even as they were intensified by it: "It is preposterous that our merchants should be compelled to pay as much for the removal of a load from Courtlandt to Canal Street as is required to bring it from Chicago to New York," fumed the *Real Estate Record*.[11] How are we to explain such self-destructive patterns of development?

For one influential tradition of urban studies, with its roots in functionalist sociology and modernization theory, the answer lies in a lag model of city building. Environmental disorders, this model posits, resulted from inevitable but transitory disjunctions between old and new; especially during the nineteenth century, the expansionary energy of capitalist development imposed demands to which an older, slower, less complex landscape could not adequately, instantly respond. "Growth outdistanced improvements," writes historian Eugene Moehring, an authority on nineteenth-century public works. "In many towns the shock of sudden and continued urbanization overwhelmed inexperienced [city] councils" and "accelerated the velocity of change beyond social control." Such an account treats economic and demographic growth as engines of change that were racing in too low a gear, exceeding the technical, market, and administrative capacities of the city-building process. Eventually the dislocations of growth pulled urban development forward, stimulating innovations in land use, design, and infrastructural technology. In the interim, however, traffic jams and rotten docks were the residua of a modernization process that had not yet run its course.[12]

Scholars have used this paradigm in various ways to analyze the disorders of nineteenth-century urbanization. Studies of transportation and technology, for instance, stress the backwardness of civil engineering and urban infrastructures in the Gilded Age. Not until the turn of the century did electrified transport, modern pavements, power and telephone grids, and steel construction enable American cities to handle their mushrooming demographic and commercial needs.[13] Similarly, political historians point to the inadequacy of older municipal institutions to the escalating demands of urban governance and city building. They argue that Gilded Age cities inherited a balkanized power structure, dispersed among weak mayors, parochial aldermen, and antiurban state legislators. It was the emergence of strong municipal executives late in the century, aided by competent bureaucracies and a new ethos of efficiency and expertise, that equipped American cities to plan, finance, and regulate their growth.[14]

Like all useful models, this account of nineteenth-century urban disorder offers ample room for diversity and disagreement. Yet it frames such debates within a common metanarrative of environmental change. Like the larger paradigm of the "organizational revolution" to which it is indebted, best known from the work of Robert Wiebe and Samuel Hays, it casts the late nineteenth century as a threshold era of modernization: a time of corrosive progress in which the juggernaut of industrial advancement rent the spatial and social fabric of city life. The central impulse of Gilded Age urbanism is thus cast as a search for technologies and institutions by which cities adjusted to what Hays calls "the innumerable dislocations of the economic revolution." City building is seen as an inexorable process of growth, disruption, and equilibration: a process whose disorders necessitated, and thereby facilitated, new means of reconstructing and regulating urban space.[15]

It is a powerful model, one that indeed helps to explain key aspects of New York's uneven growth. For much of the disorder that I have been describing *was* caused by lags in the city's technical development. The congestion and filth of the downtown streets, for instance, could only be relieved by reducing the presence of cobblestones, commuters, and horse manure on them; the later development of asphalt, electric transit, and the internal combustion engine made that possible. As Clay McShane and other scholars have shown, these technologies effected a revolution in urban circulation, transforming the inner-city street from a communal forum, an open-air store, a garbage dump, and a sort of Darwinian free-for-all into a specialized instrument of movement. Like the concurrent innovations of subway travel and the "union" station, the twentieth-century business street came to embody new Progressive ideals of efficiency, cleanliness, and social discipline.[16]

Yet the disorders of Manhattan's streets should not be reduced to a matter of unfinished technological progress. They were *emergent* results of the city's growth, by-products of the boom itself. Consider, for instance, the effect of the 1811 street plan. Even as it activated real-estate development, the grid did much to derange land use and circulation. Like the "premodern" labyrinth that it superseded, it ignored New York's topography and specific commercial needs. Its narrow cross streets impeded movement between the waterfront and the interior; its broad avenues promoted linear, distended patterns of growth, so that working-class neighborhoods on the flanks of Manhattan Island remained underdeveloped and overcrowded. Moreover, even as the grid spurred uptown resettlement, it made commuting more difficult; only a few of the new avenues debouched into existing downtown thoroughfares. It had the effect, in other words, of nullifying New York's most important topographic endowment (generalized access to water transport) and accentuating its primary disadvantage (a long, narrow landmass). "If they had done the work in the dark, or without surveying it, or even seeing it," William Martin complained, "[the 1811 commissioners] could not more completely have disregarded fundamental conditions."[17]

Similarly, lag theories of development cannot wholly account for the sorry state of the Manhattan waterfront. The congestion, dilapidation, and inefficiency of the docks worsened during the midcentury boom *despite* mechanical and design innovations that were adopted by European ports, American rivals, and New York's satellite cities. The technical backwardness of the waterfront resulted rather from the social and institutional disarray of its property, administrative, and market arrangements, a disarray that had both "residual" and "emergent" causes.

On one hand, a crazy-quilt pattern of municipal, private, and joint ownership made systematic redevelopment or berth reallocation nearly impossible. City-owned docks suffered the most. Officials long held that New York's competitive advantage depended on underpricing its rivals; they set rents and wharfage rates so low that neither the City Corporation nor its lessees could afford to improve or maintain their facilities. The Albany legislature further discouraged investment on the East River by reserving its prime locations for Erie Canal boats and mandating low wharfage fees to boost the volume (and toll revenue) of the state canal system.[18] Such inefficiencies were compounded by a fragmented administrative regime. Federal customs officials oversaw foreign trade and tariffs. The governor appointed pilot commissioners to direct harbor navigation, harbormasters to control access to berths, and port wardens to supervise damaged craft and cargoes. The municipal street commissioner was responsible for construction and repair of the wharves; the commissioners of the Sinking Fund, for leasing municipal property; the dockmasters, for collecting wharfage fees. The Metropolitan Police patrolled the rivers against dock thieves. Needless to

say, this divided governance hampered improvements: it took twenty years of jurisdictional bickering, inadequate funding, and technical delays to get the Army Corps
of Engineers to blast the treacherous strait at Hell Gate clear of rocks.[19]

On the other hand, New York's boom intensified the complexity and fragmentation of the port economy, perversely reinforcing the obstacles to modernization. As
the press lamented, the "variety of interest and almost inevitable conflict of ownership" on the waterfront "tended directly to the . . . decay of [its] wharves and piers."
Here was a classic prisoner's dilemma: the aggregate pursuit of divergent interests
stalemated collective action. For New York's shipowners, the primary needs were
faster turnaround times and more systematic locational arrangements; for merchants,
lower transshipment and storage costs; for wharf owners, more lucrative rates; for insurers, improved protection against fire, weather, and theft; for the canal interest, am-
pler berthing facilities; for rail and steamship companies, better terminals; for ferry
lines, improved links to street transit. Everyone had a stake in "dock reform," but a
different stake. As the "multiform wants of commerce" heightened the need for waterfront reconstruction, they also heightened disagreement over how to harmonize
such conflicting demands. The result, as we shall see, was a planning debate as energetic, heterogeneous, and deadlocked as the waterfront itself.[20]

The disorders of lower Manhattan, in short, were caused less by the incompleteness of urban development than by its contradictory effects. Precisely as—precisely
because—New York was growing into a modern metropolis, its streets and docks became more crowded, more disorganized, less adequate to that growth. The midcentury boom escalated the volume, speed, and complexity of trade, but in so doing, it
made the waterfront more resistant to redevelopment. It caused a sharp rise in land
values, but in so doing, created a landscape whose haphazard intricacy encouraged
landowners and land users to gridlock one another. The rewards of growth made
much of Manhattan, ironically, too valuable to improve.

Students of Victorian America will find this conjuncture of unstable dynamism and
paralyzing disorder familiar; it mirrors the larger story of national economic development in leading sectors like railroading and commercial agriculture. In the case of
the Manhattan landscape, however, uneven development was reinforced by problems specific to capitalist city building: by the peculiarities of urban space as a commodity. More than other sectors, I would argue, real estate was subject to disabilities
that hindered it from responding fluently to economic and environmental change. In
the face of complex, escalating demands for land use, circulation, and construction,
key aspects of the city-building process broke down.[21]

Several tendencies of the real-estate market hobbled its efficacy as a determinant of
spatial change. First of all, the very dynamism of New York's growth encouraged a
monopolistic, unresponsive attitude toward land use. Especially in lower Manhattan,
property owners (and long-term lessees) possessed what amounted to a corner on a
scarce, supervalued good. Even the most intensive program of construction could not
augment the supply of central locations commensurate with demand for them. The
paradoxical result was to encourage some owners and leaseholders to *resist* the in-

visible hand. For every Appleton who obeyed the dictates of price discipline, others withheld land from its "best and highest use": either reserving it against a further rise in the market or extracting immediate gain from it without enhancing its physical or locational value. Tenants of city-owned piers, for instance, consistently violated the terms of their leases by renting bulkhead space to barges that sold hay and straw to Manhattan teamsters; the growing horse traffic made it more profitable in the short term to leave ships languishing in the harbor.[22] Sidewalk encumbrances proliferated for the same reason: entrepreneurs sought to claim the "monopoly power" of locations whose ground rent they could not afford, but whose centrality they could not afford to pass up. Wherever landowners and land users could externalize the commercial or environmental costs of a dysfunctional market choice, prosperity made it attractive to hoard land without enhancing collective land value.

It also magnified the cost and difficulty of improving space. Wages in the building trades nearly doubled in the 1860s, and carrying costs on property rose even more dramatically: the expansion of public works and services multiplied tax rates threefold during the third quarter of the nineteenth century. At the same time, the sluggishness of land development, with its heavy initial investment and slow income stream, meant that new construction had trouble keeping pace with volatile shifts in demand. For less wealthy owners and tenants, this sluggishness encouraged two different, but equally dysfunctional strategies. On one hand, it promoted the overuse or patchwork recycling of existing structures. We saw the result on the waterfront, with its tumbledown piers, lack of up-to-date facilities, and piecemeal but entrenched locational patterns. On the other hand, high entry costs and slow returns encouraged rapid turnover of unimproved property, especially on the unbuilt margin of the city. These may seem opposite responses—disinvestment versus speculative investment —but both amounted to ways of "sweating the land." Each extracted value from real estate without improving it, and each tended to retard the city-building process.[23]

The most powerful impediment to systematic development, however, was the *interdependence* of the location market. Unlike most commodities, the exchange value of urban space is almost completely relational, its price set by the larger geography of activities and contiguities in which it is embedded. The "rationality" of the real-estate economy thus depends on its collective stability, its capacity to generate regions of development within which the uses and prices of specific locations can be calculated and secured. Yet, as we have seen, urban development in Victorian New York was anything but stable. The city's volatile growth exposed property to the constant threat of "external" devaluation, usually from industrial or working-class neighbors. "Numerous manufactories" clung to downtown addresses, fumed the *Real Estate Record*, "which, if they were removed, would immediately increase in market value for other purposes." Frederick Law Olmsted decried similar disruptions in the genteel neighborhoods of upper Manhattan. "Where five years ago there was nothing but elegance & fashion," he wrote in an 1860 letter to an uptown owner, "you now see unmistakeable signs of the advance guard of squalor, an anxiety to sell out on the part of the owners of the finest villas, no sales except for public houses, and an absolute deterioration in value of property. . . ." Such intrusions defeated the sorting process by which the location market was meant to secure functional efficiency and social harmony. Indeed, it seems to have encouraged a mode of land extortion: "Men will often buy lots and keep them, until the neighborhood is handsomely improved," reported the superintendent of buildings, "and then, by threatening to build tenements, levy blackmail upon their wealthy neighbors and compel them to buy their property at fabulous prices."[24]

Land value, in short, was both the most robust and fragile of goods. Its paradoxical mixture of exclusiveness and interdependence enabled it to function as a powerful arbiter of spatial change; but these qualities also promoted self-seeking, blinkered, economically perverse choices. The cues of the real-estate market could encourage either improvement or stagnation, the inscribing or the effacing of boundaries. The resulting "heteroscape" posed a threat not only to New York's efficiency and economic power but also to its social stability. It made the built environment a theater of class conflict and communal violence that, precisely at its time of triumph, brought New York to the verge of catastrophe.

Boundaries and Boundarilessness

For Victorian New Yorkers, the interconnection between spatial and social disorder was self-evident; they invoked it constantly in accounts of the Manhattan landscape. Journalists and illustrators, for instance, portrayed the corner of Broadway and Fulton—ground zero of Manhattan gridlock—as a "Babel scene" of social disruption: the streets full of swearing teamsters and careening omnibuses, the sidewalks clogged with tourists, hawkers, businessmen, beggars, and—sole point of order in a mad world—a uniformed policeman guiding a lady through the maelstrom (Figure 4.6). For all the Brueghelian humor of such scenes, they expressed an alarming message about the civic costs of environmental disorder. "Not the least of the bad results of the shortsightedness of our ancestors in making narrow streets is found in the fact that it has produced an exceeding demoralization," the *Real Estate Record* lamented. "The golden rule has been utterly abolished by your representative New York driver." *Harper's Weekly* similarly portrayed public transit as a threat to public virtue. After a gruesome wave of streetcar crime, the journal published an engraving of a genteel mother and daughter pausing fearfully before "a car crowded with murderers and thieves." On the front bumper were blazoned words from Dante: "ALL HOPE ABANDON YE WHO ENTER HERE" (Figure 4.7).[25]

Invocations of the Sermon on the Mount or the *Inferno* may seem overwrought in accounts of traffic jams or horse car rides. Yet bourgeois New Yorkers believed that spatial disorder eroded the moral and social boundaries on which civilization depended. Two complementary scenes of disorder provoked special concern. First of all, the city's public landscape—most notably the downtown streetscape—seemed a boundariless space of corrosive self-seeking. "Commerce requires a character of

FIGURE 4.6   This magazine illustration offers a satirical account of a police officer guiding a genteel lady through the maelstrom of Broadway, warding off importunate street children, unruly horses, aggressive teamsters, and other threats to her decorum and respectability. (*Harper's Weekly*, August 27, 1859; image courtesy of HarpWeek, LLC)

FIGURE 4.7   Like Figure 4.6, this illustration dramatizes the social risks of spatial disorder, but in a more melodramatic register. Here the Manhattan horse car is a Dantesque scene of moral, class, and sexual danger, a threat to the civilizing order embodied by the mother and daughter in public. (*Harper's Weekly*, May 20, 1871; image courtesy of HarpWeek, LLC)

streets and traffic" whose congestion and hurry socialized citizens "to regard others in a hard if not always hardening way," Frederick Law Olmsted cautioned in *Public Parks and the Enlargement of Towns*. "This involves . . . a calculation of their strength and weakness, which is not so much for their benefit as our own." Given New York's deepening class inequality and ethnoreligious heterogeneity, such atomism and antagonism threatened to explode into violence; an otherwise light sketch of Broadway warned with deadly seriousness: "Walk down this thronged avenue on a holiday, when the Irish crowd the sidewalks . . . , and all you have read or dreamed of savagery will gleam . . . from those myriads of sullen or daredevil eyes. . . . The materials of riot in the heart of the vast and populous city then strike one with terror. . . ." Here was a public sphere where civility might dissolve in an instant, leaving only competition, disguise, and open struggle.[26]

At the same time, bourgeois New Yorkers feared the teeming districts into which the "materials of riot" disappeared each night. Not until the 1890s did the world of working-class Manhattan come to seem picturesque to genteel flaneurs. Earlier observers portrayed it rather as a moral antipodes whose mean streets, vile groggeries, and crowded slums promoted wretchedness, violence, and vice (Figure 4.8). It was the tenement that most keenly provoked the outrage, anxiety, and distaste characteristic of Victorian jeremiads. "The elements of popular discord are gathered in those wretchedly-constructed tenant-houses," one journalist wrote in 1863. "Here disease in its most loathsome forms propagates itself. Unholy passions rule in the domestic circle. Everything, within and without, tends to physical and moral degradation."[27] The working-class landscape represented a sort of antimetropolis, an inversion of civilized ideals of public and domestic virtue.

Genteel representations of spatial disorder thus projected a complex map of class disorder. They portrayed New York as simultaneously fluid and divided, a place whose "nether side" was too distant for supervision but too close for comfort. "It is strange," a *Times* reporter commented, "how widely the two halves [of the city] may be separated by social barriers, and how near together they may be at the same time in their local habitations." This combination of boundaries and boundarilessness evoked sharp anxiety among urbanists, journalists, and reformers. They feared the presence of "a vast, explosive, dangerous mass of poor and ignorant human beings," withdrawn from the oversight of its betters, but (as a result) capable of overrunning the common institutions and spaces of New York. For Charles Loring Brace, founder of the Children's Aid Society, the mix of physical proximity with social and moral distance represented a standing threat to civic order. "Let . . . the civilizing influences of American life fail to reach them," Brace warned in *The Dangerous Classes of New York*, "and . . . we should see an explosion from this class which might leave the city in ashes and blood."[28]

This mental map was shaped by twenty-five years of civil disorder. The city streets had seen crowd violence throughout the nineteenth century, but from the Astor Place riot of 1849 to the Orange Day and Tompkins Square battles of the early 1870s, New York was especially rife with it. Both the frequency and the geography

FIGURE 4.8   This January 1871 engraving from *Harper's Weekly*
depicts a horrific inversion of one of New York's most important
genteel rituals, the New Year's Day visit. A drunken man stumbles
into a cellar tenement of unprotected women, one of whom sleeps
on a straw mat on the floor. Middle-class observers often represented working-class New York as a moral otherworld: a subterranean place where domestic order, sexual virtue, privacy, and respectability were undermined. (*Harper's Weekly*, January 7, 1871; image
courtesy of HarpWeek, LLC)

of these outbreaks provoked concern. On one hand, they made clear to genteel New
Yorkers the vulnerability of their property, social enclaves, and public institutions:
the Astor Place violence besieged the city's "best" theater, and elite mansions, stores,
and newspapers were torched in the 1863 draft riot (Figure 4.9). On the other hand,
riots seemed to erupt from behind the barriers of an occluded, class-riven cityscape.
"The high brick blocks and closely-packed houses where the mobs originated
seemed to be literally *hives of sickness and vice*," one journalist wrote in 1863. "It was
. . . difficult to believe that so much misery, disease, and wretchedness can be huddled together and hidden by high walls, unvisited and unthought of, so near our
own abode . . ."[29]

The draft riot was the signal event in translating this geography of working-class
violence into a cartography of bourgeois fear. For four days, roving crowds brought

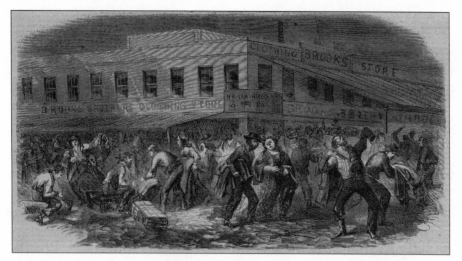

FIGURE 4.9   On August 1, 1863, *Harper's Weekly* published eyewitness sketches of the New York draft riot, which had taken place only two weeks earlier. The illustrations portrayed class targets such as the Brooks Brothers clothing store; racial targets such as the Colored Orphans Asylum (Figure 4.10); and other buildings associated with the war effort, the federal government, and the Republican Party. (*Harper's Weekly*, August 1, 1863; image courtesy of HarpWeek, LLC)

FIGURE 4.10   Episodes like the destruction of the Colored Orphans Asylum during the draft riots conveyed the sense of an immediate and widespread threat to civilization itself, ready to erupt across the New York cityscape. (*Harper's Weekly*, August 1, 1863; image courtesy of HarpWeek, LLC)

not only federal conscription but the whole city to a halt, engaging in mass strikes, armory raids, arson against bourgeois Unionists, sabotage against telegraph and transit lines, lynching of African Americans, and open warfare with the police and militia (Figure 4.10). The riot offered propertied New Yorkers a nightmare vision of insurrectionary violence, obscure and subterranean in its origins, but contagious and ubiquitous in its effects. "Who will ever forget the marvelous rapidity," Charles Loring Brace wrote nine years later, "with which the better streets were filled with a ruffianly and desperate multitude" that "crept [from] its burrows and dens to join in the plunder of the city?"[30]

It was a lesson that Brace's peers learned repeatedly over the next decade. In 1866, cholera outbreaks turned the image of social contagion into epidemiological fact. As disease threatened to spread from tenement to townhouse, George Templeton Strong traced its course with the familiar tropes of distance and contiguity, borders drawn and breached: "Cholera multiplies. Cases are confined as yet to our disgraceful tenement houses and foul side streets," Strong noted darkly. "We are letting [the poor] perish and . . . they will prove their . . . common humanity by killing us with the same disease." Sometimes the contagion was industrial: eight-hour strikes spread through the building trades and other sectors in 1868 and 1872, bringing as many as a hundred thousand journeymen off the job. At other times, it was ethnocultural: in 1870 and 1871, Irish Catholics set upon Ulstermen celebrating the historic "Orange" victory at Boyne. The cumulative effect of such crises was to make the discourse of boundaries and boundarilessness into a commonplace of urban commentary. "We have warned the public so much of the perilous material which underlies the surface of society in New-York, that the subject becomes almost monotonous," the *Times* wrote in July 1871, after the second Orangemen riot and the concurrent exposure of Tweed's courthouse frauds. "And yet every fresh event . . . should remind our citizens that we are in this City over the crust of a volcano. . . . There is in every large city, and especially in this, a powerful 'dangerous class' who care nothing for our liberty or civilization, . . . who burrow at the roots of society, and only come forth . . . in times of disturbance, to plunder and prey . . ."[31]

We are in this City over the crust of a volcano: for bourgeois New Yorkers, class conflict was like a geological catastrophe, a subterranean cataclysm that could—with horrific speed and without warning—erupt out of nowhere and spread havoc everywhere. It is a mystification, of course, to give social disorder the form and force of natural disaster. Yet the imagery of cataclysm or contagion does convey something accurate and important about violence in the Victorian metropolis: it tacitly points back to the city-building process, to the dynamics of New York's development. For the midcentury boom *did* produce a landscape that was at once bounded and boundariless, highly differentiated but explosive and unstable in its growth. As we saw in the last chapter, the geography of class was particularly contradictory; land and labor markets worked to segregate propertied and plebeian New Yorkers *and* to throw them into unexpected contact with one another. That interplay of separation and contiguity was most marked in upper Manhattan; and it was there, significantly, that much of the new violence took place. Where earlier disturbances like the antiabolition or bread riots of the 1830s usually occurred in the lower working-class wards, the midcentury boom shifted the locus of disorder uptown. Thus, the draft riot began with mass walkouts from factories and construction sites on Eighth and Ninth avenues, an indignation meeting in Central Park, and raids on draft offices at Third Avenue and Forty-seventh Street and Broadway and Twenty-ninth Street. The first Orange Day riot occurred on West Ninetieth Street, where Irish Catholic bands attacked a picnic ground full of Protestants; the second one broke out when Orangemen marched through a "green" tenement district on upper Eighth Avenue.[32]

The geography of riot thus mirrored the patterns of settlement, sociability, and wage work produced by the midcentury boom. Violence tended to begin on the border avenues that divided upper Manhattan into class corridors. "The rioters . . . are in full possession of the western and eastern sides of the city, from Tenth Street upward, and of a good many districts besides," George Templeton Strong reported in his Gramercy Park study during the draft insurrection. "I could not walk four blocks eastward from this house without peril." Equally interesting, civil violence tended to involve workers who were engaged in *building* the new uptown landscape. As Iver Bernstein has shown, antidraft crowds were disproportionately filled with construction artisans and street laborers. Bricklayers, carpenters, and woodworkers led the strike waves of 1868 and 1872, and the 1870 Orange Day riot was begun by a crew of road workers on upper Broadway (Figure 4.11). Moreover construction labor was not only a primary scene, but often a key *aim* of popular mobilization: during the panic of 1857, crowds gathered in the new Central Park to demand "Bread or Work" from Superintendent Olmsted. Similar calls for public-works employment were answered with a police riot in Tompkins Square during the depression winter of 1874.[33]

Such close links between city-building and civil disorder should not surprise us. Construction sites and public improvements were visible scenes of communal labor from which the collective assertion of grievances could readily spill into the streets. Workers at such sites, employed in one of the most profitable sectors of an inflationary economy, were well poised to recognize the unequal benefits of the midcentury boom and their own strategic power within it. Especially uptown, they worked in, and on, a built environment where wealth, volatility, and social antagonism came together in an astonishingly compressed space. If lower Manhattan made palpable the economic and technical disorders of New York's growth, then the new uptown landscape underscored its social frictions. Conflict in the built environment—and over the terms of its making—represented a growing cost of imperium.

The New Urbanism

The midcentury boom transformed Manhattan in paradoxical ways, both stimulating the development process and stalemating it. The boom imposed demands on construction and land use that encouraged the consolidation of land, building, money,

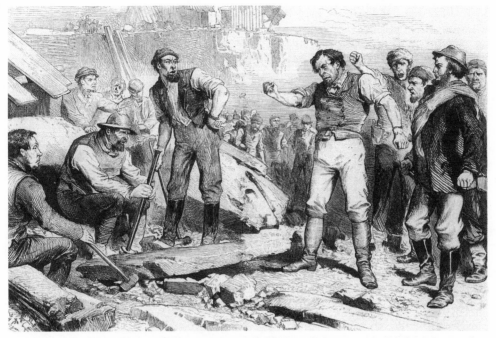

FIGURE 4.11   This engraving from *Frank Leslie's Illustrated Newspaper*, published during the eight-hour strike movement of 1872, dramatizes the links between class conflict, spatial change, and city building in New York. Here, striking workers, probably from the building trades, angrily call street laborers off a public works job site in upper Manhattan. Street work, especially on the uptown frontier of development, was a recurrent scene of class confrontation. (*Frank Leslie's Illustrated Newspaper*, June 8, 1872; negative no. 74690; © Collection of the New-York Historical Society)

and location markets; but it also enhanced the vested privileges of property ownership, rewarding "free riders" and predatory land users. It amassed a massive fund for improving the built environment, but magnified the costs and difficulties of improvement. It subjected city building to a market regime that promoted both the fixing and effacing of sociospatial boundaries; as a result, those boundaries became sites of class conflict and communal violence.

In this and the preceding chapters, I have sketched the results of this uneven development on the ground: a mixed landscape of dynamism and inertia, grandeur and dilapidation, boundaries and boundarilessness. Victorian New York juxtaposed monuments of commercial growth, civic refinement, and technological progress with ragged spaces of inefficiency, decay, overuse, and underdevelopment, sometimes in close proximity to each other. The city's environmental and social disorders—traffic jams, rotting piers, riotous streets—represented more than just residua in a bumpy road toward greatness. They were the fruits of that greatness. Even as the midcentury boom seemed to confirm New York's imperial stature, it subjected the cityscape to two linked crises.

The first was economic. As we have seen, New York came to play a dominant role in national capitalist consolidation during the mid-nineteenth century. The metropolitan real-estate economy was particularly important to the American "social structure of accumulation," as economists David Gordon, Richard Edwards, and Michael Reich put it. Capitalist production, these authors argue, requires a "stable and favorable external environment," without which it "take[s] place either in a vacuum or in chaos." Their analysis stresses the role of political-legal regimes, institutions of social discipline, and appropriate moral norms in ensuring capitalist stability. But the story of Victorian New York suggests that the built environment is equally salient to the social structure of accumulation. Especially during the midcentury boom, when the city's population, territory, and national power were all enlarging, city building offered a key means of organizing and catalyzing economic growth.[34]

At the same time, growth insinuated its own irrationalities into the city-building process. As Gordon, Edwards, and Reich argue, the social structure of accumulation tends dialectically to break down, generating disorders that it is unable to manage; new institutional and ideological arrangements are needed to restabilize market and class relations. Something like this breakdown began to take place in New York during the 1860s and 1870s. The boom reinforced the disorders of improvement, rewarding the "sweating" of land, dysfunctional land use, and the use of public space for the pursuit of private interests or class grievances. As a result, the city streets grew more deadlocked, chaotic, and unruly; the port devolved into a shambles of congestion and disarray; and market mechanisms that were meant to order the city-building process became stalemated. Especially along the margins of Manhattan Island, the spatial structure of accumulation undermined itself, becoming too rigid and too makeshift to regulate land values, capital flows, commerce, and class relations.[35]

These frictions implied a second type of crisis: an ideological and moral crisis for those who viewed the landscape as a prophetic text. As bourgeois New Yorkers understood, spatial disorder threatened the city's prospects as the metropolis of a far-flung empire of commerce and civilization. "When we look at the city of New-York," proclaimed the Citizens' Association in an appeal for port improvements, "a whole country tributary to its power, a whole nation concerned in its welfare, the centre of science, art, and wealth . . . —when we . . . see how [nature's] laws . . . are striving to raise it . . . to a pinnacle of commercial imperium grandeur and glory, and when we then turn and contemplate what little has been done by art . . . to improve the commercial advantages which nature affords, we cannot but stand amazed . . ." The congestion and squalor of the working-class environment was even more troubling to bourgeois observers. "Tenement life has destroyed . . . the safeguards which a genuine home erects around a people," Edward Crapsey warned in his widely read expose *The Nether Side of New York*. "It must brutalize its victims, and leave vice and ignorance as the foundation stones of the municipality." For George Templeton Strong, such evils threatened not only civic virtue but the very legitimacy of New York's existence: "It is shameful that men, women, and children should be permitted to live in such holes as thousands of them occupy this night in the city," he mused during the cholera outbreak. "The epidemic is God's judgment on the poor for neglecting His sanitary laws. It will soon appear as His judgment on the rich for tolerating that neglect. . . . And the judgment will be not on the owners of tenements houses alone, but on the whole community."[36]

Uneven development, in short, challenged the most cherished material and moral ambitions of the metropolitan bourgeoisie. They responded by reimagining how New York should look and how they should build and rule it. Beginning with the formation of Central Park in the mid-1850s, a diverse array of city-building elites—landowners and merchants, politicians and administrators, genteel intellectuals and reformers, journalists and design professionals—pursued a novel effort to plan the new cityscape, coordinate its growth, and regulate its disorders. Their initiatives were by no means all of a piece. Merchants like those in the Citizens' Association called for systematic improvement of the docks and commercial district. Editors discussed the "scientific method of laying out thoroughfares" and debated the merits of enlarging or extending various downtown arteries to relieve Broadway. Reports on paving experiments proliferated in the engineering, real-estate, and popular press. Boosters and trade journalists offered proposals for modernizing New York's freight and terminal facilities. Rapid transit advocates floated plans for elevated, viaduct, underground, arcade, and circumferential railroads. Sanitarians and public officials raised the cry for the environmental regulation of property development through tenement, health, fire, and building codes. Most important, a coalition of reformers, property owners, politicians, and publicists sought to transform upper Manhattan—and the metropolitan periphery as a whole—into a utopian terrain of parks, promenades, tutelary institutions, and planned suburban districts.[37]

Many of these ideas had been broached before the Civil War era. Yet never had real-estate boosters, commercial interests, building and design experts, journalists, officials, and reform intellectuals devoted such wide-ranging attention to the shaping of the urban landscape. Out of a congeries of reform tracts, agitational pamphlets, bureaucratic reports, and editorial columns, a relatively programmatic urbanism took shape: a call for unified metropolitan development guided by centralized institutions. "The work is one, and can be managed most efficiently if treated as a unit," the New York *Times* argued in support of the Citizens' Association plan for port improvement. "NO PIECEMEAL IMPROVEMENT WANTED," agreed the *Real Estate Record* in an 1870 editorial on street extensions. "What is wanted is one, general, comprehensive plan for . . . the thoroughfares of the whole city."[38]

Implicit in the new urbanism was a consciousness of space and city building quite different from the habitus of the real-estate economy. Although bourgeois city builders understood that capitalist development would remain the engine of New York's transformation, they did not view the cityscape simply as an atomized grid of locational commodities. The integrative effects of growth taught them to "construct" the cityscape—conceptually as well as physically—as a distinct, unified artifact, a totality defined by its interdependence and metropolitan scale. It is telling that *Harper's Weekly* published in 1871 perhaps the first attempt to represent what would come to

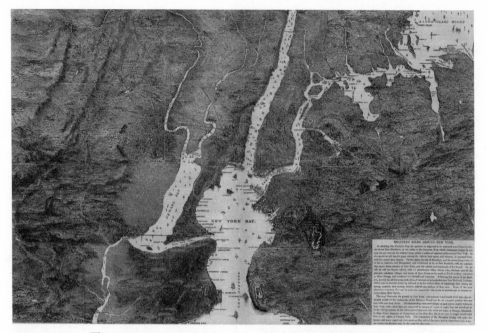

FIGURE 4.12   This sumptuous engraving, issued by *Harper's Weekly*, offers perhaps the ultimate booster fantasy of New York's growth: an impossibly high bird's-eye view of a vast, unified metropolitan area. (*Harper's Weekly*, May 6, 1871 [Supplement]; image courtesy of HarpWeek, LLC)

be Greater New York: a fantastical bird's-eye view that showed the "territorial extent of the metropolis of the Western World" reaching to "the surrounding cities and villages on each side" for "eighteen miles around" (Figure 4.12) Among boosters and city officials, this sense of an emerging metropolitan totality led to the first calls for the unification of Manhattan, Brooklyn, and the environs: "Westchester is demanding ways to transmit her population to the city; [Staten Island,] by her ferries and railways, is exerting herself in the same direction," park commissioner Andrew Haswell Green argued in 1868. "All progress points toward eventual consolidation and unity of administration" among "communities that are striving by all material means . . . to become one . . ."[39]

The *dis*integrative effects of growth tempered this totalizing sense of space, but did not undermine it. They underscored that the metropolis remained an unfinished project, one that required the interposition of administrative will. Officials must "act on broad and comprehensive ideas" in laying out streets, parks, and infrastructures, William Martin told the West Side Association, instead of "attempting city improvements upon an inadequate plan" as they had long done.[40] Ironically, then, spatial disorder taught city builders to view the New York landscape as their collective product. It compelled them to move beyond the rule of real estate into a *politics* of space. It made them ask, *Can a City Be Planned?*

As the next chapters will argue, New York's urbanists answered this question with a twofold effort of imaginative and institutional creation. They elaborated a sophisticated discourse of metropolitan portraiture, composing an ideal "map" of the Empire City out of booster fantasies, reform surveys, editorial polemics, aesthetic sketches, and bird's-eye views. At the same time, they founded a set of institutions that concentrated power over the city-building process in unprecedented ways and launched ambitious plans for New York's growth. These institutions included elite voluntary associations and new governmental agencies that contended for political control of the city-building process during the 1860s and 1870s. The complex rivalries and alliances among these institutions made New York an important laboratory for state-building initiatives in nineteenth-century America. They also produced a novel program of landscape design, environmental regulation, and planned growth, one that did much to inscribe the imperial ideal on the metropolitan landscape.

CHAPTER 5

Imagining the Imperial Metropolis

New York is a theater of progress. . . . Its plot is: barbarism giving way to refinement.

—Rem Koolhaas, *Delirious New York* (1978)

Imagined Prospects

One Wednesday evening in January 1871, many of New York's leading landowners and developers braved the cold to convene at West Side Hall, above Ford's New Market, in Longacre (now Times) Square. The gathering was one of a monthly series of indignation meetings organized by the West Side Association to agitate for uptown improvements. The assemblage heard addresses by President William Martin and others on the need for mortgage tax relief, the renaming of the avenues west of Central Park, and, most important, rapid transit to open upper Manhattan to development. The concluding speaker, real-estate lawyer Simeon Church, pressed the transit question with particular urgency, taking the unusual position that the city should build and run its own steam railway up the west side of Manhattan. Church carefully laid out the demographic and fiscal projections that justified a publicly owned line. Then, shifting his register from budgets to boosterism, he summoned all the firepower that the rhetoric of empire, nation, and civilization had to offer: "Not merely as lot owners and tax payers . . . do we demand this improvement. We are true citizens of New York. . . . With pride we see her reach her iron arms across the Continent . . . and send her commercial flag unto every Sea and Ocean. Still greater is the pride with which we contemplate in the future her rocky heights and waste places filled with palaces, and monuments dedicated to Art and Science, . . . her commerce enriching, and her civilization blessing every Nation."[1]

By now, I hope, the banality of Church's language is clear. It was common for Manhattan urbanists to portray the cityscape as an expression of New York's imperial prospects. "The beauty of our modern metropolitan architecture," wrote John Kennion in an 1868 guide, provides "evidenc[e] not alone [of] our past and present progress, but the unerring index as well, of our city's future greatness." Such views informed debates over New York's growth; even the most practical proposals came wrapped in the mantle of destiny. "The first city of the Western Hemisphere, wielding the commerce of the continent, should wear an imperial front to the whole world," the *Real Estate Record* argued in support of the consolidation of Brooklyn and Manhattan. It was utterly conventional for Simeon Church to end his call for rapid transit by casting himself and his audience as the stewards of New York's commerce, civilization, and greatness.[2]

Church understood that building the Empire City was first of all a work of imagination. He and his interlocutors drew on a complex set of assumptions about what a great metropolis should look like, a design ideal with which they measured the New York cityscape and sought to improve it. Their efforts were saturated with ideology; debates over transit, parks, and tenements represented a displaced conversation about history, civility, and legitimate authority in New York. My aim in this chapter is to elucidate that conversation, to unpack the assumptions with which urbanists imagined the metropolis.

Several general notions about the linkages among landscape, culture, and power informed the discourse of city building. Most fundamental was the peculiarly Victorian conviction that some scholars have called *moral environmentalism*: the belief that natural and built environments exert a profound influence over the ideals and inward capacities of those who experience or inhabit them. "You might almost write out the creeds, the probity, the sentimentality, of any community," one magazine essayist commented, "by only going through the streets and inspecting the habitations." Calvert Vaux agreed, arguing in an 1857 pattern book that "architectur[e] . . . can not help being a friend or enemy to the improvement of civilized beings all the days of their lives." This belief in the spiritual efficacy of landscape and design was grounded in English theories of moral psychology and environmental determinism; it informed a wide array of cultural, reform, and aesthetic practices in Britain and the United States, from rural tourism to arts education to suburban design and wilderness preservation.[3] American intellectuals and social critics brought it to bear especially on the urban environment. "Our country has entered upon a stage of progress in which its welfare is to depend on the convenience, safety, order, and economy of life in its great cities," Frederick Law Olmsted mused. "It cannot . . . gain in virtue, wisdom, comfort, except as they also advance." Even as most Americans remained in smaller towns and rural settlements, Victorian intellectuals believed that drama of cultural legitimation had shifted scenes. It was in urban space that American civilization would be forged and tested.[4]

As the nation's economic and cultural center, New York was subjected to the most intense scrutiny. Representations of Manhattan's life and landscape flooded the cultural marketplace during the midcentury boom. Genteel monthlies like *Harper's*, *Putnam's*, the *Atlantic*, and the *Galaxy* published essays on the city's growth, sketches of its streets, views of its architectural monuments, and serial portraits of its "nether side."[5] Lithographers issued images of Broadway, Central Park, Brooklyn Bridge, and other landmarks.[6] Trade journalists and booster pamphleteers reported on the heady progress of New York's commercial growth and construction boom; intellectual journals like *The Nation* and reform tracts like Brace's *Dangerous Classes of New York* detailed its sanitary, housing, and social crises. A new literature of middle-class exposé laid bare the "sunshine and shadow" of New York life, offering the respectable public a prurient but sanitized tour of "the great metropolis."[7]

The results of this scrutiny were complex and ambivalent. On one hand, journalists, artists, reformers, city builders, and tastemakers elaborated their vision of what New York should look like. They imagined a metropolis that projected the values of bourgeois civilization—virtue, enterprise, refinement—across the cityscape. Much of New York seemed to embody this ideal, and observers celebrated the landscape for its progressive energies and civilizing influences: "We see . . . the improved tastes of our people everywhere," *Leslie's Illustrated Weekly* declared with satisfaction. "Who will deny that New York, with its magnificent harbor, its vast warehouses, its palatial dwellings, its parks and its drives, may yet become the grandest city on the face of the globe?" On the other hand, it was clear that the city's uneven development put the lie to such claims: "Notwithstanding New York has been proudly termed 'The Metropolis of the World,' it is painfully evident to the most casual observer, that she is not finished," wrote the city's superintendent of buildings at the height of the postwar development frenzy. "Her narrow streets, frightful tenements, and filthy markets yet remain in vivid contrast to her Broadway, 5th avenue and Central Park."[8]

A belief in moral environmentalism; obsessive attention to the New York scene; an imperial landscape ideal tempered by conflicted accounts of the actual environment—these habits of mind shaped the discourse of city building in New York. They made the consequences of urban growth seem both fateful and uncertain to Victorian observers. "There is not a structure erected in this huge metropolis . . . that but adds its quantum to the good or bad impression to be indelibly stamped upon the public mind," the New York *World* warned. "Every one who builds is unwittingly enhancing or deteriorating the public taste." Metropolitan space was not only an index but an instrument of moral and civic progress—and not only for New York, but for the nation as a whole. Thus, even the most technical city-building issue was fraught with significance. "Elevated" railroads and "central" parks were props in a world-historical drama.[9]

Simeon Church understood all this. After dilating about New York's greatness to his listeners, Church brought his prophecy to bear on more immediate concerns: how a city-owned steam railway would propel uptown development. New York's extraordinary prospects were being stifled by Manhattan's backwardness, he lamented; only rapid transit could free up the energies of growth, could unfetter History itself. "Great abroad, [the city] struggles now for breath at home," Church concluded.

"Break these gyves that bind her. Give New York a chance to grow, and she will achieve her own destiny, and become, not merely the Queen City of the Continent, but THE IMPERIAL METROPOLIS OF THE WORLD."[10]

But what did "The Imperial Metropolis of the World" look like?

The Bridge Between Capital and Culture

In answering this question, Victorian urbanists began with a twofold ideal: they believed that New York should foster capitalist energy and civilizational order. On one hand, they sought to create a landscape that would embody the city's economic dynamism and dominance: "New York cannot stand still," proclaimed the *Real Estate Record* in an 1873 plea for dock improvements, "it must go forward in the work of improvement. To remain stationary is to retrograde. The commerce of this continent is to be transacted here, and we must prepare the city for its imperial destiny." On the other, they viewed the environment as a means of educating taste, inculcating virtue, and refining public sociability. "To teach and induce habits of orderly, tranquil, contemplative, or social amusement . . . has been the most needed 'mission' for New York," the Reverend Henry Bellows wrote in the *Atlantic Monthly*. "[Central] Park accomplishes not a little in this way."[11]

"Commerce" and "culture," then, were the twin foundations of the metropolitan landscape ideal, as they were of New York's rise to power. The task of projecting them in space informed every aspect of city building, from park design to tenement reform to property speculation and architectural style. We can begin to trace their influence by looking at perhaps the most celebrated structure in the new metropolitan landscape: Brooklyn Bridge. Aesthetically, structurally, and functionally, the bridge represented a précis of the dualisms of the imperial ideal.

Begun in 1867 and completed in 1883, the East River bridge linked the first and third largest cities of the nation; its scale and technical sophistication were unprecedented in the history of engineering. Thus, it was vested with massive significance by its builders and the public: "[It] will not only be the greatest Bridge in existence," designer John Roebling assured potential investors, "but . . . the great engineering work of this continent, and of the age." From the start, the design, promotion, and reception of the structure were shaped by notions about New York's dominion and destiny. Roebling's prospectus rang all the changes of booster discourse to justify the expense and daring of the project:

> New York will . . . become the great commercial emporium, not of this continent only, but of the world. . . . This is no futile speculation, but the natural and legitimate result of natural causes. As the great flow of civilization has ever been from the East towards the West, with the same certainty will the greatest commercial emporium be located on this continent, which links the East to the West, and whose mission it is in the history of mankind to blend the most ancient civilization with the most modern.

Roebling moves effortlessly here between the roles of booster prophet and practical builder, promoting the bridge as an instrument and symbol of New York's "mission . . . in the history of mankind." In part his pitch is nakedly instrumental: New York must "accommodate the vastness of travel" that would attend its growth as a world capital. In part, he sells the work as an imperial icon, a monument to New York's place in "the great flow of civilization." In linking the two shores of the East River, the bridge would embody the confluence of East and West, modernity and tradition, that New York was destined to oversee.[12]

Roebling encoded these themes in the shape of the thing itself. The famed dualism of his design, combining steel cables and masonry towers, made the bridge very much a "blend [of] the most ancient civilization with the modern" (Figure 5.1). Since the 1880s, critics have faulted Roebling's work for this aesthetic heterogeneity, attacking the neo-Gothic towers in particular as a surrender of functionalist "honesty" to historicist ornament. Yet if we view Brooklyn Bridge as an artifact of Victorian design ideals, it *was* an organic unity; it conjoined the elements that formed the basis of New York's metropolitan stature. Most obviously, it joined Manhattan and Brooklyn; contemporaries viewed the bridge as a prefiguration of the "incorporation of these two cities into one grand municipality." More subtly it embodied a spatiotemporal synthesis that linked East and West, past and present. "The old and the new are to meet on this continent," Roebling told his board of directors, "and this will be effected through the means of commerce." The bridge was meant as a microcosm, in short, of booster notions about world geography and the westering flow of history. As a sign in a shopwindow on opening day made clear, Roebling was not the only one who thought this way: "Babylon had her hanging garden, Egypt her pyramid, Athens her Acropolis, Rome her Athenaeum; so Brooklyn has her Bridge."[13]

Moreover the bridge's aesthetic dualism can be read as a commentary on the ideological binaries that defined a great metropolis for Victorian Americans: most of all, the opposition between energy and order, market dynamism and moral discipline. The symbolic work of the bridge was to mediate these values, to synthesize their competing claims in monumental form. On one hand, the explosion of cables and stays, held in tension by the invisible hand of modern engineering, signified the concatenation of private interests that would enable New York to become "the great commercial emporium . . . of the world." On the other hand, the great Gothic towers, with their noninstrumental arches, stood for the grounding role of what Roebling and other Victorians meant by "culture": a canon of public standards and legacies that would anchor the commercial life, channel its lines of force, and clothe it in forms that made it recognizable, legitimate, civilized. The monumentality of Brooklyn Bridge came not only from its physical massiveness but also from the symbolic virtuosity with which these tensions were handled and resolved. It is for this reason that criticisms of Roebling's towers are beside the point. The bridge represented New York as a heterogeneous unity of capital and culture: a concretization of the imperial ideal.

FIGURE 5.1   John Roebling's design for the East River bridge used a series of oppositions—between steel and masonry, monumental architecture and avant-garde engineering—to present the bridge as a synthesis of modernity and tradition, European civilization and American destiny. In the process it also recast New York as a synthesis of opposites, uniting Manhattan and Brooklyn into a metropolis that bridged commerce and culture. (*Harper's Weekly*, May 26, 1883; image courtesy of HarpWeek, LLC)

The same mediation of different modes of value is evident in the ways that Brooklyn Bridge was meant to be used. As a roadway, the bridge was both an "economic" and a "cultural" infrastructure, "private" and "public" property. Roebling designed it first and foremost to service commercial and commuter traffic—and, as the property of a franchised corporation, to profit its investors as well as its users. "To the American business man time is money," he wrote, urging his backers to finance a shuttle railway across the bridge. "He will not hesitate to pay . . . five cents for one mile of steam travel, when he can traverse this distance . . . inside of five minutes." At the same time, the design went beyond mere utility: between and above the traffic roads, an "elevated promenade" was added "to allow people of leisure, and old and young invalids, to . . . enjoy the beautiful views and the pure air" (Figure 5.2). Even here, in the "elevated" realm of urbane sociability and healthful recreation, market values were never far away: Roebling estimated that toll "receipts of the Bridge Company from this source" would make "such a promenade . . . of incalculable value." The bridge served the claims of both public culture and private interest; it defined New York as a place where both claims, both modes of circulation, could be grandly accommodated.[14]

FIGURE 5.2   Like the New York cityscape as a whole, Brooklyn Bridge was designed to unify material and moral values. As a thoroughfare, it serviced commercial and commuting traffic; as a promenade, it supported health and refinement.
(*Harper's Weekly*, May 26, 1883; image courtesy of HarpWeek, LLC)

A similar play of contraries characterized its effect on land use in the metropolitan
area. Observers understood that, by facilitating commuter traffic across the East
River, the bridge would encourage the functional differentiation of Manhattan and
Brooklyn. In downtown New York, the result would be a more intensive and specialized commercial landscape, higher ground rents, and residential displacement.
"With the building of the bridge across the East River," the *Real Estate Record* reported, "New York Island is becoming more and more a great wholesale merchandise
and financial centre, and less relatively a place of residence." Across the river, the
bridge would foster suburban growth and Brooklyn's evolution from an industrial
port to a middle-class City of Homes—a place "set apart and guarded by nature," as
Olmsted and Vaux told the Brooklyn park board, "for the tranquil habitation of those
[for] whom the business of the world requires . . . convenient access [to] the waters of
the New York harbor." Quite literally, the bridge separated the metropolis into realms
of "commerce" and "culture," and reintegrated them in a common landscape.[15]

In function and style, then, Brooklyn Bridge lived a double life. It was at once a
business artery and genteel promenade, a civic landmark and commercial investment, a timeless monument and modern infrastructure. That dualism was what
made it such an apt icon of New York's imperial stature: "As a great work of art, and
as a successful specimen of advanced Bridge engineering," Roebling claimed, "this
structure will forever testify to the energy, enterprise and wealth of that community,

which shall secure its erection."[16] Just as the bridge bound Manhattan and Brooklyn together in a single metropolitan landscape, so it mediated the divergent values that those regions symbolized. With its gateways, vistas, and gigantic scale, it transformed an apparatus of urban mobility into an allegory of metropolitan grandeur.

Eros and Civilization

What Roebling built in stone and steel, other New Yorkers elaborated in print and speech. Bourgeois urbanists portrayed the city as a center of economic power and moral influence—"her commerce enriching, and her civilization blessing every Nation," as Simeon Church had put it. As they debated New York's development, they envisioned a landscape that embodied both modes of power.

First of all, Victorian commentators celebrated New York's dynamism and growth. Essays, illustrations, and oratory from the mid-nineteenth century portray a city charged with a sublime, intoxicating energy. "[To] look down the swarming length of Broadway, on the movement and the numbers, while the Niagara roar swelled and swelled from those human rapids, was always like strong new wine to me," Basil March exclaims in *Their Wedding Journey*. "I don't think the world affords such another sight. . . ." This restlessness seemed inscribed in the city-building process itself. Real-estate boosters, journalists, and officials reveled in the calculi of growth, documenting New York's gains in population, land values, and building rates in table after table. Such growth curves served as a kind of analogy to the soaring cables of Brooklyn Bridge, a "statistical sublime" that traced the arc of New York's ascendance. "Since the organization of the science of statistics, no city in the world has ever multiplied its population, wealth, and internal resources . . . with a [similar] rapidity," an essayist in the *Atlantic Monthly* wrote. "The advance by New York in less than a century toward the position of the world's metropolis is a more important one than has been gained by London [since] the time of Julius Caesar . . ."[17]

Statistical tables and street vignettes represented more than simply evidentiary reports. They were a kind of capitalist erotica, aimed at exciting urban growth as much as recording it. They portrayed New York from the standpoint of futurity, a vantage from which the declaration *we are growing* and the desire *we must grow* were indistinguishable. City builders thus invoked New York's dynamism partly to incite the policies that would make it come true. "New York must expand not only to Westchester, not only to Brooklyn, but all around," the *Real Estate Record* argued in tones reminiscent of the exponents of Manifest Destiny. "The Jersey shore of the Hudson will be ours in due course of time. . . . The march of improvement must go on, and whoever doubts this mistakes the mission of the great American metropolis." Municipal expansionism did in fact win the day. New York annexed southern Westchester in 1874, and a few years later, the elevated railway opened uptown land to development. One guidebook, describing the new el, conveys the sense of imperial command that Victorian observers associated with such expansion: "It is as if the lower part of the city were the palm of a great hand with gigantic iron fingers stretched out to grasp West-chester County."[18]

The erotics of growth was tempered by a second discourse, equally central to the Victorian landscape ideal: the discourse of *civilization*. Here was one of the god terms of nineteenth-century culture—and one of the most protean in meaning. When New York's urbanists used it, they tended to refer to the project of refining, disciplining, and legitimizing the energies unleashed by the city's economic ascendance. "A city takes the rank in the world of a metropolis," Frederick Law Olmsted argued, by attending to "the higher results of human labor" rather than "purely money-making occupations"; its landscape should be "rich . . . in libraries, churches, clubs, and hotels" and "adapted to serve . . . not [only] ordinary commerce . . . but humanity, religion, art, and scholarship." To many New Yorkers, the work of Olmsted himself seemed a benchmark of this uplifting ideal; Henry Bellows praised Central Park for "exercising a good influence upon the character of the people" that made "rude, noisy fellows . . . become hushed, moderate, and careful."[19]

The idea that urban space should serve as a civilizing agency formed part of a larger social ideal throughout the capitalist world in the latter half of the nineteenth century. For the cosmopolitan bourgeoisie who rose to preeminence during this era, the discourse of *civilization* and its antitypes, *barbarism* and *savagery*, carried enormous ideological weight. They used it to differentiate themselves from the proletarian and colonial masses; to manage social and moral fractures within their own class world; and to define a set of tutelary and reform projects that asserted their claim to political and cultural stewardship.[20]

Among these was the project of city building. From the political upheavals of the late 1840s to the business crisis of the mid-1870s, governmental, economic, and cultural elites in Europe and the Americas sought to inscribe "civilization" on the fabric of great cities. Rulers like Napoleon III and Franz Joseph of Austria undertook massive campaigns of reconstruction, laying out landscapes that enforced new modes of social and state discipline and dramatized the legitimacy of their regimes. Haussmann's rebuilding of central Paris (1852–70) and the creation of the Viennese Ringstrasse (1857–73) were the boldest of these interventions; but large stretches of Berlin, Budapest, London, Buenos Aires, and other metropolitan centers were also transformed. These initiatives were by no means identical in their design program, their physical effects, or the political conditions that animated them. Yet they codified what might be called the Bourgeois International Style, a neobaroque urbanism of broad avenues, palatial architecture, grand public squares, scenic pleasure grounds, and massive infrastructures. The aesthetic markers of the style—monumental scale, lavish adornment, theatricalized public space, refined opulence—informed the spatial imagination of urban elites in the United States as well as elsewhere.[21]

New York's development boom coincided precisely with this global *mission civilisatrice*. The Bourgeois International Style offered New Yorkers a lexicon of forms and a heroic past against which to measure their own prospects and present achievements. "The history both of Paris and London teaches . . . how splendid [the city] may be made," William Martin argued. "There is no reason, save our own indifference, why the future New York, so soon to surpass them in population, should be in any respect inferior." New York's urbanists did not all turn to the same models, however, or draw the same lessons from them. For some, the essence of a civilized metropolis was its capacity for splendor and spectacle, values particularly identified with French architectural design and the Parisian cityscape. New York was becoming "as luxurious as Paris," architect A. B. Mullett told an interviewer, "noted for [its] magnificent and spacious edifices." Realtor V. K. Stevenson agreed, boasting that "the *Bois de Boulogne* is nothing compared with [Riverside] Park."[22] Others stressed the use of the urban landscape to inculcate morality and taste, an ideal drawn from British associationist psychology and landscape aesthetics and associated with English park and scenic design. It was in the pleasure grounds and promenades of New York's periphery that urbanists were most apt to claim this project of tutelary influence: "[Central Park] will stand for ages before the civilized world as a noble organ of education," wrote the developer Samuel Ruggles, "advancing the general culture and refinement . . . [of] the common metropolitan capital of the Western Continent."[23]

Two key discourses thus grounded elite conceptions of metropolitan space: a capitalist erotics that stressed New York's dynamism and growth and a civilizational vision of its splendor and elevating influence. These discourses were both descriptive and prescriptive; they offered imaginative resources for depicting the urban environment *and* directing its transformation. The claims and aspirations that they expressed were often in tension with each other. The discourse of dynamism stressed the power of market values and the glory of futurity; that of civilization underscored the authority of moral values and the grandeur of the past. And different urbanists, of course, foregrounded different aspects of the imperial ideal. The loudest ideologues of growth and splendor tended to be development boosters whose interests were often linked with Democratic politics and uptown land speculation. Advocates of moral "influence" were often intellectuals, reformers, and journalists from New York's patrician-Republican subculture, for whom land values and moral values seemed often in conflict.[24]

Yet it would be wrong to overdraw the divide between "booster" and "genteel" versions of the imperial ideal. Whatever their differences in emphasis, most urbanists conceived of "commerce" and "civilization" as interdependent values. Even the most hardheaded landowner understood that "the development of art . . . is one of the chief stimulants of progress," as the *Real Estate Record* put it. "To give cities a rapid and at the same time a healthful growth they must be made beautiful." Conversely, even the most high-minded reformer took pains to calculate the benefits of "civilizing design" to local markets. "The cost of forming [Central] Park . . . has been great," Olmsted noted in 1870, but it was "more than compensated by the additional capital drawn to the city through [its] influence." Bourgeois urbanists did not view market values and moral values as identical, merely as inseparable. They sought to create a landscape that, like Brooklyn Bridge, accommodated both sets of values on the ground.[25]

The accommodation took place, first of all, through the medium of design, the structure and style of built forms. This was especially true of the city's transportation infrastructures: with their stylistic eclecticism and their synthesis of architecture and engineering, they provided apt occasions to express and symbolically resolve the antinomies of the imperial ideal. Steamship lines erected cast-iron palazzi for passenger terminals; Grand Central Depot joined a functionalist train shed to a neobaroque station house (see Figures 2.7 and 2.10).[26] Yet the most interesting case of the integration of "commerce" and "civilization" was the elevated railroad. Built in the mid-1870s, the el was an amalgam of virtuoso engineering, romantic architecture, and urbane interior decoration—each design element embodying a different form of space and value in the imperial metropolis.

To begin with, the roadway trestle was a feat of structural design. Contemporary views accentuated its height and sublimity; especially at Coenties Slip and Central Park, where the tracks turned dramatically, the el seemed a tableau of technical prowess and heroic modernization: "It curves around the upper end of the Park . . . at an almost dazzling elevation," the *Real Estate Record* gushed, "present[ing] a picture . . . such as our illustrated journals ought to have placed before all of their readers long ago" (Figure 5.3). Perched on the tracks were the stations, "tasteful cottages" in the manner of Swiss chalets—all steep roofs, angles, and tracery—from which "a light and graceful iron pavilion roof" extended along the platform. The domestic associations of these structures offered a visual counterpoint to the rigidities of the railway and the street grid underneath: they evoked the *morally* elevated realm of home life to which the el supposedly whisked its riders away. At the same time, the cars that those riders entered conveyed another, more cosmopolitan message. Designed "after the style of the Pullman palace cars," they offered a workaday version of the fantasy of luxury and adventure associated with high-class travel. Plush seats, sumptuous appointments, and plate-glass windows elicited a sense of voyeuristic freedom that observers like William Dean Howells described as the el's contribution to New York's public culture. Rapid transit, these cars implied, enlarged not only the city's territory but also its capacity for refinement and urbane spectacle.[27]

The design of public works like Brooklyn Bridge or the elevated railway thus joined together the different claims of metropolitan life. They accommodated these claims in another, more literal way as well: by sorting them into discrete geographic regions of their own. As we have seen, the new infrastructures enabled the development of an expansive, specialized metropolitan area. Within it, all the various elements of the imperial ideal could find their place—or so Victorian urbanists argued. New York's growth had caused a "crystallization of localities" according to "principles of natural affinity and selection," the *Real Estate Record* noted with satisfaction; Manhattan was now segmented into a downtown "appropriated by wholesale business," a domestic uptown of "undisturbed seclusion," and a luxurious shopping district in between. Olmsted similarly confirmed the "constant increasing distinctness"

FIGURE 5.3   Very few images capture as eloquently as this illustration from
E. Zeisloft's *New Metropolis* (1899) the exhilaration and even sublimity with which
the elevated railway—and other New York infrastructures—was associated.
(University of Michigan–Flint Archives)

of New York's business center and residential periphery; the "tendency . . . to separate domestic from commercial life," he concluded, represented one of the "fixed laws of civilized progress."[28]

The segregationist patterns of the midcentury boom, in short, seemed to many urbanists a blueprint for the metropolitan ideal. Of course this mental map of a city neatly divided into downtown commerce and uptown civility effaced a good many realities, particularly the landscape of workshops, tenements, and saloons that ran the length of Manhattan. The laboring majority tended to be consigned to interstitiality: "Interwoven with and around these distinctive localities," the *Real Estate Record* wrote in its sketch of New York's development zones, "in spots and gaps unsuited for the use of any of them, will be built up the tenement house, the inevitable dwellings of the poor . . ." Such marginalization merely underscores how ideologically charged this image of Manhattan was. Geographic differentiation seemed to Victorian urbanists more than just a technical effect of urban growth. It was a "law of civilized progress," the sine qua non of metropolitan greatness. "So far as the plan of New York remains to be formed," Frederick Law Olmsted argued in an 1875 proposal for the laying out of the Annexed District, "it would be inexcusable that it should not be the plan of a Metropolis; adapted to serve, and serve well, every legitimate interest of the wide world. . . . If a house to be used for many different purposes must have many rooms and passages of various dimensions and variously lighted and furnished, not less must such a metropolis be specially adapted at different points to different ends."[29]

The Empire City was thus a place of boundaries, of functional divisions and social distinctions inscribed in space. Not surprisingly: Victorian Americans conceived of civilization itself as a regime of boundaries, sequestering women from men, class from class, virtue from vice, moral values from material interests, (private) home from (public) market, (private) property from (public) politics. Bourgeois urbanists sought to incorporate that geography of "lines" and "spheres" into the spatial fabric of New York. They envisioned the Empire City as a house of many rooms, in Olmsted's striking image, each "specially adapted" to different modes of value and authority.[30] I want to explore three such "rooms," three sites of the imperial ideal, in more detail: the monumental commercial building, the well-ordered public street, and the refined city home. Together these spaces composed a utopian geography, a vision of progressive and virtuous urbanity, that informed the work of Manhattan's city builders.

Second Empire

In the spring of 1872, the Western Union company bought a parcel of land at Broadway and Dey Street, the heart of downtown Manhattan. Razing the existing buildings, the telegraph monopoly put up one of the tallest and most imposing edifices in Victorian New York: a Second Empire pile topped by a steep Mansard roof (Figure 3.8). The "Parisian" style of the ten-and-a-half-story "Telegraph Palace" was ironically apropos, for the seller of the Broadway site was none other than Louis Napoleon himself. Acting through a certain Dr. Evans ("the American dentist at the late court of France," the *Times* reported), the recently deposed emperor had purchased the property only months before, paying less than half a million dollars. Now he turned it around for $840,000—the largest consideration then paid for a building site in the city. Yet to contemporaries, this financial history was less notable than the structure itself: "It is a matter of just pride to our citizens that the erection of substantial and tasteful edifices is multiplying so rapidly," one daily wrote of the Western Union building. "[New York] ought to be a city of business palaces, inviting as well as accommodating the commerce of all the world."[31]

Such comments testify to a shift in the aesthetics of commercial design during the midcentury boom. As downtown Manhattan grew more geographically complex, physically dense, and economically powerful, builders, landowners, and tastemakers sought to endow it with a grandeur that would rival the Paris of Louis Napoleon. They abandoned the republican aesthetic of the older mercantile center, with its horizontal lines and visual restraint. In its place came a turn toward verticality, massiveness, ornament, and the supremacy of building over setting—an aesthetic of hierarchy and spectacle that served as an emblem of New York's imperium. The results generally dazzled Victorian observers. "The quiet and plain business houses" of the antebellum city "are disappearing for . . . edifices of immense size, beautiful in appearance, and rich in design," reported architectural and building experts. "New York in a few years can put in a claim to be called the City of Magnificent Buildings."[32]

As with the city's infrastructures, historicist style was central to this architecture. Lower Manhattan became a potpourri of revivalist extravagance during the midcentury boom, including such monuments as the neoclassical Tweed Courthouse, the Italianate Equitable Life headquarters, and the Second Empire *Herald* building. The results could be quite ludicrous—"Classic pillars and Gothic pinnacles stuck on ad libitum," complained an English visitor—as builders clothed utilitarian structures in a congeries of grandiose gestures. Yet, as architecture critic Paul Goldberger has asserted, this sort of eclectic historicism was typical of New York's brand of civic ambition. It pointed to the multiple pasts to which New Yorkers looked for legitimacy; at the same time, it melded those pasts into an exorbitant celebration of the city's dynamism and destiny. "The beauty of our modern metropolitan architecture is of the old classic period," wrote John Kennion, but "present improvements are the shadows cast before" even "greater wealth and prosperity." Simeon Church agreed, cataloging the downtown "improvements which point to . . . [New York's] rank with the older and prouder cities of Europe." City builders envisioned lower Manhattan as an aesthetic synthesis of (American) capital and (European) culture. The styles of the Old World were to contain—but not *too* successfully—the lavish energy of the New.[33]

Yet one model did have special cachet: that of Second Empire Paris. There Louis Napoleon and Baron Haussmann had set a new standard for the impress of capital, culture, and power on urban space; bourgeois New Yorkers embraced its canon of monumental, urbane, integrative design. "The City Hall Park . . . looks exactly as if a park, a fountain, and half a dozen public buildings had been shaken together in a huge dice-box," the *Real Estate Record* complained. "The city fathers should adopt the idea of forming a 'Louvre' out of the park" and "transform this unsightly place of incongruities into a palatial pile of elegant buildings." No architectural development typified the imperial ideal so clearly as this appropriation of Second Empire style in lower Manhattan. Before the postwar boom, Italianate palazzi like the Harpers Building or Stewart's emporium had represented the crowning statements of New York's commercial supremacy (Figure 5.4). By the early 1870s, these were displaced by Parisian "piles" like the post office, the Staats-Zeitung Building, Lord and Taylor's midtown store, and the Western Union tower.[34]

In part the vogue for the Second Empire represented a response to the changing needs of commercial land users. The Italianate palazzo, with its horizontal line and iterative use of window and wall elements, fit the street-based, smaller-firm economy of the antebellum downtown. It could not accommodate the more intensive land use that postwar growth made necessary and the postwar elevator made possible. Here the massive scale and Mansard roof of the Second Empire palace served admirably.

FIGURE 5.4   Downtown buildings erected during the early part of
the midcentury boom, like the offices of Harper and Brothers in
Franklin Square, invoked the civic associations of Italianate design,
with its horizontal line and street orientation, to express the role of
commerce in a republican community. (*Franklin Square Front*, engraving:
J. N. Allan, Harper & Brothers; Museum of the City of New York; Print
Archives)

FIGURE 5.5   In contrast to antebellum commercial buildings
(*above*), postwar edifices such as
the federal Post Office at City Hall
Park used the verticality, scale,
and opulence of "the Parisian
style" to set themselves apart as
imperial statements. (*Old Post Office*,
stereograph; Museum of the City of
New York; bequest of Dr. Henry A.
Cone)

Thus, it was the vanguard institutions of the new downtown—department stores, commercial hotels, publishers, financial corporations, and the Federal bureaucracy— that did the most to popularize the Parisian aesthetic.

But Second Empire design reflected symbolic as well as functional needs. It signaled New York's transformation from a maritime port to an imperial capital—from Venice to Paris, so to speak—and it emblematized the new modes of authority on which that imperium was based. Second Empire architecture was grounded in an aesthetic of dominance and display; it made the act of viewing into a drama of subordination. The massiveness of the style, its elaborate treatment of roof lines and walls, and its mélange of porches, portals, statuary, and cupolas all worked to make a fetish of the individual edifice, to endow it with visual supremacy over onlooker and setting. "The style . . . give[s] a colossal air to the general proportions of the building," one journalist wrote of the Park Bank, "completely dwarf[ing] everything in [the] immediate neighborhood."[35] This aesthetic helps to explain why so many Second Empire structures went up at focal intersections of the new downtown: the Park Bank at Broadway and Fulton, the Staats-Zeitung Building at the north end of Printing-House Square, the post office at the tip of City Hall Park (Figure 5.5). These edifices recomposed the cityscape around themselves, establishing themselves as landmarks in a geography of prestige. They stood for the hierarchies of capital, information, and merchandising on which New York's dominance depended— for the corporations, bureaucracies, and emporia whose centralizing, supervisory activities they housed.

Downtown design, in short, made a spectacle of capital. Part of what defined a metropolis, after all, was its capacity to theatricalize the forms of its power. In Europe, that power was mainly political and military, and (as Lewis Mumford has brilliantly argued) imperial city building served to legitimize the absolutist state. In New York, the forms of power were primarily commercial, and downtown elites used grand architecture to proclaim a "second empire" of capitalist dominion. "The City of New York—the Eastern Gateway of the American Continent," Mayor Franklin Edson toasted at a Chamber of Commerce banquet, "to its natural advantages are now added the triumph of architecture and the graces of art." Such sentiments help to explain the opulent busyness of the new commercial palaces. Their proliferation of ornament served to celebrate the multiplication of profit; their reappropriation of historical styles stood for the reproduction of wealth. Commercial developers and corporate tenants sought to produce tableaux that could arrest the gaze of the public and turn looking into a form of consent. "At all times," an 1871 guidebook gushed during the building of the Park Bank, "crowds of people pause . . . to stare up at its elaborate and massive marble front, its colossal features, and its columns and pediments. It is likely for a long time to rank as an architectural boast of the metropolis."[36]

Buildings like the Park Bank did *not* long remain "an architectural boast of the metropolis." They came to stand for a sort of nouveau-riche grandiosity that seemed meretricious to later tastemakers. Manhattan's tall buildings were "crowned not only with no history, but with no credible possibility of time for history," Henry James wrote in *The American Scene*, "and consecrated by no uses save the commercial at any cost." From such a viewpoint, the extravagant historicism of the city's nineteenth-century "bonanza buildings" was little more than a cloak thrown over the nakedness of the profit motive. "'Commodity' . . . is as strictly subserved by those towering structures," the great turn-of-the-century architecture critic Montgomery Schuyler wrote of New York's early skyscrapers, "as comity is defied."[37]

Yet Victorian urbanists did not always divide commodity from comity quite so sharply. They celebrated commercial palaces as icons of New York's civic grandeur and historic prospects. "These structures [are] evidence of the wealth, growth and promise of the future magnificence of the city," proclaimed a leading booster. Architecture critic John Kennion agreed, citing the Park Bank and other downtown edifices as "the *avant-courriers* of a future to be marked by bolder views, more stirring enterprise, more audacity of business." Downtown monuments were captivating precisely because they displayed, rather than disguising, the second empire of capital. That is why it made perfect sense for Western Union to build its "Telegraph Palace" as a Parisian *hôtel*. Surmounted by a chateaulike roof, enclosed in a thicket of telegraph poles and a Gorgon's-head of cables, fronted with statues of Franklin and Morse, the building identified itself simultaneously with French civilization, American democracy, and scientific progress. It presented Western Union as the heir and master of History: grounded in a heroic past but overlooking Broadway as if from the future itself.[38]

Disciplining the Streets

Making a spectacle of capital was a key element of the imperial ideal, but it was not sufficient by itself. A great metropolis also submitted its wealth and power to the influences of refinement and virtue. Two settings were especially important to this civilizing ideal: the public realm of street life and the private realm of domestic life. New York urbanists envisioned a cityscape that would separate, discipline, and elevate both.

City streets represented a primary arena of public sociability in nineteenth-century America; New York's streets in particular seemed to embody contradictory prospects for a shared public life. Guidebooks, magazines, lithographs, and exposé narratives portrayed the Manhattan streetscape as a microcosm of the city's dynamism and urbanity—but also its fluidity and disorder. Broadway was the locus classicus for this theme: its "almost endless variety" represented at once "an epitome of the civilized world" and "a very Babel of excitement and confusion." Such kaleidoscopic diversity by all accounts exhilarated genteel observers, but it could seem fearfully disorienting as well. Much of the literature of urban portraiture concerned itself with navigating readers through the tumult of cosmopolitanism that Broadway embodied. "Persons who . . . visit [the] great city," one tour book wrote, "would gladly accept the services of some . . . guide, who could conduct them through its perplexing mazes, pointing out what there is to see, and how to see it."[39]

What there is to see, and how to see it: as such language suggests, street sketches did more than just represent the New York landscape; they made it *capable* of representation for a public that equated visibility with social legibility. Observers composed the streets into a landscape by offering what Walter Benjamin called "a physiognomics of the crowd." "The moving panorama of human life . . . on the Broadway Pave, presents a curious . . . picture to the student of ethnology," an English visitor noted in 1865. "There you may see the lean lanky Puritan from the east, with keen eye and demure aspect, rubbing shoulders with a coloured dandy, whose ebony figures are hooped in gold." An essay in the *Atlantic Monthly* took this classificatory impulse even further, transmuting a Broadway stroll into a veritable gallery of illustrious civic types:

> You behold . . . an eminent representative of each . . . phase of high civilization;—wealth vested in real estate in the person of an Astor; . . . volunteer heroes . . . of the Union war; merchants, whose names are synonymous with beneficence and integrity; artists, whose landscapes have revealed the loveliness of this hemisphere to the Old World; women who lend grace to society and feed the poor; men of science, who alleviate, and of literature, who console, the sorrows of humanity . . . —the redeeming and recuperative elements of civic society.

Portraying the streets thus became a *mission civilisatrice* in itself, an inscription of boundaries and distinctions on a fluid, unregulated field.[40]

These anxieties about representation registered actual disorders in the city streets. Precisely because the streets channeled so much economic and ideological power, they seemed charged with danger to bourgeois New Yorkers. The scale and complexity of urban development intensified this danger: as the metropolis grew more differentiated, its boundaries and integuments were seen as liminal, precarious spaces. Anthropologist Mary Douglas argues that taboos often mark the anomalous elements of a classificatory system; fear and disgust get attached to the borderlands, to the monstrous thing that slips between the categories. For bourgeois urbanists, disorderly streets were just such a place-out-of-place: a promiscuous shambles where all the repressed and unspeakable conditions of metropolitan life might erupt into visibility (Figure 5.6).[41]

Two aspects of street life were especially threatening to genteel visions of a virtuous, decorous public life. First, the streets seemed to enforce a corrosive competitiveness and market individualism. Olmsted portrayed downtown thoroughfares as a sort of Hobbesian theater, habituating city people to the commercial war of all against all: "To merely avoid collision with those we meet . . . , we have constantly to watch, to foresee, and to guard against their movements. . . . Much of the intercourse between men when engaged in the pursuits of commerce has the same tendency. . . . Men who have been brought up, as the saying is, in the streets . . . generally show, along with a remarkable quickness of apprehension, a peculiarly hard sort of selfishness." Like Simmel's classic essay, "The Metropolis and Mental Life," Olmsted stresses the atomistic, alienating effect of street life on modern interiority. Yet down-

FIGURE 5.6   *Harper's Weekly* wryly depicts middle-class anxiety about the eruption of disorder on the city streets. As a policeman smugly guides two fair ladies across Broadway, a crowd of unruly horses harries the gentry behind him. On the margins, a black street boy whips up trouble, causing an elderly shopper to drop her packages. (*Harper's Weekly*, March 12, 1870; image courtesy of HarpWeek, LLC)

town Manhattan was a school for self-seeking in a more literal sense: congestion and land pressure encouraged the "use [of] the public walks, streets, and parks for private advantage" by hucksters, teamsters, shopkeepers, and construction crews. Such appropriation of space was a significant element of the downtown economy, providing storage, sales, parking, and publicity to marginal but functionally necessary entrepreneurs. As we saw in Chapter 4, it was also self-defeating, for it jammed the flow of commodities that constituted the primary function of the downtown streets. Such blockage represented more than just an inefficiency to bourgeois observers; it was a violation of the public-private boundary that ensured property rights and civic order. Remove the "incumbrances in Broadway" and "rescue . . . the public property from the individuals who have seized it," proclaimed the *Times*—no doubt in an edition that newsboys hawked on downtown corners.[42]

Second, the city streets provoked elite anxiety because they were a site of class tension. As I have noted, popular grievances, labor insurgency, and communal violence recurred there throughout the mid-nineteenth century. Even in quiet times, the daily needs of working-class life made the streets a theater of public disorder, according to genteel norms. As Christine Stansell and other scholars have shown, poor women, casual laborers, and vagrant children used the streets for wage work, relief, food, and stolen or scavenged goods. Working-class New Yorkers claimed them for sociability and leisure, often in ways that seemed barbaric to their social betters: "How often you see young men in . . . lounging attitudes rudely obstructing the sidewalks," Olmsted lamented. "There is nothing about them which is adapted to bring into play a spark of admiration, of delicacy, manliness, or tenderness." In hard times, such anxieties grew sharper: "The streets of New York became thronged with [a] ragged, needy crowd," a group of charity reformers reported in the Panic of 1874. "Street-begging, to the point of importunity, became a custom. Ladies were robbed, even on their own doorstop, by these mendicants."[43]

The most disturbing figure of class disorder was the street child. Vagrant boys and girls—newsboys, message runners, bootblacks, peddlers, performers, prostitutes—composed an essential "informal sector" of the downtown economy, and thousands roamed the streets of Victorian Manhattan in quest of shelter and subsistence. They had long been lightning rods of class anxiety in New York, but during the midcentury boom, they entered the mainstream of urban portraiture through popular melodrama, the best-sellers of Horatio Alger, the engravings of *Harper's* and other weeklies, and the growing fame of Charles Loring Brace's Children's Aid Society (Figures 5.7 and 5.8). At once demonic and sentimentalized, "these wild and untutored young Arabs" served as emblems of the "demoralization" that characterized life on the unregulated streets. "The immense number of boys and girls floating and drifting about our streets, with hardly any assignable home or occupation," Brace wrote in his celebrated 1872 memoir, *The Dangerous Classes of New York*, "continually swell . . . the multitude of criminals, prostitutes, and vagrants."[44]

Bourgeois New Yorkers thus feared that street life eroded civic and moral order. On one hand, it displaced "private" pursuits like trade, labor, sexuality, and subsistence from the workplace, storeroom, and home, milieus where they could be supervised and infused with the virtues of honesty, thrift, hard work, and self-mastery. On the other hand, it transformed the streets into a boundariless realm where "public" meant anonymous and undisciplined, and all manner of deceits and debasements became possible. The cautionary tales of exposé narratives, reform tracts, and children's stories spelled out the consequences of such a devolution. They depicted a city where market relations degenerated into confidence games; where work was pursued as a desultory means of earning idle time; where the public presence of women signified sexual vice; where the presence of private property induced thievery; where personal independence took the debased form of vagrancy. When street life went undisciplined, all the touchstones of bourgeois morality were threatened.

Not surprisingly, journalists, reformers, and public administrators engaged in a broad campaign during the 1860s and 1870s to rid the city streets of predatory trade, casualized labor, sexually independent women, and vagrant children. The daily press called for the removal of "street obstructions," "incumbrances," and "all other forms of the abuse by which private persons obtain public property for their own use." Officials undertook campaigns against sidewalk peddlers, unlicensed carters, and other street entrepreneurs: "Thanks in part to an effective police, the nuisance of

FIGURE 5.7   Victorian culture was deeply ambivalent toward figures of social marginality or suffering. That ambivalence was especially acute in por-
trayals of children on the street. Middle-class artists, writers, and social observers sometimes demonized "street Arabs" as brutish creatures outside
the civilized order of things (compare Figure 5.8). (*Harper's Weekly*, August 12,
1871; image courtesy of HarpWeek, LLC)

street eating-centers are not often found on Broadway," *Harper's Weekly* reported in
1868. Genteel intellectuals like E. L. Godkin agitated for the suppression of public
soup kitchens and "outdoor relief" and the enforcement of antitramp ordinances.
Moral reformers and exposé writers like Edward Crapsey, George Warren, and Anthony Comstock raised the cry against commercialized vice and public sexuality.
Charles Loring Brace's Children's Aid Society sought to resettle street boys on upstate and western farms, and to place vagrant girls in industrial schools and domestic service.[45]

   These efforts to order and purify the streets had uneven success. Although they
yielded some important accomplishments—the passage of state compulsory-educa-
tion laws "to put some decisive check on youthful vagrancy," for instance, and the
growth of preventive organizations like Comstock's Society for the Suppression of
Vice—New York remained as full of peddlers, prostitutes, newsboys, and tramps in
the 1880s as in the 1860s.[46] What makes the campaign relevant here is the ideal of
space and civic order that informed it. It envisioned a metropolis whose streets were
the scene of a capacious, disciplined public sphere. Culturally such a sphere would
be a *civil* realm of refined endeavor and decorous sociability. Politically it would be a
civic realm of disinterested duty, free of the blandishments of self-seeking. Spatially it
would be purged of "Babel-like" disorder, social and sexual promiscuity, and "private" market pursuits. Well-ordered streets, in short, would embody the authority of
genteel culture and suppress more populist uses of public space.

FIGURE 5.8   Unlike Figure 5.7, in "The Hearthstone of the Poor," street children are seen as sentimental embodiments of naked, virtuous humanity; their similarity to the middle-class public in everything but material comfort is meant to prick the viewer's conscience. (*Harper's Weekly*, February 12, 1876; image courtesy of HarpWeek, LLC)

More specifically, disciplining the streets meant the creation of two quite different landscapes of movement, roughly corresponding to the "uptown" and "downtown" ideals of metropolitan space. On one hand, the city's commercial arteries had to be free of obstacles to frictionless circulation. "The law of the street is motion, not rest," park commissioner Andrew Haswell Green argued in 1866. Business interests attacked sidewalk nuisances in the same language: "The merchant now finds himself unable to get his goods through the streets," warned one trade journal. "The universal cry down-town is for 'more elbow-room.'"[47] On the other, city builders imagined a second type of "ideal street," usually on the metropolitan perimeter, where movement served the needs of civilized sociability (Figure 5.9). "The present street arrangements," Olmsted and Vaux advised the Brooklyn park board, "require . . . a series of ways designed [for] the pleasure . . . [of] walking, riding, and the driving of carriages; for rest, recreation, refreshment, and social intercourse." As I have argued elsewhere, such processional spaces were key settings of respectable publicness in Victorian America, enabling bourgeois men and women to constitute themselves as

FIGURE 5.9   Riverside Drive was designed to embody the ideals of a virtuous and refined public life. Its free but decorous sociability and expansive vistas of the Hudson River were to be an antidote to the commercial and class disorders of the downtown streets. (*Frank Leslie's Illustrated Newspaper*, June 19, 1880; negative no. 74691; © Collection of the New-York Historical Society)

the guardians and guides of civilization. As such, promenades were essential features of a great metropolis: "[Broadway] is not merely a means of communication between Wall Street street and the up-town squares," Charles Astor Bristed argued. "It is a place to lounge in, . . . a show street. And such streets are of . . . indispensable advantage to a city. It can scarcely be a city without some of them." Promenades transformed movement from an instrumental to a transcendental act, from a means of commodity exchange to a ritual of community purification; they staged a literal rite of passage into a public sphere of free but self-disciplined sociability.[48]

Bourgeois New Yorkers thus envisioned a streetscape that would balance dynamism and refinement. It would retain the energy and kaleidoscopic diversity of Manhattan's actual street life, but purge it of its predatory individualism and barbarous class disorders. Like the imagined city of urban sketches, it would recompose the streets into a tableau of civilization.

Urbane Domesticity

"Decent, wholesome, tidy dwellings for people who are struggling to maintain an honorable independence are more to be desired in a city than great churches, convents, or colleges," wrote Frederick Law Olmsted and civil engineer J.J.R. Croes in an

1876 plan for the Annexed District. "They are sadly wanting in New York, and why?" Like most Victorian Americans, urbanists such as Olmsted and Croes took it for granted that virtuous domesticity was the touchstone of a stable, legitimate social order. As a (female) scene of private influence, the home provided a moralizing, refining intimacy, set apart from the scrutiny of strangers; as a (male) scene of proprietorship, it offered a manly autonomy, set apart from the competition of rivals. Such domesticity was especially needed in great cities. Precisely because they withdrew families from the heterogeneity and commercialism of urban life, city homes established the ground on which a decorous, virtuous public sphere might be secured. "It has been truly said that the home is the last analysis of the state," journalist Edward Crapsey wrote in *The Nether Side of New York*. "The civic virtues decay in a community where . . . people have no home in the true meaning of the word."[49]

Unfortunately New York seemed to be just such a homeless community. "Family privacy, which is the foundation of public morality and intelligence, is within reach of but a small fraction of the [city's] population," Crapsey feared. "It requires at least $5,000 per annum for . . . even a small family to live in the metropolis with the domesticity necessary to the successful propagation of the home virtues." The development boom, far from provisioning Manhattan with "the home virtues," had made matters worse. It increased the cost and congestion of housing, driving middle-class families off Manhattan, encouraging extravagance and display among the wealthy households that remained, and consigning the working-class masses to tenement life. The result, decried critics, was a landscape of demoralizing luxury and debasing need. Metropolitan growth eroded the domesticity on which metropolitan greatness depended. Thus, city homes, like the city streets, had to be recomposed.[50]

As bourgeois New Yorkers debated what "decent, wholesome, tidy dwellings" should look like, they drew on and revised widely held beliefs about home life and household design. Indeed, New York's preeminence in American literary culture and genteel reform meant that some of the most influential voices of Victorian domestic ideology—among them, Harriet Beecher Stowe, Andrew Jackson Downing, and Downing's protégés Vaux, Olmsted, Charles Wyllys Elliott, and Clarence Cook—lived in, designed, or commented on city homes. They and other urbanists elaborated a metropolitan variant of the domestic ideal, with its own distinctive aesthetic and moral values.[51]

The metropolitan ideal shared several key assumptions with other versions of Victorian domesticity. It stressed, for instance, the need for seclusion from the hurlyburly of public life. "Privacy is . . . one of the luxuries of civilization," E. L. Godkin wrote. "One of the greatest attractions of the dwellings of the rich is the provision they make for the segregation of the occupants. . . . In no ways does poverty make itself more painfully felt by people of refinement or cultivation, than in the loss of seclusion and the social promiscuousness it entails." Architects, builders, and homeowners took such sentiments to heart; townhouse design in upper Manhattan accented the separateness of the genteel home. Calvert Vaux's Fifth Avenue residence for banker and Central Park commissioner John A.C. Gray (1856–57) was typical:

FIGURE 5.10   The exterior face of elite domesticity in Victorian
New York: a perspective view of the Fifth Avenue townhouse that
Calvert Vaux designed for banker (and soon-to-be Central Park
Commissioner) John Gray in 1856. (University Library, University of
Michigan)

stoop, railing, porch, bays, and window accents all reinforced the interiority of domestic life and its withdrawal from the street (Figure 5.10). So did the proliferation of
vestibules, hallways, dark woods, draperies, and fabric coverings for which Victorian
interior design was celebrated.[52]

Indeed, as nineteenth-century tastemakers and modern scholars make clear, the internal ecology of the ideal Victorian home was an elaborate matrix of the "seclusions"
and "segregations" praised by Godkin. Design experts like Downing and Stowe
imagined domestic space as a honeycomb of discrete settings for formal entertaining,
family intimacy, personal conversation, household work, and bodily care.[53] Both the
Gray residence and New York real-estate circulars illustrate the Manhattan townhouse version of this layout: a first floor with parlor, dining room, butler's pantry,
and library; second- and perhaps third-floor bedrooms, baths, and children's areas; a
basement work area with kitchen and laundry; and servants' quarters in the attic.[54]
Such a plan distributed family, acquaintances, servants, and possessions in a complex
array of gender, generational, affectional, and class hierarchies. It provided male- and
female-defined spaces for formal sociability, "withdrawing" rooms for informal and
juvenile recreation, areas for eating, sleeping, and physical care, and a variety of bays,
nooks, and other liminal spaces. The halls and stairways that connected these rooms
were themselves bifurcated into "public" processional spaces and service corridors,

FIGURE 5.11   The interior face of elite domesticity in Victorian New York: a photograph from the 1880s shows the front hall of James Morgan's home in Brooklyn. This image, along with Figure 5.10, underscores the interplay of public display and private withdrawal that defined the bourgeois city home. (*Home of Mr. & Mrs. James Lancaster Morgan, Hall*, photograph: B. J. Smith, circa 1880; Museum of the City of New York, 27.118.42)

marking the class divisions and labor power on which the ideal home depended. Behind the front hall, below the "parlor floor," and above the family apartments lay a backstage realm where "help" produced the perquisites of hospitality and refinement. Wealthy New Yorkers might employ a half dozen or more servants under their roof; even the merely "comfortable" needed at least a cook and maid to maintain themselves.[55]

Like the metropolis that surrounded and opposed it, then, the ideal city residence was "a house with many rooms." Its logic of segregations and boundaries mirrored the discourse of lines and spheres in Victorian domestic orthodoxy. Yet metropolitan canons of domesticity also diverged from that orthodoxy in two significant ways. First of all, unlike the suburban villa that represented the "model home" of Victorian plan books, the city residence was architecturally embedded in a public sphere of elite sociability. Manhattan townhouses were built in clusters and composed into "monumental streetscapes," as Charles Lockwood puts it; contiguous homes were visually unified through the use of string courses and other decorations that announced the collective status and fellowship of the occupants (see Figure 3.11). Interior design also stressed the connection between private domesticity and public sociability. The front hallway and parlor provided the stage for a ceremonial drama of courtesy calls, at homes, and card exchanges governed by complex codes of propriety, recognition, and exclusion (Figure 5.11). Genteel women used these gatekeeping rituals to arbitrate not only the "private" negotiations of courtship and friendship but also inclusion in the respectable public. Only someone with entrée to the parlor could legitimately gain recognition on the promenade or admittance to the social club.[56]

The interpenetration of urban domesticity and elite sociability points to a second difference between the ideal city home and its country cousin. It was meant to be far more sumptuous. Influenced by the triumphalism of booster discourse and the abundance of luxury goods in mid-Manhattan stores, New Yorkers seasoned their version of domestic ideology with more than a dash of splendor and spectacle. Builders' advertising stressed such elegant appointments as "Hardwood Cabinet-work," "handsome Mirror frames," "Bric-a-Brac Shelves," and "Basin Slabs of Statuary Marble"; New York parlors were noted for the opulence of their gilt, plush, lace, mahogany, and marble. "The lavish adornment of metropolitan interiors is a marvel," one guidebook wrote, making explicit the links between luxury consumption, display, and metropolitan domesticity: "Bronzes, pictures, vases, rare and costly furniture, and articles of *vertu* generally, have one of their best markets in New York. Through the plate-glass windows the promenader may occasionally catch a glimpse of the interior elegance. . . . Fashion is here; rank is here; taste is here; wealth is here; supreme elegance is here; social exclusiveness is here; all the virtues are here."[57]

As such language suggests, the splendor of the city home was not thought to be at odds with its civilizing mission. "Nothing denotes more greatly a nation's advancement in civilization," one New York paper wrote, "than . . . the erection of palatial private residences." Harriet Beecher Stowe offered a similar view in her 1871 courtship novel *My Wife and I;* when narrator Harry Henderson meets the adorable Eva Van Arsdel at her father's elegant soiree, the scene connects domestic piety and tasteful acquisitiveness:

> "Now," she said, as the rooms were rapidly filling, "let me show you if I have not been able to read aright some of your tastes. Come in what I call my 'Italy.'" She lifted a *portiere*, and we stepped into a charming little boudoir, furnished in blue satin, whose walls were finished in compartments, in each of which hung a copy of one of Fra Angelico's angels. Over the white marble mantel was a superb copy of "The Paradise." "There," she said, turning to me, with a frank smile, "am I not right?"

Eva's "Italy" prefigures the home that she and Harry will make together: a shrine of privacy and cultivation presided over by angels, replete with a marble altar to the paradise of domestic life. Stowe was mindful, of course, that the splendor glimpsed here was extravagant even for her respectable public. When Harry finally gets the girl—despite his modest income as a city journalist—they settle in St. John's Park, transforming a shabby-genteel house into a temple of unpretentious refinements:

> Dear reader, fancy now a low-studded room, with crimson curtains and carpet, a deep recess filled by a crimson divan with pillows, the lower part of the room taken up by a row of book-shelves. . . . The top of this formed a convenient shelf, on which all our pretty little wedding presents—statuettes, bronzes, and articles of *vertu*—were arranged. A fire-

place . . . exhibits a wood fire, all laid in order to be lighted at the touch of the match. My wife has dressed the house with flowers . . . the arrangements of which . . . I pronounce to be perfect. I have come home from my office an hour earlier to see if she has any commands.

Stowe ends the story by democratizing the ideal of urbane domesticity. Eva's sumptuous boudoir is now a tasteful sitting room, but its aesthetic and moral topography remains the same: a "deep recess" of thick fabrics, dark hues, and well-ordered adornments, in which masculine and feminine arts and powers are separated and blended. It is a middle-class utopia of respectable, affordable splendor.[58]

And yet there is something wrong with this tableau, something that any New Yorker would have recognized as distorted. For one thing, St. John's Park no longer existed when *My Wife and I* was published: it had already devolved into a freight and tenement district. More important, genteel New Yorkers were coming to fear that the domestic idyll described by Harry Henderson was equally nonexistent throughout the city. "The average New Yorker . . . has no expectation of a home," *Tribune* reporter Junius Henri Browne lamented. "The most he dares to hope for is a sojourning place for six months, or a year or two at the furthest. . . . Moving from place to place is his custom and his curse." The emblematic scene of Manhattan's residential life was not Harry Henderson's shrine of virtuous pleasures, but the May Day traffic jam. New York was "a collection of Bedouins," Edward Crapsey worried, "a camping ground rather than a city."[59]

Genteel commentators attributed the lack of metropolitan domesticity to several causes. New York's population growth, narrow shape, distended development, and inadequate public transit "affected rents so disproportionately," Crapsey argued, "that [no]thing less than the revenues of a principality would suffice to keep a roof over a man's head." Others blamed the Manhattan grid for the cost and inadequacy of city housing. "The rigid uniformity of the system of 1807 requires that no building lot shall be more than 100 feet in depth, none less," Olmsted and Croes noted in their 1876 report. "In New York, [such] lots . . . cannot be afforded for small, cheap houses. The ground-rent would be in too large proportion to . . . the betterments." Everything that contributed to the dynamism and complexity of the development boom, in short, also made New York a metropolis of transients. "There is something here for everybody," Browne wrote, "everything, indeed, except a home, with what befits it, independence, freedom, and a fair chance."[60]

The "domesticity crisis" affected different New Yorkers in different ways—all of them troubling to Victorian reformers and cultural arbiters. For the middle classes, it had the effect of an eviction notice, casting many out of Manhattan altogether. "That large class . . . between the rich and the very poor" were fleeing across the rivers, journalists reported, "justify[ing] the painful, dispiriting averment that [New York] is a city of paupers or of millionaires." By 1871, it was estimated, three-fifths of the city's businessmen lived in New Jersey, Long Island, or Westchester. Those who remained confronted high costs and cramped quarters; it was nearly impossible to fit the perquisites of refinement into the dimensions of a Manhattan lot. For all but the wealthiest householder, the minister and reformer Henry W. Bellows complained, a city residence meant "a slice of furnished house, fifteen feet wide, slid into a block, with seven flights between the places where the cook works and sleeps."[61]

In the face of these discontents, otherwise respectable New Yorkers turned to "a life of flaring exposure," as *Harper's Weekly* wrote, at odds with "the retirement of home." Many middle-class families were drawn into "the publicity and indolence of boarding-house life," and the city's wealthy indulged a taste for luxury and fashion that disturbed genteel commentators. "The fever of display has consumed comfort," George W. Curtis wrote in a jeremiad on "The Best Society of New-York." "Every new house is the counterpart of every other, with the exception of more gilt, if the owner can afford it. . . . [Parties are] full of senseless display . . . and all the spacious splendor that a thirty foot front can afford." To such critics, the dramaturgy and consumerism of uptown residential life did not seem an urbane version of "the domestic virtues," but an inversion of them.[62]

It was the laboring classes who suffered most from New York's congestion and transience, and bourgeois New Yorkers expressed horror at the "demoralizing influences" to which tenement life was thought to expose wage-earning families. "Thousands of the industrious poor . . . are wandering about to-day from house to house or floor to floor," the *Commercial and Financial Chronicle* warned, "while their children, for want of A HOME, A REAL HOME . . . , grow up like the nomads of Arabia or the Bohemians of Europe, houseless, shiftless, and scornful of all moral ties and holy attachments." The racialized imagery of rootlessness here should be taken almost literally: just as "A HOME, A REAL HOME" civilized its inhabitants, so its absence was thought to make the working-class city a barbarous and alien world, "devoid of every appliance for health, privacy, or decency." Charles Loring Brace laid bare the sexual devolution to which the indiscriminate mixing of tenement life subjected poor girls: "If a female child be born and brought up in a room of one of these tenement-houses, she loses very early the modesty which is the great shield of purity. . . . Living, sleeping, and doing her work in the same apartment with men and boys of various ages, it is well-nigh impossible for her to retain any feminine reserve, and she passes almost unconsciously the line of purity." Others underscored the corrosive effect of such homelessness on *public* institutions. "The tenement-house . . . [is] the primary cause of whatever is peculiarly disgraceful in New-York City politics," Olmsted told an interviewer, "through the demoralization which it works in the more incapable class of working-people." Like plebeian street life, tenement life erased "the line of purity" that defined the sexual virtue of women and the civic virtue of men.[63]

As New York grew into a metropolis, then, reformers, writers, and city builders codified an urbane vision of domesticity that melded older ideals of virtue and seclusion with a new accent on public sociability and refined consumption. At the same time, they worried that the market demands and class divisions of the midcentury boom undermined New York's capacity to provide well-ordered, affordable homes. Urban growth seemed to have produced middle-class flight, elite withdrawal into a life of fashion and display, and the "demoralization" of the masses. In the wake of the class and civic disorders of the early 1870s—strike waves, riots, Wall Street scandals, Tammany corruption—the effects of this "domesticity crisis" were fearfully evident. "With its middle classes in large part self-exiled, its laboring population being bru- talized in tenements, and its citizens of the highest class indifferent to the common weal," Edward Crapsey worried, "New York [has] drifted from bad to worse, and bec[o]me the prey of professional thieves . . . and political jugglers."[64] The implica- tion for bourgeois urbanists was clear: if New York were to achieve its destiny as a great metropolis, it must create decent, refined, virtuous homes for all its classes.

Melodrama

At the heart of the new urbanism—and bourgeois culture in Victorian America more generally—lay a striking amalgam of confidence and anxiety. Like Charles Dickens's French revolutionaries, bourgeois New Yorkers felt themselves to be living in the best of times and the worst of times. They were poised on the threshold of an epoch of civic achievement and imperial power, the heirs of History itself. Yet they feared that progress had taken them to the edge of a legitimation crisis, a breakdown of moral values and social order inscribed in the very fabric of the Manhattan landscape. "Peo- ple talk of the pride a New Yorker must feel in his great city!" George Templeton Strong wrote bitterly one December night in 1868. "To be a citizen of New York is a disgrace. A domicile on Manhattan Island is a thing to be confessed with apologies and humility. The New Yorker belongs to a community worse governed . . . than any city in Western Christendom, or in the world. . . ."[65] It was in this space between op- timism and disgust that New York's urbanists imagined their ideal landscape and surveyed the actual one.

Their aim was to make New York into a center of capitalist energy and civiliza- tional progress. To that end they envisioned a cityscape that integrated the claims of "commerce" and "culture" in the aesthetics of its built forms and the geography of its social life. Such a built environment would embody bourgeois norms of commercial, civic, and domestic order by projecting them in space. Even as this design ideal as- serted the authority of bourgeois values, however, it also helped to change them. The physical reconstruction of New York provided an important occasion for the reimag- ining of Victorian culture. Older commitments to honesty, austerity, sexual and republican virtue—the touchstones of the antebellum middle class—were inflected with a new stress on hierarchy, refinement, and display. Thus, the business palaces of lower Manhattan dramatized New York's evolution from mercantile port to national money market. The new ideal of the street as a scene of frictionless circulation and decorous sociability marked a turn away from the rowdy heterogeneity of the early- nineteenth-century city. Instead of the "republican forum" of antebellum street life, as Elizabeth Blackmar puts it, bourgeois urbanists envisioned a pacified landscape of well-paved thoroughfares and well-policed sidewalks.[66] The same accent on specta- cle and hierarchy was evident in the canons of urbane domesticity. The city home was still seen as an enclave of male proprietorship, female virtue, and moral uplift. Yet now its "civilizing influences" required elegant commodities, domestic servants, and rituals of class sociability.

These changes in bourgeois culture provoked much concern among city builders and tastemakers. Aesthetic and social critics decried the opulence of Manhattan's commercial and residential architecture as meretricious and debasing. Genteel reformers who preached the gospel of decorous streets and affordable homes were sometimes at odds with developers who called for grand public works and high land values. Yet, for the most part, these debates did not represent incompatible notions of urban space and bourgeois culture so much as diverse strands of a complex discourse. In an 1879 interview on New York's "metropolitan position," for instance, Frederick Law Olmsted moved seamlessly between the claims of civilization and consumerism: "As to the higher results of human labor, in general attractiveness to cultivated minds and as a place of luxury, New-York has probably been gaining of late . . . more rapidly than any other city in the world." Olmsted was right: nearly every setting in the metropolis testified to a shift in bourgeois taste and values. From the East River bridge and the Western Union building to uptown parlors and promenades, established codes of commercial, civic, and domestic virtue were making room for new norms of opulence and refinement.[67]

Yet if the cityscape embodied key aspects of the imperial ideal, it also did much to undermine them. At its best, Manhattan confirmed the aspirations of bourgeois New Yorkers to build, rule, and live in a center of capitalist civilization. At its worst, the city seemed a place where social divisions had grown too strong and moral distinctions too weak. I began this chapter by saying that the new urbanism was first of all a work of imagination; New Yorkers had to envision the Empire City before they could create it. What should be clear by now is that it was a work of Victorian melodrama. Bourgeois urbanists imagined city building as a contest between virtue and vice, refinement and wretchedness, civilization and barbarism. Given New York's economic and cultural power, it was a melodrama played out on a national stage—in magazine sketches and lithographs, reform best-sellers and investment circulars— with consequences of enormous importance. For the denouement of the melodrama was not "merely" imaginary. It involved the making of political institutions, physical spaces, and money. In the 1860s and 1870s, a variety of reformers, officials, property owners, and opinion makers sought to script the sequel: a drama of the cityscape redeemed.

CHAPTER 6

The Politics of
City Building

You may be Nap III in disguise.
—Calvert Vaux to Frederick Law Olmsted, May 22, 1865

The Emperor of New York

Elite New Yorkers' vision of the Empire City included one final idea that was central to the city-building process: a heroic conception of the city builder who would direct it. An imperial metropolis required an imperial urbanist, someone capable of ordering New York's sublime energy and giving form to its destiny as a center of capital and culture. It required an American Haussmann. "The daily experience of New York," an 1868 *Times* editorial argued, "leads to the wish that some Haus[s]mann had presided at [its] planning."[1]

It is not surprising that the figure of Baron Georges Haussmann, the prefect of the Seine under Napoleon III (1851–70), hovered over the wish for a heroic city builder in New York. "Haussmannization"—the unified construction of new boulevards, quays, transit facilities, housing, and public gathering places in Second Empire Paris—represented the most stunning achievement of what I have called the Bourgeois International Style in the mid-nineteenth century. It offered New York city builders an apt measure for their own visions. The work that Haussmann oversaw proved the feasibility of comprehensive urban planning and construction informed by an aesthetic of magnificence and scale; moreover, it effectively linked this city-building program to the agenda of imperial nation building. Haussmann and Napoleon III accomplished much of what New York's urbanists aspired to, and their example was held up as a sort of rhetorical promissory note, attesting to the ambition of metropolitan city builders. Thus, in an 1869 report to the Brooklyn park board, Olmsted and Vaux cited the Avenue de l'Impératrice, the new promenade of fashion in Paris, as a precursor for their own boulevard projects. The *Real Estate Record* donned the prefect's mantle a year later: "There is a good deal of work to be done to make the metropolis what it should be, and we want a Haus[s]mann who will do for New York what that great reconstructor did for Paris."[2]

Yet there was something ambiguous and often uneasy in these appeals to Haussmann as hero. For one thing, the "great reconstructor" tended to show up in the context of elite *anxiety* over the disorders of New York's growth, not in celebrations of its imperial grandeur (Figure 6.1). "If we are to become the noble capital we are always boasting ourselves to be, we *must* have a system of quays and wharves as grand as those of Paris or St. Petersburg," one city trade journal complained. "It surely cannot be that, in this country, democracy will be found wholly unequal to doing what despotism has so splendidly done in Europe."[3] Moreover, as the passage makes clear, worry over New York's environmental discontents was linked to a fear of *political* failure, a fear of the inadequacy of republican institutions. Haussmann's boulevards, plazas, and quays—and similar improvements in St. Petersburg, Vienna, and Berlin —challenged the pretensions of American democracy. They posed the question of whether the Republic lacked the political, economic, and civilizational wherewithal to build a metropolis commensurate with its claims to civic virtue and commercial sublimity. They implied that only autocratic power could build a great city.

Observers of New York were haunted by this prospect. "Liberty [the people] want, and equality, and fair play; but do they . . . desire beautiful buildings and clean streets?" mused *Harper's Monthly* editor George Curtis in an essay on Manhattan's streets. He answered by summoning up a dream figure of benevolent urban rule: "Might not a good-natured despot of fine taste . . . give his dominions nobler public works and a better municipal administration than a republic . . . in which there is easy and indolent indifference to public beauty and public order?" Such rhetoric came close to cultural treason; it put in question the interdependence of civilization and democracy, imperial nationhood and republican citizenship, that was a touchstone of mainstream patriotism in Victorian America. It hinted at an unspeakable political desire, one that New York's city builders sometimes openly indulged: "Despotic governments are generally bad governments," the *Real Estate Record* wrote in 1868, "but when one hears of the marvels Napoleon has accomplished in Paris, in the way of street improvements, it makes us wish that he, or some one like him, could be made Emperor of New York for about ten years. What a superb city we could have if re-planned and re-built aright! In view of the imperial destiny of the metropolis, is it not a shame that its buildings and streets should be left to chance?"[4]

The Emperor of New York—this figure expresses what can only be called a guilty longing for political will. It is all the more striking for showing up in both a booster trade journal with Democratic leanings and a genteel, Republican monthly. Like most utopian fantasies, it manifests a desire to be delivered from the flux of history: in this case, the physical, market, and institutional disorders that plagued the city-building process. Only an imperial urbanist could "re-plan and re-build the city aright," as the *Record* put it, freeing New York from the contradictions that blocked its mastery of

FIGURE 6.1   This diptych of the streets of Paris and New York points to the worry that often underlay comparisons of metropolitan life in Europe and America. (*Harper's Weekly*, April 9, 1881; image courtesy of HarpWeek, LLC)

time and space. "New-York is at an epoch when splendid and grand ideas to fit it for the site of the Metropolis of the country are being carried into execution," William Martin told his fellow West Siders. "A vigorous government is needed to rise above the poverty of plan and execution which has heretofore characterized [its] work."[5]

The Emperor of New York, in short, stood for the notion that new mobilizations of state power were needed to order the cityscape and guide New York into its future. The figure helps to pose three sets of questions about the politics of spatial change, questions that this chapter tries to answer. First of all, what constituencies sought public power over the city-building process? Who tried to claim the mantle of the American Haussmann? Second, what public institutions and coalitions did they create in the pursuit of a politics of planning? What links do we find between city building and state building in the nineteenth-century metropolis? Finally, what ideology of political authority was implicit in the program of bourgeois urbanism? What vision of the legitimate aims and uses of public power—especially elite power in a democratic society—did the imperial planner represent?

This last question was especially crucial to the legitimacy of the new urbanism. As George Curtis and the *Real Estate Record* make clear in the passages just quoted, New Yorkers were deeply ambivalent about the idea of an imperial planner. It raised the specter of a Hobson's choice between democracy and civilization: the possibility that building a great American metropolis might require an enlightened despot. Bourgeois urbanists went to great lengths to allay this concern, to elide the gap between their "imperial" and "republican" impulses. On one hand, they argued, metropolitan growth required new forms of public authority and new concentrations of elite prerogative; on the other, the politics of city building offered a novel means of civilizing the urban masses and incorporating them into a virtuous citizenry. Far from undermining democracy, the imperial urbanist would vindicate it, protecting civic virtue and social decorum in a city where both were at risk.

Best Men, Businessmen, and Boosters

"It would be a wise and timely event, if some ten or twelve of our leading Real Estate owners and public spirited men would examine all the various proposals looking towards the permanent improvement of New York," the *Real Estate Record* told its readers in 1869. Unlike "the present haphazard system," such a "voluntary commission" could "decide upon some general plan which the people at large could be induced to endorse."[6] The editorial offers an important clue to the politics of planning in New York; for the groups that most programmatically sought power over the cityscape correspond roughly to the "Real Estate owners" and "public spirited men" of the proposed commission. The turn to planning was the product of a dialogue between exponents of "civilization" and those of capitalist growth. Three constituencies were especially influential in this dialogue: a cultural gentry of reformers, journalists, and intellectuals, typically patrician and Republican in their affiliations; a downtown elite of merchants and other business leaders, active in reform associations and administrative work, who often mediated between conflicting partisan coalitions; and finally a cadre of real-estate developers, often active in local Democratic politics, but allied with a classwide range of investors and builders. Each of these constituencies had its own institutions, social networks, values, and occupational niches in the city-building process; but each also had important linkages to the others.

First of all, the new urbanism was theorized and publicized by an influential cadre of reformers, professionals, and journalists. Included in this genteel intelligentsia were literati like George W. Curtis of *Harper's Weekly* and *The Nation*'s E. L. Godkin; moral and sanitary reformers such as Charles Loring Brace of the Children's Aid Society and Dr. Elisha Harris of the Citizens' Association; liberal religious leaders like Henry W. Bellows; and design professionals such as Downing, Olmsted, Vaux, and Roebling. Generally middle-class, Anglo-Saxon, and Protestant in origin, and Republican by conviction, these men were bound together in metropolitan and national networks of friendship, profession, reform work, and political agitation. As I discussed in the first chapter, they lived the 1860s and 1870s as a time of vocational crisis and ideological opportunity. Many took part in wartime projects of elite stewardship aimed at fostering a militant, civic-minded nationalism. In the process they invented an array of new vocations, organizations, and cultural media that institutionalized their program of public activism in the service of public uplift.[7]

The "best men" turned from national culture building to local city building out of the same impulse. The growing significance of city life meant that urbanism represented a key front in the genteel campaign for an orderly, virtuous American civilization. "The immense proportions which great cities are assuming," Godkin wrote in *The Nation*, "promise to make the arrangement and management of them the most important of all the problems of social science." New York in particular offered a laboratory for the proper "arrangement and management" of cities, not least because its uneven growth coincided with its emergence as a center of Victorian journalism and reform. Genteel intellectuals participated actively in local voluntary and governmental initiatives; urban-reform projects like Brace's Children's Aid Society or Elisha Harris's sanitary survey of New York tenements, undertaken for the Citizens' Association in 1864, garnered wide publicity in the national press. So did the landscape improvements of Olmsted, Vaux, Roebling, and other design professionals.[8]

Olmsted was without question the most influential member of this city-building gentry. Along with Vaux, he served as landscape architect to the Prospect Park Commission (1865–73), the Central Park Commission (1857–61, 1865–70), and its successor, the municipal Department of Public Parks (1871–78). He codesigned the most novel and ambitious planned landscapes in greater New York: Central Park (1857), Morningside Park (1873), and Riverside Drive (1875) in Manhattan, and Prospect Park (1866) and the Eastern and Ocean parkways (1868) in Brooklyn. As superintendent of Central Park (1857–61, 1875–78), he established himself as the preeminent American authority on park use, maintenance, and policing. Finally, he collaborated on three of the most ambitious ventures in comprehensive planning in mid-nineteenth century America: proposals for the suburban development of outer Brooklyn (undertaken for the Prospect Park Commission in 1868), Staten Island (for a state commission in 1870), and New York's Annexed District (for the city parks department in 1875–77).[9]

Not all of these projects bore fruit; and of course Olmsted and Vaux created parks, parkways, and suburbs in many other North American cities in the same period. Nonetheless, greater New York provided Olmsted with the most important site for articulating and disseminating his theories of planning and design. His idiosyncratic mix of practical competence, intellectual daring, and cranky assertiveness suited him perfectly for the omnibus role of metropolitan adminstrator, national ideologue, and public gadfly. To study his New York design writings in the 1860s and 1870s is to segue from technical discussions of plantations or policing to theoretical asides on city form or social psychology. The result was that in various contexts—published manifestos, personal correspondence, professional reports, and working papers— Olmsted used New York to generalize about the dynamics of urban growth and the aims and methods of landscape design. Not only did the reshaping of the metropolis anchor his career as a founder of American landscape architecture, but it also served as a national showcase for genteel planning thought. Throughout the country, people were coming to accept the need for "systematic prearranged plans" to "provid[e] for the growth of cities," he told the Central Park Commission with satisfaction. "It is not difficult in these movements to perceive the influence of works executed . . . in this city."[10]

Such ambitions would have been stillborn, however, without another group of more practical city builders. These were "bourgeois urbanists" in a more strictly economic sense, driven to the politics of planning by a commitment to managing the real-estate economy or the city's commercial growth. They included trade journalists like C. W. Sweet, editor of the *Real Estate Record and Builders' Guide*, real-estate developers such as Samuel Ruggles or William Martin, reform-minded businessmen like the leadership of the Citizens' Association, and capitalist administrators like Andrew Haswell Green and James Stranahan of the New York and Brooklyn park commissions. The social and political milieu of these "practical men" differed subtly from that of the cultural gentry. They tended to be financially rather than professionally invested in the city-building process, either in real-estate or infrastructural development, and so were typically well connected to Democratic Party circles. Even wealthy Republicans like Stranahan and Ruggles inhabited a local world of coalition building and deal making alien to the "best men." Wall Street businessmen had their own national networks, of course, but their lives were less cosmopolitan and itinerant than those of genteel professionals and intellectuals: where Olmsted migrated from Staten Island to Manhattan to Washington to the California mining country and back to New York during the midcentury boom, Andrew Green moved from the New York school board to the park board to the comptroller's office, while serving for most of the period as law partner to Democratic politico Samuel Tilden. It was precisely this settled base of power that enabled boosters and businessmen to translate the ideological ambitions of the new urbanism into concrete schemes of development.

The "practical men" fell into two types, each with distinctive roles and interests. The first could be called *civic-minded capitalists*: men whose investments or fiduciary responsibilities propelled them into the leadership of reform organizations, cultural or charitable institutions, and public commissions. Their activism often took the form of voluntary associations: indeed the class-based civic or reform club, intervening in public affairs from a "disinterested" vantage point in civil society, represents their distinctive contribution to nineteenth-century urban politics. The most important example of this elite voluntarism in Victorian New York was the Citizens' Association. Formed after the 1863 draft riots, the association comprised conservative men of property with diverse party affiliations and economic interests; its leaders ranged from anti-Tammany Democrats like glue maker Peter Cooper and attorney Charles O'Conor to patrician Republicans like merchant William Dodge and rentier Robert Roosevelt. In the 1860s the association was not only the leading reform group in New York, but one of the most powerful forces in city politics. Like its "goo-goo" successors, it sought to counteract Democratic machine politics through charter revision, fiscal retrenchment, and efficient administration. Yet it also melded this agenda with calls for strong municipal government and the active improvement of the urban landscape.[11]

Indeed the association's most effective work centered on New York's environmental disorders. In the summer of 1864 it undertook a pathbreaking survey of the city's tenement districts. Prepared by a "Council of Hygiene" under the leadership of Dr. Elisha Harris, the *Report . . . upon the Sanitary Condition of the City* made a powerful case for housing and health regulation, and it led to the passage of pioneering health and building codes. At the same time, the association lobbied for improvement of the New York waterfront. Using all the classic tactics of elite voluntarism—pamphleteering, control of public hearings, special access to editorial columns, and alliances with business organizations—it agitated for an independent harbor commission with "entire and exclusive control . . . of the wharves and piers." Tammany boss William Tweed blocked the harbor bill in Albany. Yet he drew on the association's proposal in the home-rule charter of 1870, placing the waterfront under the aegis of a centralized Department of Docks headed by a board of merchants.[12]

Such official power was of course the point. Civic businessmen dominated city-building agencies like the dock board or Central Park commission, often playing the role of institution builders. Brooklynite James Stranahan illustrates the linkages between commercial leadership, civic influence, and new forms of administrative power. Stranahan was a principal investor in his city's leading infrastructural companies (the Atlantic Docks, Union Ferry, and Brooklyn City Railroad), a director of the East River bridge company and the public board that replaced it, a trustee of Brooklyn's Academy of Music and Historical Society, and the guiding force of the Prospect Park Commission in its first two decades of existence (1859–82). As historian David Hammack argues, such a vita was typical of the men who oversaw planning initiatives in many Gilded Age cities. They moved fluidly between public boards and private enterprise, formal and informal networks of influence, seeking to integrate local interests and resources into stable growth coalitions. Urbanism offered them "the best way to reconcile the conflicting interests of competing property-owners with one another," as Hammack puts it, "and with the interest of the public-at-large."[13]

Thus, civic capitalists intervened in the politics of city building quite differently from the "best men." When one of the cultural gentry held official power, it was typically as an appointed expert, subordinate to a board of merchant-administrators, but free of their entanglements. Genteel professionals had to balance multiple clients and projects, but they remained ideologically (and often geographically) distant from each. Civic business leaders, however, held power by moderating conflict and building alliances in an urban class world that was at once intensely solidary and intensely factionalized. They were skilled at brokering deals and coalitions among the "wealth and intelligence" of both parties. Perhaps as a result, their vision of planning stressed the integration of interests rather than the elevation of manners. Where genteel professionals tended to view the new urbanism as a dialogue between culture and politics, a means of inscribing civilizational order, civic businessmen saw it as a dialogue between private interests and public needs, a means of imposing economic rationality.

And yet it is striking how wide-ranging and culturally ambitious this model of capitalist coordination could be. Nowhere is this clearer than in the career of Andrew Haswell Green, the leading candidate for "American Haussmann" among these businessmen. Like Olmsted, Green hailed from the old-stock elite of a small New England city (Worcester, Massachusetts); unlike him, Green came to city building by way of the Manhattan business district. In the 1850s he had risen from a wholesale clerk to a Wall Street attorney and politico, serving as head of the New York school board. A reform Democrat opposed to the machine politics of Mayor Fernando Wood, Green was appointed to the Central Park Commission by Albany Republicans after the GOP electoral sweep of 1856. Building an interparty bloc with the Republican majority, he served variously as the board's president, treasurer, and comptroller—and by all accounts, its guiding spirit—until its reorganization in 1870. "Nowhere else in this or any country have such rigid economy, such scrupulous integrity, so fine a taste, and so disciplined an organization been devoted to the public service as in the Central Park," the *World* wrote in 1868. "In this career, by universal consent, [Mr. Green] has no compeer . . ."[14]

The paper captures something of Green's contradictions. On one hand, he was possessed of an obsessive commitment to economy and honesty, qualities reinforced by his work in corporate and estate law. Green's stinginess and humorless probity were legendary in city politics: even before serving as a penny-pinching city comptroller in the wake of the Tweed scandals (1871–74), he drove park employees—most notably Olmsted—to distraction with his parsimony. On the other hand, Green melded this fiduciary ethic with an activist vision of planned growth. Unlike his partner and mentor Tilden, who repudiated mercantilist models of state action in favor of laissez-faire governance, Green had a "Whiggish" faith in the exercise of public power on behalf of New York's physical and civic improvement. "Reform," he argued in 1872, "meant good schools, clean streets . . . , proper facilities for rapid transit, beautiful parks for the recreation and health of all classes of citizens, adequate accommodation for commerce along our docks, and everything, in fine, to render our city worthy of its career as the metropolis of the western world."[15] Such views demanded a strong, unified agenda of municipal administration and city building. Hence Green was an early supporter of the annexation of Westchester and Brooklyn, a leader of the five-borough consolidation movement, and a moving spirit behind the Metropolitan Museum of Art and the American Museum of Natural History. Most important here, he sought persistently (some said voraciously) to extend the power of the Central Park Commission over the development of upper Manhattan as a whole. He conceived the commission as a protoplanning agency, charged with the comprehensive design of the metropolitan periphery, and his reports ranged freely from uptown street plans to Harlem River bridge connections to the use of the park for scientific study and education.[16]

Green was not the only claimant to the mantle of capitalist planner, however. Besides administrators like him or Stranahan—and often at odds with them—there was a group of more entrepreneurial city builders whose backgrounds were in real estate:

developers like Samuel Ruggles, boosters like the *Real Estate Record*, landowners like the West Side Association. For this group, the new urbanism offered a means of saving New York from the contradictions of its booming growth. They did not turn to planning as an extension of centralized power in the real-estate economy. To the contrary: as I have argued, New York's land, location, and building markets were highly fragmented, and real-estate elites created a set of institutions aimed at consolidating them. These fostered a surprisingly open attitude toward public design and government regulation of the urban environment. Alongside its weekly lists of conveyances, mortgages, and building costs, the *Real Estate Record* published detailed discussions of transit franchises, street improvements, park planning, tenement codes, and the creation of administrative agencies capable of guiding these projects. Thus, unlike the incrementalism that historians have found to typify real-estate discourse in other midcentury cities, New York's most active developers lobbied for planned growth and urban landscape design with the zeal of visionaries.[17]

The most important of these visionaries was undoubtedly the West Side Association. Organized in 1866 "for the purpose of promoting West Side improvements, and protecting the interests of property owners," the association was open to all landholders west of Central Park and north of Fifty-ninth Street. As I have noted, its leadership spanned bourgeois New York, including ex-mayors (and adversaries) Fernando Wood and Daniel Tiemann, merchants H. B. Claflin and Marshall O. Roberts, financiers Russell Sage and Joseph Drexel, rail baron William B. Ogden, and rentier Benjamin Beekman. The real power, however, lay in a cadre of less famous lawyers, brokers, and developers—Simeon Church, Dwight Olmstead, John McClave, and especially William R. Martin—whose names recur at the top of the association's pamphlets and the bottom of its letters to the editor. Under their direction, the group became the uptown counterpart to the Citizens' Association, New York's leading advocates for an urbanism of the periphery. The results were impressive: the West Siders led the push for approval of Riverside and Morningside parks, won the transfer of planning authority over upper Manhattan to public-parks officials, agitated for street and transit extensions, and succeeded in getting much of the fiscal burden for this growth borne by the city as a whole, not local property owners. As one journal wrote, "No organization . . . has done so much toward encouraging uptown improvements as the West Side Assocation."[18]

The association's success spurred the formation of landowners' groups east of Central Park and along the East River waterfront. Indeed it seemed to augur a new type of development regime, an oligarchy of propertied planners exercising "private" but collective control over the landscape: "We hope in time to chronicle a North-End Association, a Middle Section Association, and a Down Town Association," the *Record* observed. "When these come into existence . . . , New York city will for the first time be on the road to really good government." This ambition was never realized, but it did inform the assumptions of the West Siders. Even as they pursued their own local interests and needs, they equated the prosperity of their district with the imperial prospects of the metropolis as a whole. Uptown parks and boulevards "are now laying broad and deep the foundations of the future glory . . . of New York," argued the association's leaders, making the West Side "the site of the future magnificence of this metropolis." Such claims were more than simply window dressing for particularist interests; they reflected a commitment to systematic planning that was to be pursued even at the expense of landholders' prerogatives. "Act on broad and comprehensive ideas," William Martin told his members in an 1871 speech on rapid transit, not on "incomplete and narrow-minded" proposals that were "settled upon by local or individual property interests."[19]

Martin was the closest thing to an "Haussmann" among these boosters. One of the most impressive—yet maddeningly obscure—of New York's urbanists, he was a real-estate lawyer and president of the West Side Association throughout most of the post-war building craze. His 1865 manifesto *The Growth of New York* represents the most complete statement of booster urbanism in the period; it laid out Manhattan's demographic and territorial expansion, argued for comprehensive park, transit, and street improvements, and articulated the imperial politics and aesthetics that underlay these proposals. Martin used the West Side Association to lobby for this program, and, as head of the New York parks board under Tammany Mayor William Wickham, he tried to implement it in the mid-1870s. Struggling bitterly against Green's stranglehold on the city treasury—and the fiscal constraints of the depression itself—Martin offered a bold program of public works and planned growth for the upper city. "[Let us] mak[e] this region the most attractive, the most valuable, and the most healthful suburb of the city," he argued in a sweeping plan for Washington Heights and the Annexed District. "A broad, comprehensive, positive policy will accomplish results which a narrow, piecemeal obstructive [one] will never reach. This latter policy has prevailed for too long, to the great damage . . . of the interests of the property."[20]

Like his adversary Green, Martin conceived of the new urbanism as a way to coordinate real-estate markets and protect property. Yet he inflected this notion of capitalist planning in a different way. Green sought to *rationalize* growth through the consolidation of administrative power and metropolitan space; Martin wanted to *stimulate* it by monumental public improvements that would open uptown land and downtown capital to profitable exploitation. Where Green and his allies tried to discipline the marketplace, booster visionaries like Martin sought to unleash it. For it was dynamism, not order, that they loved best. Their conception of city building was both heroic and anxious: New York was always on the verge of greatness, always at the edge of disaster, and only booster will could turn the balance. What they feared was not the market's tendency toward anarchy, but rather its capacity for stagnation.

This vivid mixture of confidence and worry enabled the real-estate activists to recognize the catalytic role of public authority in guiding urban growth. More than we might expect of such freebooting marketeers, they were willing to embrace quite radical forms of state activism. In lobbying for rapid transit, for instance, the West Side Association endorsed not only public construction of an uptown line but also the lowest possible fares: "It should seek to make no dividends, but should run at the bare cost of running," Simeon Church argued. "It would thus in time become practically *a great free public highway.*" Even more astonishing, the *Real Estate Record* backed the 1871 proposal of "the Internationals"—as it called the New York sections of the Communist movement—for municipal takeover of Manhattan's gas and transit utilities. Like good Marxists, the boosters understood that property values were shaped collectively by the overall fabric of urban space. They supported a robust program of public works and government regulation as a means of booming those values.[21]

Indeed all three groups of urbanists shared the conviction that New York's transformation had to become a self-consciously political process. Each conceived the politics of city building in light of its own values, interests, and ambitions. A genteel reformer like Olmsted viewed planning as a *mission civilisatrice* to be entrusted to technical and tutelary experts like himself. To a real-estate booster like Martin, it offered a way of catalyzing and canalizing growth in the hands of a bold directorate of public investment. A civic capitalist like Green saw it as a way to master the marketplace through the cementing of growth coalitions and the imposing of fiscal and administrative discipline. The result was not a unified regime of planning and design, but a complex drama of public activism that (as we shall see) produced both bitter discord and surprising alliances.

On one point, however, New York's urbanists were agreed: building the Empire City required novel institutions and concentrations of public authority. "All the governments of the world are assuming powers in the interests of the people which would have been thought dangerous . . . in the days of the old Democracy," the *Real Estate Record* wrote in opposition to "the antiquated rubbish" of laissez-faire. "The new school of political thought gives a much larger measure of authority to governments than the old *doctrinnaires* would ever have dreamed of tolerating. Thus the world moves."[22] State building was in fact a precondition for the city-building experiments advocated by urbanists like the *Record*. They were able to pursue initiatives in landscape design, public works, and environmental regulation during the 1860s and 1870s because these coincided with, and reinforced, political initiatives in administration and governance. The midcentury boom was a time of innovative state building and intensive partisan conflict in New York, and urban space proved a key laboratory for the former and a key battleground in the latter. Manhattan's would-be Haussmanns played pivotal roles in both dramas.

City Building and State Building

Late in 1857, two months after Frederick Law Olmsted was appointed superintendent of Central Park, the New York Common Council authorized a quarter of a million dollars for work on the still unbuilt site. The city was in the throes of a severe business panic, with tens of thousands of workers out of work as winter approached; the aldermen's order had more to do with emergency relief than landscape design. The next morning Olmsted found his office blocked by several thousand job seekers. At their head was "a candidate for reelection as a local magistrate," he later wrote, who "urged that those before him . . . demand employment of me"—and who brandished a hangman's rope should Olmsted refuse. Over the next few days, the superintendent was besieged by "an organized mob carrying a banner inscribed Bread or Blood" with "a list of 10,000 . . . men alleged to have starving families," who "should be immediately put to work." If politics and the panic caused Olmsted some anxiety, however, they made his job easier. Construction accelerated on the languishing park, fueled by relief funds and a surplus of workers too needy to resist the superintendent's rigorous notions of job discipline. "Within a week," he recalled with satisfaction, "I had a thousand men *economically* employed, & rigidly discharged any man who failed to work industriously & to behave in a quiet & orderly manner."[23]

It is an instructive skirmish, one that initiated Olmsted into two decades of hardball municipal politics. Indeed the episode registers many of the conditions and conflicts that shaped the politics of city building in Victorian New York. It shows a massing of public power over the built environment, as government agencies mobilized money and labor on behalf of urban spatial change. It shows such power to have been sharply contested between two political blocs, each with its own base of support and model of social consent. It makes clear that issues of class order—of bourgeois authority, popular resistance, and interclass negotiation—lay at the heart of these contentions. Finally, it hints at some ironic alliances that underlay the turbulence of city politics and city building. For both Olmsted and the demagogic ward heeler were committed to an activist program of public works; despite the contempt between them, they served each other's needs in the progress of Central Park.

The reshaping of New York depended on a convergence of new forms of state and political power. These included not only the public funds, partisan demonstrations, and managerial prerogatives at play in Olmsted's story but also the granting of utility franchises, the promulgation of health and building codes, and the construction of public improvements—all supported by the massive use of eminent domain and bonded debt. As historians Eric Monkkonen and Jon Teaford argue, such interventionism was typical of urban growth in nineteenth-century America; it promoted an era of strong municipal governance and the emergence of what Monkkonen calls the "service city."[24]

The change was especially acute in New York. Governance in early nineteenth-century Manhattan was largely defined by the city's status as a proprietary corporation with extensive land grants. The core issues of public and fiscal policy involved the use and management of New York's estate. Conversely, the public powers that we now think definitive of local government—to tax, regulate, and provide services— were weak and fragmentary. In 1840, for instance, New Yorkers relied on ineffective voluntary companies for fire protection; they obtained water from dozens of wells across Manhattan Island; they looked to a nonuniformed, part-time "watch" to fight crime and civil disorder; and (as we have seen) they entrusted the control and financing of public works to local landowners.[25] Political institutions reinforced this dispersal of power. New York's streets, docks, and schools were overseen by local, shifting, sometimes overlapping agencies, mainly appointed by the Common Council (or directly elected) and independent of the mayor. Party organizations were equally fragmented: the city's most powerful political club, the Democratic Tammany Society, was a congeries of cliques and factions, without stable leadership, a consistent platform, or the organizational discipline for which it would later be notorious. The "amazing fluidity of the city's political scene," as political historian Jerome Mushkat puts it, and the corresponding ineffectuality of municipal government, made planned city building all but impossible.[26]

Between the opening of the Croton Aqueduct in 1842 and the "home-rule" charter of 1870, however, state and party power in New York grew stronger, more centralized, and more effective. It was during this era, as I noted, that the Corporation of the City subdivided and auctioned off most of its real-estate holdings. The "privatization" of urban land was mirrored by a "publicization" of civic authority: municipal government recast itself from a proprietary grantee with particular estates and resources to an agency of the liberal state with general duties and powers. The transformation was both fiscal and institutional. Public spending ballooned in the midnineteenth century, as did New York's reliance on taxes, rather than rents, to pay for it. Gross municipal expenditures increased from $1.6 million to $26.5 million between 1840 and 1869; millage rates rose more than fourfold. This budgetary growth mirrored a reorganization of municipal authority. New York's charter was revised five times during the midcentury boom, haltingly replacing the older, localistic regime of aldermanic power with a strong mayoralty and an appointed cabinet of department heads.[27]

Beneath these constitutional changes lay a more uneven, hard-edged process of partisan consolidation. In the mid-1850s, Mayor Fernando Wood began to mobilize city Democrats behind an ambitious program of public services and public works. Wood modernized the municipal police, created the first Central Park Commission, and distributed patronage with the aggressive discipline that Olmsted encountered in the episode described earlier. At the same time, leaders of the new Republican Party—which had won control of the state government in the election of 1856—challenged Wood's populist agenda with their own program of urban services and administrative centralism. In 1857, 1865, and 1866, Albany lawmakers created independent commissions to administer police and fire protection, excise regulations, public health, and park building in the metropolitan area.[28] As I will argue, these rival programs engendered bitter political struggle, involving not only partisan competition but alternative visions of state and class order as well. Underlying the conflict, however, was a shared sense that political authority needed to be concentrated and activated in New York. By the late 1860s, it was. Centralized public agencies were piping fresh water from upstate reservoirs directly into city buildings, providing New York with professional police and fire service, conforming the city's streets and buildings to new health and safety codes, and laying out parks and promenades that were open to, and financed by, the citizens of New York and Brooklyn as a whole.[29]

As this list suggests, the urban landscape was a core concern of the new activism. City building and state building catalyzed each other: political change produced massive effects in the landscape, and the landscape served as a laboratory of administrative innovation. At the heart of the dialectic was the growing capacity of local government to command land, labor, and capital for spatial change. The midcentury boom, for instance, saw a sharp increase in the legal taking of private property for public works. Before 1850 eminent domain awards for new parks in Manhattan had totaled $444,106. By contrast, the commission of estimate for Central Park awarded landholders $5.4 million for the park site. Postwar projects were even costlier: uptown owners received more than $21 million during 1870–71 for real estate incorporated into Riverside Drive, Morningside Park, the Boulevard, the widening of Broadway, and extensions of Madison and Lexington avenues.[30] These public works spurred an equally sharp expansion of the municipal workforce. In the mid-1840s all of city government employed fewer than four thousand people; twenty years later, some five thousand employees worked each summer on the New York parks alone. (As I will discuss later, managing this public workforce was a key bone of contention between "machine" Democrats and "reform" advocates of commission rule.)[31]

State mobilization of *capital* was even more striking. Metropolitan growth required legislators in New York, Brooklyn, and Albany to deploy property rights and fiscal resources to an unprecedented degree. Two different strategies of capital formation were especially effective. First of all, municipal and state governments coordinated infrastructure development through the widespread granting of franchises to horse cars, ferries, gas utilities, bridge companies, rapid-transit projects, and other ventures. Franchise policy was by no means uniformly effective or "rational." The obligations, privileges, geographic extent, financial terms, and official sources of particular grants varied widely. Some franchises were mutually inconsistent; some were later rescinded; many remained unused. Indeed legislative records from the 1860s and 1870s are filled with grants for bridges, tunnels, dock basins, arcade railroads, underground railroads, viaduct railroads, and other schemes that were never built. Moreover, as I noted in Chapter 3, many franchises were obtained by bribery and inside dealing; it was the corruption of the New York Common Council in granting horse car routes that led state lawmakers to withdraw the city's powers of enfranchisement in the 1850s. Yet, by ceding property rights over streets, slips, and other public spaces to corporate developers, franchises proved an indispensable way to guide metropolitan growth without directly paying for it. Costly, complex infrastructures like Brooklyn Bridge or the elevated railway would not have been undertaken without them.[32]

When city and state governments *did* finance their own improvements—parks, boulevards, street extensions—they relied on a second strategy of public capital formation: public debt. It was massive borrowing, not taxes or local assessments, that underwrote the grandest projects of the new urbanism. At midcentury, the net bonded debt for the city of New York stood at $12.2 million, nearly all of which had been used to build the Croton Aqueduct. By 1868 the debt tripled, and it tripled again in the next three years—the heyday of the Tweed regime—to reach $97.3 million. Municipal bonds paid for many things: the Union war effort, new upstate reservoirs, the corruption of Tweed and his cronies. They funded public works as well. The Corporation of the City issued $11 million in bonds for park construction between 1850 and 1871, $6.4 million for public buildings, $6.5 million for street and boulevard improvements, and several million for the construction of the Brooklyn Bridge.[33]

The growing reliance on public debt changed both the scale and the institutional logic of city building. Earlier in the nineteenth century, it will be recalled, public works were financed by local assessments: the decision to pave a street or lay out a park, and the obligation to pay for it, rested with the landowners who benefited directly from it. Of $444,106 laid out for new parks in this period, for instance—including Washington, Union, Tompkins, and Madison squares—all but $500 was assessed on local proprietors. Starting with bond issues for the Croton Aqueduct, however, the assessment system broke down. In the late 1840s, uptown landowners agitated for public works to be paid in part by the public as a whole. A pleasure ground or boulevard was not merely a local benefit, they argued, but a collective good that should be collectively financed. With Central Park, the antiassessment forces won their first major victory: in the skirmishing over the site and funding of the park, Albany lawmakers obligated local owners for only one-third of the acquisition costs. In the late 1860s, city taxpayers were assigned half the expenses of Riverside and Morningside parks and even one-third of conventional street openings.[34]

The Empire City, in short, was a debtor's paradise. Just as the modernization of the city's real-estate economy required the growth of an institutional mortgage-credit market, so the new public activism in city building depended on public borrowing. New York was not unique in this regard. As Morton Keller and Eric Monkonnen have argued, local governments across Gilded Age America used bonded debt to expand their infrastructures and services. Robin Einhorn's nuanced study of political economy in Chicago traces a similar shift in public-works finance from local assessments to municipal bonds during the 1860s and 1870s. For Einhorn the appeal to a "new public interest" that accompanied this shift marked the defeat of local landowners by a metropolitan elite of industrialists. In New York, the conjuncture of state building, city building, and debt was somewhat different. It was precisely Manhattan's real-estate boosters, especially those associated with uptown development, who sought to replace local assessments with a debt-driven urbanism in which public works served, and should be financed, by the citizenry as a whole. "Why Municipal Debts?" inquired a *Real Estate Record* editorial: "The life of a nation or a municipality is not limited to the generation now living. A great public improvement . . . is a part of the heritage of the unborn. Those who come after us should be willing to pay their share for the improvements of the property which will in time come into their possession. . . . [Debts] are a recognition not only of the solidarity but of the continuity of the human race."[35]

Looking back from an era in which public borrowing is widely viewed as a corruption of state power, we may find it hard to grasp why boosters celebrated debt with such panache. Indeed New York's debt burden would come to haunt city builders at the end of the midcentury boom; as I will discuss in Chapter 8, the frauds of the Tweed ring and the Panic of 1873 precipitated a fiscal emergency that halted public improvements and undermined the legitimacy of the new urbanism. In the heyday of New York's growth, however, public debt seemed both a means and a symbol of metropolitan stature. In the most literal sense, borrowing appealed to boosters because it was the easiest way of financing their expansive program of public works. More subtly, they celebrated debt because its spatiotemporal logic mirrored their vision of urban growth. Debt financing forced propertied New Yorkers to replace local interests with metropolitan ones; it required collective decision making about the spatial and aesthetic needs of the city as a whole. Moreover, it embodied a confidence that the present and future could rely on each other: if costly improvements were needed to deliver Manhattan into its destiny, that destiny would be able to repay the investment and confirm its wisdom. Public debt, in short, committed city politics to the booster metanarrative of centralism and progress. No less than the parks and bridges that they financed, municipal bonds were an expression of New York's greatness, the homage that the present owed the future.

City Blocs

As I have noted, two sets of institutions were central to the play of city building and state building in Victorian New York, and the rivalry between them did much to set the agenda of city politics. On one hand, the midcentury boom saw New York's fractious Democratic clubs—most notably, Tammany Hall—transformed into unified organizations. Led by skilled politicians like Fernando Wood and William Marcy Tweed, Tammany and its rivals mobilized voters with unprecedented discipline and oversaw a patronage system that provisioned local government with labor power. On the other hand, the 1850s and 1860s saw the formation of a network of independent metropolitan commissions—most notably, the Central Park Commission—by Albany lawmakers and their Republican allies in New York. Led by downtown notables and staffed by genteel professionals like Olmsted and Vaux, the commissions were vested with centralized authority over such problems as public health and urban design.

Precisely because "machine" Democrats and commission "reformers" shared the ambition to build and use state power, relations between them were anything but harmonious. The process of political consolidation in New York was largely driven by their struggle for dominance. Sometimes that struggle took the form of electoral conflict between Democrats and Republicans or between rival Democratic "halls"; sometimes it took the form of jurisdictional conflict between the (Republican) regime in Albany and (Democratic) City Hall. Yet city politics was not *only* about partisan competition or home rule. It involved rival models of state power—and rival visions of how to use that power to recast urban space. In such a contentious milieu, reconstructing the cityscape was not only a civic project but also a political battleground.[36]

A third factor intensified these conflicts over power and space: the persistence of class division and disorder in New York. As we have seen, the Manhattan cityscape bore the scars of class inequality in its patterns of uneven development, residential segregation, and public violence. Class inequality marked city politics too, but in a different way; in a regime based on universal white male suffrage, political rule required constant negotiation among diverse class constituencies. Such negotiations were especially important to the city-building process. New York's mixture of rapid growth, recurrent popular disorder, extensive public works, and a proletarianized electorate meant that urban development depended on the stability of class relations. As a result, political struggle over the built environment took the form of conflict between different blocs or class coalitions. It was these coalitions that provided the social base for the rival urbanisms of machine Democrats and commission reformers; and conversely, each bloc sought to inflect the city-building process with its own visions of class order. Democratic clubs saw development as a way to induct workingmen into electoral alliances built on public-works patronage. Genteel reformers used park and public health commissions to project their own political and cultural authority over an alien and seemingly antisocial working class. Both blocs used the city-building process to mediate class inequality, each soliciting popular consent for its own model of state authority and environmental change.[37]

For Democratic politicians, New York's social and spatial volatility was at once a problem and a resource. The shrewdest Tammany leaders understood that the city's disorders—mass immigration, class friction, uneven development—constituted an opportunity to transcend the localism and factionalism that had long hobbled the Democracy. They sought to meld the intense, clientelistic loyalties of antebellum partisan culture with a new emphasis on organizational discipline, centralized command of party resources, and citywide electoral mobilization. As I have noted, Fernando Wood was the first to institutionalize this machine politics, as leader of Tammany Hall in the mid-1850s and the breakaway Mozart Hall thereafter; his adversary William Marcy Tweed brought it to maturity when he won control of Tammany Hall in 1863 and of the municipal government five years later. By then Tammany had achieved a hegemony over New York politics that remained subtantially intact, if not unchallenged, for nearly a century.

As political scientist Amy Bridges has illuminated, a new mode of class negotiation lay at the heart of machine politics. The party won stable electoral majorities by serving as a broker among diverse socioeconomic constituencies. Workingmen were offered a compact based on clientage and protection; in exchange for votes, electoral work, and an occasional street brawl, the party provided them with coal or credit in hard times, help with the courts during naturalization proceedings or legal disputes, and especially patronage jobs. *Party* bosses in effect supplemented the subsistence that *industrial* bosses did not fully and regularly provide to wage earners. At the same time, the party brokered more lucrative deals with developers, builders, printers, and other entrepreneurs. These businessmen depended on public works, contracts, and franchises, and they were willing to pay into a campaign chest or a private bank account to secure them. Democratic politicians fashioned a class coalition, in short, that reproduced market power as political clout. They installed commodity exchange as the defining bond of public life; and in the process, they won the loyalty of masses of New York's workingmen and a broad range of the metropolitan bourgeoisie.[38]

The success of this marketplace regime depended on a conjuncture of several conditions. First of all, there was the growing residential segregation and economic casualization of city workers. As scholars have shown, it was the most vulnerable groups—common laborers, longshoremen, street workers, journeymen in threatened trades—who served as the core of the Tammany coalition. As the crowd in front of Olmsted's office suggests, these wage earners used the patron-client bonds of machine politics to defend themselves from the vagaries of the labor and rental markets. They turned to ward heelers for patronage and relief just as they turned to other neighborhood notables—grocers, builders, landlords, saloon keepers, labor contractors—for credit, housing information, and jobs. Indeed these entrepreneurs often served as the ward leadership of the Democratic organization; paver Peter Masterson represented the Thirteenth Ward in the Common Council during the 1860s, for instance, and contractor Terence Farley was alderman for the Sixteenth. Such figures embedded the party machine in the special class matrix of the tenement neighborhood; they were effective as political brokers precisely because of the everyday authority that they exercised over their constituents.[39]

At the same time, that class authority was mediated by the cultural ethos that politicians shared with their supporters, an ethos defined largely *by* their supporters. Many scholars have stressed the distinctive ethnoreligious base of the Democratic coalition in New York: immigrant, often Catholic wage earners, fiercely protective of their "liberties," resentful of any moral policing from evangelicals or patricians in the Whig, Know-Nothing, or Republican parties. This cultural politics was inflected with a distinctive class and gender style. It invoked a "rough" code of manly independence, braggadocio, and rowdy camaraderie, learned in the saloon, the street gang, the fire brigade, and the target company, places where party politics penetrated the associational life of the working-class neighborhood. This code gave the Democracy a plebeian—and sometimes militantly workerist—tone at odds with the distribution of power within its organization. "Is not the pending contest preeminently one of capital against labor?" Tammany orators proclaimed in the election of 1868, "of money against popular rights?"[40]

What the Democratic machine actually offered its constituents was not class struggle, but jobs. It found those jobs in the burgeoning demand for public services and public works that accompanied New York's boom; city schools, city police, and especially city building supplied the ore from which patronage could be minted. Starting with Wood in the mid-1850s, then, party leaders embraced a centralized program of park, transit, and street improvements. By 1859, several thousand employees worked on Central Park, many of them beneficiaries of the sort of personal pressure that Olmsted confronted in the panic of 1857. The largesse of the Tweed ring was even more striking, especially after the ascendance of Mayor A. Oakey Hall in 1868. Over the next three years, Hall, Tweed, and their allies built a patronage empire estimated at twelve thousand jobs, three-quarters of which consisted of labor in the parks and streets.[41]

The Tammany regime of organizational politics, class brokering, and public works reached its climax in April 1870, with the passage of a new city charter. The "Tweed charter" has a hallowed place in the political legendry of New York because of the sheer volume of cash—reputedly a million dollars—that State Senator Tweed spread around Albany to secure its passage. Yet it represented something more than just an episode in the history of boodle. The charter revolutionized municipal government, replacing both aldermanic localism and the Republican commission system with a strong mayor and a departmental executive accountable to him. The "home-rule" constitution worked especially to centralize city building. The administration of public improvements and landscape design were consolidated in two omnibus departments—Public Works and Public Parks—over which Mayor Hall appointed Tweed himself and his lieutenant Peter Sweeney.[42]

The ring lost no time in making use of its new administrative power. By early June, Commissioner Tweed was issuing dozens of Public Works contracts each week, many to Tammany insiders like sewer contractor James Everard and paver Terence Farley. Over the next two years, the municipal government opened long portions of eight uptown avenues and twenty-nine cross-streets; it initiated hundreds of paving, sewering, and grading projects throughout the city. The grandest improvements took place in upper Manhattan: the widening of Broadway to Fifty-ninth Street, the extension of Madison Avenue, and the creation of the Avenue St. Nicholas, Morningside Park, Riverside Drive, and the Boulevard (Figure 6.2). Uptown developers had long lobbied for a scenic promenade on the Hudson highlands; boosters like William Martin believed that it would clinch the West Side's emergence as New York's neighborhood of fashion. Tammany leaders agreed, and they oversaw the creation of Riverside Drive personally: the commission of estimate was composed of Sweeney's brother James, dock commissioner Hugh Smith, and Tweed himself. They awarded $6 million to assemble the park site, more than the cost of Central Park, much of it to Tammany insiders who had quietly speculated in West Side lots in anticipation of the public works binge. (Tweed foreclosed on several properties in Eighty-fourth Street.)[43]

Indeed, party leaders and wealthy backers profited sumptuously from the midcentury boom. Historian Eugene Moehring has traced more than a hundred real-estate purchases by Tweed and his allies during 1868–71, many concentrated east and northeast of Central Park, where public works and residential investment were most active. "East side property seems to be the favorite locality for the politicians," the *Real Estate Record* noted in 1871, "and large amounts of it are held by those supposed to be in the ring . . ." The Tammany leadership also enriched itself by commanding stock and directorships from development corporations whose projects it helped to enfranchise. As David McCullough has shown, Tweed, Sweeney, and Smith were accorded large shares of the New York Bridge Company in exchange for supporting Roebling's project. In 1871, Tweed similarly persuaded state legislators to enfran-

FIGURE 6.2   In a striking tableau of the alliance between bourgeois urbanism and machine politics, here we see patronage workers of the Tweed regime transforming upper Broadway into "the Boulevard." (*Frank Leslie's Illustrated Newspaper*, January 21, 1871; negative no. 74692; © Collection of the New-York Historical Society)

chise the Viaduct rapid transit railway—on whose board he and other leaders of the ring sat.[44]

Tammany urbanism was more than simply Tammany graft. Tweed and his cronies succeeded in reinventing local government, and to a great extent, they accomplished the booster program of public works and private development. Yet these achievements came with a price: they advanced the dialectic of city building and state building by subjecting both to the dictates of organizational politics. The result was something quite different from the autonomous elites and discrete institutional interests that scholars have often seen as the hallmark of modern state formation. Here the local state was permeable and dependent. It possessed strong, central powers, to be sure, and it effected enormous change in the built environment. Yet it was designed to meld into, and to serve, the party-dominated polity.

To a degree that subsequent events would obscure, elite New Yorkers understood how impressive Tweed's accomplishments were. The home-rule charter was endorsed by the Citizens' Association and commercial leaders of both parties; even the rabidly anti-Tammany *Times* noted, "Senator Tweed is in a fair way to distinguish himself as a reformer." Iver Bernstein has argued persuasively that, until the fiscal crisis brought on by his thefts, Tweed was widely regarded as the sole figure capable of securing class peace in the capitalist metropolis. Many boosters were similarly willing to bet on Tammany as the best guide through the eddies of the development boom. "Never before have we had such a directly responsible government," the *Real*

Estate Record wrote soon after passage of the 1870 charter. "Great confidence is being expressed in regard to the workings of the Department of Parks, and the public is satisfied with the energetic manner in which work is being laid out and executed." If New York required an Haussmann or Louis Napoleon, Tweed seemed for a time the likeliest candidate.[45]

And yet it was precisely Tweed's "Bonapartism" that disquieted the New York gentry. To the Republican *Times*, he was "HAUSSMANN THE LITTLE": as autocratic and corrupt as the Prefect of the Seine, but utterly devoid of the baron's aesthetic ambition and taste. If anything seemed redolent of Second Empire Paris to such critics, it was Tammany's mix of despotic power and demagogic appeal. "An imperialism has been established here as absolute as that of LOUIS NAPOLEON," warned *Harper's Weekly*, "and it is formally sustained, as his was, by an occasional *plebiscite* called an election." As the full extent of the ring's thefts was discovered, this imagery of imperial corruption became a staple of reform discourse: Thomas Nast regularly caricatured Tweed as a bloated Caesar subverting the Republic.[46] Even before the anti-corruption crusade of 1871, however, Republicans and reformers had offered an alternative to the Democratic regime of party discipline and public works. Beginning in the mid-1850s, they proposed their own version of local state building, organized around the ideals of stewardship, professional independence, and class uplift.

The Politics of Stewardship

In 1856 the newborn Republican party won the governorship and state house of New York, one of its first political triumphs. For all but two of the next twelve years, the party remained dominant in Albany, even as the fractious Democratic "halls" consolidated and fought over electoral control of Manhattan. This fact of persistently divided rule did much to set the battle lines of city politics in the midcentury boom. It meant that, when Republicans and "reform" Democrats challenged the ascendancy of the Democratic machine in New York City, the challenge typically came from Albany and primarily took the form of a nonelectoral politics of commission governance. Conversely, when Tammany Hall *did* win power in Albany—with the 1868 election of Governor John Hoffman—it pursued municipal reorganization under the sign of "home rule."

Until the Tweed charter dismantled and absorbed them in 1870, state commissions exercised broad authority in New York City (and to a lesser extent Brooklyn). Albany lawmakers established central boards to oversee metropolitan police protection (1857), the creation of Central Park (1857) and Prospect Park (1860), fire fighting (1865), excise taxation (1865), and public health (1866). It is only a slight exaggeration to say that these agencies constituted a counterregime to the emerging Democratic party-state. That was the intention: upstate Republicans founded the park and police commissions in 1857—and filled them with their own partisans—precisely to supplant Fernando Wood's initiatives on these issues. (The Metropolitan Police and

Wood's Municipal force engaged in jurisdictional struggle throughout the spring of 1857, culminating in a pitched battle on the steps of City Hall, as the "Municipals" resisted the effort of "Metropolitans" to arrest Mayor Wood for inciting a riot; in July the New York court of appeals affirmed the superior authority of the state, and the Municipals were disbanded.)[47]

Of course, Republican appointees could be quite as avid for patronage and party advantage as Tammany aldermen. "I am just informed that you have made some 12 or 14 new appointments for the [Park] Police and have paid no attention to my request," park commissioner John Butterworth told Superintendent Olmsted in 1859. "Your course in many matters is to me very unsatisfactory." Yet, as Olmsted's "unsatisfactory" behavior suggests, commission rule was more than just a redivision of the spoils. New York's commercial and cultural gentry endorsed it precisely as an alternative model of urban governance: "To abolish the Commissions would be to destroy all hope of our attaining good government," argued Peter Cooper, the (Democratic) chairman of the Citizens' Association. "It is not . . . the banker, the honest laborer and largest tax-payers in this city who are opposed to Commissions; but the professed politician . . . [and] the trader in contracts and jobs." For such advocates, commission rule was civic reform. What they meant by "reform," however, was not the politics of retrenchment that would dominate good-government movements after the fiscal crisis of the 1870s. Commissions were as centralized and activist as the party-state that they challenged. Yet they embodied a different notion of political, class, and environmental order from the Democratic machine: a vision of state authority as elite, civic-minded stewardship.[48]

The politics of stewardship was informed by the specific experiences and values of those who agitated for it: the elites that I have called "civic capitalists" and "the best men." It was influential businessmen like Robert Minturn and genteel intellectuals like William Cullen Bryant, for instance, who first mobilized support for a scenic park in the mid-1850s. Similarly, the founding of the Metropolitan Board of Health was mainly the work of merchants and sanitary reformers in the Citizens' Association. The commission ideal reflected the social base of these coalitions. It melded the fiduciary ethic of commercial elites with the ideal of "disinterested" expertise that typified the cultural gentry.[49]

Where party politicians treated state power as a form of market power, commission advocates conceived it as property held in trust. They viewed government as the trustee for a public that possessed transcendent interests but could not properly manage them in the blinkered play of daily politics. It was the duty of the fiduciary state to ensure citizens the benefits of their property, precisely by withdrawing it from their control. "[Park design] is a work in which private and local and special interests will be . . . so antagonistic to one another . . . that the ordinary organizations for municipal business are unsuitable," Olmsted told the American Social Science Association in an 1870 address. "The public in its own interest . . . should see to it that the problem is as soon as possible put clean out of its own hands." What justified this cession of power was the high-minded competence that elite stewards would bring to civic affairs. In contrast to the machine ethic of loyalism and reciprocity, commission rule was based on ideals of "disinterestedness" and "nonpartisanship." "I am pledged . . . to conduct the affairs committed to my charge," Olmsted stiffly replied to Commissioner Butterworth's patronage complaint, "as the servant of the whole Board, and of no individual or party in the Board." Impartial, expert oversight was the authorizing mark of this regime. Indeed, the New York commissions were among the first government agencies in the United States to hire *for* expertise, including in their leadership scientific and professional pioneers like Dr. Elisha Harris of the Board of Health, civil engineer George Waring of the Central Park staff, and of course Olmsted and Vaux.[50]

Of all the new commissions, the New York park board demonstrated most clearly the potential scope of the fiduciary state. As its work on Central Park gained acclaim, elite New Yorkers from the *Times* to the West Side Association pressed for the expansion of its powers. The Albany legislature responded by transforming the commission into something like a planning agency for the whole uptown periphery. By the late 1860s, the board was charged not only with overseeing Central Park but also with laying out a network of new squares, avenues, and pleasure grounds in upper Manhattan; planning the city's development west and north of Central Park; and guiding the commercial improvement of the Harlem River valley and the growth of southern Westchester. There were even proposals to give the commissioners centralized control over the New York waterfront.[51]

It is easy to see why the politics of stewardship proved so amenable to the problem of city building. Commission rule organized state power along precisely the lines that many observers saw as the solution to New York's uneven development. The park board subordinated local interests to the purview of a coordinating elite; it extended and centralized the territorial reach of public improvements; it encouraged long-term, large-scale decisions about spatial change, buffered from the particularism of ward politics and the election cycle. Finally it tended to empower those groups—financiers, large developers, genteel reformers—who were most influential in articulating the need for planned growth and civilizing design. Commission rule, in short, gave administrative form to the assumptions of bourgeois urbanists.

It also embodied their notions of class order. Unlike Democratic politicos, who mediated socioeconomic divisions through bargaining and clientelism, the advocates of commission rule frankly embraced the need for class hierarchy. They believed that public authority over the landscape belonged in the hands of men like themselves: the propertied, the educated, and the refined. Only gentleman capitalists and property owners had the material independence and fiduciary experience to guide spatial change with civic-minded wisdom: "A majority of [the park commissioners] were much better known from . . . banks, railroads, mining, and manufacturing enterprises, than from previous services in politics," Olmsted noted appreciatively. "Their method of work . . . was as like as possible to that of a board of directors of a commercial corporation." Similarly, only the cultural gentry had the requisite education and travel to grasp the technical tools and civilizing aims of fields like landscape design. Commission rule would thus delegate city building to "a small body of select men," as Olmsted put it, in whom property, training, taste, and virtue were conjoined. The structure of the actual Central Park commission mirrored these assumptions. With its board of commercial notables, its genteel administrators, and its cadre of trained engineers, the commission melded an older "Whig" model of class deference with an emergent "Progressive" ideal of professional expertise.[52]

Such a model of rule took an essentially disciplinary stance toward the urban working class. Where city politicians treated working people as bearers of specific interests and loyalties, from whom they had to bargain political consent, civic stewards viewed them more abstractly: as labor power for the reshaping of the metropolitan landscape or as tutelary subjects of its influence. Thus, when the park board addressed itself to ordinary New Yorkers, it tended to speak either as a potential employer or a potential civilizer. In either guise, it conceived the city-building process not as a medium for negotiating popular consent, but as a means of establishing class oversight.

Nothing makes this conception clearer than the labor practices that organized the construction of Central Park. From the start, Superintendent Olmsted was attentive to the political implications of the labor process. He viewed work discipline as more than simply a technical desideratum. It was a form of prefigurative politics, modeling the class and civic order that the park itself was designed to embody. It was for this reason that he so adamantly opposed "that form of bribery known as patronage." Patronage was doubly corrupt: it eroded both the republican ideal of disinterested citizenship and the free-labor ideal of industrious self-mastery. Olmsted was deeply committed to free-labor values (as his famous critiques of the slave South made clear); he excoriated politicians who pressured him to hire workers "unable to earn living wages in sewer and pavement work" as a reward for "the services of [their] sons and grandsons in carrying torch-lights, and stocking the primaries."[53] At the same time he worried that hard times would turn a partisan workforce into something even more dangerous: an insurrectionary crowd. As we have seen, he "defended" the park from political and class mobilizations during the panic of 1857; twenty years later, at the outbreak of the great railroad strike, he surrounded the headquarters of the park board with loaded howitzers.[54]

For the most part, however, Olmsted sought to secure labor peace through the training of workers, not the training of guns on workers. "I have got the park into a capital discipline, a perfect system, working like a machine, 1000 men now at work," he exulted to his father two months after the 1857 demonstration. That "system" was grounded in an innovative, corporatist model of work management. Olmsted won the board's permission to hire labor directly (overruling Democratic members who supported contract bidding as a source of market efficiency and patronage alliances). He imposed a strict time regimen—with foremen's logs and twice-daily roll calls—that was at odds with the traditional rhythms of outdoor construction work. He for-

bade hiring kickbacks, on-site political lobbying, and other forms of partisan or entrepreneurial behavior. And he fired any employee whom he found inadequate to his
standards. "With a single exception, when . . . two gangs [struck] and were immediately discharged," Olmsted told Brace, "there has been the most perfect order, peace
& good feeling preserved, notwithstanding the fact that the laborers are mainly from
. . . what is considered the most dangerous class of the great city's population."[55]

The same emphasis on class order and the disciplining of "dangerous" New Yorkers typified Olmsted's policies toward the public use of Central Park. As I discuss in
the next chapter, park goers were subjected to a battery of rules aimed at molding
them into a community of refinement and virtue. Olmsted organized a uniformed
force of "Park Keepers" whose "vigilant, decorous, and soldier-like" oversight "prevent[ed] heedless and untrained visitors" from indulging in proscribed behavior like
tree climbing, political oratory, unlicensed commerce, and music making. Such tutelary policies made the park a laboratory for moral environmentalism. "One is no
more likely to see ruffianism or indecencies in the [Central] Park than in the churches,"
Olmsted proudly reported to the American Social Science Association. "It exercises a
distinctly harmonizing and refining influence upon the most unfortunate and most
lawless classes of the city."[56]

In both the management of park labor and the regulation of park use, then, the politics of stewardship identified state power with class authority. It made Central Park
the stage for a great transaction between genteel provisioners of civilization and the
masses who required its discipline. "The poor need an education to refinement and
taste and the mental & moral capital of gentlemen," Olmsted wrote in an 1853 letter
to Brace (long before he turned professionally to landscape design). "Get up parks,
gardens, music, dancing schools, reunions which will be so attractive as to force into
contact the good & bad, the gentlemanly and the rowdy." Such a class transaction
was simultaneously an act of tutelage and a political compact: it traded "rowdy"
power for "gentle" culture and in so doing transferred authority to the fiduciary
state.[57]

To the advocates of stewardship, however, such an exchange was not undemo-
cratic. Popular rule, they argued, required a tutelary elite that could raise the class-
divided populace into a civilized public. "That the people should be capable of the
magnanimity of laying down their authority . . . to concentrate it in the hands of energetic and responsible trustees," Henry Bellows exulted in an *Atlantic Monthly* essay
on Central Park, "throw[s] light and cheer upon the prospects of popular institutions . . ." Patrician reformers like Bellows were by no means foes of democracy. They
were deeply concerned about the "prospects of popular institutions," on behalf of
which they fought secession and slavery. Yet they identified those prospects with
popular deference toward men like themselves. Urbanism was a way of winning
such deference, of reshaping "the people" (an unruly subject of power) into a "public" (an orderly beneficiary of power). For the essence of that "public" was precisely
its need to be protected from itself: its need for stewards.[58]

The Modern Prince

This chapter has told two stories. The first described the groups that embraced bourgeois urbanism and articulated its program of spatial change. It argued that the mantle of imperial city builder was claimed primarily by three constituencies: civic capitalists like Andrew Haswell Green, real-estate boosters like William Martin, and genteel reformers like Frederick Law Olmsted. The second described the political milieu within which these urbanists pursued their ambitions. It argued that city building in New York was inseparable from a contemporaneous process of state building. Local state formation took the form of rival projects of political consolidation: the emergence of centralized machine politics in the Democratic Party and the founding of independent commissions. These institutions embodied not only divergent party and jurisdictional interests but also alternative models of state authority and class order. Thus, when Olmsted confronted the demonstrators outside his office in the fall of 1857, he was taking part in a much larger drama: a struggle between a partisan politics of city building based on class negotiation and a fiduciary politics of city building based on class stewardship.

It is tempting, and to a great extent accurate, to lay these stories together: to map the groups of urbanists onto the political blocs. As we have seen, it was civic capitalists and genteel reformers who most vociferously advocated the politics of stewardship. Conversely, boosters tended to support the patronage and public works agenda of the Democratic Party; many Tammany leaders were themselves active in land speculation and contracting. Such patterns of affiliation help to account for some of the complexities of institutional and aesthetic conflict among New York's urbanists. After the adoption of the Greensward Plan in 1858, for example, park commissioner Robert Dillon sought to modify its design to include more "artificial" effects and monumental display spaces; like many Democratic urbanists, he viewed the park as an occasion for urbane spectacle. Conversely, the Republican majority stressed the uplifting influence of a peaceful, ruralized landscape; they defended the park's "English" aesthetic and defeated most of the amendments to revise it.[59]

And yet—as I have stressed throughout this book—Victorian New York tended always to complicate such neat divisions. The politics of city building produced surprising conflicts and unexpected commonalties. Thus the bitterest infighting during the early history of Central Park was not between "reformers" like Olmsted and "partisans" like Dillon, but rather between Andrew Haswell Green and everybody else. Olmsted hated Green's mix of bureaucratic expansionism (in which they were alike) and budgetary niggling (in which they were not). Conversely, even as he battled Democratic commissioners and politicos over the design and management of the park, he often found common ground with them. It was Robert Dillon, for instance, who first proposed separating the different traffic systems in Central Park—a feature that was not only incorporated into the Greensward Plan by Olmsted and Vaux but also hailed as one of its greatest innovations.[60]

Here was the great irony of the new urbanism: genteel reformers and Democratic partisans often needed each other more than they detested each other. To be sure, the struggle between the politics of stewardship and that of partisanship was heartfelt and passionate; the aesthetic and material stakes of the conflict were quite real. Nonetheless, urbanists of all stripes shared a set of imperial assumptions about the sort of metropolitan landscape that they were trying to make—and a set of ambitions to be the great demiurge that would shape it. That ambition to be the heroic city builder, the Emperor of New York, provided the common ground on which their political struggles took place.

Only one of New York's leading urbanists seems to have rejected this fantasy of rule: Calvert Vaux. An English émigré from a middling family, Vaux had learned drafting and design as a London apprentice; he came to the United States with republican convictions that were forged against the traditions of monarchy and privilege in his native land. Vaux viewed architecture and planning as expressions of those convictions—"the translation of the republican art idea," as he called Central Park—and he held no brief for the aesthetics or politics of empire. "The gates typify what we have been fighting against," he wrote against proposals for grand entrance gates around Central Park, "it is Nap. III in disguise all over." For Vaux, the very idea of an American Haussmann was a contradiction in terms, a contradiction that, to his dismay, he saw in his partner and friend. "I have . . . to deal with you throughout in two characters," he wrote in an 1865 letter, "as Olmsted the artist & republican with whom I could heartily act and sympathise—and with Olmsted the bureaucrat and imperialist with whom I never for a moment sympathised."[61]

In part Vaux's criticism of "Olmsted the imperialist" was personal. He complained with reason that his partner resisted sharing credit and official responsibility for their work: "the idea of a common fraternal effort," he acidly noted, "is too republican . . . for you." Yet his anger also reflected a dissenting vision of the politics of city building. Vaux believed in the legitimacy of centralized design, and he took part in some of the most ambitious projects of the new urbanism in New York; but he conceived the planner's power as a tool for composing, rather than policing, the civic community. He detested "Frederick the Great, Prince of the Park Police," as he called Olmsted's obsession with administrative and regulatory control. "Bossing jobs is one thing and art another," he warned his partner, "and I have an instinctive hate to anything of the Nap. III sort."[62]

Yet this "Vaux populi" was the exception who proved the imperial rule. For the most part, New York's leading city builders and civic intellectuals remained untroubled by the autocratic implications of bourgeois urbanism. They did not fear the rise of the imperial planner as a threat to democratic politics. Indeed, they believed the opposite: an "Haussmannian" massing of power, capital, skill, and taste would rescue New York from its notorious corruption and inefficiency. "Mr. [Andrew] Green is more to New York than the Baron Haussman to Paris," enthused the New York *World*, "exhibiting in his work the refutation of those who charge upon municipalities an essential incapacity for . . . self-government." Far from eroding popular rule, the great city builder would redeem the American metropolis, endowing it with an order and splendor formerly limited to Old World capitals: "The people do not mean to give up the advantages . . . of aristocratic governments," Henry Bellows enthused in his paean to Central Park, "but to engraft the energy, foresight, and liberality of concentrated powers upon democratic ideas." Bellows believed that New York had just the leader to do it in Frederick Law Olmsted; he extolled the superintendent for exactly the traits for which Vaux condemned him: "He is precisely the man for the place, . . . equally competent as original designer, patient executor, potent disciplinarian, and model police-officer."[63]

Whether they nominated Andrew Haswell Green, Frederick Law Olmsted, or others, New York's urbanists believed that building the Empire City required a new mode of power over politics and space: one that was at once hierarchical and inclusive, commanding and tutelary. Put in terms of current social theory, they saw city building as a hegemonic project, an effort to secure institutional authority over an unequal social order and educated consent for its legitimacy. Indeed, it is striking that when Antonio Gramsci was developing this notion of hegemony, he personified its entailments in a heroic figure not unlike the Emperor of New York. Drawing on Machiavelli's famous tract, Gramsci called his ideal ruler *the modern Prince*. The modern Prince stood for a form of power that was not merely coercive and regulatory, but renovative and world making, one that could incorporate the masses into a new national and cultural order. He would act as "the proclaimer and organizer of an intellectual and moral reform," Gramsci wrote in the *Prison Notebooks*, "creating the terrain for a . . . development of the nation['s] collective will" and "the realization of a superior, total form of modern civilization." The Italian thinker believed that the leading candidate for this historic role was the mass political party—especially his own Communist Party. Yet his account uncannily captures the ambitions of bourgeois city builders in Victorian New York. Like the modern Prince, their imperial urbanist would also "proclaim an intellectual and moral reform" that established the "terrain" for "a superior form of modern civilization."[64] He would redeem American democracy by reshaping and regulating its metropolis; he would transform a fractious people into a civilized public by building a utopian cityscape and inducting them into its ways.

CHAPTER 7

Uptown Utopia

Each city receives its form from the desert it opposes.
—Italo Calvino, *Invisible Cities* (1974)

Overruling the Grid

At the center of the new urbanism lay a vision of the urban periphery. Although Victorian city builders pursued planning initiatives throughout the city, their most ambitious goal was to transform upper Manhattan and the surrounding regions into a civilizing terrain of scenic parks, tree-lined promenades, tutelary public institutions, and planned suburbs. Such a landscape would be integrated into the larger geography of the metropolitan area. Yet it would counteract the confinement and moral corrosiveness of the older city with a topography of domestic and civic virtue, private property and public sociability. Thus, bourgeois urbanists envisioned the march uptown as a rendezvous with destiny. They sought to design a landscape there that would embody New York's future as the national center of a capitalist civilization.

To understand how Victorian city builders recast the periphery, we must start with the landscape that they fought so hard to undo: most of all, the street plan of 1811. I have argued that the grid embodied the uneven play of dynamism, rationality, and disorder in New York's growth. Not surprisingly, it was attacked by nearly every advocate for systematic planning in New York. Thus, the *Real Estate Record* railed at "the exasperating idiots who ruined New York by the street system of 1807," and Frederick Law Olmsted wondered if it had been "hit upon by the chance occurrence of a mason's sieve near the map of the ground to be laid out."[1]

Urbanists condemned the grid on several grounds. They decried its relentless homogeneity, which erased topographic variety even as it necessitated costly land preparation. "The plan was as simple as a sheet of ruled paper, . . . equally well or ill adapted for any and every location," William Martin complained, "in spite of . . . [the upper city's] advantages of summits and shores." It encouraged a commercialism that many city builders saw as morally corrosive, "feed[ing] the pernicious propensity . . . for gambling on small means," as Olmsted put it, "under the name of speculation." Moreover, the monotony and cramped dimensions of the basic block and lot rendered New York inhospitable to grand landscape effects or good architecture. There could be "no broad squares at the intersection of thoroughfares," complained real-estate boosters, "such as in Europe afford such splendid sites for groups of public buildings." Olmsted agreed, noting that the grid was unsuitable not only for "noble buildings" but also for "wholesome, tidy dwellings" for those of modest means.[2]

The 1811 plan, in short, was at odds with the ideal of a landscape that fostered commercial specialization, public grandeur, and domestic virtue. The qualities that made it a potent engine of growth—its calculability, homogeneity, and boundarilessness— also undermined the ideal of stable, hierarchical land use that Victorian urbanists thought the sine qua non of a metropolis. For New York to become a great city, then, its builders would have to use the new planning ideal—and the new powers of local government—to overrule the grid. During the midcentury boom, they began to do so, employing novel strategies of environmental regulation and public redevelopment to mitigate the disorders of the older cityscape. Many of these initiatives represented important experiments in American city building and urban reform. Yet, all in all, their effect was quite limited. Public regulatory authority remained too undeveloped in the mid-nineteenth century, and downtown property interests too entrenched, to permit the wholesale transformation of lower Manhattan.

Victorian urbanists and developers inherited a long tradition of private, local, and ad hoc efforts to control property investment and land use in New York. The most pervasive strategy was also the least visible: the inclusion of restrictive covenants in leases and conveyances to regulate property use. As Elizabeth Blackmar has shown, covenants were widely employed by Manhattan landowners, developers, and realtors to exclude workers' housing and nuisance trades from "respectable" neighborhoods. "No Smith's Shops, Tallow Chandler's or Starch Maker's Works to be erected at any time," read a 1799 lease for St. John's Park. By the 1840s, New York's growing need for food and animal power expanded the list of restrictions; one typical lease forbade any "brewery, distillery, slaughterhouse, soap, candle, or turp factory, or bakery, cow stable or livery stable." Midcentury city builders continued to use such devices to enforce their standards of class and economic hierarchy. An auction notice for property on West Thirty-fourth Street announced restrictions "against slaughterhouses, manufactories, and other noxious trade or business"—as well as "erecting a church." The Brooklyn park board included similar covenants in planning a "parkway neighborhood" near Prospect Park.[3]

Restrictive covenants imposed informal but wide-ranging controls on New York's growth; they reinforced the tendency of the location market to separate genteel residence from tenement-industrial districts. Yet even the most pervasive contractual restrictions could not protect property from the volatility of the real-estate market. Thus, throughout the nineteenth century, owners and tenants also petitioned public authorities to regulate land use, building, and nuisances on an ad hoc basis. In the 1830s, for instance, downtown proprietors lobbied the Common Council to clear the notorious Five Points slum by a campaign of street improvements. (The aldermen refused, citing the economic value of the rents brought in by local liquor dealers.) By the 1860s, such remonstrances led some public officials to call for systematic regulation of land use and construction. "There should be some restrictions as to the localities upon which tenement houses should be erected," argued the city's superintendent of buildings. "Many instances have come to my knowledge . . . in which owners of lots, situated in parts of the city where rows of costly and elegant dwellings were erected . . . commenced the erection of rough and unsightly structures of the tenement house order, thus depreciating the value of the surrounding property and marring the beauty of some of our finest streets and avenues . . ." Such sentiments only increased with the growth of New York's population and civil disorders. State and city authorities responded in the 1850s and 1860s by creating new doctrines and institutions to control the city-building process.[4]

The legal basis for this turn to regulation grew out of the process of political consolidation that I discussed in the previous chapter. In New York and elsewhere, legislators and judges enlarged the doctrine of the police power to permit cities to deal expansively with environmental and social ills. By 1872, when John Dillon's landmark treatise on U.S. municipal law was first published, the police power was construed to sanction "the suppression of nuisances, the preservation of the public health, the prevention of fires, [and] the regulation of trades and occupations." New York was among the first American cities to translate this doctrine into public controls. The first efforts were ad hoc and uncoordinated: a health official's drive to close bone-boiling shops in mid-Manhattan; an ordinance to move farther north the "fire line" below which wood building was proscribed. Starting just before the Civil War, however, the state and city governments created a series of new administrative agencies to regulate the Manhattan landscape.[5]

Three aspects of the environment in particular were subjected to new controls. First of all, buildings. In the early 1860s, Albany lawmakers expanded the size and authority of New York's Department of Buildings, giving it a full-time staff and the nation's first comprehensive code. Under the leadership of Superintendent James MacGregor, the department instituted systematic procedures for approving plans, inspecting existing structures, and enforcing the code. (These administrative innovations, especially the registering of building plans in docket books, provided much of the research base for Chapters 2, 3, and 4.) Fire fighting was similarly professionalized in 1865. At the urging of business leaders and insurance underwriters, Albany replaced volunteer companies with the Metropolitan Fire Department, which served both New York and Brooklyn. In place of the rowdy, rivalrous companies, the department instituted a paid, uniformed force, a military model of discipline, the use of up-to-date technology, and a safety code for contractors and landlords.[6]

The second target of environmental regulation was urban street life. As I noted in Chapter 5, municipal officials used the expanded police power to suppress the long-standing use of the streets for trade, sociability, subsistence, and political assembly in favor of circulatory efficiency. This privileging of *movement* as the normative activity of public space was central to the shift from local and particularist forms of governance to a liberally constituted municipal state. Streets "belong to the general, rather than the local, public," argued Dillon's treatise. "The fundamental idea of a street is not only that it is public, but public for all purposes of free and unobstructed passage. . . ." In the 1860s and 1870s, the city government acted on such doctrines. The Common Council passed regulations licensing street peddlers and enjoining sidewalk obstructions (Figure 7.1). The city's charity commissioners launched a campaign to remove truant or vagrant children to school or the poorhouse. The Metropolitan Police suppressed unlicensed assemblies, most notoriously in 1874, when mounted officers rioted against an illegal but peaceful demonstration of unemployed workers in Tompkins Square (Figure 7.2). "To go out on the street and talk politics," one labor radical would recall bitterly, "is violating a corporation ordinance."[7]

The third object of regulation was the most significant for the history of urban environmental reform: public health. As I have noted, the Metropolitan Board of Health was chartered in 1866, in the face of a cholera outbreak, but it culminated a decade of agitation by sanitary reformers, merchants, and journalists. The state gave the board wide authority to regulate conditions in both New York and Brooklyn, including the power to enjoin nuisances and to compel improvements from landlords, entrepreneurs, public franchises, and the municipalities themselves. The commission used its powers ambitiously. It shut down dozens of noxious trades, proscribing slaughtering and fat-rendering establishments everywhere except the up-island waterfront; it ordered the disinfecting of streets and slips throughout lower Manhattan; and it removed a literal mountain of horse manure—some 160,000 tons—from vacant lots along the riverfronts. The health board was widely hailed with averting cholera epidemics in both 1866 and 1871. Equally relevant for a history of city building, it transformed sanitary reform from the ad hoc suppression of nuisances to a systematic, if rudimentary, regulation of land use and construction.[8]

These initiatives reflected the same mixture of state building and class politics that we saw in the new urbanism as a whole. On one hand, bodies like the Department of Buildings and the Board of Health—permanent, professionalized, vested with police powers, and theoretically independent of local and partisan interests—furthered the growth of a local regulatory state. On the other hand, they defined regulation in light of bourgeois concerns with property rights and class order. The modernization of fire protection, for instance, was largely shaped by the desire of business proprietors to safeguard downtown property. The Fire Department concentrated its energies in the commercial wards, to the neglect of nearby tenements and uptown residential areas. More subtly the professionalization of fire fighting was meant to defend propertied New Yorkers from the threat of the firefighters themselves. As *Harper's Weekly* put it, "Whatever faults attach to the new department, it is certainly a vast improvement over . . . the rowdy volunteer system. Then there was but little choice between being burned out and robbed of every thing of value that they could lay their hands on.

FIGURE 7.1 The streets were seen as a barometer of social order. The efforts of the Commissioners of Charity to eradicate child peddling were part of a broad campaign to regulate street life in the 1860s and 1870s. (*Harper's Weekly*, January 30, 1869; image courtesy of HarpWeek, LLC)

FIGURE 7.2 An unemployed workers' demonstration is suppressed in the Tompkins Square police riot of 1874. (*Frank Leslie's Illustrated Newspaper*, January 31, 1874; negative no. 70957; © Collection of the New-York Historical Society)

Sometimes, indeed, a false alarm would be given for no other purpose than to give an opportunity for plundering . . ." Such class anxieties were political as well as economic. The volunteer companies had long been a base of plebeian support for ward politicians. (Tweed helped to found the Americus Engine Company, whose symbol, the tiger, gave Thomas Nast his anti-Tammany icon.) Republicans in Albany and New York thus reorganized fire protection partly to *disorganize* the political culture of class patronage that it buttressed.[9]

Building codes, street ordinances, and health boards represented an ambitious program of environmental and social improvement. And yet—compared to contemporaneous uptown planning and modern environmental controls—the turn to regulation proved surprisingly limited in effect. Nowhere are its ambitions and limits clearer than in the most innovative regulatory law of the era: the tenement code of 1867. As a pioneering effort to set standards for working-class housing, the code might have formed the basis for a full-blown regulatory urbanism, based on the improvement of the existing cityscape rather than the laying out of an alternative one. Yet it did little to ameliorate New York's most pressing environmental ill.

Moral and sanitary reformers had investigated and decried New York's tenements for two decades. Agitation reached a peak in 1865, when the Citizens' Association issued its pathbreaking *Report . . . upon the Sanitary Condition of the City*. As I have noted, the association had been founded in the wake of the 1863 draft riots to mobilize genteel intellectuals and civic businessmen on behalf of New York's political and environmental renovation. Its first campaign was for tenement reform. In the summer of 1864, the association's Council of Hygiene surveyed housing conditions throughout Manhattan; its findings caused an overnight sensation. Filled with vital statistics, site maps, and Dickensian vignettes, the *Report* exposed the world of the tenements to middle-class view and schooled middle-class New Yorkers on how to view them (Figure 7.3). It carried a simple message: medically, the tenements were a prolific source of disease and death; socially, they bred disorder and vice. Indeed the *Report* portrayed these threats as almost identical, linking them in a rhetoric of contagion. "To the physical and moral degradation . . . of these miserable abodes, where decay reigns supreme over habitation and inhabitant alike, may be plainly traced much of the immorality and crime which prevail among us," Dr. Ezra Pulling wrote in his account of the Fourth Ward. "Under such influences have been reared a large class, already so numerous as . . . to endanger the safety of our social and political fabric."[10]

For twenty years, such apocalyptic warnings had fallen on deaf ears. Yet during the 1860s they coincided with two catastrophes that made legislators and metropolitan elites take seriously the epidemiology of disorder: the draft riots and the threat of a cholera epidemic three years later. It was clear to all that tenement life posed a threat to the public health, public order, and the integrity of the body politic. Thus, at the urging of the Citizens' Association, the Board of Health, and New York's leading dailies, Albany lawmakers passed the Tenement House Act of 1867, the first such code in the nation. The act mandated minimum standards for the construction and

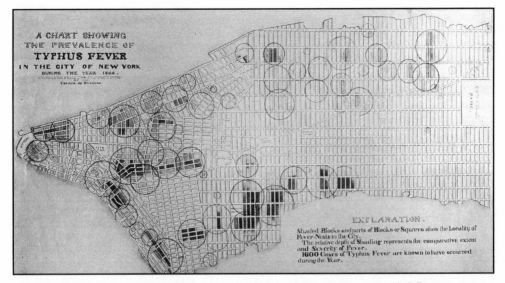

FIGURE 7.3   A survey map published by the Citizens' Association in its 1865 *Report . . . upon the Sanitary Condition of the City* charts outbreaks of typhus in Manhattan, vividly illustrating the association between disease and class geography. (*A Chart Showing the Prevalence of Typhus Fever in the City of New York During the Year 1864*, map, 1864; Museum of the City of New York, 29.100.3172)

maintenance of tenant and lodging houses. It required the ventilation of all sleeping quarters, the provision of fire escapes, and the cleansing of infectious apartments. It set limits on the distance between buildings, the height of rooms, and the provision of privies and water closets (one facility for every twenty occupants). Finally, it authorized the Board of Health to enforce its provisions. The board prosecuted thousands of code violations by city landlords—more than three thousand suits in 1868 alone. The following year it undertook a comprehensive survey of Manhattan's tenements, and it closed hundreds of cellar tenements, displacing perhaps half of the twenty thousand people who lived in them.[11]

Yet the tenement code failed to significantly improve housing for New York's working people. To begin with, the law was weakly drawn. It did not set limits on lot and room densities, for instance, the worst aspects of the housing crisis. It also lacked a dependable mechanism of enforcement, for the Board of Health was accorded at once too much legal discretion and too few resources. Landlords and nuisance owners evaded the commission's reach by obtaining injunctions from friendly judges or pressure from local politicos. "If I am a landlord and have five or six blocks of tenement houses, I am not afraid of the board of health," one labor activist told a U.S. Senate hearing. "The political system of New York is so elastic that we can make it of any length . . . by the force of greenbacks." This elasticity increased in 1870, when the "home rule" charter replaced the metropolitan commission with a municipal Health Department. In contrast to the activism of the parks and public-works departments, Tammany health administrators assuaged real-estate interests by stalemating en-

FIGURE 7.4   A reform-minded *Harper's* illustrator attacks landlords and Tammany politicians for colluding to block enforcement of sanitary codes. (*Harper's Weekly*, February 26, 1881; image courtesy of HarpWeek, LLC)

forcement of the 1867 act (Figure 7.4). "The laws . . . regulating the erection of tenements in the city [are] . . . a dead letter," claimed Joseph Haight, a spokesmen for tenement landlords. "Not a single house in this city has been erected in conformity with those laws. Tenement property would not net four per cent. if th[ey] were complied with."[12]

As Haight's comment suggests, the obstacles to reform were as much economic as political. Beneath partisan and legal inertia, there was the deeper intractability of housing and labor markets that enforced strategies of overcrowding by tenants and rewarded it by landlords. The result was the working-class landscape described in Chapter 2: a world of brick barracks and fire escapes that rationalized congestion rather than diminishing it. Only a well-established, regulatory state, wielding broad welfare powers and backed by a strong municipal coalition, could have overruled these market forces. Victorian environmentalists possessed neither the institutional nor the ideological resources to do so. Battling a secure and rooted tradition of property rights with new and relatively weak state powers, they could not undo the tangle of interests knotted into the built environment of lower Manhattan—especially when Democratic partisans used *their* growing power to render tenement regulation a dead letter.

This story of economic entrenchment and political stalemate was also evident in the other great effort to transform the older cityscape: port redevelopment. As I discussed in Chapter 3, the disorder of the waterfront posed a grave environmental and commercial threat to New York, spurring calls for comprehensive improvements among officials, business leaders, and planning advocates. Yet the debate over "dock reform" proved to be fragmented and contentious. Three different visions of how to rebuild the waterfront dominated public discussion, but none was fully adopted.

The least popular proposals came from Manhattan's wharf and water lot owners, who sought unfettered market development along the shore. Such proprietors supported deregulation of dock rates and land use, attacking waterfront planning as "demagogue[ry] . . . which strikes at the rights of property." For the most part, however, New York's commercial leadership opposed laissez-faire growth and stressed the need for coordination of the port's manifold activities. Some businessmen, notably financiers and merchants linked to the rail economy, called for a franchised corporation to pursue "a comprehensive system of dock improvement." Dozens of such schemes were floated in public hearings and the press during the 1860s and 1870s, some receiving substantial political and financial support. In 1873, for instance, a Vanderbilt-led consortium won legislative approval for a waterfront railway that would encircle New York with a belt of terminal and warehouse complexes. Downtown business interests and upstate political leaders, however, rebelled against giving the nation's richest commercial asset to its most powerful corporation. "I can regard it in no other light than a sacrifice of the commercial interests of the city and of its business classes to private gain," Governor John Dix wrote in vetoing the Vanderbilt franchise.[13]

Dix's veto message articulated the third strand of business opinion concerning the redevelopment of New York's waterfront: a downtown version of the politics of stewardship. Drawing on the widely held mercantilist assumption that the business community as a whole—as a class—incarnated the public interest, merchants' organizations like the Produce Exchange and the Chamber of Commerce called for the comprehensive administration of the harbor by a disinterested commercial elite. Not surprisingly, the leading advocate for this view was the Citizens' Association. Throughout the late 1860s, the association's Subcommittee on Wharves and Piers agitated for a state-appointed harbor commission overseen by a board of merchants. Like the health board, it would unite Manhattan and Brooklyn into a single metropolitan district, supervising wharfage rates, dock access, and infrastructural requirements for the port as a whole. The commission would not directly reconstruct the waterfront as a public work, the association urged, but spur integrated private investment.[14]

The proposal gained "the active support of the leading commercial interests of New-York," as well as much of the non-Democratic press. The Democratic machine, however, proved a fatal stumbling block. Tammany Hall saw no need to forgo the patronage windfall that rebuilding the docks would provide. Tweed defeated the Citizens' Association bill in Albany, and in the "home-rule" charter of 1870 he won passage for a more partisan version of dock reform: a municipal department of docks whose board was appointed by the mayor. Unlike the original proposal, the city department was mandated to acquire privately owned piers by purchase or condemnation; to approve a comprehensive plan of improvement to which all subsequent development must conform; and to implement its plan as a public work, financed by bond issues of up to $3 million annually. Tammany Hall, in short, attached its party-building agenda to a more ambitious version of port development.[15]

The debate over the waterfront thus rehearsed many of the interests and ideologies that shaped the politics of city building as a whole. It included advocates for market-driven growth, franchised corporations, elite stewardship, and party machines. In contrast to upper Manhattan, however, where these divergent voices sometimes concatenated powerfully to reshape the built environment, a solution to the port's disorders proved elusive. Despite the legal authority of the Tammany Department of Docks, de facto power over the waterfront remained so fragmented as to block decisive improvements. More any other sector of municipal politics, the success of the dock board depended on mercantile support. Mayor Oakey Hall was constrained to fill it with downtown notables who curbed Tammany's ambitions. After extensive hearings, the board approved in 1871 a cautious proposal for the widening of the river streets and the construction of a masonry seawall. No provision was made for building integrated dock basins like Brooklyn's Erie complex; no support was offered for ambitious schemes of rail terminals and warehouse complexes.[16]

Even this modest, incremental program was undermined in the fiscal crisis of the 1870s. When the Tweed frauds were exposed, the city's business leadership threw its support behind the anti-Tammany Committee of Seventy; when the reform administration of merchant William Havemeyer won office in 1872, its zeal for fiscal retrenchment trumped any desire for continuing waterfront improvements. "The ambitious schemes that were afoot when the present [dock] Commissioners took office . . . would, if carried out, have swamped the credit of the city," Mayor Havemeyer reported in 1874, adding with some satisfaction, "[they] have not made much progress." By the end of the 1870s depression, only the section of seawall between Canal and West Tenth streets had been completed, and neither the city government nor the business community had done much to arrest the port's decline. "When we consider the great extent of our water front, and its capabilities, we cannot help but wonder at the many incongruous spectacles that must be witnessed [there,]" one port expert concluded in the mid-1880s. "West Street and its later thoroughfares are at times almost impassable," while "[a]long other sections . . . , there is an appearance of something very nearly approaching stagnation." It was a comment that might have been made thirty years earlier or any time in between.[17]

Both tenement codes and waterfront development, in short, marked the limits of bourgeois urbanism in the existing landscape. Where regulatory or development initiatives were congruent with the protection of downtown property rights or the maintenance of class order—as in the improvement of fire fighting—they succeeded in reshaping the city-building process. Where such efforts confronted entrenched or fragmented interests—as with tenement and dock reform—comprehensive environmental change was defeated or downscaled. And so bourgeois urbanists looked uptown for the setting of their planned utopia. Of course, similar impulses were at play in both arenas. Both uptown and downtown planning represented an effort to subordinate market forces to systematic controls and civilizing values; both embraced commission rule as the best model for metropolitan growth. Like downtown regulators, the advocates of uptown design sought to overrule the grid; but they looked beyond the grid to do so. They sought to create a peripheral utopia of civility and order, an otherworld of open spaces and secure boundaries, where the oppressions of the grid could be suspended. They began with Central Park.

Inside Out: The Paradoxes of Central Park

At its inception in the mid-1850s, "the Central Park," as it was called, was considerably more central to the ambitions of its makers than to the New York cityscape. It was in laying out the park that the city's most influential urbanists first developed their theories and program of landscape design. Indeed, laying out the park was what constituted them as a community of urbanists to begin with. Central Park provided the occasion on which genteel intellectuals made common cause with New York's commercial and propertied elite to reconstruct the cityscape and uplift the civic order.

Since the mid-1840s, an influential array of reformers, journalists, and businessmen had lobbied for a grand scenic park; these included the sanitarian John Griscom, the editor-poet William Cullen Bryant, merchant Robert Minturn, and especially Andrew Jackson Downing. Downing was the most influential exponent of moral environmentalism in the antebellum United States. He preached the gospel of civilizing design in his own commissions, his best-selling residential pattern books, and *The Horticulturalist*, a monthly that he edited from his home in Newburgh, New York. Urban pleasure grounds were a key element in his program of environmental uplift. Downing praised parks as tutelary institutions that were essential to the preservation of civic life in an increasingly urbanized and class-divided republic—most of all, in a burgeoning city like New York. "[A park] is republican in its very idea and tendency," he wrote in an 1851 column. "It takes up popular education where the common school and the ballot-box leave it, and raises up the working-man to the same level of enjoyment with the man of leisure and accomplishment. . . . Plant spacious parks in your cities, and unloose their gates as wide as the gates of morning to the whole people. And as there are dark places at noon, so education and culture . . . will banish the plague-spots of democracy . . ."[18]

By the late 1850s, such a view had become part of the common sense of New York's cultural gentry. Indeed, the prestige of its proponents was part of what made the ideal of moral environmentalism so influential. The creation of a great, civilizing park was supported by every organ of elite opinion in the metropolis—the genteel press, the liberal pulpit, the leading reform associations—and its advocates were bound in a dense web of personal, professional, and associational bonds. Such networks played a crucial role in the success of both the park and its superintendent. Olmsted's friendship with Vaux, for instance, began at a chance meeting in Downing's Newburgh home in 1851; it was also through Downing that he met Charles Wyllys Elliott, the park commissioner who alerted him to the superintendent's job opening at another chance meeting in a Connecticut seaside inn six years later. When Olmsted applied for the position, his supporters included leading journalists and literary figures like William Cullen Bryant, Horace Greeley, poet Bayard Taylor, and Washington Irving. Such networks of reciprocity and influence—the counterpart to the partisan loyalties of machine politics—reinforced the gentry's experience of the park as a collective project of cultural stewardship.[19]

Yet the "best men" could not have pursued park making had they not been allied with other metropolitan elites. The enterprise was endorsed by nearly every faction in New York politics. Indeed, as historians of Central Park have detailed, the early 1850s saw a complex struggle among competing political and real-estate elites over the siting and administration of the new park. The skirmishing reached a denouement in 1856, when Republican lawmakers selected the "central" park site over its rival, Jones' Wood on the upper East River, and established the Board of Commissioners for Central Park to oversee its development.[20] In so doing, as I have discussed, they removed control of the project from Mayor Fernando Wood—who had earlier appointed his own commission—and vested it in a "nonpartisan" elite of civic capitalists. The eleven members of the Central Park commission, appointed by Governor John King, included five wealthy businessmen (among them, banker John Gray, merchant John Butterworth, and ironmonger Charles Wyllys Elliott) and four lawyers (among them, Robert Dillon and Andrew Green). The appointments showed a careful attention to the ecology of political forces in New York City. There were six Republicans, four Democrats, and one Know-Nothing, and within the major parties, a balance of "reform" and "partisan" figures.[21]

These intricacies notwithstanding, the park board resolved itself almost immediately into two blocs, roughly corresponding to the political divide discussed in the previous chapter. In the minority was a Democratic bloc that included the conservative attorney Dillon, financier August Belmont (an anti-Tammanyite who was national chair of the Democracy), Tammany lawyer Thomas Field, and Know-Nothing Waldo Hutchins. Often led by Dillon, they contested many of the aesthetic and administrative decisions taken by the board majority, Olmsted, and Vaux. They sought to defeat the Greensward Plan in the 1858 design competition; to amend the plan to include more "artificial" scenic effects; to organize the construction of the park by competitive contracting rather than public labor; and, finally, to instigate an 1860 state legislative investigation of park financing. The minority tended to assert the clientelistic politics and spectacular aesthetics that characterized the urbanism of the New York Democracy. Although it succeeded in introducing several changes into the Greensward Plan—most importantly, the segregated transportation circuits—its efforts were largely defeated by the commission majority. (The State Senate hearings of 1860 not only exonerated the park board of fiscal irresponsibility, but declared its work a "triumphant success.")[22]

The majority coalition comprised the board's six Republicans and one anti-Tammany Democrat. These men had their differences; they included capitalist gentry like Gray and Elliott and Republican partisans like John Butterworth. Yet their aesthetic and administrative decisions—most of all the hiring of Olmsted and the selection of the Greensward Plan—reflected a shared vision of the park as an agency of public refinement and of themselves as the trustees of a divided and heterogeneous metropolis. At the center of this bloc, ironically, was its sole Democrat, Andrew Haswell Green. Green was a corporate attorney with wide-ranging downtown contacts, a patrician Democrat opposed to the Tammany machine, and a tireless, capable, and controlling administrator. He took the leadership of the park board almost immediately, serving as its president and treasurer; in 1859 he suspended his law practice to devote himself to the paid office of comptroller of the park. Although his battles with Olmsted were notorious—mainly efforts to micromanage the latter's expenditures—Green did more than anyone else to institutionalize the alliance between the reform gentry and the business elites whose values and interests he represented. His advocacy was instrumental in winning Olmsted the post of superintendent in 1857; he cast a key vote in favor of the Greensward Plan in the design competition a year later; and he consistently defended the plan's pastoral aesthetics against its critics.[23]

It was with the victory of "Greensward" that the cultural gentry and the civic businessmen cemented their alliance. The commission had announced a public contest to design the park in October 1857; Olmsted and Vaux worked in secret throughout the winter, submitting their pseudonymous design on April 1, the closing day of the contest. They were the thirty-third in an eclectic array of entries. As Roy Rosenzweig and Elizabeth Blackmar have shown brilliantly, the proposals displayed an astonishing range of aesthetic and social visions, from extravagant leasure gardens to formal parade grounds to expositional settings for museums and crystal palaces. Not surprisingly, however, the commission's awards reflected the predominance of two landscape traditions. The Democratic minority supported several proposals that foregrounded formal promenading, monumental architectural effects, and occasions for mass display. The seven members of the majority coalition awarded first place (and a prize of two thousand dollars) to "Greensward." The plan was the first great expression of the majority's aims, techniques, and design ideals: the first précis of what the uptown utopia of genteel urbanists would look like.[24]

As designed and modified by Olmsted and Vaux, the plan for Central Park made a curiously ambiguous statement about the metropolis that was to surround it (Figure 7.5). It was intended to serve as an anticity, a pastoral otherworld within which Manhattan's "noise, bustle, confinement, and noxious qualities" would be replaced by "an opposite class of conditions . . . remedial of the influences of urban life." To enter that world was literally to overrule the grid: to go through the looking glass into a therapeutic space where confining streets gave way to sinuous drives, crowded sidewalks to peaceful promenades, atomistic competition to refined sociability. At the same time, the park remained indubitably an artifact of the metropolis against which

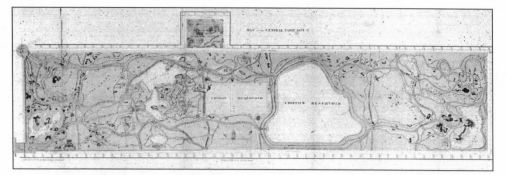

FIGURE 7.5   The Greensward Plan for Central Park, reproduced here, is a slight modification of Olmsted and Vaux's original 1858 design, amended to reflect the extension of the park boundary from 106th Street to 110th Street. (Courtesy of the Central Park Conservancy)

it was designed. Celebrated as an emblem of New York's urbanity and metropolitan grandeur, it would have been out of context—useless and unrecognizable—anywhere else. Its very success as a pleasure ground depended on the booster dynamism and straight-edged growth that its design seemed, visually, to suspend: "The Park is not planned for such use as is now made of it," Olmsted argued in 1870, "but with regard to the future use, when it will be in the centre of a population of two millions hemmed in by water at a short distance on all sides." Similarly the design and governance of the park implied a model for the larger reconstruction of urban space and sociability. Just as boulevards and landscaped residential districts spread out from the parkscape itself, so its scenic order, rules of use, and modes of administration embodied a new planning ideal in embryo: an urbanism clothed in the idiom of rustic leisure.[25]

Central Park was designed, in short, in a dialectical relationship with New York: at once oppositional and prefigurative, anticity and antecity, pastoral refuge and booster prophecy. This relationship was rooted in the double vision of urban life that I have called the imperial ideal: the idea that a metropolitan center like New York should embody and integrate capitalist energy and civilizational order. It was this dualism of great cities that made landscapes like Central Park at once possible and necessary.

In a series of theoretical writings—most importantly, the 1870 lecture *Public Parks and the Enlargement of Towns*—Olmsted analyzed the double knot between urban development and park design. On one hand, he wrote, "the enlargement of towns" was a sign and cause of the progress of civilization; it fostered "the dying-out of slavery and feudal customs," "the multiplication of books, newspapers, schools, and other means of popular education," and "the accumulation of wealth in . . . seats of learning, of science, and of art." Parks and other resorts of refined leisure depended on this growth of prosperity and taste. On the other hand, even as urban life enabled "the emancipation of both men and women from petty, confining, and narrowing cares," it substituted other, new confinements. The economic development that paid the bills of Progress "require[d] . . . an arrangement of buildings, and a character of streets and of traffic . . . which [created] conditions of corruption and of irritation, physical and mental." Such degrading "conditions," embodied in the Manhattan street grid, made the antithetical landscape of the park necessary.[26]

What was it about the existing cityscape that produced "corruption and irritation"? Like other reformers and writers, Olmsted decried the demoralizing influence of the city's sanitary problems, tenements, and class divisions. Yet he reserved his most direct and vehement critique for the debasement of public sociability. Parks were essential, he insisted, to counteract the anonymity and competitiveness that were the defining marks of urban social life. Like Engels's famous account of central Manchester, Olmsted inscribed this critique in the tableau of the downtown street crowd: "Whenever we walk through the denser part of a town," he lamented, "our minds are . . . brought into close dealings with other minds without any friendly flowing toward them, but rather a drawing from them. . . . [We] have seen thousands of [our] fellow-men, have met them face to face, have brushed against them, and yet have had no experience of anything in common with them." Such street theater dissolved all bonds of civic fellowship, enforcing an ethos of mental sharpness and moral dullness. For city dwellers "to maintain a temperate, good-natured, and healthy state of mind" within such a landscape, Olmsted concluded, city builders and reformers had to provide "opportunities of relief from it."[27]

The happy irony was that "the enlargement of towns" enabled such opportunities of relief. Especially in commercial centers like New York, the processes of capital accumulation, administrative centralization, and geographic growth opened up the wealth, expertise, and land with which to construct an otherworld of civilizing public intercourse. Olmsted and Vaux designed Central Park, and all their parks, to do just that: to turn the landscape of the capitalist metropolis against its own disorders. Such a therapeutic space would act as "the lungs of the city" and a source of "pure and wholesome air." Against the psychosocial "shock" of urban life—to borrow Walter Benjamin's concept—it would "dispel from the mind of the visitor . . . thoughts of business and memories calculated to sadden or oppress." Against the solvent of market competition and the friction of class enmity, it would renew civic community. A park "withdraw[s] us from those engrossing mercenary pursuits by which we are too apt to be absorbed," enthused the Prospect Park commission in its 1869 report, "contributing alike to the pleasure and improvement of . . . the man of business and the man of work."[28]

The medium for this metamorphosis of city life was a landscape of leisure, but it called for landscape and leisure of a specific sort. Olmsted and Vaux construed the restorative experience of a park to come primarily through visual effects—as opposed, for instance, to the physical exertion stressed by Progressive play reformers or the rituals of mass assembly so central to nineteenth-century republican culture. They figured the evils of urban living as deprivations of the eye: on one hand, the occluding of vision by the sheer density of the cityscape, on the other, the constant watchfulness demanded by such congestion. Central Park, in contrast, was meant "to secure an antithesis of objects of vision to those of the streets and houses." Open

FIGURE 7.6   Olmsted and Vaux used both landscape and architectural elements (such as the Terrace depicted here) to organize spectacles of decorous leisure in Central Park. Enabling park goers both to enact and view such scenes was one of the primary aims of the Greensward Plan. (*Valentine's Manual of the Corporation of the City of New York*, 1864; University Library, University of Michigan)

greensward and broad lake views would compensate for the inability to glimpse a clean horizon line in Manhattan. The mystery and variety of "undulating meadow without defined edge, its turf lost in a haze of shadows of scattered trees," would overcome the confinement of the grid. Finally, and in some ways most importantly, not only rustic scenery but also one's fellow citizens would become "the natural food and refreshment of the human eye." The system of prospects and terraces that Olmsted and Vaux built into the park was designed to transform other people from (social and spatial) competitors into objects of genteel spectacle—indeed to define leisure *as* genteel spectacle (Figure 7.6). The modal urban encounter would become not the traffic jam, but the promenade.[29]

Central Park's organizing strategy, in other words, was scenic. The park composed both nature and society into visual fields within which the rigors of city life were suspended. "As what is well designed to nourish the body makes a meal a meal," the designers told the New York park board in an 1872 memorandum, "so what is well designed to recreate the mind from urban oppressions through the eye, makes the Park the Park." *To recreate the mind from urban oppressions through the eye*: the park performed its work by placing a series of visual frames around the visitor's experience, frames that distanced the familiar elements of the urban landscape and enclosed unfamiliar ones. By delineating the park as an inner realm of vision against an outer realm of occlusion, this act of framing dramatized the park's oppositional stance to the city. Reversing the usual relationship, it nested rural life inside urban space, nature inside culture, and it exiled market exchange, the "core" activity of New York, to the periphery of the visible. An island within an island, Central Park turned Manhattan inside out. It transformed the rectilinear confinement of the street grid into a frame within which the eye might be free to play, and the community might be mended.[30]

This conception of the park as a (visual and moral) frame pervades the details of the Greensward Plan and Superintendent Olmsted's policies for its regulation and use. Not only was all evidence of trade and labor—"any pretence of utility," as the 1864 annual report put it—banished from the grounds. So too was any rival conception of recreation that might adulterate the park's scenic and restorative character. In contrast to the use of Central Park in the twentieth century, the original board held athletic activity to a minimum, resisting both popular desires for ball fields and upper-class efforts to use the western drives as an equestrian speedway. Even where limited provision was made for sports, as in the Cricket Ground and the boating and skating facilities, Olmsted and Vaux landscaped the spaces to encourage spectatorship and to assimilate the active participants as elements of the "scene." Indeed, contemporaneous accounts suggest that winter visitors went as often to watch skating from the terraced shore as to skate themselves; the activity had more of the flavor of a promenade than of exercise (Figure 7.7). The park's transportation system similarly worked to subdue movement: except for one exceptional stretch dictated by the shape of the Croton Reservoir inside the park, the sinuous carriageways and bridle paths allowed no scope for amateur racing. Roads existed in the park primarily to move the eye effortlessly from prospect to prospect (Figure 7.8).[31]

Along with this suppression of "exertive" recreation, Olmsted and Vaux lavished infinite attention on the succession of vistas that a visitor would experience—differently with each mode of transportation—on the grounds. In an 1865 report to the Prospect Park board, for instance, they offered a detailed exegesis of the southwestern entry into Central Park; the result is a unique glimpse of the technical choices by which the designers enacted the park's program:

> Entering by [Eighth Avenue and Fifty-ninth Street], in a few moments the visitor's eye falls upon the open space called the Cricket-Ground, . . . which extends before the observer to a distance of nearly a thousand feet. Here is a suggestion of freedom and repose which must itself be refreshing and tranquilizing to the visitor coming from the confinement and bustle of the crowded streets. But this is not all. The observer, resting for a moment to enjoy the scene, which he is induced to do by the arrangement of the planting, cannot but hope for still greater space than is obvious before him, and this hope is encouraged, first, by the fact, that though bodies of rock and foliage to the right and left obstruct his direct vision, no limit is seen to the extension of the meadow in a lateral direction; while beyond the low shrubs, which form an indefinite border to it in front, there are no trees or other impediments to vision for a distance of half a mile or more, and the only distinct object is the wooded knoll of Vista Rock, nearly a mile away, upon the summit of which it is an important point in the design, not yet realized, to erect a slight artificial structure for the purpose of catching the eye, and the better holding it in this direction. The imagination of the visitor is thus led instinctively to form the idea that a broad expanse is opening before him, and the more surely to accomplish this, a glimpse of a slope of turf beyond the border of shrub in the middle distance has been secured.

As the forward rhythm of the prose itself dramatizes, Olmsted and Vaux staged the entry into the park as an unfolding sweep of views marked off by wood, rock, turf, and water. They choreographed a processional sequence in which each vista consti-

FIGURE 7.7   Like carriage driving, horseback riding, and strolling in the warmer months, ice-skating on the Lake at Central Park was more a form of promenade than of exercise—a way of turning movement into sociability and spectacle. (*Harper's Weekly*, January 28, 1860; image courtesy of HarpWeek, LLC)

FIGURE 7.8   An emphasis on visual scenography translated the park-scape into a carefully choreographed sequence of prospects and vistas. (*Valentine's Manual of the Corporation of the City of New York*, 1861; University Library, University of Michigan)

tutes a frame for the next one and invites the viewer into it. The experience was to be heightened yet unhurried, one that left the cityscape behind and impelled the viewer into an otherworld of "freedom and repose." Here mobility connoted play rather than compulsion, social intercourse rather than strategic calculation. Even as the visitor rounded the Cricket Ground, its curving paths and hillocks denied the fixity of boundaries that were so ironclad outside. The glimpse of the Sheep Meadow beyond, and of Vista Rock beyond that, seemed to guarantee that borders were there simply to be transcended, simply to draw the visitor on toward even freer expanses of "rural spaciousness." Despite being inside the city, the park promised infinite extension. Its various edges and horizon lines seemed never to limit vision, but to hint at its enlargement.[32]

Now this was brilliant spectacle, but like much spectacle, it rested on illusion. Olmsted and Vaux were able to achieve "the constant suggestion . . . of an unlimited range of rural conditions" precisely because they cannily assimilated the urban conditions circumscribing the park. They minutely calibrated the details of their design to the constraints of the cityscape outside. In the example from the preceding paragraph, for instance, the sweeping curve of the carriageway around the Cricket Ground, so "suggestive of freedom and repose," carefully steered the visitor away from the Eighth Avenue edge of the park. The designers knew that the narrowness of the site posed the greatest threat to the experience of spaciousness and ease. They took pains "to render the lateral boundaries . . . as inconspicuous as possible," girdling the park with plantings "which, while excluding the buildings . . . from view, would leave an uncertainty as to the occupation of the space beyond." Similarly, they placed an "artificial structure" atop Vista Rock to direct the visitor's eye inward and northward; even here architectural illusionism, however, represented an implicit acknowledgment of the city's confining presence. Olmsted and Vaux deliberately underscaled the Belvedere Castle in order to enhance the sense of its distance, and they proliferated the windings of the carriageways approaching the rock for the same reason: "To the visitor, carried by occasional defiles from one field of landscape to another . . . , the extent of the Park is practically much greater than it would be otherwise be." This use of "defiles" and boundaries to enhance the illusion of magnitude is especially important—and ironic—in the example we have been examining. The shallow rise at the northern end of the Cricket Ground, beyond which "a glimpse of a slope of turf" could be discerned, was the border for the Sixty-fifth street sunken transverse road carrying commercial traffic through the park. Even as the park directed visitors away from one city street, it drew them toward another—but this street was costumed in rural scenery.[33]

In short, the park did not expel urban conditions; it incorporated them by effacing their presence. The city remained ineradicably inside, but Olmsted and Vaux developed a repertory of scenic and dramaturgical conceits to assimilate it and cover it over. The most important example of this double relation to the urban environment was the park's treatment of the transverse roads, and by implication the transportation system as a whole. The commission's requirement of four crosstown thoroughfares constituted the severest constraint imposed by the cityscape on the park's design; it "subdivided [the park] definitely, although it is to be hoped . . . invisibly," as the Greensward proposal wrote, "into five separate and distinct sections." The roads posed a fundamental challenge to the idea of the park as an "inside-out" space; they were an indelible sign that the park remained embedded in and structured by the urban grid. As is well known, Olmsted and Vaux solved the problem by sinking the roadbeds and throwing camouflaged bridges over them at ground level—a technique so liberating that it became the basis for the entire transportation network of the park. On one hand, their system of over- and underpasses enabled the designers to unify the fragmented site by making all boundaries passable. On the other hand, it worked to separate and disperse people through that space, to mediate conflicts between different types of users, at once shielding them from each other and making them figures in one another's scene.[34]

What was illusionistic about such strategies of movement, use, and scenic composition was not the sense of expansiveness or freedom or commonalty that they induced. This was real enough, as both nineteenth-century accounts and a current-day ramble in the park make clear. Rather, it was that such a protected and apparently pastoral experience could belong to a rural landscape. In reality, the park was as citified as the grid that it was designed to overrule. It used techniques of segregation, movement control, and visual occlusion that mirrored the spatial regime of its surroundings. To enter the park, no matter how quiet, winding, or shaded the carriageway, was not to leave urbanity behind, but to turn it against itself. Put another way, the moral and spatial dualisms that defined metropolitan life for bourgeois New Yorkers provided Central Park not only with its ideological rationale, but with its principle of design as well. The park performed its restorative mission by appropriating aspects of the very conditions it was designed to suppress. The result was paradoxical: a landscape where regimentation enhanced the experience of freedom, where the impeding of vision produced an expansive sense of vista, where boundaries seemed to betoken open space.

This design paradox embodied a cultural paradox. Precisely because it was an enclave of refined leisure within and against the city, Central Park served as the setting for a new ideal of urbanity. Nothing makes this fact clearer than its role in metropolitan rituals of sociability. As I have written elsewhere, the park was laid out when promenading was being elaborated into a public ceremony of class affiliation and sexual respectability. Olmsted and Vaux designed it to stage such dramas of recognition. They considered "the Promenade" (as the Mall was first called) "the central feature in our plan . . . for the lower park" and laid out a carriage circuit that immediately became New York's great parade of fashion.[35] By the late 1860s, some 1,500 carriages circulated through the grounds each day: "Fifth Avenue . . . was absolutely thronged with costly new equipages on their way to Central Park," George Templeton Strong noted acidly. "It was a broad torrent of vehicular gentility, wherein the profits of shoddy and petroleum were largely represented." Strong's condescension needs to be taken with a grain of salt; his wife Ellie was as apt to appear on the drive as clothing or oil parvenus. Yet he was right that the park encouraged the elaboration of class performances: "One would hardly believe he was in a republican country," journalist Junius Henri Browne wrote, "to see the escutcheoned panels of the carriages, the liveried coachmen, and the supercilious air of the occupants . . . as they go . . . flaringly by." The drives thus served as a great convocation for the metropolitan bourgeoisie, the gathering place where elite migrants, arrivistes, and Knickerbockers could see themselves as—make themselves into—a national class (Figure 7.9).[36]

Yet the park's urbanity was not meant for the bourgeois public alone. Its makers and advocates conceived it as a blueprint for the renovation of the whole civic community, a surrogate for nearly every "civilizing" institution in Victorian culture. For Andrew Haswell Green, a former head of the city Board of Education, the park was a vast outdoor school: "The value of the Central Park . . . for attractive and elegant recreation . . . is well known," he wrote in 1868. "But its uses as a means of popular intellectual improvement, and its importance as an educational agency in connexion with the great school system of the city are by no means yet fully recognized." Green sought to promote the tutelary function of the park. He persuaded the board to grant play privileges to public school children whose good standing was certified by their teachers, and he helped to found several scientific and educative institutions on or near the park grounds: the Meteorological Observatory, the Arboretum, and the Zoo.[37]

For Olmsted, the dominant models were congregational and domestic. He hailed Central and Prospect parks in almost ecclesiastical terms—"the only places . . . where, in this eighteen hundred and seventieth year after Christ, you will find a body of Christians coming together, and with an evident glee in coming together." Similarly he described the New York park as a homelike refuge, a sanctuary for the familial seclusion that was so central to Victorian ideals of a civilized metropolis (Figure 7.10): "There is one large American town, in which . . . a man of any class shall say to his wife . . . : 'My dear, when the children come home from school, put some bread and butter and salad in a basket, and go to the spring under the chestnut-tree where we found the Johnsons last week. I will join you there as soon as I can get away from the office. We will walk to the dairy-man's cottage and get some tea, and some fresh milk for the children, and take our supper by the brook-side;' and this shall be no joke." As such language makes clear, Olmsted associated the pastoral framing of the park scenery ("chestnut-tree," "brook-side") with domesticity, that most "interior" of Victorian ideals. He and Vaux designed much of the lower park as a family setting, a "Children's District" with a dairy, playhouses, and other facilities designed as rustic cottages. In a metropolis that undermined respectable home life, such a district represented a sort of environmental Children's Aid Society, a counterweight to the evil influences of the tenement and street. Poor children "will be all the better for having been brought up even as park vagrants," the *Real Estate Record* asserted in the racialized language of the time, "rather than the enforced Arabs of the slums."[38]

Thus, Central Park stood for much of what genteel culture meant by "culture." These associations were more than just metaphorical. The ideals of stewardship and environmental "influence" meant that the park literally served in loco parentis, as a

FIGURE 7.9   Central Park was designed to be an inclusive public space, but its conception of "the public" gave scope for class-based sociability as well. This illustration depicts the daily carriage drive that constituted the great community ritual of the metropolitan bourgeoisie (compare Figure 7.10). (*Harper's Weekly*, December 16, 1865; image courtesy of HarpWeek, LLC)

FIGURE 7.10   This stereograph celebrates the park as a setting for domestic intimacy in nature (compare Figure 7.9). (*Central Park, The Music Stand*, stereograph, 1865; Museum of the City of New York; bequest of Dr. Henry A. Cone)

custodian of refined intercourse and moral order. It was the sole commons in a class-divided metropolis; as Olmsted argued in *Public Parks and the Enlargement of Towns,* "Consider that the New York Park and the Brooklyn Park are the only places in those associated cities where . . . all classes [are] largely represented . . . , competitive with none . . . , each individual adding by his mere presence to the pleasure of all others, all helping to the greater happiness of each." Only in such a landscape, at once open and bounded, inclusive but orderly, could the rules and values of civilized life be passed on.[39]

As I argued in the preceding chapter, the parks' offer of common ground and civic fellowship was inseparable from its projection of class power. Olmsted and Vaux did not view such an assertion of genteel values and authority as inimical to the inclusive mission of the park; they sought precisely to give working people access to the same civilizing influences that bourgeois New Yorkers gained through private travel and leisure: "It is one great purpose of the Park to supply to the hundreds of thousands of tired workers, who have no opportunity to spend their summers in the country, a specimen of God's handiwork . . ." Yet such democratic commitments did not mean that the park was a classless space. Rather, just as the design of the park incorporated the surrounding city in its pastoral performance, so it accommodated—and used—class differences to compose a public sphere defined by genteel norms of social hierarchy and cultural refinement. Olmsted and Vaux, for instance, used various techniques of framing and circulation to differentiate the parkscape and screen different social groups from one another. The park's most celebrated design innovation—the segregation of its various traffic circuits—was the most class-inflected of these strategies of dispersal. Elite visitors were drawn throughout the park on carriage drives and bridle paths, while less well-to-do pedestrians congregated in the picnics and playgrounds of the lower park. Even at the Mall, the most explicitly communal space in Central Park, carriage users had the opportunity to listen to the weekly concerts from a screened terrace that overlooked the music stage. Spaces of civic intercourse, in short, were designed with the practices of distinction in mind.[40]

The park also inscribed class authority by the regulation of public activity and demeanor. As I have noted, Olmsted devoted great attention to these issues; he believed his work as superintendent to be his greatest contribution to the park, more valuable than his role as codesigner. At his urging, the commission promulgated an elaborate code governing public use of the park. It proscribed not only activities injurious to the delicate ecology of the ground, such as rock climbing or flower picking, but anything at odds with genteel norms of "orderliness and decorum": commercial trade and traffic, disreputable pastimes like gambling or fortune-telling, peaceable but informal pursuits like spontaneous music making. Not even the most orthodox rituals of republican civic culture and mass politics—fireworks, militia displays, patriotic processions, and oratory—were permitted to disturb the park's decorous, pacified ideal of sociability: an ideal embodied in the family picnic, the band concert, and the promenade. Needless to say, this also excluded most working-class pastimes. Athletic contests, rowdy celebrations, and drinking—the "rough" amusements typical of plebeian sporting, fraternal, or labor outings—were all forbidden. (So too were the elite vices of "sporting culture" like racing trotters on the park drives.)[41] The agents of this code were uniformed Park Keepers, upon whose management Olmsted lavished infinite care. The Keepers' charge was not so much to police misbehavior as to preempt it, correcting visitors "in a respectful, courteous, and propitiating way when they may be seen to be going wrong." They were the human embodiment of the park's tutelary mission, translating its genteel program of uplift into an everyday system of social management that would be as inconspicuous but essential as, say, the transverse roads.[42]

Central Park's overseers, in short, meant it to transit the values of bourgeois culture. With its ecology of vistas and borders, inclusion and regulation, the park was to be a genteel protectorate of decorum and virtue. Set apart from New York's boundarilessness, atomism, and conflict, it would shelter a civilizing ecology of enclosure, harmony, and restraint.[43] And yet—as I noted in the design of the parkscape itself—the idea that the park effected a social and moral transvaluation, a reversal of culture and commerce, seems a bit too pat. Bourgeois urbanists were as wedded to the "outside" claims of capitalist development as they were to the "inside" claims of Arnoldian culture. They understood that their civilization was embedded in the market, like the park in the urban grid. A pleasure ground was, after all, prime real estate and a substantial public-works project; planners and reformers knew that it had to be sold in the language of land values as well as genteel values, municipal bonds as well as familial bonds. "The Commissioners entertain the hope that if these improvements are made," the Brooklyn park board argued in its proposal for Prospect Park, "the increased taxable value of the real estate lying in the vicinity . . . will prevent the payment of the interest upon the debt created and gradual[ly] extinguish . . . the debt itself."[44]

Economically no less than spatially, then, the commercial metropolis remained inside the park. The "nature" that soothed visitors within its precincts was not so alien from the "natural laws" of the market that threatened them from without. This is why genteel reformers, civic capitalists, and development boosters could come together so readily behind the project of park design: all were agreed that its value was simultaneously moral *and* pecuniary. To say this is not to deny the restorative project that New York's urbanists conceived Central Park to embody. The park was indeed a space that renewed and perhaps even civilized its users. Yet it did not do so by casting back to a pre-urban world. Rather it projected a new world of metropolitan culture and power in disguise. Like the builders' advertisements that touted real estate on its borders, the park looked toward the future. It prefigured the city that would come to surround it, support it, and require it.

An Urbanism of the Periphery

Central and Prospect parks were fragments of utopia, enclaves within which the divergent claims of bourgeois urbanism could be accommodated. They melded democratic inclusiveness with class stewardship, refined leisured with dynamic growth; and in so doing they modeled the larger metropolitan regime that bourgeois urbanists sought to create. During the 1860s and 1870s, city builders set about trying to realize that model, extending the synecdochic meaning of park design into a program of comprehensive urban planning. The movement from park to city was both institutional and spatial.[45] Genteel professionals and administrators—most notably, Olmsted, Vaux, Green, and Brooklyn park commissioner James Stranahan—began to foray into the surrounding landscape, laying out scenic drives, promenades, and planned suburban districts. Their projects actualized the implications of the pleasure ground, creating extensive landscapes of domestic intimacy, decorous circulation, class order, and tutelary improvement. In Manhattan, Brooklyn, and elsewhere, they composed a counterurbanism to the world of the grid: an urbanism of the periphery.

The initiatives of the Prospect Park commission in the late 1860s exemplify this process of spatial and ideological expansion. Olmsted and Vaux had served as landscape architects to the Brooklyn board since Olmsted's return from the California gold country in 1865; the next year, when the partners presented their plan for Prospect Park, they added "a few suggestions with regard to . . . the ground outside the park boundaries." They urged the commission to design the surrounding neighborhood for "residences of a first-class character" and recommended that one of the border avenues be reserved for "museums and other educational edifices." Finally, they suggested laying out "a shaded pleasure-drive in extension to that of the park," even proposing a network of "sylvan roads" that would link Prospect and Central parks, the Brooklyn oceanfront and the Hudson shoreline in "a grand municipal promenade."[46] Two years later, these ideas coalesced into a plan, replete with "a general scheme of routes," for the creation of a "parkway neighborhood" surrounding Prospect Park. As designed by Olmsted and Vaux and adopted by the board, it would be a district of broad, tree-lined "parkways," pedestrian promenades, spacious lots, and commercial byroads, extending the pleasures of leisured sociability, family repose, and segregated circulation beyond the park boundaries. Ultimately, the board was told, such a parkway district could provide "spacious and healthful accommodations for a population of 500,000." It would meld urbanity with "a certain amount of rural satisfaction"—like the park itself—offering benefits that were both moral and material. "Wealthy and influential citizens" would enjoy "tranquil habitation" without "loss of town-privileges," and the concomitant increases in land values and tax revenues would allay "the financial burden of the [City] Corporation" in creating Prospect Park.[47]

The proposal dramatizes the speed with which metropolitan urbanists expanded park design into urban design. No sooner had Olmsted and Vaux mastered the aesthetic and ideological contours of one setting than they began to formulate broader aims and projects. They turned to the parkway neighborhood as a way of extruding the restorative influence of greenery and sociability into the surrounding streetscape. Yet, in so doing, they opened up questions of landscape design and cultural stewardship that had been expressed only figuratively in the park. Answering those questions engaged Olmsted, Vaux, and the park board in a process that edged toward comprehensive planning. The parkway proposal required them to integrate the needs of business traffic, pleasure driving, public leisure, domestic seclusion, property development, home ownership, and public cultural institutions. The new parkways were to be "the trunk lines of all future improvements in the suburbs," the commissioners announced, "so that afterwards these would all progress in some degree of harmonious relation one with another, as well as with the completed portions of the city." Thus, Olmsted and Vaux had to make sense of the larger dynamics of Brooklyn's growth, to clarify how the parkway neighborhood would function in what they called "a plan fully adapted to the most intelligent requirements of modern town life."[48]

They responded in their 1868 report to the Prospect Park board with one of the foundational statements of Victorian urban design. In an astonishing metahistory of the street form from ancient cattle paths to the Avenue de l'Impératrice, Olmsted and Vaux based the parkway proposal on an analysis of the segregative logic of urban growth. The "separation of business and domestic life" in modern cities, they argued, called for a new type of street: a parklike drive, linked to scenic resorts, lined with deep lawns and beautiful villas, filled with pleasure drivers and strollers who were distributed into distinct circuits of movement and sociability. The plan transformed the aesthetics of the park, in short, into a blueprint for a peripheral cityscape of domesticity, leisure, and public culture. It was this document—so unlike the typical annual reports of civic administrators—that provoked William Cullen Bryant to ask in the *Evening Post*, "CAN A CITY BE PLANNED?"[49]

Moreover, the growing intellectual ambition of Brooklyn's protoplanners was mirrored in the expansion of their political authority. Spurred by the parkway proposal (and by the board's Republican majority), the Albany legislature enlarged the duties and powers of the Brooklyn commission in the late 1860s. In 1869 the state approved the taking of lands for the "Eastern" and "Ocean" parkways in Brooklyn, creating a special district under the legal and fiscal control of the Prospect Park commission. Displacing the established authority of the city government, Albany granted the board extraordinary powers to open and improve streets, take property, restrict nuisances, enforce residential development, and regulate public use of the new "Eastern Parkway and Boulevards." Thus, just as the park itself served as a microcosm for larger questions of urban design and cultural stewardship, so the Prospect Park commission seemed the appropriate location to vest expansive new powers over urban space.[50]

The New York City park commission gained even wider responsibilities. As in Brooklyn, the process began modestly, with the extension of scenic drives from the park. In 1864 state lawmakers asked the board to create a carriageway on Seventh Avenue north of Central Park. They mandated similar improvements on Sixth Avenue the following year, along with the creation of a tree-lined "Boulevard" on upper Broadway and a street plan for the rugged terrain north of 155th Street (the only part of Manhattan that was unplatted in the original grid). In 1866 the board was given comprehensive authority over all streets north of Fifty-ninth Street and west of Central Park. A host of landscape, architectural, and educative projects were added over the next several years: a racing lane along the Harlem River, new boulevards north and east of Central Park, the "Grand Circle" at its southwest corner (later named for Columbus), a meteorological observatory, a museum of natural history, a metropolitan art gallery, a zoo, and Riverside and Morningside parks on the bluffs of the Hudson River. In 1868 the board was charged with improving the Harlem waterfront and dredging a shipping canal at Spuyten Duyvil Creek; the next year, it was asked to lay out bridge and road connections across the Harlem and a street plan for the adjacent regions of Westchester County.[51]

In sum, by the time Tweed replaced it with the "home-rule" Department of Public Parks in 1870, the Central Park commission directed the development of New York's northern periphery. In five years, it had evolved into a full-blown planning agency with broad authority over landscape design, street plans, civic institutions, and commercial development in upper Manhattan and much of lower Westchester. Elite observers seemed delighted with the board's power and centralizing agenda; they increasingly turned to it as the default solution for any problems of metropolitan growth and environmental disorder. "The people of [Staten] Island are singularly lethargic," the *Real Estate Record* complained in 1870. "Let the Commissioners of our Central Park be authorized . . . [to develop] a plan for laying out all necessary roads and desirable parks on the Island."[52]

Yet the park board's power and popularity also exposed the divergent ideals and interests of New York's urbanists. The expansion of park design into urban planning made upper Manhattan a terrain of conflict among business leaders, boosters, reformers, and politicians. The most important impetus for the board's activism came from Andrew Haswell Green, the president and leading light of the Central Park commission in the 1860s. Green instigated many of the projects that I have listed, and he responded to the enlargement of the board's purview with a series of official "Communications" that offered ambitious plans for the West Side, Washington Heights, and the Harlem valley. His report on the district above 155th Street, for instance, cataloged the functions that had to be integrated if "the planning of a city" were "done with any degree of foresight": civil defense, public health, food supply, and "the means of movement and circulation of its population and property." The complexity of such requirements made central administration essential: "The apportioning of expenditures for great works built in the [public] interest," Green wrote in his 1867 report on the growth of Westchester County, "should be . . . left to the determination of some body with comprehensive powers." Clearly the Central Park commission was to model, if not to become, that body.[53]

The intellectual ambition of Green's writings mirrors that of Olmsted and Vaux's Prospect Park reports, written in the same years. Yet Green's concerns were somewhat different. He embraced public planning less as a means of civilizing urban culture than as a frame for organizing urban growth. To be sure, he believed in the tutelary value of uptown improvements: he was a trustee of the American Museum of Natural History and the Metropolitan Museum of Art (both built on the borders of

Central Park in the 1870s) and a president of the park's Zoological Society. Yet the magnetic north of Green's urbanism was the need to "accommodat[e] rapid growth" and "provide for the growing wants of a great people." Where Olmsted and Vaux sought to embed capitalist city building in a moral geography of bounded districts, Green envisioned a cityscape that could adjust to the shifting imperatives of the market. He was impatient with schemes of improvement that he considered extravagant or wastefully decorative. In a tacit critique of Olmsted and Vaux's Brooklyn parkway proposals, he rejected "fanciful" plans for "street[s] ornamented with . . . spaces of green" where "the portion used for travel [is] very limited"; in a swipe at Martin and other boosters, he rebuked those who "encourage the imagination with visions of parks, groves, terraces, fountains, statuary and palatial residences." City builders had "to deal with practical things and not to excite unattainable expectations," Green sniffed in his "Communication" on Washington Heights. Indeed his street plan for the Heights (eventually adopted) was as prosaic and gridlike as the broken terrain of the district would allow.[54]

Real-estate boosters also endorsed the ambitions of the Central Park board, but for quite different reasons. Uptown landholders founded the West Side Association in 1866 precisely to support commission rule over their district, and they lobbied vigorously for Green's program of public works. For property developers, such activism made good sense. Comprehensive street, park, and boulevard improvements were key to opening the upper city to active investment. "His review of the future destiny of this city, and the vast scope of its requirements . . . is positively electrifying," the *Real Estate Record* commented on Green's plan for the upper island, and it "will give a life and activity to real estate movements, which within a year will double the area of marketable and speculative lots around the city." At the same time, however, New York's boosters sought to inflect uptown planning with a more baroque vision of urban design. With "Boulevards and drives extending far into the country," the *Record* enthused, New York would become a center of "pomp and elegance and the glittering exhibition of the fair and fashionable of the world's new imperial city." For real-estate promoters, such spectacles—not Green's efficient street plans—were the great goal of bourgeois urbanism.[55]

For the Tweed regime, on the other hand, the prize was party building through public works and property speculation. Although Tammany dismantled the park commission in the home-rule charter of 1870, the municipal department that replaced it did not abandon the movement toward comprehensive uptown planning. To the contrary: under the leadership of Tweed's ally Peter Sweeney, the Department of Public Parks embraced the urbanism of the periphery with open arms. Indeed, it was Sweeney who actually undertook most of the agenda for which Andrew Haswell Green had lobbied the state. The Boulevard, the Great Circle at Fifty-ninth Street and Eighth Avenue, the Sixth and Seventh Avenue drives, the Avenue St. Nicholas, Morningside and Riverside parks: all of these grand improvements had first been promulgated by the "reform" Central Park commission, but they were prosecuted under the rule of Tammany.[56]

Two names remained surprisingly absent from this story of expansive uptown planning: those of Olmsted and Vaux. The designers of Central Park played only limited roles in Manhattan city building in the 1860s. Although still employed by the Central Park board, they found their administrative and aesthetic advice largely ignored by Andrew Haswell Green and his colleagues; under Sweeney's tenure, they had nominal posts but even less influence. Elsewhere, however, the partners did much to elaborate the urbanism of the periphery. Along with the Brooklyn parkway project, they laid out several planned suburbs, most notably the village of Riverside, nine miles west of Chicago, in 1869.[57] The following year Olmsted was appointed to a state "improvement commission" for the development of Staten Island. The report that he coauthored drew on the theories of urban geography and peripheral planning that he and Vaux had begun to work out in Brooklyn. Noting the "increasing distinctness of separation between the commercial division and the . . . domestic division in all large modern towns," it proposed developing Staten Island from a rural (and malarial) hinterland into "the most convenient and most beautiful suburb of New York." Systematic planning would be essential to block "ill-considered, time-serving, catch-penny plans of 'improvement,'" the commissioners argued, and they put forward a comprehensive program of villa districts, land-use controls, road and rail improvements, and extensive ground drainage. Even more than the Brooklyn parkway neighborhood, such a proposal envisioned a unified development process that placed regional planning, public works, and environmental regulations in the hands of a public commission dedicated to domesticity, civility, and orderly improvement.[58]

Olmsted and Vaux did return to the fray in New York after the fall of the Tweed ring in 1872. Reform Mayor William Havemeyer enlisted the former to serve as landscape architect and superintendent of Central Park and, for a time, as president of the park board itself. He and Vaux collaborated on a variety of official projects, most notably the plan for Morningside Park as a picturesque promenade on a steep hillside just north of Central Park (Figure 7.11). Yet these years coincided with growing friction between the two, intensified by Vaux's resentment at their unequal reputation and power, and in 1874 they finally dissolved their partnership. Each continued to play an important role in the public landscape of upper Manhattan, however. Olmsted prepared a new design for Riverside Park in 1875, fashioning an irregular, terraced drive that melded "parkway" sociability with magnificent prospects of the Hudson valley (see Figure 5.9). At the same time, Vaux was commissioned to design buildings for the American Museum of Natural History (1874–78) at Eighth Avenue and Seventy-seventh Street and the Metropolitan Museum of Art (1874–80) on the eastern edge of Central Park at Eighty-second Street. Working separately, in short, the partners did much to lay out the landscape of refined leisure and cultural uplift that had been central to their shared ambitions for the new urbanism in New York.[59]

In the 1860s and 1870s, then, a variety of city builders collaborated and fought over the development of upper Manhattan. Civic capitalists, property boosters, politicos, and genteel reformers all pursued comprehensive planning on the uptown periphery. They did so for different reasons, and they created institutions and landscapes

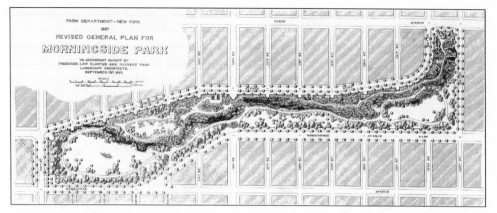

FIGURE 7.11   Shown here is Olmsted and Vaux's 1887 plan for Morningside Park, revised from their initial design of the early 1870s. Like Riverside Drive, the Brooklyn parkway system, and other projects, Morningside Park represented an effort to extend the principles of park design into a general strategy of urban planning on the metropolitan periphery. (Courtesy of the National Park Service, Frederick Law Olmsted National Historic Site)

that melded their commitments to functional integration, political patronage, civic grandeur, and moral uplift in divergent ways. Yet their efforts were grounded in two common assumptions: that New York's outward "march of improvement" required an innovative agenda of coordinated land use, scenic design, planned domesticity, public improvements, and environmental regulation; and that such an urbanism of the periphery offered the opportunity to undo the social and spatial discontents of the older city. The uptown utopia that resulted, they believed, would embody the sublimity of New York's economic growth, the moral and aesthetic grandeur of its civilization, and the legitimate power of those who built and administered it.

Cheap Trains and Cottage Suburbs

Of course this utopia was not meant for elite New Yorkers alone. It was a commonplace of Victorian urbanism that improving the uptown landscape would be a means of elevating the urban working class as well. "Walked up to Central Park this beautiful afternoon and inspected the new Museum of Natural History," George Templeton Strong wrote in his diary in the spring of 1871. "The Park is lovely and leafy. These things should exert a civilizing and humanizing influence upon 'the masses.'" Genteel observers put a similar faith in suburban homes for workers' families. "Nothing would conduce to form and continue an intelligent and moral working class," asserted the New York *Times*, than "nice little artisans' villages, where each family owned a separate and healthy dwelling." In all its settings, the urbanism of the periphery was meant to incorporate the laboring classes into a moral, inclusive, but hierarchical civic order.[60]

Such views should come as no surprise. As I argued in previous chapters, bourgeois New Yorkers deeply feared the eruption of class disorder in and over urban space. The metropolitan landscape seemed to them both divided and boundariless, riven with social inequalities whose "demoralizing influences" threatened to overrun property and public order. "It is time . . . that the intelligent and opulent classes began to reflect upon the nature of the community in which they live," warned a journalist after the draft riots. "Society must begin in earnest the work of lifting the masses out of their degradation." New York's city builders made this "work of lifting the masses" a key aim—for some, *the* key aim—of the new urbanism. Thus, the Citizens' Association urged "municipal and State authorities" to treat "the sanitary wants of the laboring classes" as "the most vitally important of all [New York's] social questions." Journalist E. L. Godkin agreed: "The most serious problem . . . connected with city life is undoubtedly the provision of dwellings for the working classes." Such assertions reflected both humanitarian concern and class anxiety. Indeed, bourgeois New Yorkers denied any conflict between the two: exposing the masses to the environmental tutelage of genteel values would benefit everyone. "The cheapest and most efficacious way of dealing with the 'Dangerous classes,'" Brace wrote in his reform tract, "is to . . . change their material circumstances, and draw them under the influence of the moral and fortunate classes." The turn to planning was partly meant to do just that.[61]

New York's urbanists pursued this program of class uplift on several fronts. In part, they sought to ameliorate the conditions of life in working-class neighborhoods. As I described at the beginning of this chapter, environmental reformers devoted much energy to tenement and health reform; the Citizens' Association in particular won passage of innovative sanitary and building codes. Yet these regulations were weakly drawn and easily evaded. Indeed, in contrast to later activists, it is striking how *little* faith Victorian urbanists placed in inner-city reform. For Progressive-era advocates like Alfred T. White, Jacob Riis, and Lawrence Veiller, tenement regulation was the sine qua non of environmental reform. For Victorian New Yorkers, by contrast, it was finally little more than a stopgap. "Overcrowding," the New York *Times* editorialized, "can never be cured . . . by law, nor by improved tenements, nor by 'model lodging-houses,' however much these measures may alleviate it. The only possible remedy is to provide more space for the laboring classes . . ."[62]

This lack of faith in inner-city environmentalism reflected a peculiarly Victorian mixture of anxiety and confidence concerning social class and spatial change. On one hand, it signaled the pessimistic belief that tenement crowding was inextricably embedded in Manhattan's street plan and property rights. For all their invocations of Haussmann, New York's urbanists did not seek and never gained the autocratic power that would have been required to nullify the property interests standing in the way of improving the inner-city landscape. On the other hand, they rejected the assumption that the laboring classes were inextricably trapped in that landscape. At the heart of their moral environmentalism was a faith in the geographic and moral plasticity of class divisions. Unlike the nativist, racialist, and anti-Catholic bent of some genteel critics, environmental reformers like Olmsted and Brace did not tend to represent the "dangerous classes of New York" as irremediably brutalized and alien. Rather they portrayed the vices of the tenement districts as debased versions of sociability. "On the curb-stones or in the dram-shops," Olmsted insisted, laboring people "are all under the influence of the same impulse which some satisfy about the tea-table . . ."[63] Working-class New Yorkers were economically fixed but morally "mobile," open to better influences if only they could be transported out of the tenements.

The class politics of Victorian urbanism, in short, was focused on the metropolitan periphery. Reformers, journalists, and developers sought to incorporate class tutelage into uptown planning, to include working-class families within the new landscape of secluded domesticity, property ownership, green space, and refined sociability. Olmsted urged the "ruralizing of *all* our urban population," including those locked in "the dense poor quarters of our great cities," and Brace called for "cheap workmen's trains" to "suburbs laid out in New Jersey or on Long Island expressly for working people." Boosters and real-estate interests echoed these sentiments. The *Real Estate Record* looked forward to the day when "legions of mechanics and laborers, instead of living in five-story tenements, will lodge in some village twenty miles away." Uptown landowner (and anti-Tweed Democrat) Charles O'Conor cited the reclamation of "the toiling millions" as a primary rationale for rapid transit: "The elevated rail . . . will snatch their wives and children from tenement-house horrors," he told the West Side Association, "and by promoting domesticity, greatly diminish the habits of intemperance and vice so liable to be forced upon the humbler classes." Cheap trains and cottage suburbs, in short, would offer domestic virtue and respectable leisure to the laboring classes, removing them from the "promiscuous" world of the tenements to an uptown landscape inscribed with moral, sexual, and property boundaries.[64]

Such aims informed the planning program that New York's urbanists pursued on the metropolitan periphery; but they did so in complex and sometimes elitist ways. Environmental reformers like Olmsted sought to use landscape design to undo not only the social distance but also the spatial proximity that made class contact so dangerous in the older cityscape. Urbanists included the working class within their uptown utopia, but at the same time they sought to curb and police its presence. For they believed that the tranquility, refinement, and domestic seclusion that were the great blessings of the city's edge required the regulation of class mixing. In an 1860 letter on Washington Heights, for instance, Olmsted decried the decline of certain "villa quarters" where unplanned growth "has given employment to numerous mechanics & laborers. . . . From a quiet & secluded neighborhood, it is growing to be a noisy, dusty, smoking, shouting, rattling and stinking one." In his own suburban projects, Olmsted tried to avert this disorder by secluding or segregating the lower classes from their betters. The Staten Island plan was the most restrictive: the commissioners proposed limiting its "suburban domestic neighborhood" to "a class of people . . . able and willing to pay an advanced price for land and for improvements." In the Brooklyn parkway district, by contrast, lots were drawn so large as to relegate "houses of inferior class" to the back streets of the district. Moreover, in an early instance of the evolution of restrictive covenants into exclusionary zoning, the enabling law for the district forbade the introduction of nuisances, places of trade, and *any* new structure "other than a stable, carriage-house, conservatory for plants, or green-house."[65]

To a great extent, these hierarchies of land use and lot size served the imperatives of the real-estate market. Victorian urbanists realized that the success of planned sub-urban districts depended on "offer[ing] some assurance to those who wish to build villas that these districts shall not be bye and bye invaded by the desolation" of anarchic growth. Yet, since that "desolation" included the workplaces and unregulated presence of wage labor, protecting land values meant policing class boundaries: "Nothing is more likely to enhance the value of . . . property for residencies," Olmsted wrote in his analysis of Washington Heights, than "its becoming associated in the minds of [people of leisure] with . . . the frequent recognition of friends of their own class." To say this is not to negate the genuine commitment of bourgeois urbanists to cheap trains and cottage suburbs, to the inclusion of working-class New Yorkers in the agenda of uptown planning. It does mean, however, that working people remained limited partners in the enterprise. Like the rules of labor and leisure that governed Central Park—and the ideology of stewardship that informed the park commission's efforts—the urbanism of the periphery offered working-class New Yorkers a mixture of democracy and class discipline: a landscape of civilizing hierarchy into which they were welcomed as subordinates.

The Uptown Prospect

When Victorian observers of New York looked north, what they often thought they saw was the future. Along the uptown frontier of development lay the prospect of New York's greatness. It was this identification of the urban periphery with metropolitan destiny that invested images like the 1876 Currier and Ives bird's-eye view and phrases like "the march of improvement" with such allegorical force. Thus, the uptown gaze had something of the same meaning for imperial city builders that the westward gaze had for imperial nationalists. It projected the movement of time in space, envisioning a utopian elsewhere, just over the horizon, that represented the culmination of history. Looking north mapped the course of empire.

Small wonder, then, that the agenda of bourgeois urbanism focused so programmatically on the shaping of the uptown landscape. It was in upper Manhattan—and the metropolitan periphery generally—that the ideals and the ideological stakes of the new urbanism were most fully articulated. New York's reformers, boosters, and civic capitalists did not ignore the existing cityscape, as their campaigns for tenement codes and dock improvements make clear. Yet it was on the edge of the metropolis that they came to envision the possibility of a new cityscape, and it was there that they created state and class institutions—park boards and landowners associations—capable of planning and building it. To drive north on the Boulevard—or out on Brooklyn's Eastern Parkway—would be to enter a utopian counterworld of well-ordered streets, stable land values, decent homes, beautiful parks, and magnificent public works. Moreover, this landscape was to be built and regulated by institutions and markets that could overcome the disorders of American capitalism and politics. Class divisions would be contained within a stable, civilized social order; the capitalist marketplace would be harnassed and disciplined; and an administrative state would rescue civic democracy from partisan corruption and shortsighted inefficiency.

It was an extraordinarily ambitious project, one that entailed a complex refashioning of spatial order, temporal change, social relations, and political power. And for a time, it was quite successful, creating new landscapes and a new politics of metropolitan city building. In the end, however, bourgeois urbanism did not meet its ambitions. During the 1870s, the unstable energies of capitalist development, the frictions of class disorder, and the corruptions of metropolitan politics worked to arrest the march of improvement. New York's urbanists failed to overcome the flux of time and space and create a national metropolis worthy of a democratic capitalist civilization.

CHAPTER 8

The Failure of
Bourgeois Urbanism

*In the center of Fedora, that grey stone metropolis, stands a metal building
with a crystal globe in every room. Looking into each globe, you see a blue
city, the model of a different Fedora. . . . In every age someone, looking at
Fedora as it was, imagined a way of making it the ideal city, but while he
constructed his miniature model, Fedora was already no longer the same as
before, and what had until yesterday a possible future became only a toy in
a glass globe. . . .*

*On the map of your empire, O Great Khan, there must be room both for
the big, stone Fedora and the little Fedoras in glass globes. Not because they
are all equally real, but because all are only assumptions. The one contains
what is accepted as necessary when it is not so; the others, what is imagined
as possible and, a moment later, is possible no longer.*

—Italo Calvino, *Invisible Cities* (1974)

The Meanings of Reconstruction

In May 1876, Franklin Sanborn, head of the American Social Science Association, the
leading genteel-reform organization in the country, published a reminiscence about
the group's founding eleven years earlier. "[We] anticipated noble results from our
venture," Sanborn recalled. "There was little we did not fancy ourselves capable of
achieving." The association had pursued manifold initiatives on behalf of civil service reform, charity organization, public health, political economy, and other issues
dear to Victorian reform intellectuals. Yet the actual results had been chastening: "I
fear we must confess now that we rather overestimated our power," Sanborn concluded. Such sentiments were typical of a larger mood and moment in centennial
America, at least for the northern gentry who had sought to guide national politics

and culture during the previous generation. Across a variety of settings, the mid-1870s were an era of retrenchment, disillusionment, and shrunken ambitions for bourgeois elites. In the face of economic depression, class division, widespread public corruption, and southern political turmoil, the expansive agenda of state building, stewardship, and tutelary reform that characterized the immediate postwar years had given way to a sense of curtailment and defeat.[1]

No one felt this shortfall of expectations more keenly than New York's urbanists. In an 1878 essay, William Martin tracked the city's recent development in terms that were strikingly similar to Sanborn's. "Twelve years ago, at the close of the rebellion, the city was emerging from a period of great depression into one of high inflation," Martin recalled in the *North American Review*. "At such eras the streams of population, business enterprise, and wealth flow toward cities . . . , and preparations were made to bring [upper Manhattan] into condition for immediate occupation . . ." Yet several factors had stymied the urbanism of the periphery: the profligacy of the Tweed ring, the stinginess of the reformers who deposed it, the slowness of transit development, and the national economic crisis. "The city of New York has passed through a long period of depression," Martin lamented, "and rests now at the bottom."[2] He was quite right: by the mid-1870s, bourgeois urbanism was in crisis. Its agenda of coordinated growth and uptown landscape design was stalemated; some of its leading adherents—notably Andrew Haswell Green—had suspended their support for planning and public improvements in favor of fiscal retrenchment and limited government. Like the reformers discussed by Franklin Sanborn, bourgeois urbanists had "anticipated noble results" from their efforts to reconstruct New York. And like Sanborn, they discovered that they had "rather overestimated" their powers of reconstruction.

I use the word "reconstruction" advisedly here. For the defeat of southern Reconstruction was the most important instance where northern elites confronted the limits of their ambitions. Indeed, we cannot fully understand the campaign to physically reshape New York except in relation to the political reshaping of the South and the nation. The new urbanism represented a key site of what Eric Foner has called "the Reconstruction of the North": the growth of new modes of public activism and social oversight by which bourgeois elites sought to organize a disciplined, virtuous citizenry and a dynamic market economy in the North as well as the ex-Confederate states.[3]

Frederick Law Olmsted's career represented the clearest case of this dialogue between metropolitan city building and the national politics of slavery and unionism. Olmsted's critical writings on the South in the 1850s had inflected his vision of Central Park as a civilizing resort and disciplined workplace; his regime of park management in turn provided the template for the quasi-military mode of philanthropic administration that he pursued as head of the U.S. Sanitary Commission. During his tenure at the Sanitary Commission, he agitated for a congressional bill establishing an experimental freedmen's commission on the (newly captured) Georgia Sea Islands; he was asked to direct the Port Royal experiment, as well as a private freed-men's aid society, after the end of the war. Although Olmsted refused both positions, he and others in the Manhattan cultural gentry provided influential support for the Freedman's Bureau in the early years of congressional Reconstruction. Indeed, the bureau's mission of directing the transition from slavery to freedom through moral tutelage, labor discipline, and multidimensional social oversight reflected precisely the same program of state, class, and cultural authority that defined the politics of stewardship in New York.[4]

Concomitantly, it is impossible to understand the sense of defeat and curtailment among bourgeois New Yorkers in the mid-1870s outside of the crisis of national Re-construction. Beginning in May 1876—the same month that Franklin Sanborn's mem-oir was published—South Carolina and other southern states were erupting into civil violence. Militant strikes among African American rice workers and armed skir-mishes between freedmen and Democratic "rifle clubs" raised the specter of a whole-sale devolution into class and race war—a specter reinforced that summer by the news of Custer's rout and labor violence in the Pennsylvania coal fields. Within a few months, the national election would set in motion the sectional, partisan, and busi-ness negotiations that ended the Union occupation of the South and ensured the elec-tion of Rutherford Hayes.[5] Yet, even before the Compromise of 1877, much of the Northern gentry had abandoned their commitment to racial equality under the su-perintendence of an activist, custodial nation-state. Thomas Nast's cartoons in *Harp-er's Weekly* track the shift: earlier images of noble African American Union veterans give way in the 1870s to minstrel-show stereotypes of black political corruption and incapacity (Figure 8.1). It was against this racial (and racist) disillusionment with Re-construction that New York's gentry made sense of their own city's discontents: "The governments of South Carolina and Louisiana are, I fear, mere nests of corrupt car-pet-baggers upheld by a brute nigger constituency," George Templeton Strong wrote in 1874. "But have we here in New York any right to look down on them? Our civic rulers are, as a class, utterly base, and a Celtocracy is as bad as a niggerocracy, and in some respects worse."[6]

As Strong's ugly rhetoric makes clear, bourgeois disaffection with Reconstruction was intensified by the fear that civic and moral order in New York was breaking down. I have already described the rising arc of disorders that underlay this fear in the 1860s and early 1870s. Riots, epidemics, strike waves, Wall Street frauds, public sex scandals like the Beecher-Tilton affair, political corruption like the Tweed thefts—all of this added up to a pervasive legitimation crisis: "We are living in a day of ruffi-anism and of almost universal corruption," Strong noted grimly. "It is a thoroughly rotten community. . . . Unless some peaceful and lawful remedy be found, a danger-ous convulsion cannot be far off." The new urbanism was meant precisely to provide such a "remedy," to lay out an elevating landscape through an elevated politics of city building. Yet for many in the metropolitan bourgeoisie, the civic crisis was com-ing to make urban reconstruction seem as tainted as southern Reconstruction. As we

FIGURE 8.1   Thomas Nast's "The Ignorant Vote," published in *Harper's Weekly* after the presidential election of 1876, underscores the disillusionment that much of the northern middle-class public came to feel toward both Reconstruction and New York politics. In contrast to Nast's earlier, sympathetic sketches of southern blacks, here a demeaning caricature of a freedman is balanced against a brutal stereotype of an Irish voter—visual shorthand for the legions of Tammany supporters. (*Harper's Weekly*, December 9, 1876; image courtesy of HarpWeek, LLC)

shall see, the most important defector was Andrew Haswell Green. In the aftermath of the Tweed fiscal crisis, Green served as a "reform" City Comptroller, where he pursued a cost-cutting crusade against many of the same uptown projects that he had first championed as parks commissioner.[7]

To trace the career of bourgeois urbanism against the larger story of Reconstruction is to do more than invoke a conceptual pun. On one hand, it underscores the importance of the argument with which I began *Empire City:* that remaking New York was a project of national consequence for the Victorian elites who undertook it. On the other hand, it points to the argument with which I want to end: that this project was, on its own terms, a failure.

Failure may seem an unduly harsh conclusion. After all, we have Central Park as palpable evidence of the achievements of New York's urbanists. Although the park has seen a century of political and cultural struggle since its creation—and is quite a different place from the orderly, rustic resort it was designed to be—we can surely credit its survival *as* contested terrain partly to the aesthetic vision and administrative tenacity of Green, Vaux, Olmsted, and others. Yet the park's survival as an urban oasis is not really the appropriate measure of success here. For, as I have stressed, New

York's urbanists intended something more than simply environmental amelioration. Assessed against their ambitions, even a grand achievement like Central Park was not the triumph that it represents for planners and park goers today. As a project of American reconstruction, bourgeois urbanism tells a story of cultural and intellectual stature clothing political and ideological defeat. In its successes and failures, we can discern a larger crisis of legitimacy, central to the experience of bourgeois Americans—and to national politics and culture—in the latter half of the nineteenth century.

The Legacies of Bourgeois Urbanism

To measure the limits of New York's urbanists, we need to begin by marking their accomplishments. Two sets of effects are especially notable in summing up their legacy. First and most obviously, the new urbanism held aesthetic and intellectual sway for forty years. Until the emergence of the City Beautiful movement and Progressive environmental reform in the first decade of the twentieth century, the Victorian program of park, promenade, and suburban planning plainly set the agenda of American urban and landscape design. As David Schuyler and others have shown, it reshaped nineteenth-century ideals of how great cities should be organized; it led to the early professionalization of landscape architecture; and it spurred the first sustained theorizing about urban form and city planning in the United States.[8]

Second, New York's urbanists produced stunning achievements on the ground. Most remarkable were the parks and drives designed by Olmsted and Vaux. Along with Central Park, there were Morningside and Riverside parks in Manhattan, and Prospect Park and Eastern and Ocean parkways (the fruits of the 1868 parkway proposal) in Brooklyn. These spaces in turn point to the administrative success of the New York and Brooklyn park boards, both of which evolved into nascent planning agencies responsible for laying out much of the metropolitan periphery. Under their aegis, residential plans for Washington Heights and Morningside Heights (1866) and the "parkway neighborhood" near Prospect Park (1868) were drawn up; a commercial blueprint for the Harlem River valley was developed (1868); and connections to southern Westchester were mapped out (1869).[9] Add to this the sanitary oversight of the Metropolitan Board of Health, the pioneering tenement code of 1867, and the planning efforts of the Staten Island Improvement Commission, and we see the lineaments of a wide-ranging metropolitan politics of planning and urban design.

As I suggested in the Introduction to *Empire City*, the rediscovery of these administrative and design achievements has revised the narrative of U.S. planning history in important ways. Earlier research typically located the origins and defining achievements of American city planning in the Progressive era. It tended to emphasize the centrality of social scientific investigation and professional expertise to planning practice, themes that privileged the contribution of Progressive reformers and reflected the functionalist theoretical commitments of both planners and the "new urban history."[10] Revisiting Victorian urbanism has changed that earlier paradigm in several ways. It has altered the periodization of planning history, pushing back by two generations the point at which research shows Americans systematically asking, "Can a City Be Planned?" It has foregrounded the role of aesthetic, cultural, and moral issues in the traditions of American urban planning. Finally, it has called attention to the role of parks and suburbs in setting the agenda of city planning, challenging the assumption of much twentieth-century planning that the city center is where "urbanity" really resides.[11]

Implicit in these changes is an alternative model of the enabling conditions for urban planning in the United States. The Progressive-functionalist paradigm traced its emergence to a series of early-twentieth-century phenomena: new urban technologies like electrification and structural steel construction, new levels of demographic congestion, and new ideals of efficiency, expertise, and instrumental technique. The story of Victorian urbanism suggests that these factors, while not absent from earlier programs of urban design and planning reform, played a less definitive role in shaping them. *Empire City* instead points to a nexus of economic, class, and cultural factors, all of them specific to the third quarter of the nineteenth century, as catalysts for the rise of urbanism in New York.

Most fundamental was the city's national economic ascendance and the simultaneous consolidation of the local real-estate economy. The boom that resulted from these twin developments transformed New York from a bustling port to an expansive metropolitan area; the uneven effects of the boom made the turn to planning at once possible and necessary. At the same time, national dominance infused the city-building process with issues of elite class formation and class ambition. Real-estate boosters, business leaders, and cultural gentry viewed the New York landscape as an arena of collective economic opportunity and ideological influence. They turned to urbanism as a way of instituting a dynamic, disciplined, virtuous social order and asserting their own stewardship over it.

These economic and class factors were matched by a growing *cultural* investment in the Manhattan landscape. As the national capital of print and public culture, New York was an object of intense scrutiny. Three linked discourses in particular raised the stakes of city building and encouraged the turn to urban planning and design. A booster discourse of empire celebrated New York's growth and grandeur and cast the metropolis as a microcosm of national progress; a reform discourse of environmental uplift stressed the moral influence of the urban environment in advancing or undermining that imperial future; and a transnational ideal of civilization defined the commercial, civic, and domestic values that the metropolis was meant to embody and project over its hinterland. What fueled Victorian urbanism, then, was not so much the Progressive ideals of efficiency and expertise but the bourgeois touchstones of booster ambition, moral environmentalism, and the *mission civilisatrice*.

Together these economic, class, and cultural factors fostered the turn toward urban planning and design in Victorian New York. They spurred a sophisticated vision of what a great metropolis should be and an unprecedented willingness by elite New Yorkers to use their capital, class sociability, professional skill, and state power to realize it. The result was a novel array of projects aimed at guiding, designing, legitimating, and ameliorating the city's growth. Most important was the project of creating a utopian otherworld on the metropolitan periphery that would embody the lineaments of a capitalist civilization.

And yet, however much these ideas and interventions help to recast the history of city planning and design in the United States, there is finally a note of pathos to the career of bourgeois urbanism. For, given the ambitions of New York's city builders, it is striking how much of their agenda remained unconsummated. I have already noted the limited effect of "downtown" efforts at health regulation, tenement inspection, and port redevelopment. Yet even the urbanism of the periphery did not match the intended reach of its advocates. Of the three suburban plans designed by Olmsted and his collaborators, two were never implemented at all. The proposal of the Staten Island Improvement Commission was derailed by local strife among the island's villages; a similar plan for the Annexed District north of the Harlem River was blocked by retrenchment forces in the Department of Public Parks, as I will detail in a subsequent section. The one plan that *was* adopted—the "parkway neighborhood" around Prospect Park—fell far short of the citywide boulevard network first envisioned by Olmsted and Vaux. Construction on the Eastern and Ocean parkways began in 1868, but work was suspended for lack of funds in 1869 and 1873; the partners terminated their relationship with the Brooklyn board in frustration.[12]

Even the much-heralded parks of upper Manhattan represented a mixed success in the eyes of their designers. Depression-era austerity, cost overruns, and poor contract work delayed progress on Riverside and Morningside parks for nearly fifteen years. Similar fiscal pressures produced cutbacks in the budget for Central Park, goading Superintendent Olmsted into a fury against Comptroller Green: "I tell you," he told *Tribune* reporter Junius Henri Browne in 1874, "I think the park is going to the devil and have grave doubt whether the undertaking ... was not a mistake, was not doomed to failure because of the general ignorance of the conditions of [its] success. ... The Park can easily become a nuisance and a curse to the city." In 1882, after his dismissal from the parks department, Olmsted published *The Spoils of the Park*, a pamphleteering jeremiad that detailed twenty years of patronage politics in New York and ridiculed the Central Park board as a "disorganized body ... masquerading before the public, a headless trunk, without policy, without order, without well-defined purpose."[13]

By the mid-1870s, in short, both the design program of bourgeois urbanism and its larger aims of political and cultural stewardship seemed stymied to many of its advocates. What had happened to defeat and disillusion them? The new urbanism received two mortal blows in these years: one delivered by Tammany Hall, the other by the capitalist business cycle. Together these setbacks undid the political and economic conditions that had encouraged planned growth and public design in New York. At the same time, they provoked an ideological crisis that led much of the metropolitan bourgeoisie to lose faith in the imperial ideal and the politics of stewardship.

The End of the Boom and the Politics of Retrenchment

The first setback to the new urbanism came on January 21, 1871: the day that New York County Auditor James Watson was killed in a sleighing accident. As auditor, Watson had played the role of public accountant to the Tammany regime, and he was a trusted confidant to Boss Tweed and his allies. His successor, Matthew O'Rourke, was not. O'Rourke quietly fed the New York *Times* detailed evidence of the kickbacks, insider contracts, and other graft with which the Tweed ring had bilked taxpayers over the previous three years. The *Times*'s revelation of the frauds in July 1871 spurred a genteel uprising, as the New York bourgeoisie awoke to the depth of the civic and fiscal crisis faced by the city. With municipal bonds increasingly difficult to market and the city government facing imminent bankruptcy—the ring's thefts were estimated as high as $75 million—a bipartisan coalition of merchants, financiers, and reform politicians organized the Committee of Seventy to investigate the frauds and organize opposition to the Tammany regime. In the elections of 1871 the reform slate swept most Democratic aldermen and legislators from office. (One of the few exceptions was State Senator Tweed himself.) The following year, Mayor A. Oakey Hall was defeated by sugar merchant William Havemeyer. Meanwhile a new era of fiscal austerity was inaugurated by the zealous reform comptroller: Andrew Haswell Green.[14]

The saga of Tweed's downfall is one of the great set pieces of nineteenth-century U.S. political history, and I will not rehearse it here. What I do want to underscore is the destructive effect that the events of 1871 had on bourgeois urbanism in New York. The exposure of the Tweed frauds and the formation of an elite political movement organized around fiscal economy fractured the uneasy (often unacknowledged) cooperation between "reform" and "partisan" urbanists on behalf of public works and landscape design. After 1871, uptown planning seemed to many civic capitalists and cultural gentry an effort to build a landscape of virtue with a politics of vice. "The upper part of the island ha[s] been laid out with parks and boulevards . . . at a ruinous cost to the people," the *Times* fulminated, "plung[ing] this City irrevocably in debt . . . for the sole purpose of enriching a band of political adventurers."[15]

The starkest case of the turn from activism to retrenchment was Andrew Green. As city comptroller from 1871 to 1876, Green enforced a massive rollback of public works and a shift of public monies into debt reduction. To be sure, he denied that his actions constituted a departure from his earlier city-building policies. Green rejected any thought that the original park board had been responsible for the public works binge of the Tweed era, and he assured New Yorkers that he still favored "liberal expenditures for the development of the city" when they were directed to "needed works, based on thoroughly matured plans." The trouble was that no actual improvements met this standard. Under his administration, all the major projects of the new urbanism either slowed to a crawl (the Hudson seawall), ground to a halt (Riverside Drive), or were canceled (Manhattan's Eastern Boulevard). In effect, Green's policies pointed to the opposite conclusion from his words: it was impossible to throw away the bathwater of Tammany Hall and still save the baby of uptown urbanism. Just as genteel reformers had feared, machine politics defeated the ideal of stewardship: not because these were at odds with each other, but because they had become so intertwined.[16]

The second blow to bourgeois urbanism was more prolonged and even more severe. Once again, it can be precisely dated: September 18, 1873. That was the day that the nation's leading investment bank, Jay Cooke and Company, shut its doors, triggering the closure of the New York Stock Exchange two days later and a six-year national business depression. I have already described the impact that the Panic of 1873 had on New York's real-estate markets. Its effect on the public agenda of bourgeois urbanism was nearly as harsh. While municipal debt service quadrupled in the 1870s, property values and city tax revenues remained flat. Even as New York's population grew by a third, the public works budget declined some 25 percent. The park and boulevard improvements of upper Manhattan in particular stagnated. "During the years of depression the West Side [was] in a large measure neglected," one real-estate chronicle recalled. "All the great public plans for improvements which had an effect so stimulating during the years of the boom were allowed to lie dormant."[17]

The combined effect of political scandal and economic depression destroyed the conditions that had enabled bourgeois urbanism to take root. The dual crisis blocked the flow of capital into metropolitan real-estate investment and public improvements; it fractured the coalition of elites that had advocated city building and state building on the city's fringe. Moreover, the crisis generated a collapse of cultural confidence. It eroded the ideological commitments that had justified the new urbanism: commitments to the booster story of New York City's dominance, the legitimacy of massing state power on behalf of that dominance, and the use of government to civilize and discipline urban life. In response, many bourgeois New Yorkers reevaluated their beliefs, joining Andrew Haswell Green in a more chastened, tightfisted politics.

Thus, for the next twenty years, "reform" in New York meant economy in the service of low taxes, not state activism in the service of public uplift. The clearest manifestation of the spirit of retrenchment was the widespread call for debt limitation: "If the power of city officials to increase debt is not closely guarded and absolute limits placed upon it," the *Commercial and Financial Chronicle* opined, "we cannot expect either prudence or honesty to prevail." Debt-limitation proposals offered an effective response to the fiscal constraints of the depression, and they were adopted by many U.S. city and state governments in the 1870s. Yet they also marked an erosion of the faith in futurity that had typified civic boosterism during the mid-nineteenth century. "It is to be accepted that New York is no longer endowed by natural advantages with the commercial supremacy which crowned her by divine right as the empress of trade," the commissioner of taxes and assessments wrote somberly in 1877. "Still a city of great resources, and of vast possibilities . . . , her future [is] darkened by circumstances yet controllable. Samson is not wholly shorn, nor yet blind."[18]

If the spirit of retrenchment reflected a loss of confidence in the future, it also signaled a growing disillusionment with civic politics and state building in the present. The Tweed debacle made it clear that political centralization had not brought compact, effective rule to New York: "The government [is] . . . in a state of disintegration, and the interests of the people in every department wasted," Mayor Havemeyer reported. "Notwithstanding the numerous and extravagantly paid officers and subordinates, official duty has been neglected. . . ." For many reform-minded New Yorkers, the culprit was not simply Tweed or party politics, but democratic governance itself in a vast, fragmented metropolis: "I wish I could flee into the wilderness as Lot fled from Sodom," George Templeton Strong wrote. "No rich and crowded community can long survive universal suffrage." Such disillusionment might have been expected from a sardonic patrician, but it is telling to find it echoed in the columns of the *Real Estate Record*: "In no civilized city on earth is the experiment of universal suffrage and republican institutions put to so severe a test as in New York."[19]

These concerns catalyzed a new style of elite politics: a muscular laissez-faire liberalism aimed at curbing the powers of government and the masses that corrupted it. In 1873 city reformers and state Republicans passed a new municipal charter that reversed the centralism and activism of the 1870 Tweed charter. Executive power was dispersed among several interdepartmental boards *and* concentrated in the hands of the comptroller as a check on public spending. Two years later, Governor Samuel Tilden—an anti-Tammany Democrat who had helped to bring Tweed down —appointed a panel to propose new models of urban governance for New York State in light of the fiscal and political turmoil of the previous years.[20]

Chaired by Republican attorney William Evarts, the "Tilden Commission" reproduced the bipartisan alliance of civic capitalists and cultural gentry that had shaped the park and health commissions of the 1860s. Indeed, its proposals did echo the older commission ideal, calling for cities to be run like business corporations according to a fiduciary model of government. Yet the *Report of the Commission to Devise a Plan for the Government of Cities* was a manifesto of retrenchment; it proposed a set of constitutional amendments aimed at *dis*abling activism in city government. The report advocated debt limits for cities of more than one hundred thousand; it called for a renewed reliance on local assessments for public works; and—most importantly— it curbed the power of the mass electorate in favor of the body of taxpayers. The ability to tax, spend, and borrow would be controlled by a municipal board of finance, elected by those who owned real property or paid rent of more than $250. The proposal disfranchised most urban workingmen from fiscal decisions, and reformers, business associations, and trade journals rushed to endorse it: "Great cities like New York require in the management of their finances the direct agency of the tax-payers," the *Commercial and Financial Chronicle* noted. "There is a vast horde who own no property and to whom the city seems a treasure-house fit for pillage."[21]

Predictably, machine Democrats opposed these antisuffrage and antipatronage proposals; Tammany boss John Kelly succeeded in blocking the commission's amendment legislation. Yet if the advocates of retrenchment lost their most ambitious battle, they won the war. After the fall of Tweed, conservative business interests took control of all wings of the Democratic Party. During the 1870s, a string of economy-minded merchants ruled City Hall; "Honest John" Kelly cleaned out Tammany Hall and wooed downtown interests by embracing low taxes and debt reduction; the city's credit was restored; and most public works ground to a halt. Thus, in the end, it was not constitutional counterrevolution but politics as usual that laid to rest the public activism and debt-driven urbanism of the 1860s.[22]

As I noted at the start of this chapter, the rise of retrenchment in New York was part of a widespread constriction of elite ambitions in Gilded Age America. The retreat from Reconstruction; the Liberal Republican and Mugwump insurgencies against organizational politics; the turn to laissez-faire orthodoxy in American jurisprudence; the rise of social Darwinism among genteel intellectuals—each of these signaled in its own way the bourgeois abandonment of robust public activism on behalf of social improvement. Nowhere was the sense of disillusionment sharper than in the New York of the 1870s. "When the majority vote in this city," warned Henry Bellows, a decade after extolling New York's masses for harmonizing democracy and civilization in Central Park, "by an almost fatal necessity it is always against those very principles that lie at the bottom of American freedom and of American institutions."[23]

Of course, not everybody abandoned Victorian urbanism or the larger ambitions that were inscribed in it. Real-estate interests continued to lobby for public works with all the zeal their boosterism could muster. In June 1875, in the depths of the depression, the West Side Association held a mass meeting at Harvard Hall to agitate for the renewal of uptown improvements and the reclaiming of New York's destiny. "There was hardly a seat vacant in the large hall," reported the *Real Estate Record*, "and at no time since the history of the association [began] was such a determination evinced . . . to urge upon the authorities the necessity of improving the West Side and continuing to make the metropolis what it is destined to be, under able management, the fairest city on the face of the globe."[24] At just the same time, the Victorian growth coalition of boosters and genteel environmental reformers revived once more, pursuing one last effort to lay out a progressive, civilizing landscape on the outskirts of the metropolis. Their campaign represented the first and only time that all three of our key "Haussmannian" figures—Frederick Law Olmsted, William R. Martin, and Andrew Haswell Green—confronted each other openly. The ensuing struggle represented the last hurrah of bourgeois urbanism. It concerned the laying out of the Annexed District across the Harlem River.

The Battle for the Annexed District

In 1874, New York had annexed a large tract of Westchester County between the Bronx and Hudson Rivers (the western half of what would become the Borough of the Bronx). The district was divided into two new wards (the Twenty-third and Twenty-fourth) and, like the rest of the uptown periphery, placed under the aegis of the Department of Public Parks. Department engineers at first proposed platting the territory on a grid. Given the city's fiscal straits, that proposal made sense; the grid was the most economical street plan from the viewpoint of public investment, and it was supported on that basis by Comptroller Green and his ally on the parks board, Commissioner Henry Stebbins. The proposal was decried, however, by the incoming president of the park board: none other than William Martin. In 1875, Martin moved from real-estate lobbying to public administration; Tammany Hall had just regained control of City Hall, and the incoming Mayor, William Wickham, named him commissioner. It is not surprising that a Tammany leader should have placed the city's most influential uptown booster at the head of the parks department. What *is* surprising is that Martin turned to the patrician Olmsted to implement his plans.[25]

Martin saw the Annexed District as an ideal site for the revival of the booster urbanism advocated by the West Side Association. He envisioned a design that would meld the region's varied topography with a bold program of parks, drives, villa suburbs, and steam transit, and he instructed Olmsted and staff engineer J.J.R. Croes to prepare an alternative plan for the mainland wards. Given the long, conflicted history between Olmsted and Green, the request was something of a provocation. Indeed, it formed part of a broader campaign to wrest control of the park department from Green and his allies. In 1875, Green and Martin fought a bitter publicity war over the comptroller's efforts to cut the wages of public day laborers.[26] At the same time, Green went after Olmsted, seeking (unsuccessfully) to have him fired from the parks department for accepting a minor post with the state government.[27] It was in this context of tactical skirmishing and ideological conflict that Olmsted and Croes presented three reports laying out their plan for the Annexed District in late 1876 and 1877.[28]

As with the Brooklyn and Staten Island projects discussed in Chapter 7, the collaborators proposed a comprehensively planned suburban district. And once again that proposal was grounded in a broad analysis of urban growth and city form. Responding to the initial suggestion that the annexed wards be platted on a grid, Olmsted and Croes subjected the 1811 street plan to a withering critique as inflexible, confining, and corrosive to civilized life. By contrast, "the Plan of a metropolis" should be varied and capacious, "specially adapted at different points" to foster "every legitimate interest in the wide world." Such social and spatial diversity was especially needed in the Annexed District, they argued, for the region's irregular terrain made the grid particularly unsuitable and expensive. In response, the reports offered an array of topographically appropriate interventions. Olmsted and Croes called for the development of middle- and working-class housing tracts and village business centers in the central corridor of the district. They proposed a "picturesque" highland suburb of villas and curving drives on the Riverdale shore. They laid out a steam transit system linking the new wards with Manhattan, routing the lines to cross all streets below grade, like the transverse roads in Central Park (Figure 8.2). Finally they prepared but never completed a fourth report planning a park system for the uptown wards.[29]

Historian David Schuyler has argued that the plan for the Annexed District represents "the most complete articulation of the vision of a new urban landscape" by nineteenth-century urbanists. Certainly it was Olmsted's most ambitious effort to integrate suburban residential development, scenic landscaping, street platting, and

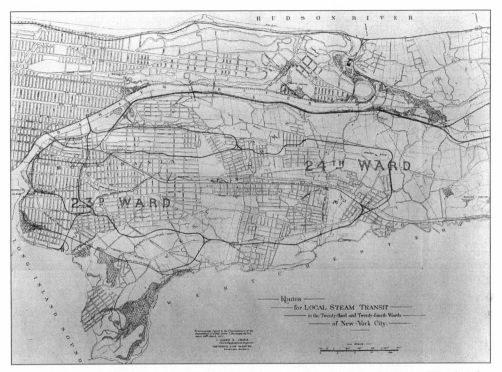

FIGURE 8.2   As part of their plan for the development of the "Annexed District," Frederick Law Olmsted and J.R.R. Croes proposed a system of steam-driven rapid transit, separated from the local streets and integrated with Manhattan's public transportation. (Courtesy of David Schuyler)

transit planning, and its design rehearses all the key themes of what I have called the urbanism of the periphery. Here was a civilizing otherworld of private domesticity, public sociability, and pastoral scenery, connected to the commercial center by efficient but unobtrusive transportation. It was an inclusive landscape to which all classes were given entrée; but at the same time it segregated elite villa districts from plebeian neighborhoods that would be filled with "houses of low rent for families of small means."[30]

Perhaps most intriguingly, it was a plan that embodied the complex and often surprising political solidarities that underlay bourgeois urbanism. For it is surely counterintuitive to see a local Tammany speculator and a renowned genteel planner making common cause against a "reform" civil servant. In part, as I have noted, these battle lines reflected the personal enmity between Olmsted and Green and the personal ties between Olmsted and Martin: the latter's brother Howard was a friend and trusted assistant of the landscape architect.[31] Yet more was at stake in this alliance than individual bonds. What drew Olmsted and Martin together was a common mode of ambition, a shared sense of the ideological stakes of city building. Despite their differences in party affiliation and aesthetic taste—and despite the crises of depression and fiscal collapse that hobbled their work—both men continued to view the reconstruction of New York as a world-historical project. Both invoked the grandest comparisons of the Bourgeois International Style to sound the call for activist planning in the Annexed District. "New York can combine" the "commercial advantages" of London with the "attractions as a place of residence" associated with Paris, Martin insisted in his endorsement of the new plan. "This fixes on us the inevitable duty, in future plans of the city . . . , to turn these natural advantages to account." Olmsted and Croes were even more pointed in citing the great centers of European urbanism: "So far as the plan of New York remains to be formed, it would be inexcusable that it should not be the plan of a Metropolis," they asserted. "This [will happen] . . . more surely if [it is] laid out . . . with carefully directed intention to the purpose, such as is now being used . . . in London, Paris, Vienna, Florence, and Rome."[32]

The plan for the Annexed District was the most comprehensive single expression of the values and ambitions that informed urban planning and landscape design during the midcentury boom. It also proved to be the last such expression. For the boom was over, and the conjuncture of economic resources, political power, and cultural vision that underwrote bourgeois urbanism had come undone. This is not to say that Olmsted and Croes's plan went unsupported. The (normally pro-Green) New York *Times* warmly applauded the proposal, opining that "[a] suburban quarter . . . is precisely what [New York] wants to make its attractions more like those of the European capitals." For a time, the Department of Public Parks adopted the plan. Yet it was blocked in 1877 by the city comptroller, still the most powerful official in the depression-era government.[33]

The episode's final irony is that that recalcitrant official was no longer Andrew Haswell Green. Green's term had ended the year before, and with the regular Democrats back in power, Tammany boss John Kelly had himself named comptroller. Kelly was determined to win the backing of downtown business interests through a Green-like policy of austerity. Combining the goads of fiscal and party discipline, he moved against the planning activists in the park department. In early January 1878, Kelly's allies on the park board abolished the salaried Office of Design and Superintendence that Olmsted had occupied. Five days later, Tammany Mayor Smith Ely demanded William Martin's resignation. Martin's brother Howard—Olmsted's clerk—was purged as well, and so, six months later, was J.J.R. Croes.[34]

Predictably, as they had done often since the late 1850s, New York's cultural and commercial gentry mobilized to protect Frederick Law Olmsted and restore him to office. E. L. Godkin and Henry W. Bellows led a protest campaign, and a petition signed by such luminaries as painter Albert Bierstadt, geologist Clarence King, and banker August Belmont appeared in the daily papers.[35] Yet for the first time, such efforts were unavailing—in part because Kelly's alliance with New York business elites made him a more formidable power, in part because Olmsted himself wished to leave Manhattan. In the summer of 1878, after two decades of activism in the reshaping of New York, he moved his family and his practice to Boston. Olmsted would go on to many significant landscape projects, most famously the design of the Boston park system, but he never again played a central role in the making of the New York cityscape. Nor would William Martin: he disappeared from public notice after 1878, leaving not even a *Times* obituary in his wake.[36]

The March of Improvement, 1890

New York, of course, kept on growing: more powerful and wealthy, more populous and congested, more diverse and divided, more built up and built out. A visitor returning in 1890 would have found the metropolis long recovered from the city-building crises of a generation earlier. National trade and local real estate rebounded in the late 1870s, fueling a new burst of development. During the 1880s land values appreciated by nearly one-half in New York (nearly twice the growth rate of the previous decade), and the pace of construction reached the unprecedented level of three thousand buildings annually. The upper West Side and northern Manhattan at long last had their day; uptown developers built hundreds of row houses and villas west and north of Central Park in the 1880s, saturating the Manhattan grid as far north as Washington Heights.[37]

The renewal of active building was accompanied by the culmination of public works that had been stalemated during the midcentury boom. The elevated railway lines were rescued from bankruptcy and unified into a single system. By 1890, Morningside and Riverside parks were largely completed, and a cluster of civic and educational institutions—Columbia University, New York Hospital, Union Theological Seminary—made plans to move uptown, crowning Morningside Heights with the sort of monumental, civilizing acropolis envisioned by boosters and gentry alike.[38]

In short the revival of growth followed the lines laid down by the midcentury boom. For the boom had represented more than just another upturn in the cycle of capitalist city building. It was a threshold moment in New York's development, one that established the logic of a new metropolitan area through a nexus of real-estate institutions, a network of public works and infrastructures, and an expansive mosaic of specialized districts and building typologies. Over the next quarter-century, these same forces would enlarge and transform the metropolis still further: New York in 1890 was on the verge of great things. A new park system was being planned north of the Harlem River; the subway and electric trolley would replace the horse car and steam-driven el; eight-story commercial palaces would give way to steel-frame skyscrapers; and the eclectic opulence of the Second Empire style would be supplanted by the corporate grandiosity of Beaux Arts. Most significantly, leading New Yorkers and Brooklynites, led by Andrew Haswell Green and others, were discussing the political integration of the metropolitan area, a debate that led to the creation of the five-borough Greater New York in 1898.[39] All of these transformations had their roots —like Green himself—in the 1850s and 1860s, building upon the ideas and improvements of the midcentury boom.

At the same time, a returning traveler would have been struck by the *dis*continuities with Victorian New York. For the spatial and cultural order of the midcentury boom was no longer so resonant in the metropolis of 1890. Nowhere is the change clearer than in the experience of two figures (albeit fictional) who *did* return after twenty years away: Basil and Isabel March. In *A Hazard of New Fortunes* (1890), William Dean Howells brings the Marches back to Manhattan, where Basil has been asked to edit a new magazine. As the middle-class (now middle-aged) couple house-hunt, stroll, make visits, and indulge their penchant for riding the elevated lines, they confront a city quite different from the scene of their honeymoon. On one hand, New York has outgrown the raw, sublime energy of their younger days: "They . . . looked down [Broadway], and found it no longer impressive," Howells writes, and he has Basil comment, "You do not now take your life in your hand when you attempt to cross it; the Broadway policeman who supported the elbow of timorous beauty . . . and guided its little fearful boots over the crossing . . . is gone, and all that certain, processional, barbaric gaiety of the place is gone." On the other hand, this city proves to be even more disjunctive and boundariless, a place of arrivistes, radicals, aesthetes, beggars, and strikers whose intersections are unexpected, bracing, and combustible. Sometimes the resulting "hazards" of the book's title are exhilarating ventures; sometimes they bring unforeseen dangers like the deadly streetcar strike that ends the story. But either way Howells makes it clear that the project of bourgeois urbanism—the double project of bounding urban space and elevating urban culture—has failed.[40]

That failure is especially evident in the social geography of the novel. Olmsted and his peers had pursued their urbanism of the periphery precisely for people like Basil and Isabel March: genteel migrants who would ensure New York's rise as a center of culture and commerce. Yet it is striking how little attention Howells's characters pay to the uptown world of parks and boulevards. Rather the heart of the novel takes place in a crowded midtown landscape filled with strange new spaces (apartment houses, cheap restaurants, rapid transit cars) and strange new social types (bohemian, adman, New Woman). The Marches engage this world with urbane fascination, preferring its shocks and pleasures to the virtues of the civilizing periphery. When they ride the el, it is not to commute, but to catch voyeuristic glimpses of the city's masses. When they house-hunt in the novel's great opening episode, they reject the townhouses and villas of upper Manhattan for a new residential form: the "French flat." Flats in fact represented a key innovation of the building wave that followed the 1870s crisis. As the architectural historian Elizabeth Bromley has argued, their acceptance by middle- and upper-class New Yorkers required a sea change in social and aesthetic norms; builders and landlords worked hard to detach the ideal of domestic virtue from the typology of the single-family, owner-occupied residence. The Marches fully understand the moral stakes of their decision: "No child brought up in [a flat] can have any conception of home," Basil worries, "[it] is the negation of motherhood." Yet in the end, they embrace the midtown apartment house as a mode of middle-class life with its own new-fangled respectabilities. "It was not to be above Twentieth Street nor below Washington Square," Isabel instructs her husband, "it must not be higher than the third floor; it must have an elevator, steam heat, hallboy, and pleasant janitor. These were essentials."[41]

If the urbanity of New York's bourgeoisie had changed by 1890, so too had the urbanism of its environmental reformers and would-be planners. The same year that Howells published his novel, police reporter Jacob Riis transformed American urban reform with the publication of *How the Other Half Lives*. Like *A Hazard of New Fortunes*, Riis's exposé of the New York tenements drew the reader's gaze away from the otherworld of parks, drives, tutelary institutions, and suburbs that had been the centerpiece of Victorian environmentalism. The urbanism of the periphery had failed, he argued, as a strategy for ameliorating poverty, congestion, and class enmity in New York. "Rapid transit to the suburbs . . . has brought no relief. We know now that there is no way out; that the [tenement] . . . has come to stay, a storm-centre forever of our civilization. Nothing is left but to make the best of a bad bargain." Abandoning the strategy of civilizing the masses through outward mobility, Riis and a new generation of Progressive urbanists sought to penetrate the world of the "other half" with new modes of social oversight: documentary photography, surveys, crusades against vice, alcohol, and police corruption.[42]

Along with this turn toward moral regulation and surveillance of the urban masses came a new stress on their environmental relief. Reformers like Riis, Alfred T. White, and Lawrence Veiller abandoned the Victorian passivity toward the downtown cityscape—toward vested property rights in general—and agitated for local playgrounds, neighborhood bathhouses, cleaner streets, and most of all, healthier, safer tenements. An earlier generation of urbanists had sought to use cheap trains, scenic parks, and cottage suburbs to carry the mass of New Yorkers out of the tenements. Their Progressive stepchildren turned to housing inspectors, privies, and organized play as ways of carrying cleanliness and order in.[43]

Taken together, Howells's novel and Riis's jeremiad offer more than just a portrait of the New York cityscape at the turn of the century. They mark the end of bourgeois urbanism. I do not mean that real-estate development, public improvements, and landscape design ceased on the metropolitan periphery; if anything, the city's outward growth intensified. Yet no longer were upper Manhattan and the outer boroughs viewed as a setting for the most consequential ambitions of spatial and social transformation. For Frederick Law Olmsted, Andrew Haswell Green, and William Martin, such places had been scenes of a romance of global significance. For Isabel March and Jacob Riis, they had ceased to stir the imagination.

APPENDIX

Statistical Tables

TABLE A. New York City Building Statistics, 1863–71: New Buildings Commenced, by Building Type, Year, and Ward

	Ward																						
	1st	2d	3d	4th	5th	6th	7th	8th	9th	10th	11th	12th	13th	14th	15th	16th	17th	18th	19th	20th	21st	22d	Total
1863																							
First-class dwellings	0	0	0	0	0	0	0	0	0	0	0	35	0	0	2	3	0	4	35	12	61	10	162
Second-class dwellings	1	0	0	4	0	4	5	0	6	3	0	101	0	0	2	4	11	3	107	1	38	11	301
Tenements	3	0	0	5	0	1	0	2	7	55	33	1	8	21	4	4	54	1	62	48	14	16	339
Brick stores	16	9	1	2	11	5	1	1	3	0	0	2	0	5	4	0	2	2	2	3	0	4	71
Factories/workshops	2	0	1	1	3	2	4	5	23	0	4	8	3	7	2	7	2	5	6	10	12	8	115
Stables	0	0	0	0	0	2	0	1	4	0	2	8	1	0	2	21	4	1	10	34	26	25	141
Frame houses	0	0	0	0	0	0	0	0	0	0	0	72	0	0	0	0	0	0	17	0	0	20	109
Churches	0	0	0	0	0	0	0	0	0	0	0	0	0	0	0	0	0	0	1	0	4	0	5
Public buildings	0	0	0	1	0	0	1	1	0	0	0	1	0	0	0	0	0	0	0	0	0	0	4
Total	22	9	2	13	14	14	11	10	43	58	39	228	12	33	16	39	71	16	240	108	155	94	1,247
1864																							
First-class dwellings	0	0	0	0	0	0	0	0	0	0	0	30	0	0	0	0	0	7	79	1	56	4	177
Second-class dwellings	0	0	1	0	0	2	1	0	2	2	0	32	1	0	0	4	4	1	33	3	25	11	122
Tenements	3	0	0	0	0	1	1	1	3	9	10	0	5	2	0	0	17	2	9	9	0	4	76
Brick stores	21	7	2	4	32	5	0	0	2	0	0	0	0	2	2	1	0	0	2	0	0	0	78
Factories/workshops	0	0	0	0	1	1	0	1	3	3	4	1	2	4	1	7	3	8	4	18	3	9	73
Stables	1	0	0	0	0	2	0	0	4	0	0	14	0	0	5	17	0	3	10	19	29	7	111
Frame houses	0	0	0	0	0	0	0	0	0	0	0	52	0	0	0	2	0	0	9	0	0	9	72
Churches	0	0	0	0	0	0	0	1	0	0	0	0	0	0	0	0	0	0	4	1	2	2	10
Public buildings	0	0	0	0	0	1	0	2	0	0	0	0	0	0	0	2	1	3	3	0	0	2	14
Total	25	7	3	4	33	12	2	5	14	14	14	129	8	6	8	33	25	24	153	51	115	48	733
1865																							
First-class dwellings	6	0	1	0	0	0	0	0	12	0	0	42	0	0	0	2	0	4	181	3	23	34	308
Second-class dwellings	0	1	0	0	2	0	2	1	1	0	0	17	0	0	3	6	1	1	86	4	22	20	167
Tenements	1	0	0	2	1	2	5	0	3	20	12	2	7	0	0	4	46	6	18	13	5	14	161
Brick stores	6	1	4	0	15	5	6	0	1	6	0	0	2	2	4	0	1	5	1	2	0	1	54
Factories/workshops	2	2	0	1	1	3	11	2	14	6	2	7	2	6	2	7	7	1	21	13	5	15	130
Stables	0	0	0	1	1	1	0	0	8	1	0	11	0	1	1	25	2	27	26	11	24	16	156
Frame houses	0	0	0	0	0	0	0	0	0	0	0	105	0	0	0	0	0	0	58	0	0	25	188
Churches	0	0	0	0	0	0	0	0	0	0	0	1	0	0	0	0	0	0	2	1	2	2	8
Public buildings	1	0	1	0	1	0	0	0	2	0	0	1	0	0	1	1	0	2	2	1	1	3	18
Total	16	4	6	4	21	11	24	3	41	27	14	186	9	9	11	45	57	46	395	49	82	130	1,190

TABLE A (CONTINUED)

	1st	2d	3d	4th	5th	6th	7th	8th	9th	10th	11th	12th	13th	14th	15th	16th	17th	18th	19th	20th	21st	22d	Total
1866																							
First-class dwellings	0	0	0	0	0	0	0	0	12	0	0	41	0	0	2	1	0	8	256	15	24	50	409
Second-class dwellings	0	0	1	1	0	0	1	1	8	0	1	33	0	0	6	2	2	2	7	5	9	36	115
Tenements	4	0	1	0	2	0	8	3	5	49	17	7	13	1	0	4	52	5	94	19	14	16	314
Brick stores	7	4	8	5	66	9	2	11	1	0	0	1	0	9	11	0	0	0	3	1	7	3	148
Factories/workshops	1	0	0	3	7	3	5	4	14	2	5	15	3	4	6	15	3	4	24	18	4	22	162
Stables	0	0	0	0	1	0	2	1	7	2	1	19	4	1	1	20	4	1	30	25	20	16	155
Frame houses	0	0	0	0	0	0	0	0	0	0	0	213	0	0	0	0	0	0	85	0	0	28	326
Churches	0	0	0	0	0	0	0	0	1	0	0	0	0	0	0	0	0	2	6	4	1	1	15
Public buildings	0	0	0	0	1	1	0	0	0	2	0	2	0	1	0	1	2	3	6	3	1	3	26
Total	12	4	10	9	77	13	18	20	48	55	24	331	20	16	26	43	63	25	511	90	80	175	1,670
1867																							
First-class dwellings	0	0	0	0	0	0	0	0	0	0	0	76	0	0	1	5	0	4	370	17	27	56	556
Second-class dwellings	0	0	0	2	0	0	1	0	3	2	1	33	0	0	3	8	2	4	55	12	6	19	151
Tenements	5	0	0	1	0	0	11	1	8	24	14	12	10	2	0	3	23	23	106	26	19	60	348
Brick stores	5	4	2	2	39	6	2	11	4	1	0	0	0	4	5	0	1	2	10	0	6	5	109
Factories/workshops	1	0	0	1	5	3	0	2	4	0	4	47	3	1	2	6	5	14	31	22	13	18	182
Stables	0	0	0	0	0	0	1	0	10	1	3	16	0	1	1	5	2	8	25	11	10	20	114
Frame houses	0	0	0	0	0	0	0	0	6	0	0	203	0	0	0	0	0	0	16	1	1	8	235
Churches	0	0	1	0	0	0	0	0	0	0	1	1	1	0	0	0	2	0	5	0	1	2	14
Public buildings	1	1	0	2	1	0	0	0	1	2	2	3	0	0	1	0	0	2	5	0	0	6	27
Total	12	5	3	8	45	9	15	14	36	30	25	391	14	8	13	27	35	57	623	89	83	194	1,736
1868																							
First-class dwellings	0	0	0	0	0	0	0	0	9	0	0	159	0	0	0	3	1	2	564	19	57	113	927
Second-class dwellings	0	0	0	0	0	0	1	0	9	0	1	52	1	1	4	6	0	9	126	17	12	75	314
Tenements	1	0	0	5	0	2	2	1	4	9	11	36	3	2	1	3	28	31	127	32	15	33	346
Brick stores	4	2	5	3	19	10	2	10	0	0	3	3	2	11	9	1	2	8	2	1	1	1	99
Factories/workshops	0	0	0	2	1	3	4	8	13	0	12	14	10	5	4	17	10	9	22	7	5	24	170
Stables	0	0	0	2	1	0	1	0	6	2	3	9	1	0	2	5	3	3	13	4	8	11	74
Frame houses	0	0	0	0	0	0	0	0	0	0	0	111	0	0	0	0	0	0	14	0	0	8	133
Churches	0	0	0	0	0	0	1	0	0	0	0	0	0	0	0	0	2	0	3	2	0	6	17
Public buildings	0	0	0	2	2	2	0	0	1	0	1	1	0	0	1	1	2	5	4	3	5	2	32
Total	5	2	5	14	23	17	11	19	43	11	31	387	17	19	21	36	48	67	875	85	103	273	2,112

TABLE A (CONTINUED)

	Ward																						
	1st	2d	3d	4th	5th	6th	7th	8th	9th	10th	11th	12th	13th	14th	15th	16th	17th	18th	19th	20th	21st	22d	Total
1869																							
First-class dwellings	0	0	0	0	0	0	0	0	5	0	0	121	0	0	0	0	0	1	466	10	51	131	785
Second-class dwellings	2	0	0	0	2	0	1	4	3	1	3	39	1	1	6	7	3	8	82	7	11	62	243
Tenements	3	0	0	7	2	0	9	3	6	22	19	15	25	8	2	3	56	56	129	38	27	38	468
Brick stores	5	6	5	2	45	5	1	12	7	3	0	5	3	6	3	4	0	4	6	2	6	3	134
Factories/workshops	2	2	0	1	0	0	8	4	3	2	4	5	2	5	3	13	4	6	27	7	5	28	131
Stables	1	0	0	1	0	0	5	0	9	3	6	10	4	1	2	12	1	6	25	3	10	12	111
Frame houses	0	0	0	5	0	0	0	0	0	0	1	106	0	0	0	1	0	0	23	6	4	22	168
Churches	0	1	0	0	0	0	0	1	1	0	0	4	0	0	0	0	0	2	5	2	1	5	22
Public buildings	1	0	1	0	1	1	0	0	2	0	0	5	1	0	1	0	0	2	6	4	4	5	34
Total	14	9	6	16	50	6	24	24	36	31	33	310	36	21	17	40	65	85	769	79	119	306	2,096
1871 (April 5/April 5)																							
First-class dwellings	0	0	0	1	0	1	0	0	7	0	0	173	1	0	1	6	0	1	502	6	8	97	804
Second-class dwellings	0	0	1	0	1	0	1	1	2	0	2	14	2	1	0	9	1	2	12	11	4	31	95
Tenements	7	2	0	6	1	3	51	3	36	50	37	155	26	12	2	15	38	31	226	74	63	182	1,020
Brick stores	2	4	14	4	16	6	1	13	2	0	2	3	1	4	5	5	3	1	15	5	3	7	116
Factories	1	0	0	2	0	3	1	3	8	1	10	5	2	1	1	8	3	1	13	12	5	21	101
Stables	0	0	0	0	1	1	6	2	7	2	3	8	1	1	5	4	2	1	41	6	14	11	116
Frame houses	0	0	0	0	0	0	0	0	3	0	0	37	0	0	0	0	0	0	3	1	0	3	47
Churches	0	0	0	0	0	0	0	0	0	0	0	2	0	0	0	1	0	0	5	1	0	0	9
Schoolhouses	0	0	0	0	1	0	0	2	2	0	1	1	0	0	1	1	1	1	9	0	0	5	25
Total	10	6	15	13	20	14	60	24	67	53	55	398	33	19	15	49	48	38	826	116	97	357	2,333

TABLE A (CONTINUED)

Yearly totals per ward

	1st	2d	3d	4th	5th	6th	7th	8th	9th	10th	11th	12th	13th	14th	15th	16th	17th	18th	19th	20th	21st	22d	*Total*
1863	22	9	2	13	14	14	11	10	43	58	39	228	12	33	16	39	71	16	240	108	155	94	1,247
1864	25	7	3	4	33	12	2	5	14	14	14	129	8	6	8	33	25	24	153	51	115	48	733
1865	16	4	6	4	21	11	24	3	41	27	14	186	9	9	11	45	57	46	395	49	82	130	1,190
1866	12	4	10	9	77	13	18	20	48	55	24	331	20	16	26	43	63	25	511	90	80	175	1,670
1867	12	5	3	8	45	9	15	14	36	30	25	391	14	8	13	27	35	57	623	89	83	194	1,736
1868	5	2	5	14	23	17	11	19	43	11	31	387	17	19	21	36	48	67	875	85	103	273	2,112
1869	14	9	6	16	50	6	24	24	36	31	33	310	36	21	17	40	65	85	769	79	119	306	2,096
1870	NA	NA	NA	NA	NA	NA	NA	NA	NA	NA	NA	NA	NA	NA	NA	NA	NA	NA	NA	NA	NA	NA	NA
1871	10	6	15	13	20	14	60	24	67	53	55	398	33	19	15	49	48	38	826	116	97	357	2,333
Total	116	46	50	81	283	96	165	119	328	279	235	2,360	149	131	127	312	412	358	4,392	667	834	1,577	13,117

Yearly figures per building type

	1863	1864	1865	1866	1867	1868	1869	1870	1871
First-class dwellings	162	177	308	409	556	927	785	NA	804
Second-class dwellings	301	122	167	115	151	314	243	NA	95
Tenements	339	76	161	314	348	346	468	NA	1,020
Brick stores	71	78	54	148	109	99	134	NA	116
Factories	115	73	130	162	182	170	131	NA	101
Stables	141	111	156	155	114	74	111	NA	116
Frame houses	109	72	188	326	235	133	168	NA	47
Churches	5	10	8	15	14	17	22	NA	9
Schoolhouses	4	14	18	26	27	32	34	NA	25
Yearly total	1,247	733	1,190	1,670	1,736	2,112	2,096	NA	2,333

Note: The Department of Buildings was reorganized in 1870; no complete records are available.

Source: New York City Department of Buildings, Reports of the Superintendent.

TABLE B. Assessed Valuation of Manhattan Real Estate per Ward, 1860–80 (in thousands of dollars)

Year	Ward																						Total Value
	1st	2d	3d	4th	5th	6th	7th	8th	9th	10th	11th	12th	13th	14th	15th	16th	17th	18th	19th	20th	21st	22d	
1860	36,626	21,737	26,993	9,905	17,311	12,766	13,019	18,297	15,512	8,666	8,917	11,857	5,500	12,425	28,385	17,790	17,459	37,550	16,092	16,581	29,711	14,785	397,883
1861	36,117	21,542	26,987	9,533	18,733	12,819	13,036	18,392	15,737	8,755	8,967	12,455	5,548	12,552	28,611	18,375	17,795	37,157	17,096	17,412	31,672	17,666	406,956
1862	32,585	19,727	25,766	9,191	18,757	12,966	12,455	18,146	15,729	8,685	8,956	13,100	5,450	12,367	26,934	18,486	17,775	37,017	17,903	17,569	31,949	18,042	399,556
1863																							
1864	34,293	19,909	25,536	9,198	18,622	12,901	12,350	18,088	15,981	8,925	9,262	15,515	5,513	12,522	27,141	18,645	18,587	37,554	20,462	17,971	32,964	18,759	410,695
1865	35,249	19,986	25,717	9,411	21,211	13,417	12,402	18,392	15,934	9,129	9,461	18,135	5,553	12,686	28,249	18,867	18,770	38,397	23,071	18,178	35,322	19,824	427,361
1866																							
1867	47,996	24,747	32,516	10,421	27,631	15,497	13,337	21,628	17,138	10,755	11,738	24,941	6,298	15,349	39,760	19,986	23,596	43,549	46,249	21,655	49,747	30,915	555,447
1868	52,723	27,670	34,184	11,223	35,541	18,175	13,829	25,879	18,681	12,306	11,910	28,143	6,882	18,246	41,998	23,783	23,737	47,108	53,608	24,856	56,583	36,175	623,237
1869																							
1870	53,487	29,215	32,435	12,259	41,476	20,819	14,664	31,011	22,933	13,931	13,135	48,870	7,452	20,907	48,273	28,928	25,834	60,872	71,319	27,255	64,770	53,147	742,992
1871	53,624	29,386	32,868	12,509	38,820	21,176	15,095	31,373	22,955	14,611	13,921	50,363	8,259	21,453	49,332	29,147	29,475	61,180	77,772	31,327	66,992	57,666	769,306
1872	51,216	28,092	31,637	12,572	38,671	21,210	15,589	32,285	23,571	15,226	14,335	54,569	8,530	21,426	50,350	29,579	30,038	62,544	91,284	33,245	70,996	60,186	797,149
1873	50,609	27,754	31,355	12,512	38,425	21,349	15,852	33,774	25,128	16,321	14,614	62,459	9,302	21,991	50,917	29,731	30,552	64,468	110,521	34,830	71,235	63,095	836,793
1874	51,564	28,284	31,737	12,562	38,624	21,804	16,303	34,321	25,563	17,026	14,851	67,494	9,644	22,411	51,584	32,137	31,058	65,480	113,032	35,946	72,312	63,905	857,642
1875	51,261	28,015	31,958	12,595	38,245	21,422	16,038	34,375	25,807	17,112	14,856	67,064	9,588	22,391	51,509	32,249	31,327	65,105	116,052	39,027	72,511	65,476	863,983
1876	51,004	28,012	32,692	12,686	38,562	21,432	15,986	34,438	25,920	17,362	14,871	67,239	9,770	22,305	51,713	32,454	31,705	66,045	119,157	36,985	72,707	66,420	869,463
1877	51,269	28,057	32,736	12,606	38,588	21,420	15,932	34,789	26,098	17,317	14,939	65,819	9,783	22,290	51,776	32,545	31,707	66,584	120,360	37,088	73,059	67,392	872,152
1878	50,996	27,816	32,830	12,400	38,578	21,361	16,119	34,439	26,300	17,194	15,674	65,600	9,819	22,288	50,944	33,348	31,785	67,058	123,311	37,693	74,204	68,561	878,316
1879	52,090	27,903	33,423	12,563	38,938	21,676	15,935	34,747	26,839	17,062	15,790	67,980	9,777	22,338	50,906	33,780	32,137	68,075	120,282	38,308	75,664	70,308	886,521
1880	53,057	28,106	33,818	12,606	38,949	21,812	15,931	35,127	26,923	17,135	15,834	74,923	9,742	22,493	51,419	34,000	32,703	69,342	138,545	38,591	76,624	71,986	919,668

Note: Figures from Wards Twenty-three and Twenty-four, the mainland wards annexed in 1874, are excluded. Figures for 1863, 1866, and 1869 are unavailable.
Source: Annual Reports of the Commissioners of Taxes and Assessments.

Notes

Abbreviations

AHG	Andrew Haswell Green
Alterations Docket	New York City Department of Buildings, *Docket Books for Plans for Building Alterations* (1870)
BCCP	Board of Commissioners of Central Park
BCPP	Board of Commissioners of Prospect Park
BDPP	New York City Board of the Department of Public Parks
CA	Citizens' Association of New York
CLB	Charles Loring Brace
CV	Calvert Vaux
FLO	Frederick Law Olmsted
FLOP	*The Papers of Frederick Law Olmsted* (Baltimore: Johns Hopkins University Press) 　　Volume I: *The Formative Years, 1822–1852* (1977) 　　Volume II: *Slavery and the South, 1852–1857* (1981) 　　Volume III: *Creating Central Park, 1857–1861* (1983) 　　Volume IV: *Defending the Union, 1861–1863* (1986) 　　Volume V: *The California Frontier, 1863–1865* (1990) 　　Volume VI: *The Years of Olmsted, Vaux and Company, 1865– 1874* (1992)
FLO Papers	Frederick Law Olmsted Papers, Library of Congress
New Docket	New York City Department of Buildings, *Docket Books for Plans for New Buildings*
RERBG	*Real Estate Record and Builders' Guide*
Superintendent Reports	New York City Superintendent of Buildings, *Annual Reports* (1872) (issues 1863–71 reports in single volume)
WRM	William R. Martin
WSA	West Side Association

Introduction

1. "Can a City Be Planned?" New York *Evening Post* (March 16, 1868), reprinted in *RERBG* (March 21, 1868). For William Cullen Bryant's editorial role in the *Evening Post*, see Allan Nevins, *The Evening Post: A Century of Journalism* (New York: Boni and Liverright, 1922); for Bryant's support of park improvements, see Roy Rosenzweig and Elizabeth Blackmar, *The Park and the People: A History of Central Park* (Ithaca, N.Y.: Cornell University Press, 1992), 15, 24, 26.

2. The report to which the editorial refers is Frederick Law Olmsted and Calvert Vaux, "Report of the Landscape Architects and Superintendents . . . ," BCPP, *8th Annual Report* (1868), reprinted in Albert Fein (ed.), *Landscape into Cityscape: Frederick Law Olmsted's Plans for a Greater New York City* (Ithaca, N.Y.: Cornell University Press, 1967). (Until the consolidation of Greater New York in 1898, Brooklyn and New York were separate cities; Prospect Park and Brooklyn's other public grounds were administered by the Board of Commissioners of Prospect Park.)

3. For an overview of the town-site design practices that dominated American city planning before the mid-nineteenth century, see John Reps's *The Making of Urban America: A History of City Planning in the United States* (Princeton, N.J., Princeton University Press, 1965).

4. For influential examples of this social-scientific approach to urban spatial change in the United States, see Sam Bass Warner, Jr., *Streetcar Suburbs: The Process of Growth in Boston, 1870–1900* (Cambridge, Mass.: Harvard University Press, 1962), the source of "walking city"; Warner, *The Urban Wilderness: A History of the American City* (New York: Harper and Row, 1972), and David Ward, *Cities and Immigrants: A Geography of Change in Nineteenth-Century America* (New York: Oxford University Press, 1971). For the larger modernization narrative on which this literature draws, see Robert Wiebe, *The Search for Order, 1877–1920* (New York: Hill and Wang, 1967) and Samuel D. Hays, *The Response to Industrialism, 1885–1914* (Chicago: University of Chicago Press, 1957).

5. In addition to the works cited in footnote 4, see David Ward, "The Industrial Revolution and the Emergence of Boston's Central Business District," *Economic Geography* 42:2 (April 1966): 152–71; Allan R. Pred, *Urban Growth and City-Systems in the United States, 1840–1860* (Cambridge, Mass.: Harvard University Press, 1980); and John R. Borchert, "American Metropolitan Evolution," *Geographical Review* 57:3 (July 1967): 301–32.

6. See Warner, *Streetcar Suburbs*; Melvin G. Holli, *Reform in Detroit: Hazen S. Pingree and Urban Politics* (New York: Oxford University Press, 1969); and Kenneth T. Jackson, *Crabgrass Frontier: The Suburbanization of America* (New York: Oxford University Press, 1985). For research that periodizes U.S. city form according to transportation regimes, see Warner, *Urban Wilderness*, 55–149; and Borchert, "American Metropolitan Evolution."

7. See Warner, *Streetcar Suburbs*; Theodore Hershberg et al., "The 'Journey-to-Work': An Empirical Investigation of Work, Residence, and Transportation, Philadelphia, 1850 and 1880," in Hershberg (ed.), *Philadelphia: Work, Space, Family, and Group Experience in the 19th Century* (New York: Oxford University Press, 1981), 128–73; Clay McShane, *Technology and Reform: Street Railways and the Growth of Milwaukee* (Madison: University of Wisconsin Press, 1974); and Eugene Moehring, *Public Works and the Pattern of Real Estate Growth in Manhattan, 1835–1894* (New York: Arno Press, 1981).

8. See Michael J. Doucet, "Urban Land Development in Nineteenth-Century North America," *Journal of Urban History* 8 (1982): 299–342; Elizabeth Blackmar, *Manhattan for Rent, 1785–1850* (Ithaca, N.Y.: Cornell University Press, 1989); Robin Einhorn, *Property Rules: Political Economy in Chicago, 1833–1872* (Chicago: University of Chicago Press, 1991).

9. See Marc A. Weiss, *The Rise of the Community Builders: The American Real Estate Industry and Urban Land Planning* (New York: Columbia University Press, 1987); and Jackson, *Crabgrass Frontier.*

10. See especially Henri Lefebvre, *The Production of Space* (Cambridge, Mass.: Blackwell, 1991); David Harvey, *The Limits to Capital* (Chicago: University of Chicago Press, 1982); Harvey, *The Condition of Postmodernity: An Enquiry into the Origins of Cultural Change* (Cambridge, Mass.: Blackwell, 1989); Edward Soja, *Postmodern Geographies: The Reassertion of Space in Critical Social Theory* (New York: Verso, 1989); and Neil Smith, *Uneven Development: Nature, Capital, and the Production of Space* (New York: Blackwell, 1984).

11. Soja, *Postmodern Geographies* ("sociospatial dialectic"); Harvey, *Limits to Capital.*

12. I have found Smith's theoretical analysis in *Uneven Development* especially helpful in understanding the contradictory patterns of New York's growth in the mid-nineteenth century.

13. Mel Scott, *American City Planning since* 1890 (Berkeley and Los Angeles: University of California Press, 1969). My analysis of U.S. planning historiography has benefited from Mary Corbin Sies and Christopher Silver, "Introduction: The History of Planning History," in Sies and Silver (eds.), *Planning the Twentieth-Century American City* (Baltimore: Johns Hopkins University Press, 1996), 1–34.

14. For the Victorian origins of urban design and planning in the United States, see Thomas Bender, *Toward an Urban Vision: Ideas and Institutions in Nineteenth-Century America* (Lexington: University of Kentucky Press, 1975); David Schuyler, *The New Urban Landscape: The Redefinition of City Form in Nineteenth-Century America* (Baltimore: Johns Hopkins University Press, 1986); and Daniel Schaffer (ed.), *Two Centuries of American Planning* (Baltimore: Johns Hopkins University Press, 1988). For the role of business leaders and civil engineers as "protoplanners," see David C. Hammack, "Comprehensive Planning Before the Comprehensive Plan: A New Look at the Nineteenth-Century American City," in ibid., 139–65; Joel Tarr, "The Impact of Sanitary Reform upon American Urban Planning, 1840–1890," *Journal of Social History* 13 (1979–80): 83–103; and Stanley K. Schultz and Clay McShane, "To Engineer the Metropolis: Sewers, Sanitation, and City Planning in Late-Nineteenth-Century America," *Journal of American History* 65 (September, 1978): 389–411. For "moral environmentalism" and the tutelary aims of Victorian urbanism, see also Stanley K. Schultz, *Constructing Urban Culture: American Cities and City Planning, 1800–1920* (Philadelphia: Temple University Press, 1989), 112–14; and my discussion in Chapter 5.

15. I summarize key historical, biographical, and archival publications on Olmsted in Chapter 1, note 7. For historiography that foregrounds Olmsted's role in American urban planning, see Schuyler, *New Urban Landscape*; Fein (ed.), *Landscape into Cityscape*; and William H. Wilson, *The City Beautiful Movement* (Baltimore: Johns Hopkins University Press, 1989), 9–34.

16. Charles Loring Brace, *The Dangerous Classes of New York, and Twenty Years' Work among Them* (New York: Wynkoop and Hallenbeck, 1872), ii.

17. For the cultural historiography of bourgeois and middle-class formation in nineteenth-century America, see Lawrence Levine, *Highbrow Lowbrow: The Emergence of Cultural Hierarchy in America* (Cambridge, Mass.: Harvard University Press, 1988); Stuart Blumin, *The Emergence of the Middle Class: Social Experience in the American City, 1760–1900* (New York: Cambridge University Press, 1989); Richard Brodhead, *Cultures of Letters: Scenes of Reading and Writing In Nineteenth-Century America* (Chicago: University of Chicago Press, 1993); Paul Dimaggio, "Cultural Entrepreneurship in Nineteenth-Century Boston: The Creation of an Organizational Base for High Culture in America," in Chandra Mukerji and Michael Schudson (eds.), *Rethinking Popular Culture: Contemporary Perspectives in Cultural Studies* (Berkeley and Los Angeles: University of California Press, 1991), 374–97.

18. Readers will note here the influence of Antonio Gramsci's writings on hegemony and the class politics of nation building, especially "Notes on Italian History," "The Modern Prince," and "State and Civil Society," translated and collected in Quintin Hoare and Geoffrey Nowell Smith (eds.), *Selections from the Prison Notebooks of Antonio Gramsci* (London: Lawrence and Wishart, 1971). For an exemplary use of Gramscian analysis to explore the links between class and nation formation in Germany during the same period as my study, see David Blackbourn and Geoff Eley, *The Peculiarities of German History: Bourgeois Society and Politics in Nineteenth-Century Germany* (New York: Oxford University Press, 1984).

19. The historiography of U.S. state formation has remained too focused, I think, on the growth of federal power in the twentieth century. For the *local* etiology of state building in nineteenth-century America, see Terrence McDonald, "The Burdens of Urban History: The Theory of the State in Recent American Social History," *Studies in American Political Development* 3 (1989): 3–29; and Amy Bridges, *A City in the Republic: Antebellum New York and the Origins of Machine Politics* (New York: Cambridge University Press, 1984). For the role of city building in the growth of local governmental authority, see Eric Monkkonen, *America Becomes Urban* (Berkeley and Los Angeles: University of California Press, 1989); and Jon Teaford, *The Unheralded Triumph: City Government in America, 1870–1900* (Baltimore: Johns Hopkins University Press, 1984).

Chapter 1

1. FLO to Parke Godwin, August 1, 1858, *FLOP* III, 201; CV to FLO, July 6, 1865, in *FLOP* V, 402; [Henry W. Bellows,] "Cities and Parks: With Special Reference to the New York Central Park," *Atlantic Monthly* 7 (April 1861): 421–22.

2. New York *Times* (June 18, 1994): I, 21:2; Elizabeth Barlow Rogers et al., *Rebuilding Central Park: A Management and Restoration Plan* (Cambridge, Mass.: MIT Press, 1987), quoted in Elizabeth Blackmar and Roy Rosenzweig, *The Park and the People: A History of Central Park* (Ithaca, N.Y.: Cornell University Press, 1992), 512; Elizabeth Barlow Rogers quoted in ibid., 510.

3. For the labor and environmental history of the building of Central Park, see the nuanced account in Blackmar and Rosenzweig, *Park and the People*, 150–79.

4. For the intellectual and cultural history of Olmsted's reputation, see Melvin Kalfus, *Frederick Law Olmsted: The Passion of a Public Artist* (New York: New York University Press, 1990), especially 35–52. For Olmsted's struggles with Andrew Haswell Green and other rivals, see *FLOP* III, 24–25, 30–36, 189–242; *FLOP* V, 359–66, 375–79, 383–90; David Schuyler, *The New Urban Landscape: The Redefinition of City Form in Nineteenth-Century America* (Baltimore: Johns Hopkins University Press, 1986), 95–100; Rosenzweig and Blackmar, *Park and the People*, 142–49, 180–205; and Laura Wood Roper, *FLO: A Biography of Frederick Law Olmsted* (Baltimore: Johns Hopkins University Press, 1973), 124–55 passim. For his conflicts with the public over the proper use of the park, see Frederick Law Olmsted, Jr., and Theodora Kimball (eds.), *Forty Years of Landscape Architecture: Central Park* (Cambridge, Mass.: MIT Press, 1928), 406–71; and Blackmar and Rosenzweig, *Park and the People*, 238–59.

5. CV to FLO, July 31, 1865, in *FLOP* V, 419. For the relationship between Vaux and Olmsted, key sources and overviews include *FLOP* III, 10–16, 63–68; *FLOP* V, 114–17, 144–57, 358–66, 372–79, 383–91, 402–7, 419–25, 443–45; *FLOP* VI, 1–5, 67–72; Kalfus, *Olmsted*, 44–46, 209–31, 253–55; and Roper, *FLO*, 135–37, 261–63, 291–93, 342–43, 366.

6. The quoted phrase is from Rosenzweig and Blackmar, *Park and the People*, 433. For Olmsted's influence on twentieth-century design and social thought, see also William H. Wilson, *The City Beautiful Movement* (Baltimore: Johns Hopkins University Press, 1989), 9–34; and Lewis Mumford, *The Brown Decades: A Study of the Arts in America, 1865–1895* (New York: Dover Publications, 1955). For additions to Central Park during the 1920s and 1930s, see Rosenzweig and Blackmar, *Park and the People*, 439–63.

7. For biographical studies of Olmsted, see Roper, *FLO*; and Kalfus, *Olmsted*. Important anthologies of Olmsted's design writings include Albert Fein (ed.), *Landscape into Cityscape: Frederick Law Olmsted's Plans for a Greater New York City* (Ithaca, N.Y.: Cornell University Press, 1967); S. B. Sutton (ed.), *Civilizing American Cities: A Selection of Frederick Law Olmsted's Writings on City Landscapes* (Cambridge, Mass.: MIT Press, 1971); and Olmsted, Jr., and Kimball (eds.), *Forty Years of Landscape Architecture*. For research on Olmsted's career, landscape work, and social thought, see Charles E. Beveridge, "Olmsted's Theory of Landscape Design," *Nineteenth Century* 3 (Summer 1977): 38–43; Thomas Bender, *Toward an Urban Vision: Ideas and Institutions in Nineteenth Century America* (Lexington: University of Kentucky Press, 1975); Bender, *New York Intellect: A History of Intellectual Life in New York City from 1750 to the Beginnings of Our Own Time* (New York: Knopf, 1987); Geoffrey Blodgett, "Landscape Architecture as Conservative Reform," *Journal of American History* 62 (March 1976): 869–89; Schuyler, *The New Urban Landscape*; and Cynthia Zaivzetsky, *Frederick Law Olmsted and the Boston Park System* (Cambridge, Mass.: Belknap Press, 1982). Johns Hopkins University Press has published six volumes of *The Papers of Frederick Law Olmsted*, enumerated in the abbreviations list at the start of the Notes section.

In the past decade, the "cult of Olmsted" has sparked a critical reevaluation of the designer's achievements, values, and temperament, a revisionist turn within which my own work may be situated. Among the best examples of this scholarship—although quite different in approach—are Rosenzweig and Blackmar, *Park and the People*, and Kalfus, *Olmsted*. Like the "Olmsted revival," the "Olmsted backlash" has its own history, one that reflects, I think, the political crisis of urban liberalism in the 1980s.

8. Wilson, *City Beautiful*, 9–34; Peter Hall, *Cities of Tomorrow* (London: Blackwell, 1988), 89.

9. FLO to Parke Godwin, August 1, 1858, in *FLOP*, III, 200–201. For patronage and labor pressures on Olmsted in the winter of 1857, see FLO to Charles Loring Brace, December 8, 1860, in ibid., 286; FLO, "Passages in the Life of an Unpractical Man," autobiographical manuscript published in Fein (ed.), *Landscape into Cityscape*, 54–62. For the efforts of Robert Dillon and other park commissioners to amend the Greensward Plan, see BCCP, *Minutes . . .* , May 24, 1858, 44–47; FLO to BCCP, May 31, 1858, FLO to Richard Grant White, June 3 and June 16, 1858, in *FLOP* III, 193–200. For Parke Godwin's collaboration with Olmsted in the founding of *Putnam's Monthly* in the mid-1850s and his significance as a Republican journalist, see Charles E. Beveridge and Charles Capen McLaughlin (eds.), *FLOP* II, 63, 349; and Bender, *New York Intellect*, 164–65.

10. FLO to James T. Fields, October 21, 1860, in *FLOP* III, 269; Henry Bellows, "Cities and Parks," *Atlantic Monthly* 7 (April 1861): 423. For Bellows's career and relationship with Olmsted, see *FLOP* II, 347–48, and *FLOP* IV, 83–89; and Clifford E. Clark, Jr., "Religious Beliefs and Social Reforms in the Gilded Age: The Case of Henry Whitney Bellows," *New England Quarterly* 43 (March 1970): 59–78.

11. FLO to Godwin, August 1, 1858, in *FLOP* III, 201.

12. FLO, "Passages in the Life of an Unpractical Man," in Fein (ed.), *Landscape into Cityscape*, 52; Bellows, "The Townward Tendency," *The City: An Illustrated Magazine* 1, no. 1 (January

1872): 36–40; [Bellows,] "Cities and Parks," 421. For the importance of urban issues to Victorian social thought, see Bender, *Toward an Urban Vision*. The tension between republican ideals and bourgeois civility is analyzed in John Kasson, *Rudeness and Civility: Manners in Nineteenth-Century America* (New York: Hill and Wang, 1990); and David Scobey, "Anatomy of the Promenade: The Politics of Bourgeois Sociability in Victorian New York City," *Social History* (1992): 205–27.

13. Junius Henri Browne, *The Great Metropolis: A Mirror of New York* (Hartford: American Publishing, 1869), 28; James Fenimore Cooper, "New York," *Spirit of the Fair*, April 7, 1864. *The Spirit of the Fair* was a daily paper published during the Metropolitan Sanitary Fair, an exposition organized by New York "society" women in the spring of 1864 to raise funds for the U.S. Sanitary Commission and the Union war effort.

For the cultural history of Victorian urban portraiture, see Alan Trachtenberg, *The Incorporation of America: Culture and Society in the Gilded Age* (New York: Hill and Wang, 1982), 101–39; Peter Bacon Hales, *Silver Cities: The Photography of American Urbanization, 1839–1915* (Philadelphia: Temple University Press, 1984); and Stuart Blumin, "Explaining the New Metropolis: Perception, Depiction, and Analysis in Mid-Nineteenth Century New York City," *Journal of Urban History* 11 (1984): 9–38. Important textual and visual portraits of New York include architectural studies like the "New-York Daguerrotyped" series in *Putnam's Monthly* 1–3 (1853–54); explorations of vice subcultures like Edward Crapsey, *Nether Side of New York* (New York: Sheldon, 1872); magazine sketches like [H. T. Tuckerman,] "Through Broadway," *Atlantic Monthly* 18 (December 1866): 717–27; and exposé books such as George Foster, *New York in Slices* (New York: W. F. Burgess, 1849); Browne, *Great Metropolis*; and Matthew Hale Smith, *Sunshine and Shadow in New York* (Hartford: J.B. Burr, 1869).

14. Colonel O. Vandenburgh, "The City of New York Ten Years Hence," *Hours at Home: A Popular Monthly of Instruction and Recreation* (August 1868): 350; John Roebling, Report . . . to the President and Directors of the New York Bridge Company on the Proposed East River Bridge (1870), 4; Fitz-Hugh Ludlow, "The American Metropolis," *Atlantic Monthly* 15 (January 1865); Fernando Wood, address to a public meeting of the West Side Association, May 26, 1871, published in West Side Association, *Proceedings of Six Public Meetings* . . . , Document No. 6, 14.

15. Jerome Mushkat, *Fernando Wood: A Political Biography* (Kent, Ohio: Kent State University Press, 1990), especially 41–81, details Wood's mayoral policies, ideology, and role in New York city building. For conflicts between Wood and Olmsted, see Rosenzweig and Blackmar, 153–58; and FLO to Edwin Lawrence Godkin, July 15, 1863, in *FLOP* IV, 655.

16. For the history of republican nationalism in the antebellum era, see Alexander Saxton, *Rise and Fall of the White Republic: Class Politics and Mass Culture in Nineteenth-Century America* (London: Verso, 1990); and Joel H. Sibley, *The American Political Nation, 1838–1893* (Palo Alto, Calif.: Stanford University Press, 1991). For an overview of U.S. national consolidation during the mid-nineteenth century, see D. W. Meinig, *The Shaping of America: A Geographical Perspective on 500 Years of History*, Volume II: *Continental America, 1800–1867* (New Haven, Conn.: Yale University Press, 1993). For general approaches to the history of nationalism and nation building, see Eric Hobsbawm, *Nations and Nationalism since 1780* (New York: Cambridge University Press, 1990): and Benedict Anderson, *Imagined Communities: Reflections on the Origin and Spread of Nationalism* (London: Verso, 1990).

17. For the politics of planning in Paris and Vienna, see David Pinckney, *Napoleon III and the Rebuilding of Paris* (Princeton, N.J.: Princeton University Press, 1972); David Harvey, "Paris 1850–1870," in Harvey, *Consciousness and the Urban Experience: Studies in the History and Theory of Capitalist Urbanization* (Baltimore: Johns Hopkins University Press, 1985), 63–220; Carl E. Schorske, *Fin-de-Siècle Vienna: Politics and Culture* (New York: Knopf, 1980), 24–115; and Donald J. Olsen, *The City as a Work of Art: London, Paris, Vienna* (New Haven, Conn.: Yale University Press, 1986).

18. Ludlow, "American Metropolis," 86–87. For New York's role in antiwar and antidraft politics during the Civil War, see Iver Bernstein, *The New York Draft Riots: Their Significance for American Society and Politics in the Age of the Civil War* (New York: Oxford University Press, 1990); and Mushkat, *Wood*, especially 133–51.

19. For New York politicians' influence in national party politics in the Gilded Age, see De-Alva Stanwood Alexander, *A Political History of the State of New York* (1909), especially Volumes II (1833–1861) and III (1861–1882); Irving Katz, *August Belmont: A Political Biography* (New York: Columbia University Press, 1968); Allan Nevins, *Abram S. Hewitt* (New York: Harper and Brothers, 1935); Robert Kelley, *The Trans-Atlantic Persuasion: The Liberal-Democratic Mind in the Age of Gladstone* (New York: Knopf, 1969); and John Foord, *The Life and Public Services of Andrew H. Green* (Garden City, N.Y.: Doubleday, Page, 1913).

20. Amy Bridges, "Rethinking the Origins of Machine Politics," in John Mollenkopf (ed.), *Power, Culture, and Place: Essays on New York City* (New York: Russell Sage Foundation, 1988), 69. I analyze the dialectic of city building and state building more fully in Chapter 6.

21. [WRM,] *The Growth of New York* (1865), 15, 18.

22. For New York's share of U.S. foreign trade during the Gilded Age, see New York State Commerce Commission, Annual Report (1900), I:395–96. (These statistics are for the Port of New York as a whole, comprising not only Manhattan but also Brooklyn, the New Jersey waterfront, and surrounding areas.) During the Civil War, the blockade of New Orleans and other Confederate ports made New York even more predominant. The two interior routes whose main terminus was not New York were the Baltimore and Ohio and Pennsylvania railroads, although the latter did construct a terminal complex on the Jersey City shore.

23. Margaret Myers, *The New York Money Market: Volume I, Origins and Development* (New York: Columbia University Press, 1931), 242; [WRM,] *Growth of New York,* 17. For Wall Street's emergence as the national money market, see also Robert Sobel, *The Big Board: A History of the New York Stock Market* (New York: Free Press, 1965); and Vincent Carosso, *Investment Banking in America: A History* (Cambridge, Mass.: Harvard University Press, 1970).

24. James Madison, "The Evolution of Commercial Credit Reporting Agencies in Nineteenth-Century America," *Business History Review* 48, no. 2 (Summer 1974): 164–86, traces the national ascendance of New York's credit agencies. The history of business and trade journals, among the most influential periodicals in nineteenth-century America, remains to be studied; for an introduction, see Volume III of Frank Luther Mott's magisterial *A History of American Magazines* (Cambridge, Mass.: Harvard University Press, 1938), especially 104–36, 146–47.

25. For the formation of the New York Associated Press during the late 1840s, see Oliver Gramling, *AP: The Story of News* (New York: Farrar and Rinehart, 1940), 19–25, 60–81. For the consolidation of Western Union, see A. R. Brewer, *Western Union Telegraph Company: A Retrospect* (New York: J. Kempster, 1901), 22–29; U.S. Bureau of the Census, *Historical Statistics of the United States, Colonial Times to 1957* (Washington, D.C.: n.p., 1960), 483. For Western Union's control of commercial information, see U.S. House of Representatives, 41st Congress, 2nd Session, U.S. Document 1438 (1869–70), Postal Telegraph System, 3, 7, 14–15, and Postal Telegraphy in the United States, 46–47, 101–4. The growing importance of wire reports to Gilded Age newspapers is discussed in Donald Shaw, "News Bias and the Telegraph: A Study of Historical Change," *Journalism Quarterly* 44 (Spring 1967): 6–9.

26. Henry George, *Progress and Poverty* (New York: Modern Library, 1954), 193. George's trip to New York and his unsuccessful attempt to buck the AP monopoly are told in Charles Albro Barker, *Henry George* (New York: Oxford University Press, 1955), 113–20.

27. Anderson, *Imagined Communities,* 40. I discuss the links between nation building, market building, and commercial culture in David Scobey, "What Shall We Do with Our Walls? The

Philadelphia Exposition and the Meanings of Household Design," in Robert Rydell and Nancy Gwinn (eds.), *Fair Representations: World's Fairs and the Modern World* (Amsterdam: VU University Press, 1994), 87–120.

28. Lithographer Edward Carqueville, remarks at convention of National Lithographers' Association (1891), quoted by Peter C. Marzio, *The Democratic Art: Chromolithography, 1840–1900* (Boston: D. R. Godine, 1979), 42; the estimate of New York's market share is Marzio's. For Manhattan's leadership in periodical publishing, see Mott, *History of American Magazines*, II, 103–4, and III, 25–26.

29. Ronald J. Zboray, "Antebellum Reading and the Ironies of Technological Innovation," in Cathy N. Davidson (ed.), *Reading in America: Literature and Social History* (Baltimore: Johns Hopkins University Press, 1989), 180–81 (growth and variety of new titles), 188–91 (cheapening production), and 193 ("national print culture"); *Harper's Magazine,* quoted in James D. Hart, *The Popular Book: A History of America's Literary Taste* (New York: Oxford University Press, 1950), 86; Mary Kelley, *Private Woman, Public Stage: Literary Domesticity in Nineteenth-Century America* (New York: Oxford University Press, 1984), 3–6 (sales figures for best-sellers). Along with these sources, my account of the publishing revolution draws on Richard Brodhead, *Cultures of Letters: Scenes of Reading and Writing in Nineteenth-Century America* (Chicago: University of Chicago Press, 1993); Susan Coultrap-McQuin, *Doing Literary Business: American Women Writers in the Nineteenth Century* (Chapel Hill: University of North Carolina Press, 1990); and Mott, *History of American Magazines*, II, 4–26.

30. Kelley, *Private Woman, Public Stage,* and Hart, *Popular Book,* 85–105, stress gender differences in the composition and tastes of mid-nineteenth-century readerships. For class divisions in reading publics and the role of reading practices in class formation, see Michael Denning, *Mechanic Accents: Dime Novels and Working-Class Culture in America* (London: Verso, 1987), especially 17–61; and Brodhead, *Cultures of Letters,* 13–47, 69–106. Ronald Zboray's more recent study, *A Fictive People: Antebellum Economic Development and the American Reading Public* (New York: Oxford University Press, 1993) qualifies this picture of a neatly divided reading public, arguing that male and female readers moved freely over a book market that was highly fragmented but "boundless." The suggestion that the publishing revolution penetrated the southern U.S. more slowly than it did the West comes from Zboray, "Antebellum Reading," 192.

31. For an overview of the New York story papers, see Denning, *Mechanic Accents,* 17–26; and Brodhead, *Cultures of Letters,* 77–85, 99–106. For Robert Bonner's *New York Ledger* and his arrangements with female authors, see Coultrap-McQuin, *Doing Literary Business,* 50–78, 129–30. For Street and Smith and Ned Buntline, see Peter G. Buckley, "The Case Against Ned Buntline: The 'Words, Signs, and Gestures' of Popular Authorship," *Prospects* 13 (1988): 249–72. For the American News Company, see Denning, *Mechanic Accents,* 19; and Winston Weisman, "Commercial Palaces of New York, 1845–1875," *Art Bulletin* 36 (December 1954): 296, 301.

32. Mott, *History of American Magazines,* II, 4, 30–31, 383–405, 469–87, and III, 26, 388–90. See also Eugene Exman, *The House of Harper: One Hundred and Fifty Years of Publishing* (New York: Harper and Row, 1967); and Gerard Wolfe, *The House of Appleton* (Metuchen, N.J.: Scarecrow Press, 1981).

33. "New and Cheap Goods, Phillips and Co.," Chicago *Tribune,* April 23, 1849, quoted in William Cronon, *Nature's Metropolis: Chicago and the Great West* (New York: W. W. Norton, 1991), 62; Foster, *New York in Slices,* 8; Anthony Trollope, *North America* (New York: Harper and Brothers, 1862), quoted in Mott, *History of American Magazines,* II, 121.

34. Table of Contents, *Harper's Monthly Magazine* 43 (1871). See also Marzio, *Democratic Art,* especially 59–62, 107–15; and Harry T. Peters, *Currier and Ives: Printmakers to the American People* (Garden City, N.Y.: Doubleday, Doran, 1942).

35. J. Henry Harper, *I Remember* (New York: Harper and Brothers, 1934), 25, 26.

36. Vandenburgh, "The City of New York Ten Years Hence," 357; [WRM,] *Growth of New York,* 18. For representations of the city docks, see "The Lading of a Ship," *Harper's New Monthly Magazine* 55 (September 1877): 481–93; and "Along the Hudson River at New York," *Atlantic Monthly* 22 (July 1868): 1–9.

37. Michael P. Conzen, "The Maturing Urban System in the United States, 1840–1910," *Annals of the Association of American Geographers* 67, no. 1 (March 1977): 88–108.

38. [Tuckerman,] "Through Broadway," 718; Browne, *Great Metropolis,* 29. For other accounts of Broadway as a microcosm or kaleidoscope, see also Foster, *New York in Slices,* 7–13; *Miller's New York as It Is* (New York: J. Miller, 1866), 128; James D. McCabe, Jr., *New York by Sunlight and Gaslight* (Philadelphia: Hubbard Brothers, 1882), 144.

39. Hobsbawm, *Nations and Nationalism,* 10; Denning, *Mechanic Accents*; Eric Lott, *Love and Theft: Blackface Minstrelsy and the American Working Class* (New York: Oxford University Press, 1993); Robert Snyder, *The Voice of the City: Vaudeville and Popular Culture in New York* (New York: Oxford University Press, 1989).

40. See Robert Wiebe, *The Search for Order, 1877–1920* (New York: Hill and Wang, 1967), 11–76; and Morton Keller, *Affairs of State: Public Life in Late Nineteenth Century America* (Cambridge, Mass.: Harvard University Press, 1977). For local and family patterns of investment and credit, see Diane Lindstrom, *Economic Development in the Philadelphia Region, 1810–1850* (New York: Columbia University Press, 1977). For regional publishing centers and information circuits, see Mott, *History of American Magazines,* II, 102–121; Marzio, *Democratic Art,* 23–40, 130–48; Zboray, *A Fictive People,* 65–68.

41. New York Pier and Warehouse Company, *Piers and Wharves of New York, Remedy Proposed . . .* (New York: n.p., 1869), 12.

42. John A. Dix, "The Growth of New York City," lecture before the New-York Historical Society (January 6, 1853), reprinted in Dix, *Speeches and Occasional Addresses* (New York: D. Appleton, 1864), II, 357.

43. [WRM,] *Growth of New York,* 42–3; address of President A. A. Low, published in the Chamber of Commerce of the State of New York, *Eighth Annual Report* (1865–66), 7; Charles Astor Bristed, *A Few Words of Warning to New Yorkers, on the Consequences of a Railroad in Fifth Avenue . . .* (New York: W.C. Bryant, 1863), 18.

44. I discuss class negotiations in the city-building process in Chapter 6 and the class politics of landscape reform in Chapter 7.

45. Between the mid-1880s and World War I, labor radicals and "sewer socialists" began to forge a distinctive city-building politics of their own, with a sweeping program of social planning, nonmarket development, environmental regulation, and the provision of mass public amenities. This "urbanism from the bottom up" had a deep influence on the policies of urban Progressives like Seth Low and populist politicians like Al Smith. For a rudimentary effort to sketch its lineaments, see David Scobey, "City Blocs: Social Class, Politics, and the City-Building Process in Gilded Age New York" (unpublished manuscript).

46. The proportion of landowning families in New York is calculated from New York State, Secretary of State, *Census of the State of New York for 1855* (Albany: C. Van Benthuysen, 1857), 8; *Census . . . for 1875* (Albany: Weed, Parsons, 1877), 29, 258. The 1855 population of 629,904 included 126,558 families and 14,784 landowners; the 1875 population of 1,041,886 included 213,467 families and 24,378 landowners.

Note that the numerical relationship between city landowners, families, and total population remains nearly exactly the same between the two state census years: real proprietors constitute about 11 percent of all families in New York and about 2.3 percent of the total population.

For the proportion of landowners possessing only their own place of residence, see *RERBG* (October 10, 1868).

47. For the wage and salary levels of New York employees, see Ralph Andreano (ed.), *The Economic Impact of the American Civil War* (Cambridge, Mass.: Schenkman Publishing, 1962), 179–80; U.S. Bureau of the Census, Eighth Census, 1860. Manufactures, 385; and BDPP, Document No. 30 (November 28, 1871), 9–17. For average real-estate prices and new building costs, see Real Estate Record Association, *A History of Real Estate, Building and Architecture in New York* (New York: Record and Guide, 1898), 157, 159. For mortgage terms and conditions, see for instance "Executor's Sale of Valuable Property on the Grand Boulevard, Broadway, . . . of the Estate of James Slevin . . . on Wednesday, May 22d, 1872 . . . , in James Slevin, Inventory, 1851–1870, of real estate, New York, etc." (Slevin Papers, New York Public Library).

48. At its inception in 1856, the Central Park commission included four lawyers (Robert Dillon, Thomas Fields, Andrew Haswell Green, and Waldo Hutchins), four merchants (James Cooley, Charles Russell, John Butterworth, and William Strong), a banker (John Gray), an iron maker (Charles Wyllys Elliott), and a tree nurseryman (James Hogg). For an analysis of the board's social composition, see Rosenzweig and Blackmar, *Park and the People,* 97–99.

49. The "Tweed charter" of 1870 replaced the eleven-person, state-appointed Board of Commissioners of Central Park with a Department of Public Parks led by a four-person board serving at the pleasure of the mayor. The first board was composed of four lawyers (Peter Sweeney, a Tweed ally and president of the board, Thomas Fields, Henry Hilton, and Andrew Haswell Green). The commissioners of the newly created Department of Docks had a similarly elite profile: tobacco merchant John T. Agnew, dry-goods merchant Wilson Hunt, banker William Wood, transport capitalist Hugh Smith, and lawyer Richard Henry. See CA, *Address . . . to the Public* (New York: Citizens' Association, 1871), 23–24; and Alexander B. Callow, Jr., *The Tweed Ring* (New York: Oxford University Press, 1965), 222–37.

50. For the leadership of the WSA, see its pamphlet of *Proceedings of Six Public Meetings . . .* (New York, 1871). For WRM, see below, note 52; for the Beekman family, see Philip L. White, *The Beekmans of New York in Commerce and Politics* (New York: New-York Historical Society, 1956); for James Ruggles, see D. G. Brinton Thompson, *Ruggles of New York: A Life of Samuel B. Ruggles* (New York: n.p., 1946); for Marshall Roberts, see Bernstein, *Draft Riots,* 205; for Russell Sage, see Matthew Josephson, *The Robber Barons: The Great American Capitalists, 1861–1901* (New York: Harcourt, Brace, 1934), 198, 206, 209–11; for Fernando Wood and Daniel Tiemann, see Mushkat, *Wood,* 79.

51. For information on Bristed, see New York *Times* (January 16, 1874); George Templeton Strong, *The Diary of George Templeton Strong,* ed. Allan Nevins and Milton Halsey Thomas (New York: Macmillan, 1952), IV, 357n, 510 (hereafter cited as Strong, *Diary*). For Bristed's views on urbanity and urban space, see Bristed, *A Few Words of Warning.*

52. It is easier to document Martin's political activities and city-building ideas than to reconstruct his biography. His most important statement about the links between real-estate development, urban growth, public works, and landscape design in New York was the booster pamphlet, *The Growth of New York,* published in late 1865. (The catalog of the New York Public Library attributes this anonymous tract to developer Isaac Kendall, but Gilded Age real-estate sources cite Martin as its author, and its themes echo the arguments and sweep of his speeches and reports; see for instance "The Past and Future of New York," *RERBG* [August 7, 1886].)

Other important documents include Martin's addresses as president of the West Side Association and official communications as a commissioner of the Department of Public Parks from 1875 to 1877. For the former, see WSA, *Proceedings of Six Public Meetings . . .* (1871) and Proceedings of a Public Meeting . . . on the 22d of January, 1873 (1873). For the latter, see "A Communication Relative to the Plans and Improvement of the Fort Washington District . . ." (issued March 19, 1875 and reprinted in *RERBG* [Supplement, June 19, 1875]), *A Communication Relative to the Prosecution of Public Improvements in This City* (1875), *Statement in Reference to the Operations of the Department During the Year 1875* (coauthored with Commissioner Joseph J. O'Donohue, 1876), "Report . . . upon the Treatment of the Up-Town Parks" (BDPP, Document No. 70 [June 9, 1876]), and "Report . . . upon the Subject of Laying-Out the Twenty-third and Twenty-fourth Wards" (BDPP, Document No. 73 [December 20, 1876]). See also several interviews, including "A Treatise for Speculators" *RERBG* (January 17, 1880) and "The Annexed District," ibid. (January 31, 1880). For Martin's advocacy of public transit along Broadway, see WSA, Proceedings of the . . . Public Meeting Held on the 8th of February, 1871, 11–26.

Martin's political career and conflicts as a park commissioner are discussed in Roper, *FLO*, 348–62; and Seymour Mandelbaum, *Boss Tweed's New York* (New York: J. Wiley, 1965), 114–30.

53. For John Dix's biography, see Morgan Dix, *Memoirs of John Adams Dix* (New York: Harper and Brothers, 1883). For other members of this elite of Democratic politician-capitalists, see Katz, *August Belmont*; Alexander C. Flick, *Samuel J. Tilden: A Study in Political Sagacity* (New York: Dodd, Mead, 1939); Kelley, *Transatlantic Persuasion*, 238–92; and John Foord, *Life and Public Services.* I have found Iver Bernstein's discussion of this group especially helpful in *The New York City Draft Riots*, 132–46.

54. Helpful accounts of genteel reform include John Sproat, *"The Best Men": Liberal Reformers in the Gilded Age* (New York: Oxford University Press, 1968); George Fredrickson, *The Inner Civil War: Northern Intellectuals and the Crisis of the Union* (New York: Harper and Row, 1965); David D. Hall, "The Victorian Connection," in Daniel W. Howe (ed.), *Victorian America* (Philadelphia: University of Pennsylvania Press, 1976), 81–94; and John Tomsich, *A Genteel Endeavor: American Culture and Politics in the Gilded Age* (Palo Alto, Calif.: Stanford University Press, 1971).

55. For Dix's career in the 1860s and 1870s, see Morgan Dix, *Memoirs,* II, 76–94, 171–97; Bernstein, *New York City Draft Riots*, 62–64; and Alexander, *Political History*, III, passim. For Green, see Foord, *Life and Public Services;* and Rosenzweig and Blackmar, *Park and the People,* 184–96, 273–76.

56. For Olmsted's attempts at scientific farming and contacts with the Downing circle, see Roper, *FLO*, 43–65; and Rosenzweig and Blackmar, *Park and the People,* 123–30.

57. For overviews of Olmsted's publishing venture and southern travel writings in the 1850s, see *FLOP* II; Roper, *FLO*, 86–123; and Kalfus, *Olmsted,* 149–90.

58. For Olmsted's role in the U.S. Sanitary Commission, see *FLOP* IV and Roper, *FLO,* 156–232. For an overview of the commission, see also Fredrickson, *Inner Civil War;* and Lori Ginzberg, *Women and the Work of Benevolence* (New Haven, Conn.: Yale University Press, 1990), 133–73. For the Union League Club, see FLO to Oliver Wolcott Gibbs, November 5, 1862, and January 31, 1863, in *FLOP* IV, 466–71, 505–8; and Will Irvin et al., *A History of the Union League Club of New York City* (New York: Dodd, Mead, 1952), 1–25. For the founding and significance of *The Nation* magazine, see Bender, *New York Intellect,* 181–91; Roper, *FLO,* 227, 280–81, 291–302; "Prospectus For a Weekly Journal," *FLOP* IV, 628–36; *FLOP* VI, 77–86.

59. FLO to CLB, November 1, 1884, quoted in Kalfus, *Frederick Law Olmsted,* 73. My discussion of Olmsted's vocational and identity crisis owes much to Kalfus's psychologically insightful biography.

60. For the backers of Olmsted's candidacy for superintendent in 1857, see Roper, *FLO,* 128; and Olmsted, "Passages," in Fein (ed.), *Landscape into Cityscape,* 57–59. For the campaign to

protect Olmsted from removal by the Democratic-led Department of Public Parks in 1878, see "MR. FRED LAW OLMSTED/A STRONG PROTEST LODGED AGAINST HIS REMOVAL SIGNED BY MANY PROMINENT CITIZENS," letter to the New York *World* (January 22, 1878), reprinted in Olmsted, Jr., and Kimball, *Forty Years of Landscape Architecture,* 112–13; and Roper, *FLO,* 360–62. I discuss Olmsted's 1878 dismissal in Chapter 8.

61. Roper, *FLO,* 128; "MR. FRED LAW OLMSTED/A PUBLIC PROTEST . . . ," in Olmsted, Jr., and Kimball, *Forty Years of Landscape Architecture,* 113.

62. George Templeton Strong describes the dinner party to honor Grant in Strong, *Diary,* IV, 50–1. For Dix's role in the Civil War and the draft riots, see Morgan Dix, *Memoirs,* II, 76–94; and Bernstein, *New York Draft Riots,* 62–64. For leadership roles in Trinity Church, see Morgan Dix, *Memoirs,* II, 202–3; and Strong, *Diary,* 460–62, 511–12, 529. On Samuel Ruggles and the development of Gramercy Park, see Carole Klein, *Gramercy Park: An American Bloomsbury* (Boston: Houghton Mifflin, 1987), 3–18.

63. New York *Times,* November 21, 1865; John Y. Simon (ed.), *The Papers of Ulysses S. Grant* (Carbondale: Southern Illinois University Press, 1988), XV, 405n. For Grant's visit to New York, see ibid., 403n-8n; daily coverage in the New York *Times,* November 15–22, 1865; and Strong, *Diary,* IV, 52. For the context of Grant's presidential ambitions in the aftermath of the Union victory, see William S. McFeeley, *Grant: A Biography* (New York: W. W. Norton, 1981), 231–38.

64. [WRM,] *Growth of New York,* title page; WSA, *Proceedings of Six Public Meetings . . .* (1871), iii; Simon (ed.), *Papers of Ulysses S. Grant,* XV, 406n.

65. For Olmsted's relationship with Howard Martin, see *FLOP* III, 39; *FLOP* V, 14–15, 141, 142. I discuss Olmsted and William Martin's alliance against Green in the Chapter 8.

66. "Changes in New York," *Leslie's Illustrated Weekly* 40 (May 1, 1875): 118; "The Fresh Blood in the Real Estate Market," *RERBG* (December 4, 1880). For the birthplaces of New York elites, see Fredric Cople Jaher, *The Urban Establishment: Upper Strata in Boston, New York, Charleston, Chicago, and Los Angeles* (Urbana: University of Illinois Press, 1982), 205, 254. For elite migrants to Wall Street before and after the Civil War, see Carosso, *Investment Banking in America,* 1–50; Katz, *Belmont,* 1–11; and Joseph Wall, *Andrew Carnegie* (New York: Oxford University Press, 1970), 221. Sven Beckert, *The Monied Metropolis: New York City and the Consolidation of the American Bourgeoisie* (New York: Cambridge University Press, 2001), appeared too late for me to use its insightful analysis in my discussion of bourgeois class formation.

67. For New York's rivalry with Boston and emergence as a national cultural center, see Bender, *New York Intellect,* 119–205; Gordon Milne, *George William Curtis and the Genteel Tradition* (Bloomington: Indiana University Press, 1956); Clark, "Henry Whitney Bellows"; and Coultrap-McQuin, *Doing Literary Business.* The best account of the bourgeois Great Migration to New York and its effect on the city's cultural dominance remains William Dean Howells's 1890 novel *A Hazard of New Fortunes.*

68. [WRM,] *Growth of New York,* 17. For divisions and rivalries in New York "society," see Jaher, *Urban Establishment,* 263–81.

69. Jaher's analysis is concisely presented in "Style and Status: High Society in Late Nineteenth-Century New York," in Fredric Cople Jaher (ed.), *The Rich, the Well Born, and the Powerful: Elites and Upper Classes In History* (Urbana: University of Illinois Press, 1973), 258–84.

70. Kenneth Wiggins Porter, *John Jacob Astor, Business Man* (Cambridge, Mass.: Harvard University Press, 1931), especially II, 910–52; Slevin, Inventory . . . ; "The Fresh Blood In the Real Estate Market," *RERBG* (December, 4, 1880); William B. Ogden address to the WSA, *Proceedings of Six Public Meetings . . .* (1871) , Document No. 3, 27–37; *FLOP* V, 218, 288; C. C. Martin to Frederick Law Olmsted, March 25, 1871, Olmsted Papers, General Correspondence, Reel 12.

71. My emphasis on the socioeconomic fluidity of the metropolitan bourgeoisie contrasts somewhat with the nuanced effort of Iver Bernstein to map partisan and ideological divisions onto sectoral and occupational differences among New York elites; see *New York Draft Riots*, 43–72, 125–92.

72. "The Fresh Blood In the Real Estate Market," *RERBG* (December 4, 1880); New York *Times* (March 13, 1870), quoted in Rosenzweig and Blackmar, *Park and the People*, 224–25; [WRM], *Growth of New York*, 29.

73. Browne, *Great Metropolis*, 40; Fernando Wood, address to the WSA, May 26, 1871, Document No. 6, 14, in *Proceedings of Six Public Meetings . . .* (New York, 1871); CA, *Report of the Executive Council to the Honorary Council. . . . November 17, 1866* (New York: n.p., 1866), 18; [WRM,] *Growth of New York*, 15; "Changes in New York," *Leslie's Illustrated Weekly* 40 (May 1, 1875): 118.

74. George Foster, *The Empire City* (1850). For use of the epithet by New York businesses and civic associations, see the 1851 lithograph for the Empire Stone Dressing Company in John A. Kouwenhoven, *The Columbia Historical Portrait of New York: An Essay in Graphic History* (New York: Columbia University Press, 1953), 237, and the photograph of the firehouse for the Empire Hose Company, first built in 1843, in Kenneth Holcomb Dunshee, *As You Pass By* (New York: Hastings House, 1952), 259.

75. New York Pier and Warehouse Company, *Piers and Wharves of New York,* 11–12; CA, *Report of the Executive Council,* 17, 18; *RERBG* (September 26, 1868).

76. For the racist and (and in the modern sense) imperialist ideology of nineteenth-century U.S. expansionism, see Reginald Horsman, *Race and Manifest Destiny: The Origins of American Racial Anglo-Saxonism* (Cambridge, Mass.: Harvard University Press, 1981); Meinig, *The Shaping of America,* II, 170–218; and Richard Slotkin, "Buffalo Bill's 'Wild West' and the Mythologization of the American Empire," in Amy Kaplan and Donald E. Pease (eds.), *Cultures of United States Imperialism* (Durham, N.C.: Duke University Press, 1993), 164–81.

77. Benjamin Beekman address, Union League Club, November 15, 1865, quoted in Simon (ed.), *Papers of Ulysses S. Grant,* XV, 406n.

78. Horsman, *Race and Manifest Destiny,* 245. My understanding of Cole's *Course of Empire* owes much to Angela Miller's insightful *Empire of the Eye: Landscape Representation and American Cultural Politics, 1825–1875* (Ithaca, N.Y.: Cornell University Press, 1993), 21–64.

79. William Gilpin, *Mission of the North American People* (Philadelphia: J. B. Lippincott, 1874), quoted in Cronon, *Nature's Metropolis,* 44. Cronon's reading of the discourse of empire is especially helpful (ibid., 41–46), as is Henry Nash Smith, *Virgin Land: The American West as Symbol and Myth* (New York: Vintage Books, 1957), Anders Stephanson, *Manifest Destiny: American Expansionism and the Empire of Right* (New York: Hill and Wang, 1995), and Ernest N. Paolino, *The Foundations of the American Empire: William Henry Seward and U.S. Foreign Policy* (Ithaca, N.Y.: Cornell University Press, 1973).

80. For the ideological linkages between nineteenth-century landscape art, American nationalism, and the discourse of empire, see Miller, *Empire of the Eye;* and Albert Boime, *The Magisterial Gaze: Manifest Destiny and American Landscape Painting, c. 1830–1865* (Washington, D.C.: Smithsonian Institution, 1991). Leutze's mural "Westward the Course of Empire Takes Its Way" is discussed in ibid., 43–45; and William Cronon, "Telling Tales on Canvas: Landscapes of Frontier Change," in Jules David Prown et al., *Discovered Lands, Invented Pasts: Transforming Visions of the American West* (New Haven, Conn.: Yale University Press, 1992), 37–44.

81. Stephen Douglass, quoted in George B. Forgie, *Patricide and the House Divided: A Psychological Interpretation of Lincoln and His Age* (New York: W. W. Norton, 1979), 144; James Hall, "The Commercial Growth and Greatness of the West," *Hunt's Merchant Magazine* 17 (1847),

quoted in Cronon, *Nature's Metropolis*, 44. For the view that the United States was a "naturally" continental nation, see Meinig, *The Shaping of America*, II, 211–18.

82. For the ideological contours of U.S. imperialism at the turn of the century, see Walter LaFeber, *The New Empire: An Interpretation of American Expansion, 1860–1898* (Ithaca, N.Y.: Cornell University Press, 1963), especially 62–101; Stephanson, *Manifest Destiny*, 66–111; and Richard Slotkin, *Gunfighter Nation: The Myth of the Frontier in Twentieth-Century America* (New York: Atheneum, 1992), 29–122.

83. Walt Whitman, "A Broadway Pageant" (1860); "COMMERCIAL RELATIONS OF NEW YORK," *Harper's Weekly* (May 30, 1868): 344–45. For Whitman's political and ideological links with the Democratic Party, see David Reynolds, *Walt Whitman's America: A Cultural Biography* (New York: Knopf, 1995), especially 65–67, 111–53. My attribution of the *Harper's Weekly* column to George Curtis is uncertain, but from 1863 until his death in 1892, Curtis wrote most, and oversaw all, of the current-events commentary in the *Weekly* (Milne, *Curtis and the Genteel Tradition*, 118).

84. For overviews of both Democratic and Whig-Republican strands of expansionist thought, see Stephanson, *Manifest Destiny*. For Seward's ideas in particular, see Daniel Walker Howe, *The Political Culture of the American Whigs* (Chicago: University of Chicago Press, 1979), 197–209; LaFeber, *New Empire*, 24–32; and Paolino, *Foundations of the American Empire* (in which Seward's verses are quoted on p. 9).

It needs to be stressed that a broad interparty and intersectional consensus defining the United States as an expansive, republican "empire" was not at odds with deepening divisions over the fate of slavery in America. As Michael Rogin argues, the very success of American expansionism raised the stakes of defining what sort of empire the United States was to become; see Rogin, *Subversive Genealogies: The Politics and Art of Herman Melville* (Berkeley: University of California Press, 1979).

85. My understanding of the dialectical links between national and international affiliations for the nineteenth-century bourgeoisie has been enriched by Leora Auslander, "Nationalism, Internationalism, and Bourgeois Class Formation in Nineteenth-Century France" (unpublished paper). For the idea that the Asia market was the end point of American imperial development, see Smith, *Virgin Land*, 19–34; and Paolino, *Foundation of the American Empire*, 28–30.

86. CA, *Report of the Executive Council*, 17–18.

87. My discussion of booster ideology is indebted to Cronon, *Nature's Metropolis*, 31–54. Other helpful accounts include Charles N. Glaab, "Visions of Metropolis: William Gilpin and Theories of City Growth in the American West," *Wisconsin Magazine of History* 45 (1961): 21–31; Carl Abbott, *Boosters and Businessmen: Popular Economic Thought and Urban Growth in the Antebellum Middle West* (Westport, Conn.: Greenwood Press, 1981); and D. A. Hamer, *New Towns in the New World: Images and Perceptions of the Nineteenth-Century Urban Frontier* (New York: Columbia University Press, 1990).

88. See William Gilpin, *Mission of the North American People*; and Jesup W. Scott, *A Presentation of the Causes Tending to Fix the Position of the Future Great City of the World in the Central Plain of North America . . .* (Toledo: Blade Print, 1876).

89. For boosterism and townsite speculation, see Charles N. Glaab and A. Theodore Brown, *A History of Urban America* (New York: Macmillan, 1967), 73–81; and Daniel J. Boorstin, *The Americans: The National Experience* (New York: Random House, 1965), 113–34, 161–68. For the use of booster rhetoric to encourage railroad investment in and around Chicago, see Cronon, *Nature's Metropolis*, 55–93.

90. [WRM,] *Growth of New York*, 19; *RERBG* (April 11, 1868); CA, *Report of the Executive Council*, 18.

91. Cheney Ames, quoted in the *Commercial and Financial Chronicle* 1 (1865): 324; *RERBG* (May 15, 1869).

92. CA, *Report of the Executive Council*, 18; "COMMERCIAL RELATIONS OF NEW YORK," *Harper's Weekly* (May 30, 1868): 345–46.

93. "M.," "In a Hundred Years," *Spirit of the Fair* (April 23, 1864).

94. On Olmsted's wartime activities and identity crises, see Kalfus, *Frederick Law Olmsted*, 232–55; and Roper, *FLO*, 156–290. For the offer to head up the American Freedman's Aid Union, see also FLO to James Miller McKim, September 7, 1865, in *FLOP* V, 439.

95. CV to FLO, July 6, 1865, in *FLOP* V, 402–3. For Vaux's negotiations with the Central and Prospect Park boards, as well as with his ex-partner, see CV to FLO, May 10, May 12, May 20, May 22, June 3, July 8, and July 21, in ibid., 358–59, 360–64, 372–74, 375–78, 383–78, 403–5, 405–6.

96. For the work undertaken by Olmsted, Vaux and Co., see Roper, *FLO*, 293–94; and *FLOP* VI, 20–21, 77–182.

97. Strong, *Diary*, IV, 52 (November 24, 1865).

98. Ibid., 52–53. As I discuss in Chapter 3, both Trinity Church and Columbia College had extensive landholdings in lower Manhattan.

Chapter 2

1. "Disastrous Fire," New York *Times* (July 14, 1865); George Templeton Strong, *The Diary of George Templeton Strong*, ed. Allan Nevins and Milton Halsey Thomas (New York: Macmillan, 1952), IV, 17–18. See also the discussion of the American Museum and the fire in Neil Harris, *Humbug: The Art of P. T. Barnum* (Chicago: University of Chicago Press, 1973), especially 165–72.

2. For the shift to a hierarchical public culture in the nineteenth century, see Lawrence Levine, *Highbrow Lowbrow: The Emergence of Cultural Hierarchy in America* (Cambridge, Mass.: Harvard University Press, 1988); Richard Brodhead, *Cultures of Letters: Scenes of Reading and Writing in Nineteenth-Century America* (Chicago: University of Chicago Press, 1993); and Paul Dimaggio, "Cultural Entrepreneurship in Nineteenth-Century Boston: The Creation of an Organizational Base for High Culture in America," in Chandra Mukerji and Michael Schudson (eds.), *Rethinking Popular Culture: Contemporary Perspectives in Cultural Studies* (Berkeley: University of California Press, 1991), 374–97. For the relationship between urban amusements and cultural hierarchy, see also Robert Allen, *Horrible Prettiness: Burlesque and American Culture* (Chapel Hill: University of North Carolina Press, 1991).

For the mixed commercial geography of the antebellum "walking city," see Sam Bass Warner, Jr., *The Urban Wilderness: A History of the American City* (New York: Harper and Row, 1972), 81–82; and David Ward, *Cities and Immigrants: A Geography of Change in Nineteenth Century America* (New York: Oxford University Press, 1971), 88–93.

3. On the takeover of Barnum's site by *Herald* publisher James Gordon Bennett, Jr., see Harris, *Humbug*, 171–72. On the *Herald*, Park Bank, and post office buildings, see "The New Park Bank," *RERBG* 1 (April 4, 1868); *Appleton's New York Illustrated* (1871); and Lois Craig et al., *The*

Federal Presence: Architecture, Politics, and Symbols in United States Government Building (Cambridge, Mass.: MIT Press, 1978), 158.

Barnum reopened the American Museum farther uptown at Broadway and Canal; in 1868, the new building also burned down, and the impresario did not rebuild it or move it again. See "Burning of Barnum's Museum," New York *Times* (March 3, 1868).

4. Strong, *Diary*, IV, 17; John Kennion, *The Architects' and Builders' Guide* (New York: Fitzpatrick and Hunter, 1868), III, 66–67; *Appleton's New York Illustrated*, quoted in Winston Weisman, "Commercial Palaces of New York, 1845–1875," *Art Bulletin* 36 (December 1954): 297.

5. For the American Museum of Natural History, see William Alex and George B. Tatum, *Calvert Vaux: Architect and Planner* (New York: Ink, 1994), 23–24, 202–5. For the Central Park and Bronx zoos, see Roy Rosenzweig and Elizabeth Blackmar, *The Park and the People: A History of Central Park* (Ithaca, N.Y.: Cornell University Press, 1992), 340–49. For the geography of the legitimate theater in midtown Manhattan, see Mary C. Henderson, *The City and the Theater: New York Playhouses from Bowling Green to Times Square* (Clifton, N.J.: J. T. White, 1973).

6. *Commercial and Financial Chronicle* 3 (October 12, 1866). For illustrations of the crowded intersection and the Loew pedestrian bridge, see *Harper's Weekly* (August 27, 1859, and March 12, 1870).

7. Strong, *Diary*, IV, 85–86 (May 21, 1866), and 363 (June 5, 1871).

8. New York *Times* (April 19, 1852); Samuel Sloan, *Architectural Review and American Builders' Journal* II (1869): 7.

9. Philip Hone, *The Diary of Philip Hone, 1828–1851*, ed. Allan Nevins (New York: Dodd, Mead, 1927), 395; Carl Condit, *The Port of New York*, Volume I: *A History of the Rail and Terminal System from the Beginnings to Pennsylvania Station* (Chicago: University of Chicago Press, 1980), 76.

10. *RERBG* (July 24, 1869); address of Hermann H. Cammann, reprinted in Real Estate Exchange and Auction Room, *Report of the Proceedings . . . of the Formal Opening of the . . . Room . . . on Tuesday, April 14, 1885*, 10–11 (New York: n.p., 1885).

11. John Reps, *Views and Viewmakers of Urban America: Lithographs of Towns and Cities in the United States and Canada . . . , 1825–1925* (Columbia: University of Missouri Press, 1984), 3. Reps's introductory essay offers a fascinating overview of the changing cultural context, business milieu, and aesthetic conventions of American bird's-eye views.

12. Reps discusses the evolution of a more cartographic style and the development of the "outsider's perspective," in *Views and Viewmakers*, 17–21, 65–66; he looks at the audience of bird's-eye lithographs in ibid., 39–66.

13. Isaac Newton Phelps Stokes and Daniel C. Haskell, *American Historical Prints: Early Views of American Cities . . .* (New York: New York Public Library, 1932), xv. Reps lists 173 views of Manhattan out of a total catalog of 4,480 (3.8 percent), and 216 (4.8 percent) of the immediate metropolitan area, including Brooklyn, Yonkers, Newark, Jersey City, and other neighboring areas. The next most popular cities include San Francisco (135 views), Chicago (81 views), St. Louis (47), Philadelphia (42), Boston (37), and Washington (35).

14. The following discussion draws on lithographs in the New-York Historical Society and the New York Public Library, but it relies especially on a series of bird's-eye views at the Yale University Art Gallery: "New-York and Environs, from Williamsburgh" (1848; Reps catalogue no. 2637); "New York et Brooklyn" (1848, not listed in Reps catalog); "New-York" (1849, Reps no. 2646); "View of New York, Jersey City, and Brooklyn" (1858, Reps no. 2679); and "The City of New York" (1876, Reps no. 2721). Reps des not list Yale among the holders of the last image, but it is clearly the same one.

15. "New-York et Brooklyn," drawn by Simpson, lithographed by Thomas Muller, and printed by L. Turgis in Paris. This print was evidently reissued from an American original, a sign of European interest in New World cities.

16. "The City of New York" (1876, Reps catalog no. 2721), sketched and lithographed by Parsons and Atwater, and published by Currier and Ives. For the career of these lithographers, see Reps, *Views and Viewmakers*, 196–98.

17. For a chronology of the building of the East River bridge, see David McCullough, *The Great Bridge: The Epic Story of the Building of the Brooklyn Bridge* (New York: Simon and Schuster, 1972), 565–66.

18. Reps, *Views and Viewmakers*, 70, 67.

19. For assessed property values, see Appendix, Table B; for levels of new buildings, see Table A.

20. In addition to the maps in Figures 2.5 and 2.6, information about the uptown building frontier comes from Charles H. Haswell, *Reminiscences of New York by an Octogenarian* (New York: Harper and Brothers, 1896), 459; Robert Ernst, *Immigrant Life in New York City, 1825–1863* (New York: King's Crown Press, 1949), 21; and Homer Hoyt, *The Structure and Growth of Residential Neighborhoods in American Cities* (Washington, D.C.: Federal Housing Administration, 1939) 157.

21. [WRM,] *The Growth of New York* (1865), 11; Condit, *Port of New York*, II, 343.

22. *RERBG* (September 15, 1877, and March 21, 1868); Friedrich Ratzel, *Sketches of Urban and Cultural Life in North America* (New Brunswick, N.J.: Rutgers University Press, 1988), 14–15; William Wickham, annual message (1875), *Documents of the Board of Aldermen of the City of New York* (1876), Part I, 42. On the consolidation of a greater New York, see also AHG, "Communication of the Comptroller of the Park Relative to Westchester County, Harlem River, and Spuyten Duyvil Creek," in BCCP, *Thirteenth Annual Report* (1869), 163.

23. I discuss the design of the elevated railway and Brooklyn Bridge in Chapter 5 and Grand Central Depot later in this chapter.

24. For an overview of horse car development, see Harry James Carman, *The Street Surface Railway Franchises of New York City, Columbia University Studies in History, Economics, and Public Law* 88, no. 1 (1919): 1. The effect of telegraphy on New York's geography and economy still needs to be studied, but Paul Israel, *From Machine Shop to Industrial Laboratory: Telegraphy and the Changing Context of American Invention, 1830–1920* (Baltimore: Johns Hopkins University Press, 1992) offers a helpful introduction. For Brooklyn's dock basins, see Henry R. Stiles, *A History of the City of Brooklyn* (Brooklyn: n.p., 1869), II, 578–82n. For the Hudson River terminal improvements, see New York *Times* (March 31 and June 2, 1870). For the New York Central complex on the Hudson waterfront, see the sources in note 42.

25. For the growth in horse car ridership, see Carman, *Street Surface Railway Franchises*, 145; and New York State Engineer and Surveyor, *Railroad Reports* (Albany: Weed, Parsons, 1865) 156–57, (1870) 276–77, (1875) 372–73. For the growth of freight tonnage on the New York Central and Erie railroads, see ibid. (1860) 411, (1865) 160, (1870) 246–47, (1875) 339–40. For the growth in telegraph volume, see A. R. Brewer, *Western Union Telegraph Company: A Retrospect* (New York: J. Kempster, 1901), 22–29; and U.S. Bureau of the Census, *Historical Statistics of the United States, Colonial Times to 1957* (Washington, D.C.: n.p., 1960), 483.

26. Kennion, *Architects' and Builders' Guide*, III, 27–28.

27. Statistics on property development in Ward Nineteen and the city as a whole are drawn from the annual reports of the Commissioner of Taxes and Assessments and *Superintendent Re-*

ports, which give usable figures for new construction for 1863–69 and 1871. (The office of the Superintendent of Buildings was reorganized in 1870, and its statistical records break off and begin again in midyear).

	Ward 19 (percent of city)		New York City
Rise in land values (1865–73)	$87,450,000	(21.4%)	$409,432,000
New buildings (1863–69, 1871)	4,329	(33.0%)	13,117
New nontenement housing	2,961	(52.5%)	5,636
New tenement housing	866	(28.2%)	3,072

28. *RERBG* (February 4, 1882). According to the 1880 census, the population of New York that resided north of Fortieth Street (Wards 12, 19, 22–24) was 393,223.

29. My analysis here, and indeed my larger argument about the periodization and context of New York's reconstruction, is deeply indebted to Hobsbawm, *Age of Capital, 1848–1875* (New York: Scribner, 1975), especially 27–71.

30. See especially Donald J. Olsen, *The City as a Work of Art: London, Paris, Vienna* (New Haven, Conn.: Yale University Press, 1986); David Pinckney, *Napoleon III and the Rebuilding of Paris* (Princeton, N.J.: Princeton University Press, 1972); Carl E. Schorske, *Fin-de-Siècle Vienna: Politics and Culture* (New York: Knopf, 1980), 24–115; David Owen, *The Government of Victorian London, 1855–1889: The Metropolitan Board of Works, the Vestries, and the City Corporation* (Cambridge, Mass.: Harvard University Press, 1982); Ross Miller, *American Apocalypse: The Great Fire and the Myth of Chicago* (Chicago: University of Chicago Press, 1990); and Karen Sawislak, *Smoldering City: Chicagoans and the Great Fire, 1871–1874* (Chicago: University of Chicago Press, 1995).

31. For an overview of New York's demographic growth during the mid-nineteenth century, see Ira Rosenwaike, *Population History of New York* (Syracuse, N.Y.: Syracuse University Press, 1972), 33–89. For annual levels of immigration through the Port of New York during the midcentury boom, see Chamber of Commerce of the State of New York, *Annual Report* (1865–66) 144, (1870–71) 143.

32. See Richard Stott, *Workers in the Metropolis: Class, Ethnicity, and Youth in Antebellum New York City* (Ithaca, N.Y.: Cornell University Press, 1990), especially 162–90.

33. On the experience of casualized day laborers, see U.S. Senate, Select Committee on Relations Between Labor and Capital, *Report . . .* (1885), I, 771–83 (testimony of Thomas McGuire, teamster), and II, 678–87 (testimony of Jeremiah Murphy, freight handler); and David Montgomery, *The Fall of the House of Labor* (New York: Cambridge University Press, 1987), 58–111. On sweated industrial labor in New York, see U.S. Senate, Select Committee on Relations Between Labor and Capital, *Report . . .* , I, 413–21 (testimony of Conrad Carl, tailor) and 846–52 (testimony of Robert Blissert); Jesse Eliphalet Pope, *The Clothing Industry in New York* (Columbia: University of Missouri Press, 1905), 1–27; Montgomery, *Fall of the House of Labor*, 117–23; and Christine Stansell, "The Origins of the Sweatshop: Women and Early Industrialization in New York City," in Michael Frisch and Daniel Walkowitz (eds.), *Working-Class America: Essays on Labor, Community, and American Society* (Urbana: University of Illinois Press, 1983), 78–103.

34. *RERBG* (December 5, 1868); *Superintendent Reports* (1872), 49–51; *New Dockets*, plans 46 (Seebald), 2, 110, 127, 161, 245, 374, 387, 776, 797, 798, 821, 823, 924, 976, 977, 1146, 1153, and 1183 (Burchell clan). For a helpful overview, see also Elizabeth Blackmar, *Manhattan for Rent, 1785–1850* (Ithaca, N.Y.: Cornell University Press, 1989), especially 183–249.

35. Jacob Riis, *How the Other Half Lives: Studies among the Tenements of New York* (New York: Dover, 1971), 17. The percentage of uptown tenements built in 1870 was aggregated from *New Dockets*. I elaborate on the class geography of upper Manhattan in Chapters 3 and 4.

36. On the older tenant houses and the recycling of existing buildings, see Blackmar, *Manhattan for Rent*, 69–70; on Gotham Court and other rent barracks, see "Crowding the Poor," New York *Times* (July 17, 1870); "Life in the Slums," ibid. (August 19, 1870); and Riis, *Other Half*, 27–42. The size and density of the Burchell tenements were calculated from the plans in *New Dockets*.

37. Journalist quoted in CA, *Report . . . upon the Sanitary Conditions of the City* (New York: D. Appleton, 1865), xv; Riis, *Other Half*, 32, 231–32 (population densities). For an overview of turn-of-the-century tenement reform in New York, see Roy Lubove, *The Progressives and the Slums: Tenement House Reform in New York City, 1890–1917* (Pittsburgh, Pa.: University of Pittsburgh Press, 1962).

38. New York State Commerce Commission, *Annual Report* (Albany: J. B. Lyon, 1900), I, 395 (New York's share of foreign trade); "The Lading of a Ship," *Harper's New Monthly Magazine* 55 (September 1877): 483; Chief of the Bureau of Statistics on the Commerce and Navigation of the United States, *First Annual Report on the Internal Commerce of the United States* (Washington, D.C.: n.p., 1877), 116 (growth of interior trade); David Maldwyn Ellis, "New York and the Western Trade, 1865–1910," *New York History* 33 (1952): 387 (New York's share of East-West trade, an 1882 estimate by railroad administrator Albert Fink).

39. For the volume of securities traded in the New York Stock Exchange, see Robert Sobel, *The Big Board: A History of the New York Stock Market* (New York: Free Press, 1965), 82; and Margaret Myers, *The New York Money Market*: Volume I, *Origins and Development* (New York: Columbia University Press, 1931), 36. For levels of foreign investment, see Sobel, *Big Board*, 82; and Myers, *A Financial History of the United States* (New York: Columbia University Press, 1970), 119.

40. Condit, *Port of New York*, I, 16–75, especially 60–61 (Erie facilities), 50–52 (Pennsylvania Railroad right-of-way).

41. Charles Francis Adams, Jr., "A Chapter of Erie," in Charles Francis Adams, Jr., and Henry Adams, *Chapters of Erie* (Ithaca, N.Y.: Cornell University Press, 1956), 97. Vanderbilt's takeover and consolidation of the Hudson River and New York Central roads is summarized in Condit, *Port of New York*, I, 35, 83–84. See also Wheaton Lane, *Commodore Vanderbilt: An Epic of the Steam Age* (New York: Knopf, 1942).

42. For the expansion of New York Central rail facilities on the upper West Side, see the Bromley *Atlas of New York* (New York: G. W. Bromley, 1879); *Harper's Weekly* 21 (December 22, 1877): 1008, 1010; and Lane, *Commodore Vanderbilt*, 281. Vanderbilt's transit and dock development schemes are discussed in ibid., 272; and Walker, *Fifty Years of Rapid Transit*, 98–100.

43. New York *Tribune*, quoted in *New York and Its Institutions, 1609–1873* (New York: E. B. Treat, 1872), 130; for other contemporary press responses to Grand Central Depot, see *RERBG* (June 24, 1871) and—a dissenting view—*Harper's Weekly* (February 3, 1872): 108–9. For a discussion of the site, design, engineering, and cost of the depot, see Condit, *Port of New York*, I, 81–92; Lane, *Commodore Vanderbilt*, 280–87; and Gustavus Myers, *History of the Great American Fortunes* (Chicago: C. H. Kerr, 1908–10), II, 171–75. For the growth of intercity passenger ridership, see, in addition to Condit's discussion, New York State Engineer and Surveyor, *Railroad Reports* (1865) 156–57, (1870) 240–41, (1875) 333–34, (1880) 186–87.

44. *RERBG* (June 24, 1871). For an interesting discussion of the technological, symbolic, and social functions of the great European railway stations against which Grand Central was meant to be judged, see *Les Temps des Gares* (Paris: n.p., 1978).

45. For Vanderbilt's purchase of St. John's Park, see John A. Dix and Leicester C. Lewis, *A History of the Parish of Trinity Church . . .* (New York: Columbia University Press, 1950), V, 64–70;

and Clifford P. Morehouse, *Trinity: Mother of Churches* (New York: Seabury Press, 1973), 151–53. For the building of the Hudson line's freight depot, see Condit, *Port of New York*, I, 39–40. For the New York Central's freight statistics, see the sources in note 25.

46. "The Vanderbilt Monument," *Harper's Weekly* 13 (September 25, 1869): 620–21; Strong, *Diary*, IV, 260. The statue of Commodore Vanderbilt stands today in front of Grand Central Terminal.

47. "Vanderbilt: Unvailing [*sic*] the Memorial Bronze Yesterday," New York *Times* (November 11, 1869); Strong, *Diary*, IV, 260.

48. *RERBG* (October 10, 1868).

49. For land use in the Fifth Ward at the end of the midcentury boom, see the Bromley *Atlas* (1879). Population in the ward declined from 22,686 (1850) to 15,966 (1875); see New York State Secretary of State, *Census of the State of New York for 1875* (Albany: Weed, Parsons, 1877), 129.

50. *RERBG* (June 16, 1877).

51. William Dean Howells, *Their Wedding Journey* (1870), 27; New York *Times* (April 19, 1852).

52. For population growth in the 1850s, see Rosenwaike, *Population History*, 36; for the expansion of streetcar transit, see Carman, *Street Surface Railway Franchises*, 39–77; for the housing crisis of the 1850s, see Blackmar, *Manhattan for Rent*, 183–212.

53. For building levels, compare *Superintendent Reports* for 1863 (1,247 new buildings) 1864 (733), and 1865 (1,190) with the *Annual Reports of the City Inspector on the Number and Class of New Buildings* for 1847 (1,846 new buildings), 1848 (1,191), 1849 (1,618), and 1850 (1,912); see Blackmar, *Manhattan for Rent*, 276. For the links between progress on Central Park and the Panic of 1857, see Rosenzweig and Blackmar, *Park and the People*, 150–79, and my discussion in Chapter 6. For the role of the Civil War in fostering capital accumulation in New York, see Myers, *New York Money Market*, 213–64; Vincent Carosso, *Investment Banking in America: A History* (Cambridge, Mass.: Harvard University Press, 1970), 13–23; and Matthew Josephson, *The Robber Barons: The Great American Capitalists, 1861–1901* (New York: Harcourt, Brace, 1934), 51–74.

54. Kennion, *Architects' and Builders' Guide*, III, 27–28. For the increase in assessed property values, see Appendix, Table B; for building levels, see Table A.

55. For the increase in horse car franchises and ridership, see Carman, *Street Surface Railway Franchises*, 108–47. I discuss uptown park and boulevard development in Chapters 6 and 7.

56. Real Estate Record Association, *A History of Real Estate, Building, and Architecture in New York City During the Last Quarter of a Century* (New York: Record and Guide, 1898), 58; "The Crisis in Real Estate (II)," *RERBG* (December 4, 1875). I discuss the interconnections between land speculation and Democratic public works patronage in Chapter 6.

57. Real Estate Record Association, *History of Real Estate*, 157, 159 (average conveyances and ratio of conveyances to building costs), 61 (quoted passage), 62 (tactics of deception).

58. Ibid., 62 (speculative profits); *RERBG* (June 16, 1877) ("enigmatic character" of real estate). For the history of Beekman Place, see Strong, *Diary*, IV, 375 (entry of July 26, 1871), including the editorial note. For the history of Pike's Opera House, see *Harper's Weekly* (January 25, 1868); Willoughby Jones, *The Life of James Fisk, Jr.* . . . (Philadelphia: Union Publishing, 1872), 312–18, 23–24; John Grafton, *New York in the Nineteenth Century* (New York: Dover, 1977), 139. When Fisk was assassinated in 1872 by his romantic rival and sometime business partner Edward Stokes, it was in the Opera House that his body lay in state.

59. Address of WRM, reprinted in WSA, *Proceedings of Six Public Meetings* . . . (1871), meeting of December 22, 1870, 13, 7; address of Fernando Wood, reprinted in ibid., meeting of May 26, 1871, 27.

60. Address of WRM, reprinted in ibid., meeting of December 22, 1870, 8. Assessed property values for the Twenty-second Ward (Fortieth to Eighty-sixth Street west of Central Park) increased from $19,824,000 in 1865 to $65,476,000 ten years later; see Appendix, Table B. For the underdevelopment of the upper West Side, see also the Bromley *Atlas* (1879), plates 17 and 25.

61. Address of WRM, reprinted in WSA, *Proceedings of Six Public Meetings . . .* (1871), meeting of December 22, 1870, 8; [Martin Zborowski,] *Assessments in the City of New York* (n.d.), 7; "East Side and West Side," *RERBG* (October 13, 1877).

62. "The Crisis in Real Estate (II)," *RERBG* (December 4, 1875); Real Estate Record Association, *History of Real Estate*, 68. For the decline in conveyances and new buildings, see ibid., 157, 159; for the volume of mortgage foreclosures, see ibid., 68.

63. David Harvey, "The Urban Process under Capitalism," in Michael Dear and Allen J. Scott (eds.), *Urbanization and Urban Planning in Capitalist Society* (London: Methuen, 1981), 108. My analysis of New York's growth is indebted to Harvey's theoretical work on spatial change in capitalist cities, as well as to Neil Smith, *Uneven Development: Nature, Capital, and the Production of Space* (Oxford: Blackwell, 1984).

64. Sloan, *Architectural Review and American Builders' Journal*, II, 7–8. For the importance of May Day to the economics of housing and rent, see Blackmar, *Manhattan for Rent*, 213–16.

65. Strong, *Diary*, III, 565–66 (entry of March 18, 1865); Howells, *Their Wedding Journey*, 27.

66. *Miller's New York as It Is* (New York: J. Miller, 1866), 21, 5.

67. *Harper's Weekly* (August 14, 1869): 525.

68. Ibid.; Grafton, *New York in the Nineteenth Century*, 78.

Chapter 3

1. Real Estate Exchange and Auction Room, *Report of the Proceedings . . . of the Formal Opening . . . on Tuesday, April 14, 1885* (1885), 8; the quoted phrase is from the address of James M. Varnum. The *Real Estate Record and Builders' Guide* published a partial list of subscribers to the Exchange and Auction Room on December 15, 1883. For the horse car strikes that coincided with the opening of the Room, see *John Swinton's Paper* (March 1, 1885).

2. Real Estate Exchange, *Opening*, 13 (address of Brooklyn Mayor Seth Low), 4 (address of James M. Varnum).

3. John A. Kouwenhoven, *The Columbia Historical Portrait of New York: An Essay in Graphic History* (New York: Columbia University Press, 1953), 29, gives an illustration and full translation of the letter mentioning the purchase. See also E. M. Rutterbar, *History of the Indian Tribes of Hudson's River* (1872), 77–78, and Alonson Skinner, *The Tribes of Manhattan Island and Vicinity* (Port Washington, N.Y.: Kennikat Press, 1961).

4. Mrs. Martha J. Lamb and Mrs. Burton Harrison, *History of the City of New York* (New York: A. S. Barnes, 1877), I, 53–54. For other references to the story, see the sources in note 5 and John H. Warren, Jr., *Thirty Years' Battle with Crime* (Poughkeepsie, N.Y.: A. J. White, 1875), 351. On the anachronism of the exchange rates used to translate sixty Dutch guilders into dollars, see John Fiske, *The Dutch and Quaker Colonies in America* (Boston: Houghton Mifflin, 1903), I, 106.

5. *Leslie's History of the Greater New York* (New York: Arkell Publishing, 1898), I, 19; *Miller's New York as It Is* (New York: J. Miller, 1866), 21.

6. Michael Denning, *Mechanic Accents: Dime Novels and Working-Class Culture in America* (London: Verso, 1987), 81.

7. See Elizabeth Blackmar, *Manhattan for Rent, 1785–1850* (Ithaca, N.Y.: Cornell University Press, 1989); Henrik Hartog, *Public Property and Private Power: The Corporation of the City of New York in American Law, 1730–1870* (Chapel Hill: University of North Carolina Press, 1983).

8. *RERBG* (September 26, 1868). Data about population displacement are drawn from the 1845 and 1875 New York State censuses; the following table compares population above Fourteenth Street, below Fourteenth Street, and on the lower West Side for both years. (Wards Twenty-three and Twenty-four, annexed by New York in 1874, have been included in the 1875 calculations.)

Area	1845		1875	
Above Fourteenth Street	53,728	(14.5%)	546,876	(54.3%)
Below Fourteenth Street	317,495	(85.5%)	495,010	(45.7%)
Below Fourteenth, west of Bowery	194,129	(52.3%)	208,674	(20.0%)
Below Canal, west of Bowery	91,797	(24.7%)	74,789	(7.2%)

9. For the horizontal form and tenancy patterns of the antebellum business district, see *Boyd's Pictorial Directory of Broadway* (New York: William H. Boyd, 1859) and Real Estate Record Association, *A History of Real Estate, Building, and Architecture in New York City During the Last Quarter of a Century* (New York: Record and Guide, 1898), 360. For the port's economic and spatial organization, see Robert Greenhalgh Albion's classic *The Rise of New York Port* (New York: Scribner, 1939); and Stuart M. Blumin, *The Emergence of the Middle Class: Social Experience in the American City, 1760–1900* (New York: Cambridge University Press, 1989), especially 66–107.

10. *Superintendent Reports*, 549. For the retailing landscape of Ladies' Mile, see the painstaking reconstruction in M. Christine Boyer, *Manhattan Manners: Architecture and Style, 1850–1900* (New York: Rizzoli, 1985), 43–129; Margaret Moore, *End of the Road for Ladies' Mile?* (New York: Drive to Protect the Ladies' Mile District, 1986); Elaine Abelson, *When Ladies Go A-Thieving: Middle-Class Shoplifters in the Victorian Department Store* (New York: Oxford University Press, 1989); Henry Resseguie, "Alexander Turney Stewart and the Development of the Department Store, 1823–1876," *Business History Review* (Autumn 1962); and David Scobey, "Nymphs and Satyrs: Sex and the Bourgeois Public Sphere in Victorian New York" (unpublished manuscript).

11. [WRM,] *The Growth of New York* (1865), 29. For the expansion of the west side wholesaling district, see *Superintendent Reports*, 214, 247, 343, 390–93, 428–36, 512, 627; the Bromley *Atlas of New York* (New York: G. W. Bromley, 1879); and *RERBG* (May 9, 1868).

12. On port improvements, see "The Lading of a Ship," *Harper's New Monthly Magazine* 55 (September 1877): 485–86, and "The Atlantic Docks," *Appleton's Journal* 5 (April 1, 1871): 362, for grain elevators; *Harper's Weekly* 21 (July 7, 1877): 521, 540, and New York *Times* (May 31 and November 12, 1868) for abattoirs; ibid. (March 31 and June 2, 1870) for new shipping terminals; and Henry R. Stiles, *A History of the City of Brooklyn* (Brooklyn: n.p., 1869), II, 578–82, for the Brooklyn dock basins. I discuss the Grand Central and Hudson freight depots in Chapter 2, and the Brooklyn Bridge in Chapter 5.

13. New York *Daily Graphic* (June 3, 1873). For descriptions of the new office palaces, see also *New York and Its Institutions* (New York: E. B. Treat, 1872), 125; John Kennion, *The Architects' and Builders' Guide* (New York: Fitzpatrick and Hunter, 1868), III, 52–54, 60–62; and Real Estate Record Association, *History of Real Estate*, 54–55, 66–67, 112–13, 373–95, 615. Winston Weisman analyzes the development of this architecture in "Commercial Palaces of New York, 1845–1875," *Art Bulletin* 36 (December 1954), and "New York and the Problem of the First Skyscraper," *Journal of the Society of Architectural Historians* 12 (1953).

14. Weisman, "Commercial Palaces," points to the growing role of professional architects in downtown city building during the midcentury boom.

15. For changes in the geography of wholesale merchant houses, see Albion, *New York Port*, 260–86; *RERBG* (May 9, 1868, and December 1, 1877); *Wilson's Business Directory, 1874–75* (New York: John F. Trow, 1875); and Real Estate Record Association, *History of Real Estate*, 45–54, 63–67.

16. For Claflin's activities, see Real Estate Record Association, *History of Real Estate*, 624. For the Demorests, see Ishbel Ross, *Crusades and Crinolines: The Life and Times of Ellen Curtis Demorest and William Jennings Demorest* (New York: Harper and Row, 1963), 158–59; and Boyer, *Manhattan Manners*, 101, 110.

17. *RERBG* (December 1, 1877, and October 1, 1881).

18. The analysis in this and the following paragraph is based on locational data from Albion, *New York Port*, 260–86; the *New York City Mercantile and Manufacturers' Business Directory, 1856–57* (New York: Mason Brothers, 1857); *Wilson's Business Directory, 1874–75*; and the Bromley *Atlas* (1879). For research on the changing structure of nineteenth-century commercial centers, see David Ward, *Cities and Immigrants: A Geography of Change in Nineteenth Century America* (New York: Oxford University Press, 1971), from which the quoted phrases come (88); James E. Vance, Jr., *The Merchant's World: The Geography of Wholesaling* (Englewood Cliffs, N.J.: Prentice-Hall, 1970), especially 129–37; and Allan Pred, "Manufacturing in the American Mercantile City: 1800–1840," *Annals of the Association of American Geographers* 56 (1966). For the emergence of Printing-House Square as a newspaper center, see Kouwenhoven, *Columbia Historical Portrait*, 302.

19. For the proliferation of print-linked trades near Printing-House Square, see *Wilson's Business Directory, 1874–75*; for the persistence of Knox's hat manufactory, see *Old New York in Early Photographs* (New York: Dover, 1973), 40, 41, 44.

20. Ward, *Cities and Immigrants*, 87. For other examples of this analysis and periodization of American city form, see John R. Borchert, "American Metropolitan Evolution," *Geographic Review* 57, no. 3 (July 1967): 301–32; David M. Gordon, "Capitalist Development and the History of American Cities," in William K. Tabb and Larry Sawyers (eds.), *Marxism and the Metropolis: New Perspectives in Urban Political Economy* (New York: Oxford University Press, 1978), 23–63; and Martyn J. Bowden, "Growth of the Central Districts in Large Cities," in Leo Schnore (ed.), *The New Urban History: Quantitative Explorations by American Historians* (Princeton, N.J.: Princeton University Press, 1975), 75–109.

21. I have learned much from two classics of locational economics—Robert Murray Haig, *Major Economic Factors in Metropolitan Growth and Arrangement*, Volume I of the Regional Survey of the Regional Plan Association of New York (New York: Regional Plan of New York and Its Environs, 1927), and Homer Hoyt, *The Structure and Growth of Residential Neighborhoods* (Washington, D.C.: Federal Housing Administration, 1939)—and from David Harvey's critical revision of the field in *The Limits to Capital* (Oxford: Blackwell, 1982), especially 368–69.

22. *New York Mercantile and Manufacturers' Business Directory, 1856–57* and *Wilson's Business Directory, 1869–70* (New York: John F. Trow, 1870) (technical publications, commission merchants, and lawyers); U.S. Bureau of the Census, *Historical Statistics of the United States, Colonial Times to 1957* (Washington, D.C.: n.p., 1960), 640 (bank clearances); *Merchant's and Banker's Almanac*, 1865 and 1870, cited in Vincent Carosso, *Investment Banking in America: A History* (Cambridge, Mass.: Harvard University Press, 1970), 16n (brokers and private bankers).

23. New York *Times* (February 27, 1871); "Dry Goods Trade," *Woodhull and Claflin's Weekly* (November 12, 1870), quoted in William Leach, *True Love and Perfect Union: The Feminist Reform*

of Sex and Society (New York: Basic Books, 1989), 227–28. For the uptown movement of retailing, see also New York *Times* (November 21, 1867); *RERBG* (May 9, 1868, and April 1, 1871); and Boyer, *Manhattan Manners*, 87–129. For the business and design strategies of luxury retailers, see, in addition to the sources in note 10, Neil Harris, "Museums, Merchandising, and Popular Taste: The Struggle for Influence," in *Cultural Excursions: Marketing Appetites and Cultural Tastes in Modern America* (Chicago: University of Chicago Press, 1990), 56–81.

24. For an overview of wholesaling relationships, see Albion, *New York Port*, and Vance, *Merchant's World*. For a magazine sketch of a Manhattan warehouse, see "The Lading of a Ship." For "agglomeration economies," see Ward, *Cities and Immigrants*, 85–103.

25. *RERBG* (December 1, 1877). For the commercial paper market, see Margaret Myers, *The New York Money Market*: Volume I, *Origins and Development* (New York: Columbia University Press, 1931), 315–37. On the design of cast-iron lofts see Kennion, *Architects' and Builders' Guide*, II, 129–30; Real Estate Record Association, *History of Real Estate*, 615; Margot Gayle and Edmund V. Gillon, Jr., *Cast-Iron Architecture in New York: A Photographic Survey* (New York: Dover, 1974); Weisman, "Commercial Palaces," 301; and Carl Condit, *American Building: Materials and Techniques from the Beginning of the Colonial Settlements to the Present* (Chicago: University of Chicago Press, 1968), 76–86.

26. All data about assessed land values are taken from the *Annual Reports* of the Commissioners of Taxes and Assessments; see Appendix, Table B.

27. For the Turner building, see Kennion, *Architects' and Builders' Guide*, III, 25. Trinity Church rental figures are from the manuscript rent rolls, Trinity Church Archives. Income from the church's Division I properties jumped from $64,368.87 in 1871–72 to $133,047.00 a year later.

28. *New York and Its Institutions*, 125. For the design and structural innovations involved in these early "skyscrapers," see Condit, *American Building*, 116–19; Real Estate Record Association, *History of Real Estate*, 54–55, 66–67, 112–13, 373–95; Harry W. Baehr, Jr., *The New York Tribune since the Civil War* (New York: Dodd, Mead, 1936), 127.

29. On the Equitable's use of the passenger elevator, see Weisman, "New York and the Problem," 15–16; John Burchard and Albert Bush-Brown, *The Architecture of America: A Social and Cultural History* (Boston: Little, Brown, 1961), 151–52; R. Carlyle Buley, *The Equitable Life Assurance Society of the United States, 1850–1964* (New York: Appleton-Century-Crofts, 1967), I, 101–6. The building is described in the New York *Times* (May 24, 1868).

30. For a summary of the office-building boom, see Real Estate Record Association, *History of Real Estate*, 66–67, 615; and Weisman, "Commercial Palaces," 296–99. For banks and insurance buildings, see ibid., 298, and *New York and Its Institutions*, 125. For newspaper headquarters, see Kennion, *Architects' and Builders' Guide*, III, 52–54, 60–62 (*Herald* and *Sun*); *RERBG* (November 9, 1872) (*Staats-Zeitung*); *The New York Tribune: A Sketch of Its History* (New York: n.p., 1883), 12–13; and Baehr, *New York Tribune since the Civil War*, 126–28.

31. The Western Union headquarters is described and illustrated in "A Telegraphic Palace," New York *Daily Graphic* (June 3, 1873). For the history of the company's consolidation and the postwar growth of its business, see A. R. Brewer, *Western Union Telegraph Company: A Retrospect* (New York: J. Kempster, 1901), 22–29; and Bureau of the Census, *Historical Statistics*, 483.

32. Plan Nos. 100, 45, and 204, *Alterations Docket*. Beginning in 1868, the Department of Buildings registered all plans for new or altered buildings in New York in separate docket books. For each plan, the dockets record building type, number of buildings in the project, number of units in each building, ward, address, owner, builder, and proposed cost.

33. New York *Times* (April 4, 1870).

34. Gerard R. Wolfe, *The House of Appleton* (Metuchen, N.J.: Scarecrow Press, 1981), 30–31, 35–39, 69–72, 115, 127–28, 132–33, 150–54, 165–83, 229–32.

35. Harvey, *Limits to Capital*, 369, 368. The argument in this section is indebted to Harvey's analysis of the role of land markets in capitalist urban development.

36. For the legal constraints governing real-estate transfers, see George W. Van Siclen, *Real Estate Record Guide to Buyers and Sellers of Real Estate* (New York: Real Estate Record and Builders' Guide, 1896); for the norms surrounding land ownership in colonial and early U.S. history, see James Henretta, "Family and Farms: *Mentalité* in Pre-Industrial America," *William and Mary Quarterly* 35 (January 1978): 3–32.

37. See Blackmar, *Manhattan for Rent*, especially 14–43, 183–212 (quoted phrases, 43 and 186).

38. David Rosner, *A Once Charitable Enterprise: Hospitals and Health Care in Brooklyn and New York, 1885–1915* (New York: Cambridge University Press, 1982), 165–66. For Columbia College's uptown migration, see Kouwenhoven, *Columbia Historical Portrait*, 199.

39. George Templeton Strong, *The Diary of George Templeton Strong*, ed. Allan Nevins and Milton Halsey Thomas, (New York: Macmillan, 1952), IV, 529. (The comptroller of Trinity Church was of course Strong himself.) For the church's landholdings and early development policies, see Blackmar, *Manhattan for Rent*, 30–33; for its midcentury fiscal crisis, see Moorhouse, *Trinity*, 153–54. Land sales and long-term lease renewals are detailed in *Transactions Concerning Trinity Church Property (1860–1900)*, Trinity Church Archives. For increases in the Church's rental income, see John H. Hopkins, *Poor Trinity: The Report of a Committee on the Condition of the Finances of Trinity Church Examined* . . . (New York: n.p., 1859), 8; manuscript rent rolls, 1866–1901, Trinity Church Archives.

40. *RERBG* (February 27, 1869). See also ibid. (May 2, 1885) (the history of the Merchants' Exchange and the Exchange Salesroom); ibid. (May 29, 1869) (Board of Real-Estate Brokers); and Real Estate Record Association, *History of Real Estate*, 165–235 (specialization among realtors and builders).

41. See the first number of *RERBG* (March 21, 1868); and David Scobey, "*Real Estate Record and Builders' Guide*," in *Encyclopedia of New York City* (New Haven, Conn.: Yale University Press, 1995). The *Record* remains the single most important source for any scholarly history of city real estate and building in the nineteenth century.

42. See United States Library of Congress, *Fire Insurance Maps in the Library of Congress* (Washington, D.C.: Library of Congress, 1981), 1–5. I have drawn heavily on the 1879 Bromley citywide *Atlas* and the 1880 Bromley *Atlas of the 19th and 22nd Wards* . . . (New York: G. W. Bromley, 1880).

43. *Commercial and Financial Chronicle* (July 8, 1865).

44. Real Estate Record Association, *History of Real Estate*, 355. For the history of the Astor fur and real-estate fortune, see Kenneth Wiggins Porter, *John Jacob Astor, Business Man* (Cambridge, Mass.: Harvard University Press, 1931); for the Lorillards, see *RERBG* (February 21, 1880), and Blackmar, *Manhattan for Rent*, 195–96.

45. *RERBG* (December 17, 1881) (names of petitioners for crosstown drive); ibid. (February 5, 1881) (New York Real Estate Association); and *Charter and Prospectus of the Real Estate Trust Co.* (1871).

46. *RERBG* (September 31, 1875, and October 9, 1980). See also my discussion of the flow of national capital into city real estate in Chapter 1.

47. For typical credit terms offered by property sellers in the mid-nineteenth century, see *Sale of Choice Improved and Unimproved Property in the City of New-York . . .* (February 23, 1853); *Peremptory Sale at Auction of 300 Plots of Land . . . at Oloff Park . . .* (June 22, 1869); Adrian H Muller, Auctioneer. *Maps of 62 Very Desirable Lots . . . to Be Sold at Auction . . .* (April 29, 1880); L. J. Phillips, Auctioneer. *Maps of 163 Lots on the Hamilton Grange Estate . . .* (October 25, 1887). For the suggestion that mortgage terms eased later in the century, see *RERBG* (January 10, 1885).

48. Samuel Ruggles, quoted in Blackmar, *Manhattan for Rent*, 201. For the role of savings banks, see Emerson W. Keyes, *A History of Savings Banks in the United States* (New York: B. Rhodes, 1878), II, 330–31 (increased mortgage activity); Alan L. Olmstead, *New York City Mutual Savings Banks, 1819–1861* (Chapel Hill: University of North Carolina Press, 1976), 92 (legal ceilings on lending); and Weldon Welfling, *Mutual Savings Banks: The Evolution of a Financial Intermediary* (Cleveland, Ohio: Press of Case Western Reserve University, 1963), 40 (high level of savings bank charters between 1860 and 1875). For lending by insurance companies, see *RERBG* (December 31, 1881); and Bureau of the Census, *Historical Statistics*, 676. Statistics on insurance mortgage lending are for the industry as a whole, but New York companies controlled some 85 percent of the national market; see Morton Keller, *The Life Insurance Enterprise, 1865–1910: A Study in the Limits of Corporate Power* (Cambridge, Mass.: Harvard University Press, 1963), 8.

49. Real Estate Record Association, *History of Real Estate*, 157, 159 (total resources spent on real estate and construction); Keyes, *History of Savings Banks*, 330 (mortgage lending by New York savings banks); *RERBG* (March 29, 1879) (foreclosures during the 1870s depression).

50. From 1860 to 1875, the total increase in assessed property values was approximately $466 million, of which $299 million took place in seven uptown Manhattan wards; this does not include values for the Twenty-third and Twenty-fourth wards of the Annexed District. Of 13,117 new buildings erected between 1862 and 1871, 10,500 went up in the wards north of Fourteenth Street (Wards 12, 16, 18, 20–24). See Appendix, Tables A and B.

51. *RERBG* (March 19, 1869); FLO et al., "Report to the Staten Island Improvement Commission of a Preliminary Scheme of Improvements" (1871), reprinted in Albert Fein (ed.), *Landscape into Cityscape: Frederick Law Olmsted's Plans for a Greater New York City* (Ithaca, N.Y.: Cornell University Press, 1967), 175, 178; CLB, *The Dangerous Classes of New York, and Twenty Years' Work among Them* (New York: Wynkoop and Hallenbeck, 1872), 51.

52. All building data in this paragraph are taken from annual tables in *Superintendent Reports*. There are no figures for 1870 because the city government was reorganized in the middle of that year; I discuss the 1870 charter reform in Chapter 6. The totals cited for 1863–69 and 1871 are as follows: new buildings, 13,117; new buildings north of Fourteenth Street, 10,500; new residential buildings, 8,603; new residences north of Fourteenth Street, 7,196; new first- and second-class residences, 5,636; new first- and second-class residences north of Fourteenth Street, 5,413. For the geography of property ownership, see New York State Secretary of State, *Census for the State of New York for 1875* (Albany: Weed, Parsons, 1877), 21: out of 24,378 landowners, 17,840 (73.1 percent) resided north of Fourteenth Street (including the Annexed District).

53. Kennion, *Architects' and Builders' Guide*, III, 44–45. For descriptions of new railroad suburbs, see New York *Times* (March 11, 1867, and August 15, 1871); *RERBG* (October, 17, 1868) (Hackensack); M. H. Smith, *Garden City, Long Island in Early Photographs, 1869–1919* (New York: Dover, 1987). For other instances of suburban town development, see Kennion, *Architects' and Builders' Guide*, II, 41–43, 67–69, 123–25; *RERBG* (January 23, 1870); and *Prospectus of the Pelham*

Manor and Huguenot Heights Association (New York: J. Huggins, 1874). For estimates of commuting volume, see Carl Condit, *The Port of New York,* Volume I: *A History of the Rail and Terminal System from the Beginnings to Pennsylvania Station* (Chicago: University of Chicago Press, 1980), 81 (number of trains); and John Austin Stevens, *Progress of New York in a Century, 1776–1876: An Address Delivered Before the New-York Historical Society* (New York: n.p., 1875), 63 (number of commuters).

54. [WRM,] *Growth of New York,* 23. For the consolidation of "Fifth Avenue" as an elite residential enclave, see *The Elite Private Address and Carriage Directory* (New York: W. Phillips, 1877); and Kate Simon, *Fifth Avenue: A Very Social History* (New York: Harcourt Brace Jovanovich, 1978). For the Astor and Stewart mansions, see also *Harper's Weekly* (August 14, 1869), and *Old New York in Early Photographs,* 154–56.

55. For information about first-class row houses, see *Offering of Six Elegant New Houses by Duggin and Crossman, Architects . . .* (1874), from which the quoted phrase comes; [D. and J. Jardine, Architects,] *For Sale. Five First Class Residences* (187?); and *RERBG* (December 12, 1881). Charles Lockwood, *Bricks and Brownstone: The New York Row House, 1783–1929: An Architectural and Social History* (New York: McGraw-Hill, 1972) remains the best historical introduction to this built form. I discuss the design and social organization of bourgeois row houses in Chapter 5.

56. For overviews of the building of civic and cultural institutions in the Fifth Avenue corridor, see "An Architectural Ramble," *RERBG* (September 17, 1870); Boyer, *Manhattan Manners*; Will Irvin et al., *A History of the Union League Club of New York City* (New York: Dodd, Mead, 1952). For the class rituals of bourgeois sociability, see David Scobey, "Anatomy of the Promenade: The Politics of Bourgeois Sociability in Nineteenth-Century New York," *Social History* 17, no. 2 (May 1992): 203–27; and Kenneth L. Ames, "Meaning in Artifacts: Hall Furnishings in Victorian America," in Dell Upton and John Michael Vlach (eds.), *Common Places: Readings in American Vernacular Architecture* (Athens: University of Georgia Press, 1986), 240–60. Edith Wharton's *The Age of Innocence,* much of it set in the Fifth Avenue of the early 1870s, offers perhaps the best ethnography of the class rituals and regulations of this world.

57. Information on new residential construction in the Nineteenth Ward is aggregated from *New Dockets.* For the role of Third and Eighth avenues as retail, transit, and development corridors, see James D. McCabe, Jr., *New York by Sunlight and Gaslight* (Philadelphia: Hubbard Brothers, 1882), 267–69; and New York State Engineer and Surveyor, *Railroad Reports* (1865) 156–57, (1870) 276–77, (1875) 372–73.

58. Strong, *Diary,* IV, 375; CA, *Report . . . upon the Sanitary Conditions of the City* (New York: D. Appleton, 1865), quoted in Jeanne Chase, "The Streets of New York, Worlds Apart, 1830–1870," *Revue Française d'Etudes Américaines* (April 1981) 36.

59. All locational information from this paragraph is taken from the Bromley *Atlas of the 19th and 22nd Wards.*

60. George Templeton Strong vividly describes the ragged, unfinished quality of the uptown landscape: "To Fifty-ninth Street this afternoon, traversing for the first time the newly opened section of Madison Avenue between Fortieth Street and [Columbia] College, a rough and ragged track, as yet, and hardly a thoroughfare, rich in mudholes, goats, pigs, geese, strammonium. Here and there Irish shanties 'come out' (like smallpox pustules) . . ." (Strong, *Diary,* IV, 155 [October 22, 1867]).

One important gap in my reconstruction of uptown development is the lack of attention to shanties and squatters' communities; clearing them was a perennial thorn in the side of real-estate developers. See Elizabeth Blackmar and Roy Rosenzweig, *The Park and the People: A His-*

tory of Central Park (Ithaca, N.Y.: Cornell University Press, 1992), 59–91; and CLB, *Dangerous Classes*, 147–64.

61. George W. Curtis, "Spring Pictures," *Other Essays from the Easy Chair* (New York: Harper and Brothers, 1893), 126–27.

62. Gouverneur Morris, Simeon DeWitt, and John Rutherford, "Commissioners' Remarks" (1811), reprinted in David T. Valentine, *A Compilation of the Laws of the State of New York Relating Particularly to the City of New York* (New York: E. Jones, 1862), 810. My analysis of the Manhattan street grid has been enriched by Hartog, *Public Property*, 158–67; Blackmar, *Manhattan for Rent*, 94–108; and Rem Koolhaas, *Delirious New York: A Retroactive Manifesto for Manhattan* (New York: Oxford University Press, 1978), 13–18.

63. Chapter 7 elaborates this analysis, but see especially WRM, "Communication Relative to the Plans and Improvement of the Fort Washington District and the Twenty-third and Twenty-fourth Wards," BDPP document reprinted as "The Growth of New York," *RERBG* (Supplement, June 19, 1875); and FLO and J.J.R. Croes, "Preliminary Report of the Landscape Architect and the Civil and Topographical Engineer, Upon the Laying Out of the Twenty-third and Twenty-fourth Wards," BDPP Document No. 72, reprinted in Fein (ed.), *Landscape into Cityscape*, 350–58.

64. Koolhaas, *Delirious New York*, 13, 15; Hartog, *Public Property*, 164–67.

65. The legal process of street opening is described in Hartog, *Public Property*, 167–75. For the pace of street openings in upper Manhattan, see New York City Department of Public Works, *Communication . . . , Being a Statement of Streets . . . Opened or Ceded to the City North of Fifty-ninth Street*, Board of Aldermen, Document No. 6 (1874).

66. For a summary of horse car railway franchises and routes, see Harry James Carman, *The Street Surface Railway Franchises of New York City, Columbia University Studies in History, Economics, and Public Law* 88, no. 1 (1919). For growth in aggregate ridership, see ibid., 145. For ridership statistics by line, see New York State Engineer and Surveyor, *Railroad Reports* (1865) 156–57, (1870) 276–77, (1875) 372–73. Ridership statistics for 1869 along the main uptown lines are as follows: total Manhattan ridership, 113,319,326; Second Avenue Railroad, 8,723,857; Third Avenue Railroad, 25,000,000; Sixth Avenue Railroad, 11,287,530; and Eighth Avenue Railroad, 14,009,267.

67. For important examples of the paradigm, see Warner, *Streetcar Suburbs: The Process of Growth in Boston (1870–1900)* (Cambridge, Mass.: Harvard University Press, 1967); Warner, *The Urban Wilderness: A History of the American City* (New York: Harper and Row, 1972); Clay McShane, *Technology and Reform: Street Railways and the Growth of Milwaukee, 1887–1900* (Madison: State Historical Society of Wisconsin, 1974); McShane, "Transforming the Use of the Urban Space: A Look at the Revolution in Street Pavements, 1880–1924," *Journal of Urban History* 5 (May 1979): 279–307; and McShane and Stanley Schultz, "To Engineer the Metropolis: Sewers, Sanitation, and City Planning in Late-Nineteenth Century America," *Journal of American History* 65 (September 1978): 389–411. For research that stresses the effect of infrastructural development on New York's growth, see Eugene Moehring, *Public Works and the Patterns of Urban Real Estate Growth in Manhattan, 1835–1894* (New York: Arno, 1981); and Condit, *Port of New York.*

68. For the special assessment system, see Hartog, *Public Property*, 167–75; and John F. Dillon, *Commentaries on the Law of Municipal Corporations* (Boston: Little, Brown, 1911 [5th edition]), IV, 2490–2642. I have found Robin Einhorn, *Property Rules: Political Economy in Chicago, 1833–1872* (Chicago: University of Chicago Press, 1991) useful in understanding special assessments and "proprietor sovereignty" in New York, although the experience of the two cities differs in significant ways.

69. I discuss the erosion of the assessment system and the increasing use of public debt financing in Chapter 6.

70. For an overview of changing transit technologies in New York, see Charles Cheape, *Moving the Masses: Urban Public Transit in New York, Boston, and Philadelphia, 1880–1912* (Cambridge, Mass.: Harvard University Press, 1980); and James Blaine Walker, *Fifty Years of Rapid Transit, 1864–1917* (New York: Law Printing, 1918).

71. For the legal context of the franchise system, see Dillon, *Municipal Corporations*, III, 1904–2087; Morton J. Horwitz, *The Transformation of American Law, 1780–1860* (Cambridge, Mass.: Harvard University Press, 1979), 109–39; Carman, *Street Surface Railway Franchises*.

72. For corruption in the Common Council in the granting of horse car franchises, see Edward K. Spann, *The New Metropolis: New York City, 1840–1857* (New York: Columbia University Press, 1981), 297–305. For opposition to a streetcar franchise on Broadway, see Carman, *Street Surface Railway Franchises*, 78–91; and address of WRM, reprinted in WSA, *Proceedings of Six Public Meetings . . .* (1871), meeting of February 8, 1871, 11–26.

73. New York *Times* (July 1866) and "H. G.," New York *Tribune* (February 2, 1866), quoted in *Exposé of the Facts Concerning the Proposed Patent Elevated Railway* (New York: n.p., 1866), 47; *RERBG* (January 20, 1872); address of Simeon E. Church, reprinted in WSA, *Proceedings of Six Public Meetings . . .* (1871), meeting of January 11, 1871, 40. On the new franchises and the establishment of the elevated railway system, see Carman, *Street Surface Railway Franchises*, 108–42; Cheape, *Moving the Masses*, 26–39, 72–101; and Walker, *Fifty Years*.

74. For large-scale suburban and townsite development, see Matthew Edel, Elliot D. Sclar, and Daniel Luria, *Shaky Palaces: Homeownership and Social Mobility in Boston's Suburbanization* (New York: Columbia University Press, 1984), 195–223; and James Slevin, *Inventory, 1851–1870, of Real Estate* (Slevin Papers, New York Public Library), which lists the real-estate investments of a New York– and Cincinatti-based dry-goods merchant, including both Manhattan plots and Western "additions." For suburban town development outside New York, see Richard Guy Wilson, "Idealism and the Origin of the First American Suburb: Llewellyn Park, New Jersey," *American Art Journal* 11 (October 1979): 79–90; Smith, *Garden City, Long Island*; and *Peremptory Sale . . . at Oloff Park*.

75. For Ruggles's development of Gramercy Park, see *Map of the Lower Division of the Lands of Samuel B. Ruggles in the Twelfth Ward of the City of New York. . . . December 31, 1831*; Carole Klein, *Gramercy Park: An American Bloomsbury* (Boston: Houghton Mifflin, 1987), 3–18; and Blackmar, *Manhattan for Rent*, 196–204.

My emphasis on the dispersed pattern of Manhattan property development echoes the analysis of Boston's growth as "a weave of small patterns" in Warner's *Streetcar Suburbs*. My view of New York differs from Warner's account of Boston, however, in deemphasizing the role of transportation improvements and stressing the self-organization of real-estate interests in response to the fragmentation of the market.

76. See New York State Secretary of State, *Census of the State of New York for 1855* (Albany: C. Van Benthuysen, 1857); and *Census of the State of New York for 1875* (Albany: Weed, Parsons, 1877), 21 (number and ward of property owners in Manhattan); *RERBG* (October 10, 1868) (proportion of proprietors who own only their own residence); T. W., "Our Millionaires," *Galaxy* 5 (1868): 529 (value of New York's largest estates); *RERBG* (July 31, 1880) (size of upper West Side parcels); AHG, "Communication . . . Relative to the Laying Out of the Island above 155th Street, and Other Subjects," BCCP, *10th Annual Report* (1866), 135–37; *New Dockets* (scale of property development in 1870).

77. For an overview of property ownership in upper Manhattan in the eighteenth and early nineteenth centuries, see Blackmar, *Manhattan for Rent*, 14–43.

78. George Ashton Black, *The History of Municipal Ownership of Land on Manhattan Island . . .* , *Columbia Studies in History, Economics, and Public Law*, 1, no. 3 (New York, 1897): 62–63 (land sales to reduce debt); *Maps of Real Estate Belonging to the Corporation of the City of New York to Be Sold at Auction on Monday, May 21st, 1866* (New York: E. B. Clayton's, 1866) (location of lots for sale in 1866). See also *Maps of Real Estate Belonging to the Corporation of the City of New York, to Be Sold at Auction . . .* (May 19, 1850). For the legal history of the landholdings of the Corporation of the City of New York, see Hartog's nuanced *Public Property*.

79. *RERBG* (May 17, 1873); the Bradhurst auction was also publicized in *Auction Sale. Bradhurst Estate . . . Consisting of 127 Lots . . .* (May 20, 1873). For the Dyckman estate, see *Sale at Auction of Part of the Dyckman Estate* (1868); *Executors' Sale at Auction. James M. Miller, Auctioneer. . . . Will Sell by Order of the Executors of Isaac Dyckman, Deceased, 128 Acres at Fort Washington . . .* (1868); *Executors' Sale at Auction. V. K. Stevenson, Son and Co. . . .* (1870); and *RERBG* (May 28, 1870). For an overview of Gilded Age estate auctions, see Real Estate Record Association, *History of Real Estate*, 130–53. For a general analysis of land preparation in nineteenth-century North America, see Michael J. Doucet, "Urban Land Development in Nineteenth-Century North America," *Journal of Urban History* 8 (1982): 299–342.

80. *RERBG* (January 17, 1880) (Beekman estate strategies); *Adrian H. Muller, Auctioneer. Executor's Sale of Valuable Property . . . Being a Portion of the Estate of James Slevin, Dec'd . . . on Tuesday, October 14, 1873 . . .* (Slevin Papers, New York Public Library); *RERBG* (April 24, 1880), and Real Estate Record Association, *History of Real Estate*, 132–33 (Mutual Life foreclosures sale). The Beekmans' relationship with "Mr. Zittel, of Third Avenue"—presumably a German or Jewish developer of East Side flats and tenements—poses the question of the ethnic composition of real-estate entrepreneurs and their relationship to different class and geographic markets. The building records in the 1870 *New Docket* and *Alterations Docket* offer a wealth of information on these issues.

81. For the use of long-term leases and the development of a secondary leasehold market, see *Transactions Concerning Trinity Church Property (1860–1900)*, Trinity Church Archive; Blackmar, *Manhattan for Rent*, 31–37; Porter, *Astor*, II, 935.

82. *RERBG* (April 19, 1884); ibid. (February 21, 1880).

83. For the geography of tailors and piano makers, see Franklin B. Hough, *Statistics of Population of the City and County of New York as Shown by the State Census of 1865 . . .* (New York: New York Printing, 1866), 267, 276; Jessie Eliphalet Pope, *The Clothing Industry in New York* (Columbia: University of Missouri Press, 1905), 1–13; and *Frank Leslie's Illustrated Weekly* (May 28, 1864). My understanding of the bifurcation of industry in New York owes much to Richard Stott, "Hinterland Development and Differences in Work Setting: The New York City Region, 1820–1870" (unpublished paper).

84. For the Vanderbilts' development of the upper West Side riverfront, see Wheaton J. Lane, *Commodore Vanderbilt: An Epic of the Steam Age* (New York: Knopf, 1942), 281; *Harper's Weekly* 21 (December 22, 1877): 1008, 1010; and the 1879 Bromley *Atlas*. The *Atlas* also documents the clustering of nuisance industries near slaughterhouses.

85. *Peremptory Sale at Auction. . . . Estate of Lewis G. Morris* (Monday, March 15, 1869); *The City Real Estate Company. Builders of New York* (n.d.). See also Robert Fishman, *Bourgeois Utopias: The Rise and Fall of Suburbia* (New York: Basic Books, 1987), especially 103–33.

86. Allan Nevins (ed.), *The Diary of Philip Hone, 1828–1851* (New York: Dodd, Mead, 1927), 202 (March 9, 1836). I discuss the use of deed restrictions to control land use in Chapter 7.

87. *RERBG* (October 13, 1877). The cost of residential construction in the central and river-front development corridors is calculated from *New Docket*. For the location of servants, drivers, and hostlers, see Hough, *Statistics of Population*, 252, 257, 273. The number and location of new stables were calculated from *Superintendent Reports*.

88. *Executors' Sale at Auction. V. K. Stevenson, Son and Company . . . Will Sell . . . 92 Acres at Fort Washington . . .* (1870).

89. Haig, *Major Economic Factors*, 39; *RERBG* (October 13, 1877).

Chapter 4

1. New York *Evening Post* (March 20, 1867), quoted in Carl Condit, *The Port of New York,* Volume I: *A History of the Rail and Terminal System from the Beginnings to Pennsylvania Station* (Chicago: University of Chicago Press, 1980), 78; *RERBG* (February 8, 1873); *Commercial and Financial Chronicle* (January 13, 1866); Special Committee of the New York State Senate on the Wharves and Piers of New York, quoted in New York *Times* (January 25, 1867); and *RERBG* (October 13, 1877).

2. CA, *The Address of George F. Noyes . . . Before the Committee of the Senate, on the Subject of Wharves and Piers* (New York: Citizens' Association, 1866), 12; New York *Times* (July 5, 1871, and February 16, 1868); Chamber of Commerce of the State of New York, *Annual Report* (New York: Press of the Chamber of Commerce, 1870–71), 18; New York *Evening Post*, quoted in *Address of the Citizens' Association of New York to the Public* (New York: Citizens' Association, 1871), 22; *Harper's Weekly* (February 16, 1884); New York *Times* (July 5, 1871).

3. New York *Times* (November 21, 1872) (receptacles for garbage); Dr. Swinburne, Health Officer of the Port, quoted in Chamber of Commerce, *Annual Report* (1865–66), 107 (health hazard); New York Common Council, report of March 23, 1863, quoted in CA, *Address of George F. Noyes*, 11 (dilapidation); Pilot Commissioners, report of December 20, 1864, quoted in ibid., 12 (survey); "Our Wharves and Piers—The Meeting To-Morrow Afternoon," New York *Times* (November 7, 1867), and CA, *Address of George F. Noyes*, 12 (collapse of docks); New York *Times* (February 16, 1869) (tumbledown structures).

4. New York *Times* (December 2, 1870); Chamber of Commerce, *Annual Report* (1865–66), 106–7; New York *Evening Post*, quoted in Condit, *Port of New York*, I, 78; *Harper's Weekly* (July 14, 1877); "The Lading of a Ship," *Harper's New Monthly Magazine* 55 (September 1877): 487–88; CA, *Address of George F. Noyes*, 12; communication of F.J.W. Hurst to the Dock Commissioners, quoted in New York *Times* (December 2, 1870); Henry R. Stiles, *A History of the City of Brooklyn* (Brooklyn: n.p., 1869), II, 574; *RERBG* (April 16, 1870); Christine Stansell, "Women, Children, and the Uses of the Streets: Class and Gender Conflict in New York City, 1850–1860," *Feminist Studies* 8, no. 2 (Summer 1982): 309–53.

5. New York *Times* (June 2 and March 31, 1870) (improvements on the Hudson riverfront); Stiles, *History of Brooklyn*, II, 575–82 (Brooklyn dock basins); Chief of the Bureau of Statistics on the Commerce and Navigation of the United States, *First Annual Report on the Internal Commerce of the United States* (Washington, D.C.: n.p., 1877), 87–88 (facilities of other ports); New York *Times* (June 24, 1870) (merchant worries).

6. New York *Times* (November 29, 1868); James D. McCabe, Jr., *New York by Sunlight and Gaslight* (Philadelphia: Hubbard Brothers, 1882), 136–37 (inadequacy of Broadway); *RERBG* (March 1, 1873, and April 11, 1868).

7. French visitor, quoted in Jon C. Teaford, *The Unheralded Triumph: City Government in America, 1870–1900* (Baltimore: Johns Hopkins University Press, 1984), 228. For debates about street pavements in New York, see letter from Peter Cooper to George W. McLean, Street Commissioner, New York *Times* (September 2, 1868); Eugene Moehring, *Public Works and the Patterns of Urban Real Estate Growth in Manhattan, 1835–1894* (New York: Arno, 1981), 110–15, 320–21; and Edward P. North, "The Construction and Maintenance of Roads," *Transactions of the American Society of Civil Engineers* 8 (May 1879): 113. For the history of street paving in nineteenth-century cities, see Clay McShane, "Transforming the Use of Urban Space: A Look at the Revolution in Street Pavements, 1880–1924," *Journal of Urban History* 5, no. 3 (May 1979): 279–307; and Teaford, *Unheralded Triumph*, 227–29.

8. Lawrence H. Larsen, "Nineteenth-Century Street Sanitation: A Study of Filth and Frustration," *Wisconsin Magazine of History* 52 (Spring 1962): 239; New York *Times* (April 9, 1871). For estimates of the horse population and animal wastes, see Mayor Oakey Hall's annual message, 1871, quoted in *RERBG* (June 17, 1871); Larsen, "Nineteenth-Century Street Sanitation," 245; and U.S. Bureau of the Census, *Tenth Census (1880)*, Volume 18: *Social Statistics on Cities*, 591. For problems of snow and snow removal, see *RERBG* (April 4, 1868); *Harper's Weekly* (March 3, 1871); and George Templeton Strong, *The Diary of George Templeton Strong*, ed. Allan Nevins and Milton Halsey Thomas (New York: Macmillan, 1952), IV, 336–37, 465.

9. The formation of the Department of Street Cleaning is recounted in George E. Waring, Jr., *Street Cleaning* (New York: Doubleday and McClure, 1899); and Richard Skolnick, "George Edwin Waring, Jr.: A Model for Reformers," *New-York Historical Society Quarterly* 52, no. 4 (October 1968): 354–78. For the unequal distribution of street services, see New York *Times* (February 23, 1871) and New York *World* (October 6, 1886).

10. *Manual of the City of New York* (1852) 286, (1860) 424, (1867) 770, and Mayor A. Oakey Hall, annual message (1871), quoted in *RERBG* (June 17, 1871) (increases in licensed carts); New York *Times* (October 2, 1869) (Fulton and Washington markets); ibid. (August 25, 1867; March 21, 1869; March 20, 1870; and March 27, 1870) (City Hall Park); *RERBG* (December 7, 1872) (construction sites). For municipal efforts to regulate street obstructions, see New York *Times* (March 9 and August 10, 1869).

11. *RERBG* (February 3, 1872).

12. Moehring, *Public Works*, 356, 360.

13. See Condit, *The Port of New York*; McShane, "Transforming the Use of Urban Space"; McShane and Stanley Schultz, "To Engineer the Metropolis: Sewers, Sanitation and City Planning in Late-Nineteenth-Century America," *Journal of American History* 65 (September 1978): 389–411; Charles Cheape, *Moving the Masses: Urban Public Transit in New York, Boston, and Philadelphia, 1880–1912* (Cambridge, Mass.: Harvard University Press, 1980), 3–6, 25–39; and Seymour Mandelbaum, *Boss Tweed's New York* (New York: J. Wiley, 1965), 1–26, 155–85.

14. See Jon Teaford, *Unheralded Triumph*; and Martin J. Schiesl, *The Politics of Efficiency: Municipal Administration and Reform In America, 1880–1920* (Berkeley: University of California Press, 1977). Eric Monkkonen, *America Becomes Urban: The Development of U.S. Cities and Towns, 1780–1980* (Berkeley: University of California Press, 1988), revises this view, stressing the proactive, experimental, and entrepreneurial quality of urban administration in the mid-nineteenth century; my own account of the politics of city building in Chapter 6 draws on Monkkonen's argument.

15. Samuel Hays, *The Response to Industrialism, 1885–1914* (Chicago: University of Chicago Press, 1957), 94.

16. See McShane, "Transforming the Use of Urban Space"; Teaford, *Unheralded Triumph*, 227–40; Larsen, "Nineteenth-Century Street Sanitation"; and Waring, *Street Cleaning*.

17. Address of WRM, reprinted in WSA, *Proceedings of Six Public Meetings . . .* (1871), meeting of April 12, 1871, 11. See also WRM, "Communication Relative to the Plans and Improvement of the Fort Washington District and the Twenty-third and Twenty-fourth Wards," reprinted as "The Growth of New York," *RERBG*, Supplement (June 19, 1875): 6; and New York *Times* (February 23, 1871). I discuss the critique of the 1811 street grid by New York's urbanists in Chapter 7.

18. For fragmentation of dock ownership, see CA, *Address of George F. Noyes*, 14; *Address of the Citizens' Association*, 20; and Peter Cooper, letter to New York *Times* (September 26, 1867). For wharfage rates, see Robert Greenhalgh Albion, *The Rise of New York Port* (New York: Scribner, 1939), 222–23; and Special Committee of the New York State Senate on the Wharves and Piers of New York, *Report* (1867), quoted in *Public Meetings of the Department of Docks to Hear Persons Interested in Improving the River Front* (New York: n.p., 1870), 10. For the condition of the private docks, see New York *Times* (August 31, 1865, and April 22, 1870). For the activities of Erie Canal boats, see *Address of the Citizens' Association*, 22; and A. W. Craven, letter to New York *Times* (February 11, 1868). Of the nearly 160 piers around Manhattan Island in 1870, the Corporation of the City of New York owned sixty-four, an additional fifty-four were privately owned, and the rest were owned by the city on one side and by private proprietors on the other (ibid., June 24, 1870).

19. On the fragmented administration of the port, see R.A.C. Smith, *The Commerce and Other Business of the Waterways of the State of New York, Their Relation to the Port of New York and the Ports of the World: A Tabulation of Facts about Waterborne Trade . . .* (New York: n.p., 1914), 48, 54–55; *Report of the Committee on Wharves and Piers, Appointed at a Public Meeting of Merchants . . .* (New York: n.p., 1868), 6; New York *Times* (February 6, 1869); and Albion, *Rise of New York Port*, 223–27.

20. New York *Times* (November 12, 1866); New York *Evening Post*, quoted in *Address of the Citizens' Association*, 20. I discuss the debate over waterfront development in Chapter 7.

21. My analysis of the uneven effects of market-driven growth in Victorian New York is indebted to Shoukry T. Roweis and Allen J. Scott, "The Urban Land Question," in Michael Dear and Allen J. Scott (eds.), *Urbanization and Urban Planning in Capitalist Society* (London: Methuen, 1981), especially 140–48.

22. New York *Times* (February 6, 1869).

23. For the rising costs of construction and land ownership, see Ralph Andreano (ed.), *The Economic Impact of the American Civil War* (Cambridge, Mass.: Harvard University Press, 1962), 179–80 (wages); Real Estate Record Association, *A History of Real Estate, Building, and Architecture in New York City During the Last Quarter of a Century* (New York: Record and Guide, 1898), 159 (construction costs); Edward Dana Durand, *The Finances of New York City* (New York: Macmillan, 1898), 373 (mill rates).

24. *RERBG* (November 8, 1873); FLO to Henry H. Elliott, August 27, 1860, in *FLOP* III, 262; *Superintendent Reports* (1871–72), 70.

25. *Harper's Weekly* (August 27, 1859); "Crossing Broadway," ibid. (March 12, 1870); *RERBG* (March 8, 1873); *Harper's Weekly* (May 20, 1871). For other middle-class responses to the dangers of public transit, see *Exposé of the Facts Concerning the Proposed Patent Elevated Railway* (New York: n.p., 1866); and letters to the editor, New York *Times* (May 1 and May 20, 1871).

26. FLO, *Public Parks and the Enlargement of Towns* (1870), 11, 14; [H. T. Tuckerman,] "Through Broadway," *Atlantic Monthly* 18 (December 1866): 727.

27. Unnamed journalist quoted in CA, *Report . . . upon the Sanitary Conditions of the City* (New York: D. Appleton, 1865), lxxxi.

28. "Life in the Slums," New York *Times* (August 21, 1870); CLB, *The Dangerous Classes of New York, and Twenty Years' Work among Them* (New York: Wynkoop and Hallenbeck, 1872), 29.

29. Unnamed journalist quoted in CA, *Report . . . upon the Sanitary Conditions*, xv. For a brilliant analysis of the Astor Place riot, see Peter Buckley, "To the Opera House: Culture and Society in New York City, 1820–1860" (Ph.D. dissertation, State University of New York at Stony Brook, 1984).

30. CLB, *Dangerous Classes*, 30. For an insightful study of the draft riots, see Iver Bernstein, *The New York City Draft Riots: Their Significance for American Society and Politics in the Age of the Civil War* (New York: Oxford University Press, 1990); Adrian Cook, *The Armies of the Streets: The New York City Draft Riots of 1863* (Lexington: University of Kentucky Press, 1963) also offers a helpful reconstruction of the events. For a contemporary account, see Joel Tyler Headley, *The Great Riots of New York* (New York: E. B. Treat, 1873), 136–288.

31. Strong, *Diary*, IV, 96; "'The Dangerous Classes,'" New York *Times* (July 16, 1871). On the cholera outbreak of 1866, see Charles E. Rosenberg, *The Cholera Years: The United States in 1832, 1849, and 1866* (Chicago: University of Chicago Press, 1962), 185–91. The labor unrest in postwar New York is discussed in "The Eight Hour Strikes," *Commercial and Financial Chronicle* (July 18, 1868): 70–71; George E. McNeill, *The Labor Movement: The Problem of To-Day* (Boston: A. M. Bridgeman, 1887), 143, 146; David Montgomery, *Beyond Equality: Labor and the Radical Republicans, 1862–1872* (New York: Knopf, 1967), 323–34; and Bernstein, *Draft Riots*, especially 209–15, 246–55. For the Orange Day riots of 1870 and 1871, see Headley, *The Great Riots of New York*, 289–306; and Michael Gordon, *The Orange Riots: Irish Political Violence in New York City, 1870 and 1871* (Ithaca, N.Y.: Cornell University Press, 1993). For an overview of the Tweed courthouse frauds, see Alexander Callow, *The Tweed Ring* (New York: Oxford University Press, 1965), 198–206, 259–61.

32. For the geography of rioting before the midcentury boom, see Bernstein, *Draft Riots*, 24; for the geography of the first skirmishes in the draft riots, see ibid., 17–25; for the locales of the Orange Day outbreaks, see Headley, *Great Riots*, 289–306.

33. Strong, *Diary*, III, 341; Bernstein, *Draft Riots*, 18–25, 41 (building workers in draft riots); Headley, *Great Riots*, 291 (road workers in 1870 Orange Day skirmish); FLO to CLB (December 8, 1860), in *FLOP* III, 286–87 (1857 demonstration for public works employment); Herbert Gutman, "The Tompkins Square 'Riot' In New York City on January 13, 1874: A Re-examination of Its Causes and Its Aftermath," *Labor History* 6 (1965): 44–70 (Tompkins Square demonstration).

34. See David M. Gordon, Richard Edwards, and Michael Reich, *Segmented Work, Divided Workers: The Historical Transformation of Labor in the United States* (New York: Cambridge University Press, 1982), 23

35. Ibid., 26–32, 94–99.

36. CA, *Report of the Executive Committee to the Honorary Council . . .* (November 17, 1866), 7; Edward Crapsey, *The Nether Side of New York* (New York: Sheldon, 1872), 116; Strong, *Diary*, IV, 96.

37. The quoted passage is from New York *Times* (October 16, 1868). For debates over dock and terminal improvements, see *Public Meetings of the Department of Docks*; New York Pier and Warehouse Company, *Piers and Wharves of New York, Remedy Proposed* (New York: n.p., 1869); and *Commercial and Financial Chronicle* (August 22, 1874, and May 19, 1877). On street improvements, see New York *World* (February 15, 1868) and New York *Times* (February 16, 1868; March 8, 1868; and January 3, 1869). For discussion of pavements, see the sources cited in note

7. The history of the many rapid-transit schemes broached in the 1860s and 1870s is summarized in Walker, *Fifty Years of Rapid Transit, 1864–1917* (New York: Law Printing, 1918). I discuss health and building reform and the effort to plan the metropolitan periphery in Chapter 7.

38. New York *Times* (September 8, 1867); *RERBG* (January 29, 1870).

39. *Harper's Weekly* (May 6, 1871), Supplement; AHG, "Communication of the Comptroller of the Park Relative to Westchester County, Harlem River, and Spuyten Duyvil Creek," BCCP, *Thirteenth Annual Report* (1869), 163. Green was a leading advocate of metropolitan consolidation throughout the late nineteenth century and a prime mover behind the creation of Greater New York during the 1890s; see Barry J. Kaplan, "Andrew H. Green and the Creation of a Planning Rationale: The Formation of Greater New York City, 1865–1890," *Urbanism Past and Present* 8 (Summer 1979): 32–39, and David Hammack, *Power and Society: Greater New York at the Turn of the Century* (New York: Russell Sage Foundation, 1982), 187–229.

40. Address of WRM, reprinted in WSA, *Proceedings of Six Public Meetings . . .* (1871), meeting of April 12, 1871, 11, 13.

Chapter 5

1. Address of Simeon Church, reprinted in WSA, *Proceedings of Six Public Meetings . . .* (1871), meeting of January 11, 1871, 55.

2. John Kennion, *The Architects' and Builders' Guide* (New York: Fitzpatrick and Hunter, 1868), ix; *RERBG* (December 16, 1871).

3. Joel Benton, "The Physiognomy of the House," *Appleton's Journal* n.s. 1 (October 1876): 364; CV, *Villas and Cottages: A Series of Designs Prepared for Execution in the United States* (New York: Harper and Brothers, 1857), 21. For a somewhat different use of the idea of "moral environmentalism" in urban reform, stressing its sanitary and medical associations, see Stanley Schultz, *Constructing Urban Culture: American Cities and City Planning, 1800–1920* (Philadelphia: Temple University Press, 1989), 112–14. For the aesthetic and psychological assumptions of moral environmentalism, see also David Schuyler, *The New Urban Landscape: The Redefinition of City Form in Nineteenth-Century America* (Baltimore: Johns Hopkins University Press, 1986), 40–56; Charles E. Beveridge, "Frederick Law Olmsted's Theory of Landscape Design," *Nineteenth Century* 3 (Summer 1977): 38–43; and James A. Schmiechen, "The Victorians, the Historians, and the Idea of Modernism," *American Historical Review* 93 (April 1988): 287–316.

4. FLO, "Passages in the Life of an Unpractical Man" (ca. 1877), reprinted in Albert Fein (ed.), *Landscape into Cityscape: Frederick Law Olmsted's Plans for a Greater New York* (Ithaca, N.Y.: Cornell University Press, 1967), 52.

5. The best introduction to Victorian genteel journalism remains Frank Luther Mott's encyclopedic *A History of American Magazines* (Cambridge, Mass.: Harvard University Press, 1938), especially II, 4–26, 30–31, 383–405, 469–87, and III, 26, 388–90. See also Ann Douglas, *The Feminization of American Culture* (New York: Knopf, 1977), 229–40; and Eugene Exman, *The House of Harper: One Hundred and Fifty Years of Publishing* (New York: Harper and Row, 1967).

6. For the history of urban lithography, see Peter C. Marzio, *The Democratic Art: Chromolithography, 1840–1900* (Boston: D. R. Godine, 1979); and John Reps, *Views and Viewmakers of Urban America: Lithographs of Towns and Cities in the United States . . .* (Columbia: University of Missouri Press, 1984).

7. Important examples of exposé writing include Matthew Hale Smith, *Sunshine and Shadow in New York* (Hartford, Conn.: J. B. Burr, 1869); Junius Henri Browne, *The Great Metropolis: A*

Mirror of New York (Hartford, Conn.: American Publishing, 1869); and James D. McCabe, Jr., *New York by Sunlight and Gaslight* (Philadelphia: Hubbard Brothers, 1882).

8. "Changes In New York," *Leslie's Illustrated Weekly* 40 (May 22, 1875): 167; *Superintendent Reports* (1871–72), 54.

9. New York *World*, quoted in Kennion, *Architects' and Builders' Guide*, I, 36.

10. Address of Simeon Church, reprinted in WSA, *Proceedings of Six Public Meetings . . .* (1871), meeting of January 11, 1871, 55.

11. *RERBG* (July 28, 1883); [Henry Whitney Bellows,] "Cities and Parks: With Special Reference to the New York Central Park," *Atlantic Monthly* 7 (April 1861): 429.

12. *Report of John Roebling, C.E., to the President and Directors of the New York Bridge Company, on the Proposed East River Bridge* (Brooklyn: Daily Eagle Print, 1870), 3–4, 40–41, 46. The bridge was originally a franchised company; this report was Roebling's design proposal to the directors. In 1875 ownership and governance of the bridge were assumed by the municipalities of Brooklyn and New York. For the construction, governance, and financing of the bridge, see David McCullough, *The Great Bridge: The Epic Story of the Building of the Brooklyn Bridge* (New York: Simon and Schuster, 1972). My reading of Roebling's design and proposal to the New York Bridge Company builds on Alan Trachtenberg, *Brooklyn Bridge, Fact and Symbol* (Chicago: University of Chicago Press, 1979), 71–77.

13. "New York and Brooklyn," *RERBG* (December 16, 1871); *Report of John Roebling*, 41; shopwindow sign quoted in McCullough, *The Great Bridge*, 528.

The classic critique of the bridge's aesthetic heterogeneity is Montgomery Schuyler, "Brooklyn Bridge as a Monument," *Harper's Weekly* 27 (May 26, 1883). Lewis Mumford demurs from Schuyler's view in *The Brown Decades: A Study of the Arts in America, 1865–1895* (New York: Dover, 1971), 46–47. See also Alan Trachtenberg, "Brooklyn Bridge as a Cultural Text," *Bridge to the Future: A Centennial Celebration of the Brooklyn Bridge. Annals of the New York Academy of Sciences* 424 (1984): 213–17.

14. *Report of John Roebling*, 46, 18.

15. "The Bridge and Tunnel Era," *RERBG* (October 4, 1879); Olmsted, Vaux and Co., "Report of the Landscape Architects and Superintendents," in BCPP, *Eighth Annual Report* (Brooklyn: n.p., 1869), republished in Fein (ed.), *Landscape into Cityscape*, 155. For Brooklyn's reputation as a "City of Homes," see *RERBG*` (April 28, 1883): "While New York is a cosmopolitan city with a vast floating population . . . , Brooklyn is essentially a city of homes. . . . If it can give to our laboring and middle classes homes where their children can be brought up amidst healthy surroundings, both moral and physical . . . , allowing at the same time the head of the household . . . easy access to his daily toil, it will have done much for the benefit of the metropolis."

16. *Report of John Roebling*, 4.

17. William Dean Howells, *Their Wedding Journey* (Boston: J. R. Osgood, 1871), 28–29; Fitz-Hugh Ludlow, "The American Metropolis," *Atlantic Monthly* 15 (January 1865): 75, 74. For other examples of the "statistical sublime," see [WRM,] *The Growth of New York* (New York: George W. Wood, 1865), 5–11; *Report of John Roebling*, 41–44; address of Simeon E. Church, reprinted in WSA, *Proceedings of Six Public Meetings . . .* (New York, 1871), meeting of January 11, 1871, 41–55.

18. *RERBG* (July 5, 1873); Matthew Hale Smith et al., *Wonders of a Great City: or, The Sights, Secrets, and Sins of New York* (Chicago: People's, 1887), 794. I discuss the debate over the design of the Annexed District in Chapter 8.

19. FLO and J. James R. Croes, "Preliminary Report of the Landscape Architect and the Civil and Topographical Engineer, upon the Laying Out of the Twenty-third and Twenty-fourth Wards," BDPP, *Document No. 72* (1876), republished in Fein (ed.), *Landscape into Cityscape*, 352; [Bellows,] "Cities and Parks," 428.

20. Despite its significance to nineteenth-century culture and politics, scholars have not fully studied the role of "civilization" in the making of the bourgeois world. My own thinking has been enriched by two clusters of work. The first focuses on the racial and sexual hierarchies embedded in the discourse. See Robert Rydell, *All the World's a Fair: Visions of Empire at American International Expositions, 1876–1916* (Chicago: University of Chicago Press, 1984); Gail Bederman, *Manliness and Civilization: A Cultural History of Gender and Race in the United States, 1880–1917* (Chicago: University of Chicago Press, 1995); and Ann Laura Stoler, *Race and the Education of Desire: Foucault's History of Sexuality and the Colonial Order of Things* (Durham, N.C.: Duke University Press, 1995). The second looks at the history of "civilization" as a process of class differentiation based on techniques of self-management and bodily self-control. See especially Norbert Elias, *The Civilizing Process,* Volume I: *The History of Manners* (New York: Urizen Books, 1978); and John Kasson, *Rudeness and Civility: Manners in Nineteenth-Century Urban America* (New York: Hill and Wang, 1990).

New research on the discourse of "civilization" in nineteenth-century America will profit from exploring a book-length manuscript by FLO, "The Pioneer Condition and the Drift of Civilization in America," begun in the spring of 1865, while he was managing the Mariposa mining estate in California. The manuscript has been edited, assembled, and published for the first time in *FLOP* V, 577–763; for a useful gloss, see Melvin Kalfus, *Frederick Law Olmsted: The Passion of a Public Artist* (New York: New York University Press, 1990), 259–75.

21. For the reconstruction of nineteenth-century Paris, Vienna, London, and elsewhere, see the works cited in Chapter 1, note 17, as well as David P. Jordan, *Transforming Paris: The Life and Labors of Baron Haussmann* (New York: Free Press, 1995); David Owen, *The Government of Victorian London, 1855–1889: The Metropolitan Board of Works, the Vestries, and the City Corporation* (Cambridge, Mass.: Harvard University Press, 1982); Daniel M. Blustone, *Constructing Chicago* (New Haven, Conn.: Yale University Press, 1991); and Thomas Bender and Carl Schorske (eds.), *Budapest and New York: Studies in Metropolitan Transformation, 1870–1930* (New York: Russell Sage Foundation, 1994).

22. [WRM,] *Growth of New York*, 12, 14; "New York's Future" (interview with A. B. Mullett), *RERBG* (June 4, 1881); *Mr. V. K. Stevenson, Jr.'s, Views of City Real Estate, As Published in the "Daily Graphic"* (September 1879), 5.

23. Samuel B. Ruggles, *Letters on Rapid Transit* (New York: n.p., 1875), 14. For the links between the discourse of "civilization" and English theories of moral psychology and landscape aesthetics, see the sources cited in note 3.

24. I discuss these patterns of aesthetic and political conflict in Chapters 6 and 7.

25. *RERBG* (June 27, 1885); FLO, *Public Parks and the Enlargement of Towns* (1870), 35.

26. For the new steamship terminals, see "River Front Improvements," New York *Times* (March 31, 1870); for Grand Central Depot, see Carl Condit, *The Port of New York,* Volume I: *A History of the Rail and Terminal System from the Beginnings to Pennsylvania Station* (Chicago: University of Chicago Press, 1980), 86–92, and Carroll L.V. Meeks, *The Railroad Station: An Architectural History* (New Haven, Conn.: Yale University Press, 86–87, 100–101.

27. "New York's Grand West End," *RERBG* 24 (1879), 871; McCabe, *New York by Sunlight and Gaslight*, 182 (station design and interior style). The association of the el cars with voyeurism

and bourgeois *flânerie* is best known from William Dean Howells's *A Hazard of New Fortunes* (1890), but see also McCabe, *New York by Sunlight and Gaslight*, 185–94.

28. "The Growth of New York," *RERBG* (May 19, 1977); FLO et al., "Report to the Staten Island Improvement Commission . . ." (1870), reprinted in Fein (ed.), *Landscape into Cityscape*, 183, 205.

29. "The Growth of New York," *RERBG* (May 19, 1877); FLO and Croes, "Preliminary Report," in Fein (ed.), *Landscape into Cityscape*, 352.

30. Schuyler, *New Urban Landscape*, 167–79, similarly uses Olmsted and Croes's image of "a house with many rooms" as the anchor for his analysis of Olmsted's ideal of urban design; my own interpretation of the larger group of bourgeois urbanists owes much to his insightful reading.

31. "A Telegraph Palace," New York *Daily Graphic* (June 3, 1873); New York *Times* (March 8, 1872). Winston Weisman discusses the history and design of the Western Union building in "Commercial Palaces of New York, 1845–1875," *Art Bulletin* 36 (December 1954): 299, and "New York and the Problem of the First Skyscraper," *Journal of the Society of Architectural Historians* 12 (1953): 13–21.

32. *RERBG* (July 23, 1870); ibid. (March 19, 1881).

33. English visitor quoted in M. Christine Boyer, *Manhattan Manners: Architecture and Style, 1850–1900* (New York: Rizzoli, 1985); Paul Goldberger, *The Skyscraper* (New York: Knopf, 1981), 37–47; Kennion, *Architects' and Builders' Guide*, ix, x; Simeon Church, letter to *RERBG* (December 18, 1875). My reading of the shift in commercial architecture also relies on Weisman, "Commercial Palaces," and Meeks, *Railway Station*, 2–25.

34. *RERBG* (July 18, 1868). For the diffusion of the Second Empire style, see Henry-Russell Hitchcock, *Architecture: Nineteenth and Twentieth Centuries* (Baltimore: Johns Hopkins University Press, 1958), 151–70; and Charles Lockwood, *Bricks and Brownstone: The New York Rowhouse, 1783–1929: An Architectural and Social History* (New York: McGraw-Hill, 1972), 161–63.

35. *RERBG* (April 4, 1868).

36. *New York, the Eastern Gateway of the American Continent: Mayor Edson's Address . . .* (1883); *Appleton's New York Illustrated* (New York: D. Appleton, 1871), quoted in Weisman, "Commercial Palaces," 297. My thinking here has been inspired by Lewis Mumford's analysis of the links between imperial politics and urban spectacle in the baroque city; see *The City in History: Its Origins, Its Transformations, and Its Prospects* (New York: Harcourt, Brace, and World, 1961), 344–409.

37. Henry James, *The American Scene* (New York: Horizon Press, 1968), 77; "Big Bonanza Buildings," *RERBG* (April 8, 1876); Montgomery Schuyler, "The Evolution of the Skyscraper," *Scribner's Monthly* 46 (September 1909): 259.

38. Simeon Church, letter to *RERBG* (December 18, 1875); Kennion, *Architects' and Builders' Guide*, ix, x.

39. *Miller's New York as It Is* (New York: J. Miller, 1866), 128. For similar accounts of the Broadway scene, see Browne, *Great Metropolis*, 29; and McCabe, *New York by Sunlight and Gaslight*, 144.

40. Walter Benjamin, "Paris, Capital of the Nineteenth Century," *Reflections* (New York: Schocken Books, 1978), 156; James Burn, *Three Years among the Working-Classes in the United States* (London: Smith, Elder, 1865), 117–18; [H. T. Tuckerman,] "Through Broadway," *Atlantic Monthly* 18 (December 1866): 727.

41. See Mary Douglas, *Purity and Danger: An Analysis of the Concepts of Pollution and Taboo* (London: Routledge and Kegan Paul, 1966).

42. FLO, *Public Parks and the Enlargement of Towns*, 11; Georg Simmel, "The Metropolis and Mental Life" (1902), reprinted in Georg Simmel, *On Individuality and Social Forms* (Chicago: University of Chicago Press, 1971); "The Public Streets—A Step Toward a Useful Reform," New York *Times* (March 9, 1869).

43. FLO, *Public Parks and the Enlargement of Towns*, 20; "Pauperism in the City of New York," *Journal of Social Science* (1875), 76. For the use of the streets by the laboring poor, see Christine Stansell, "Women, Children, and the Uses of the Streets: Class and Gender Conflict in New York City, 1850–1860," *Feminist Studies* 8, no. 2 (Summer 1982): 309–35.

44. CLB, *The Dangerous Classes of New York, and Twenty Years' Work among Them* (New York: Wynkoop and Hallenbeck, 1872), 79, 78. For other examples of the preoccupation with street children, see Charles Dawson Shanly, "The Small Arabs of New York," *Atlantic Monthly* 23 (March 1869): 279–86; "The Hearth-Stone of the Poor," *Harper's Weekly* (February 12, 1876); Edward Crapsey, *The Nether Side of New York* (New York: Sheldon, 1872), 119–27; and, most importantly, early Horatio Alger stories like *Ragged Dick* (Boston: Loring, 1867).

45. "The Public Streets—A Step Toward a Useful Reform," New York *Times* (March 9, 1869); "Street Obstructions," ibid. (August 10, 1869); "The Sidewalk Trade," ibid. (August 25, 1867); "Sidewalk Nuisances and Obstructions," ibid. (March 31, 1869); *Harper's Weekly* (August 15, 1868); Christine Stansell, *City of Women: Sex and Class in New York, 1789–1860* (New York: Knopf, 1986). For the campaign against "outdoor relief," see "Pauperism in the City of New York"; and [E. L. Godkin,] "The Educational Influence of Free Soup," *The Nation* (May 9, 1876): 155. For the movement against vice, see Crapsey, *Nether Side*; and Timothy Gilfoyle, *City of Eros: New York City, Prostitution, and the Commercialization of Sex, 1790–1920* (New York: W. W. Norton, 1992), 181–96.

46. *Report of the New York City Council of Political Reform, 1872–74* (1874), 22.

47. AHG, "Communication . . . Relative to the Laying Out of the Island above 155th Street . . . , and Other Subjects," BCCP, *Tenth Annual Report* (1866), 142; *RERBG* (March 8, 1873).

48. Olmsted, Vaux and Co., "Report of the Landscape Architects," in Fein (ed.), *Landscape into Cityscape*, 152; Charles Astor Bristed, *A Few Words of Warning to New Yorkers, on the Consequences of a Railroad in Fifth Avenue . . .* (New York: W. C. Bryant, 1863), 11–12. For other examples of the centrality of promenading to elite ideals of street life and public culture, see AHG, "Communication . . . Relative to the Laying Out of the Island," 106; and [WRM,] *Growth of New York*, 34, 38–40. I analyze the centrality of promenading to bourgeois culture in "Anatomy of the Promenade: The Politics of Bourgeois Sociability in Nineteenth-Century New York," *Social History* 17, no. 2 (May 1992): 203–28.

49. Olmsted and Croes, "Preliminary Report," in Fein (ed.), *Landscape into Cityscape*, 353; Crapsey, *Nether Side*, 115.

50. Crapsey, *Nether Side*, 115.

51. For the links between Victorian domestic ideology and home design, see Clifford E. Clark, Jr., *The American Family Home, 1800–1960* (Chapel Hill: University of North Carolina Press, 1986); Gwendolyn Wright, *Moralism and the Model Home* (Chicago: University of Chicago Press, 1979); and David Scobey, "What Shall We Do with Our Walls? The Philadelphia Centennial and the Meaning of Household Design," in Robert W. Rydell and Nancy E. Gwinn (eds.), *Fair Representations: World's Fairs and the Modern World* (Amsterdam: VU University Press, 1994), 87–120. For statements on household design by New York–based tastemakers and professionals, see Catherine Beecher and Harriet Beecher Stowe, *The American Woman's Home* (New York: J. B. Ford, 1869); CV, *Villas and Cottages: A Series of Designs Prepared for Execution in the United States* (New York: Harper and Brothers, 1857); Clarence Cook, *The House Beautiful:*

Essays on Bed and Tables, Stools and Candlesticks (New York: Scribner's Sons, 1877); and Charles Wyllys Elliott, *The Book of American Interiors* (Boston: J. R. Osgood, 1876). Elliott was one of the original members of the Central Park board and the commissioner who told Olmsted about the opening of the post of superintendent in 1857.

52. E. L. Godkin, "The Rights of the Citizen . . . to His Own Reputation," *Scribner's Magazine* 8, no. 1 (July 1890): 65. For the proliferation of interior surfaces in Victorian interior design, see Scobey, "What Shall We Do with Our Walls," 111–12; and Jean-Christophe Agnew, "A House of Fiction: Domestic Interiors and the Commodity Aesthetic," in Simon Bronner (ed.), *Consuming Visions: Accumulation and Display of Goods in America, 1880–1920* (New York: W. W. Norton, 1989), 133–56.

53. On the multiplication of specialized spaces in bourgeois domestic design, see the sources cited in note 51, as well as Lockwood, *Bricks and Brownstone*, 164–83; and Gwendolyn Wright, *Building the Dream: A Social History of Housing in America* (Cambridge, Mass.: MIT Press, 1981), 38–46, 62.

54. For the interior plan of Manhattan row houses, see William Alex and George B. Tatum, *Calvert Vaux: Architect and Planner* (New York: Ink, 1994), 94–95 (Gray residence); Lockwood, *Bricks and Brownstone*, 164–83; and *Description of a New York Gentleman's Dwelling House* (1871).

55. On the experience of servants in New York households, see Lockwood, *Bricks and Brownstone*, 180–89; and David M. Katzman, *Seven Days a Week: Women and Domestic Service in Industrializing America* (Urbana: University of Illinois Press, 1981), 18–20, 59, 64, 66, 84–85, 101–4, 114, 138, 162–63, 207–11.

56. For the monumental treatment of the row house street facade, see Lockwood, *Bricks and Brownstone*, 143; for the use of hallways as ceremonial spaces, see Kenneth L. Ames, "Meaning in Artifacts: Hall Furnishings in Victorian America," in Dell Upton and John Michael Vlach (eds.), *Common Places: Readings in American Vernacular Architecture* (Athens: University of Georgia Press, 1986), 240–60. For parlor culture, see Karen Halttunen, *Confidence Men and Painted Women: A Study of Middle-Class Culture in America, 1830–1879* (New Haven, Conn.: Yale University Press, 1982), 59–60, 101–6; and Katherine C. Grier, *Culture and Comfort: People, Parlors, and Upholstery, 1850–1930* (Rochester, N.Y.: Strong Museum, 1988).

57. *Offering of Six Elegant New Houses by Duggin and Crossman, Architects . . .* (November 24, 1874); *Description, Diagrams and Prices of an Assortment of Choice New Dwellings for Sale Built by Charles Buek, Architect . . .* (1880); *New York Illustrated* (1885), 31. Ann Douglas stresses the trend toward splendor and consumer acquisitiveness in urban norms of domesticity in *The Feminization of American Culture* (New York: Knopf, 1977), 70–80.

58. *RERBG* (May 15, 1883); Harriet Beecher Stowe, *My Wife and I* (New York: J. B. Ford, 1871), 189–90, 471. See also Douglas's reading of this novel and its sequel, *We and Our Neighbors* (New York: J. B. Ford, 1875), in *Feminization of American Culture*, 76, 169, 300–305.

59. Junius Henri Browne, "The Problem of Living in New York," *Harper's New Monthly Magazine* 65 (November 1882): 918; Crapsey, *Nether Side*, 7. I discuss the redevelopment of St. John's Park as a freight terminal and the ritual of May Day moving in Chapter 2.

60. Crapsey, *Nether Side*, 8; FLO and Croes, "Preliminary Report," in Fein (ed.), *Landscape into Cityscape*, 354; Browne, "Problem of Living in New York," 924

61. Crapsey, *Nether Side*, 8; Browne, "Problem of Living in New York," 920; *Superintendent Reports* (1871–72), 54–55 (estimate of businessmen living outside of Manhattan); Henry W. Bellows, "The Townward Tendency," *The City: An Illustrated Magazine* (January 1872): 38–39.

62. "Boarding Out," *Harper's Weekly* (March 7, 1857): 146; George W. Curtis, "The Best Society of New York," *Putnam's Monthly*, reprinted in New York *Tribune Semi-Weekly* (February 3,

1853). For an analysis of this reform critique of urbane domesticity, see Scobey, "What Shall We Do with Our Walls," 112–14.

63. "Houses and Rents in New-York," *Commercial and Financial Chronicle* (July 8, 1865); Brace, *Dangerous Classes*, 55; FLO, "The Future of New-York," New York *Daily Tribune* (December 28, 1879). See also Crapsey, *Nether Side,* 110–37.

64. Crapsey, *Nether Side,* 9. Crapsey's introduction, 5–13, offers perhaps the best summary statement of bourgeois anxiety over New York's crises in the early 1870s and its relationship to the failure of domesticity in Manhattan.

65. George Templeton Strong, *The Diary of George Templeton Strong*, ed. Allan Nevins and Milton Halsey Thomas (New York: Macmillan, 1952), IV, 236. Strong's diary offers a vivid record of this legitimation crisis among the metropolitan gentry—often expressed, in Strong's case, with growing racism. See, for instance, the entries for May 20, 1869 (ibid., 245–46), September 16, 1874 (ibid., 538), and this comment on February 3, 1872 (ibid., 411): "We are living in a day of ruffianism and of almost universal corruption. Life and property are as insecure here in New York as in Mexico. It is a thoroughly rotten community . . ."

66. Elizabeth Blackmar, "Housing and Property Relations In New York City, 1785–1850," (Ph.D. dissertation, Harvard University, 1981), 262.

67. FLO, "Future of New-York."

Chapter 6

1. "The Street Question," New York *Times* (October 16, 1868).

2. *RERBG* (June 19, 1869). For references to the Avenue de l'Impératrice by Olmsted and Vaux, see Olmsted, Vaux and Co., "Report of the Landscape Architects," BCPP, *Eighth Annual Report*, 158; and Olmsted, Vaux and Co., "Report of the Landscape Architects and Superintendents," BCPP, *Eleventh Annual Report* (1871), in *FLOP* VI, 411. For overviews of "Haussmannization," see David Pinckney, *Napoleon III and the Rebuilding of Paris* (Princeton, N.J.: Princeton University Press, 1972); and David Harvey, "Paris 1850–1870," in Harvey, *Consciousness and the Urban Experience: Studies in the History and Theory of Capitalist Urbanization* (Baltimore: Johns Hopkins University Press, 1985), 63–220.

3. *Commercial and Financial Chronicle* (December 22, 1866).

4. George W. Curtis, "The Streets of New York," in *Other Essays from the Easy Chair* (New York: Harper and Brothers, 1893), 75; *RERBG* (September 26, 1868).

5. Address of WRM, reprinted in WSA, *Proceedings of Six Public Meetings . . .* (1871), meeting of May 26, 1871, 9.

6. *RERBG* (June 12, 1869).

7. For the values, networks, and reform initiatives of this gentry, see George Fredrickson, *The Inner Civil War: Northern Intellectuals and the Crisis of the Union* (New York: Harper and Row, 1965), especially 98–112, 183–238; John Sproat, *"The Best Men": Liberal Reformers in the Gilded Age* (New York: Oxford University Press, 1968); John Tomsich, *A Genteel Endeavor: American Culture and Politics in the Gilded Age* (Stanford, Calif.: Stanford University Press, 1971); and David D. Hall, "The Victorian Connection," in Daniel W. Howe (ed.), *Victorian America* (Philadelphia: University of Pennsylvania Press, 1976), 81–94.

8. [E. L. Godkin,] "The Future of Great Cities," *The Nation* (February 22, 1866).

9. The most detailed and useful treatment of Olmsted's life remains Laura Wood Roper, *FLO: A Biography of Frederick Law Olmsted* (Baltimore: Johns Hopkins University Press, 1973).

Melvin Kalfus, *Frederick Law Olmsted: The Passion of a Public Artist* (New York: New York University Press, 1990) offers an insightful psychological interpretation of Olmsted's career crises. The editors' introductions to *FLOP* III and VI—which concern Central Park and the design partnership with Calvert Vaux, respectively—provide a helpful overview of Olmsted's city-building work in New York.

10. FLO, "Report . . . ," in BCCP, *12th Annual Report* (1868), 51. For the social and design theories that informed Olmsted and Vaux's work, the most important documents include Olmsted's 1870 lecture to the American Social Science Association, *Public Parks and the Enlargement of Towns* (Boston: American Social Science Association, 1870); Olmsted, Vaux and Co., "Preliminary Report . . . for Laying Out a Park in Brooklyn," BCPP, *6th Annual Report* (1866), reprinted in Albert Fein (ed.), *Landscape into Cityscape: Frederick Law Olmsted's Plans for a Greater New York City* (Ithaca, N.Y.: Cornell University Press, 1967), 95–127; Olmsted, Vaux and Co., "Report of the Landscape Architects," BCPP, *8th Annual Report* (1868), reprinted in ibid., 129–64; and FLO and J.J.R. Croes, "Preliminary Report . . . upon the Laying Out of the Twenty-third and Twenty-fourth Wards," reprinted in ibid., 349–58. The most relevant scholarship on his design and reform work in New York includes David Schuyler, *The New Urban Landscape: The Redefinition of City Form in Nineteenth-Century America* (Baltimore: Johns Hopkins University Press, 1986), especially 77–100, 114–30, 167–79; Geoffrey Blodgett, "Frederick Law Olmsted: Landscape Architecture as Conservative Reform," *Journal of American History* 62 (March 1976): 869–89; and Albert Fein's introduction to *Landscape into Cityscape*, 1–42.

11. The Citizens' Association has not been systematically studied; my account derives mainly from its voluminous pamphlet literature. It is treated briefly in Iver Bernstein, *The New York City Draft Riots: Their Significance for American Society and Politics in the Age of the Civil War* (New York: Oxford University Press, 1990), 187–90; and Charles Rosenberg, *The Cholera Years: The United States in 1832, 1849, and 1866* (Chicago: University of Chicago Press, 1962), 187–88.

12. *Report of the Committee on Wharves and Piers, Appointed at a Public Meeting of Merchants . . .* (New York: n.p., 1868), 7. I discuss initiatives for tenement reform and dock improvement in the next chapter.

13. David C. Hammack, "Comprehensive Planning Before the Comprehensive Plan: A New Look at the Nineteenth Century American City," in Daniel Schaffer (ed.), *Two Centuries of American Planning* (Baltimore: Johns Hopkins University Press, 1988), 139–65. For the life and career of James Stranahan, see Donald Simon, "The Public Park Movement in Brooklyn, 1824–1873" (Ph.D. dissertation, New York University, 1972); and Harold Coffin Syrett, *The City of Brooklyn: A Political History* (New York: Columbia University Press, 1944), 139–58.

14. New York *World* (1868), quoted in John Foord, *The Life and Public Services of Andrew H. Green* (New York: Doubleday, Page, 1913), 86. For Green's background and early legal and political career, see ibid., 3–39. For his work on the Central Park commission, see ibid., 48–76; *FLOP* III, 26–40, 55–59; and Roy Rosenzweig and Elizabeth Blackmar, *The Park and the People: A History of Central Park* (Ithaca, N.Y., 1992), 180–205. Other helpful scholarship includes Hammack, "Comprehensive Planning"; Hammack, *Power and Society: Greater New York at the Turn of the Century* (New York: Russell Sage Foundation, 1982), 185–229; and Barry J. Kaplan, "Andrew H. Green and the Creation of a Planning Rationale: The Formation of Greater New York, 1865–1890," *Urbanism Past and Present* 8 (Summer 1979).

15. AHG address to stall owners in Washington Market in March 1872, quoted in Foord, *Life and Public Services*, 122. I discuss Green's parsimonious record as city comptroller in Chapter 8.

16. I discuss Green's efforts to transform the Central Park board into a planning agency in Chapter 7. For his role in the founding of cultural and educational institutions, see Hammack, "Comprehensive Planning," and Foord, *Life and Public Services*, 204.

17. For Samuel Ruggles's real-estate and planning efforts, see D. G. Brinton Thompson, *Ruggles of New York: A Life of Samuel B. Ruggles* (New York: Columbia University Press, 1946), 56–72; Carole Klein, *Gramercy Park: An American Bloomsbury* (Boston: Houghton Mifflin, 1987), 3–73; and Samuel B. Ruggles, *Letters on Rapid Transit* (New York: n.p., 1875). For a brief sketch of the *Real Estate Record*, see David Scobey, "*Real Estate Record and Builders' Guide*," in Kenneth Jackson (ed.), *Encyclopedia of New York City* (New Haven, Conn.: Yale University Press, 1995). Robin Einhorn stresses the incrementalism of real-estate development in midcentury Chicago in *Property Rules: Political Economy in Chicago, 1833–1872* (Chicago: University of Chicago Press, 1991).

18. Statement of purpose and leadership roster taken from WSA, *Proceedings of Six Public Meetings . . .* (1871); *RERBG* (March 29, 1873). The West Side Association has not received a full-blown scholarly analysis, but it is briefly discussed in Bernstein, *New York Draft Riots*, 205–9; Rozenzweig and Blackmar, *Park and the People*, 268, 275; and M. Christine Boyer, *Manhattan Manners: Architecture and Style, 1850–1900* (New York: Rizzoli, 1985), 152–53.

19. "East and West Side Associations," *RERBG* (May 9, 1868); "The East Side Association," ibid., (June 27, 1868); address of Simeon E. Church, reprinted in WSA, *Meeting at Harvard Hall* (March 18, 1875), 22–23; address of WRM, reprinted in WSA, Proceedings . . . , Meeting of April 12, 1877, 11, 13.

20. WRM, "Communication . . . Relative to the Plans and Improvement of the Fort Washington District and the Twenty-third and Twenty-fourth Wards," BDPP document reprinted as "The Growth of New York," *RERBG Supplement* (June 19, 1875), 6. Martin's most important statements are *The Growth of New York* (New York: George W. Wood, 1865); "The Financial Resources of New York," *North American Review* 127 (1878): 427–43; the addresses in WSA, *Proceedings of Six Public Meetings . . . ; A Communication Relative to the Prosecution of Public Improvements in This City* (New York: n.p., 1875); "Communication . . . Relative to . . . the Fort Washington District"; and Martin and Joseph J. O'Donohue, *Statement in Reference to the Operations of the Department During the Year 1875* (New York: n.p., 1876). Martin has received scant attention from scholars, with the exception of Seymour J. Mandelbaum, *Boss Tweed's New York* (New York: J. Wiley, 1965), 114–30; Roper, *FLO*, 348–62; and Bernstein, *New York Draft Riots*, 207–8.

21. S. E. Church, *Rapid Transit in the City of New York* (New York: Great American Engineering and Printing, 1872); *RERBG* (January 6, 1872).

22. *RERBG* (December 30, 1871).

23. FLO, "Influence," unpublished manuscript in FLO Papers; FLO to CLB (December 6, 1860) in *FLOP* III, 286. See also the helpful reconstruction of this episode in Rosenzweig and Blackmar, *Park and the People*, 151–54.

24. See Eric Monkkonen, *America Becomes Urban: The Development of U.S. Cities and Towns, 1780–1980* (Berkeley: University of California Press, 1988); Jon Teaford, *The Unheralded Triumph: City Government in America, 1870–1900* (Baltimore: Johns Hopkins University Press, 1984); and Terrence McDonald, "The Burdens of Urban History: The Theory of the State in Recent American History," *Studies in American Political Development* 3 (1989): 3–29.

25. For New York's behavior as a proprietary corporation in the colonial and early national period, see Hendrik Hartog, *Public Property and Private Power: The Corporation of the City of New York in American Law, 1730–1870* (Chapel Hill: University of North Carolina Press, 1983). On

volunteer fire fighting, see Richard Calhoun, "New York City Fire Department Reorganization, 1865–1870," *New-York Historical Society Quarterly* 60 (January/April 1876): 6–34. On water supply before the opening of the Croton Aqueduct in 1842, see Edward K. Spann, *The New Metropolis: New York City, 1840–1857* (New York: Columbia University Press, 1981), 117. On the watch system, see ibid., 54–55. I discuss local assessments for public works in Chapter 3.

26. On the localism and incoherence of municipal government prior to the 1850s, see Spann, *New Metropolis,* 45–66, and Eugene Moehring, *Public Works and the Patterns of Urban Real Estate Growth in Manhattan, 1835–1894* (New York: Arno, 1981), 369; on the fluidity and fragmentation of Democratic Party politics, see Jerome Mushkat, *Tammany: The Evolution of a Political Machine, 1789–1865* (Syracuse, N.Y.: Syracuse University Press) (quoted phrase is from p. 237).

27. See Edward Dana Durand, *The Finances of New York City* (New York: Macmillan, 1898), 376 (budget expenditures), 372–73 (property tax rates); Durand is an indispensable starting point for research into the fiscal history of nineteenth-century New York. For an overview of the era's multiple charter revisions, see Spann, *New Metropolis,* 60–64, 324–55, 385–87; and Alexander B. Callow, Jr., *The Tweed Ring* (New York: Oxford University Press, 1965), 78–80, 222–35.

28. For Wood's consolidation of partisan rule, see Jerome Mushkat, *Fernando Wood: A Political Biography* (Kent, Ohio: Kent State University Press, 1990), 41–81; Spann, *New Metropolis,* 358–400; and Blackmar and Rosenzweig, *Park and the People,* 56–57, 96–97. For the rise of commission rule, see ibid., 95–99; James Mohr, *The Radical Republicans and Reform in New York During Reconstruction* (Ithaca, N.Y.: Cornell University Press, 1973), 21–114; and Mandelbaum, *Boss Tweed's New York,* 59–66.

29. See, in addition to the sources in the previous note, Nelson M. Blake, *Water for the Cities* (Syracuse, N.Y.: Syracuse University Press, 1956); and Wilbur Miller, *Cops and Bobbies: Police Authority in New York and London, 1830–1870* (Chicago: University of Chicago Press, 1977). I discuss health regulations, building codes, and park design in the next chapter.

30. Report of the Committee of Seventy by Samuel B. Ruggles, Henry Nicoll, and James M. Brown, reprinted in New York *Times* (February 12, 1872) (eminent domain takings prior to 1850); AHG, *Public Improvements in the City of New York* (1874), 5–6 (land acquisition costs for Central Park and other uptown improvements).

31. Spann, *New Metropolis,* 46–47 (government employment in the 1840s); BCCP, *Annual Report* (1867), 22 (levels of employment in Central Park); Rosenzweig and Blackmar, *Park and the People.*

32. For the legal history of the franchise system, see John F. Dillon, *Commentaries on the Law of Municipal Corporations,* 5th ed. (Boston: Little, Brown, 1911), III, 1904–2087; Morton J. Horwitz, *The Transformation of American Law, 1780–1860* (Cambridge, Mass.: Harvard University Press, 1979), 109–39. For transit franchises in New York, see Harry James Carman, *The Street Surface Railway Franchises of New York City, Columbia University Studies in History, Economics, and Public Law* 88, no. 1 (1919); and James Blaine Walker, *Fifty Years of Rapid Transit* (New York: Law Printing, 1918). Spann discusses corruption in the granting of horse car franchises in *New Metropolis,* 297–305. For projects that were enfranchised but remained unbuilt, see Rebecca Read Shanor, *The City That Never Was* (New York: Viking, 1988).

33. Durand, *Finances,* 374–75, 379.

34. Report of the Committee of Seventy by Samuel B. Ruggles, Henry Nicoll, and James M. Brown, reprinted in New York *Times* (February 12, 1872), details the changing share of land acquisition costs paid through local assessments from antebellum parks and squares to the up-

town improvements of the 1870s. Rosenzweig and Blackmar, *Park and the People*, discuss the antiassessment movement (33) and the negotiations over the siting and finance of the New York park (45–54).

35. "Why Municipal Debts?" *RERBG* (March 28, 1885). For the centrality of debt finance to nineteenth-century urban development and politics, see Eric Monkkonen, *America Becomes Urban*, especially 138–44; Morton Keller, *Affairs of State: Public Life in Late Nineteenth Century America* (Cambridge, Mass.: Harvard University Press, 1977), 115–17; and Einhorn, *Property Rules*.

36. This section and the next one engage one of the classic themes of urban historiography: the relationship between "machine politics" and "reform." It should be noted that some scholars, notably David Hammack, argue for the jettisoning of the machine/reform binary as a self-serving ideological fiction of antiparty elites at the turn of the century. In the late nineteenth and early twentieth centuries, Hammack argues, urban politics was structured around competition among relatively fluid—but also relatively interconnected—elites; its hallmark was the pluralistic, hardheaded pursuit of interests, not a morally inflected struggle between two opposing modes of political organization. See Hammack, *Power and Society*, especially 307–26.

Other scholars, notably Amy Bridges, have sought to rehabilitate the dualistic paradigm by combining it with an analysis of class relations in the capitalist city; see especially Bridges, *A City in the Republic: Antebellum New York and the Origins of Machine Politics* (New York: Cambridge University Press, 1984). While I agree with Hammack's critique of the elite moralism tacit in the machine/reform model, my argument follows Bridges in seeking to reactivate it. The machine/reform binary is useful, I argue, because it refers not only to rival coalitions but also to alternative conceptions of state power and class order. At the same time, city building in New York tended to complicate any clear-cut sense of political divisions; as I argue at the end of the chapter, persistent, classwide commonalties underlay the conflicts between "reformers" and "politicos" over spatial change in New York.

37. For the centrality of class negotiations in a city marked by both volatile growth and mass suffrage, see Bridges, *A City in the Republic*. On the notion of "blocs" as heterogeneous class formations, see Antonio Gramsci, "The Modern Prince," *Selections from the Prison Notebooks* (London: Lawrence and Wishart, 1971), 123–205.

38. My analysis of the party organization as a brokering institution relies on William Ivins, *Machine Politics and Money in New York City* (New York: Harper and Brothers, 1887); Keller, *Affairs of State*, 238–68; and Robert Merton's classic article, "The Latent Functions of the Machine," reprinted in Alexander B. Callow, Jr., *American Urban History* (New York: Oxford University Press, 1969), 291–300.

39. On the success with which the Democratic halls mobilized working-class (especially immigrant) voters, see Jon Allswang, *Bosses, Machines, and Urban Voters* (Baltimore: Johns Hopkins University Press, 1986), especially 45–52. For the entrepreneurs (often in the building trades) who tended to become Democratic ward leaders, see Moehring, *Public Works*, 256–67; and Bernstein, *New York Draft Riots*, 285.

40. Quoted from Bridges, *City in the Republic*, 151. For the antimoralistic, rough culture from which machine politics drew its style and recruitment strategies, see Richard Stott, *Workers in the Metropolis: Class, Ethnicity, and Youth in Antebellum New York City* (Ithaca, N.Y.: Cornell University Press, 1990), 247–76; and Elliot Gorn, *The Manly Art: Bare-Knuckle Prize Fighting in America* (Ithaca, N.Y.: Cornell University Press, 1986).

41. On patronage levels in the first years of Central Park, see FLO to CLB (December 6, 1860) in *FLOP* III, 286, and Rosenzweig and Blackmar, *Park and the People,* 151–58; for the Tweed era, see BDPP, *Report . . . Relative to the Condition of the Accounts . . .* Document No. 30, November 28, 1871, 19. The estimate of twelve thousand patronage jobs comes from the (admittedly biased) *Nation* (October 12, 1871).

42. On the passage and provisions of the 1870 city charter, see Callow, *Tweed Ring,* 222–35; and Mandelbaum, *Boss Tweed's New York,* 71–72.

43. *RERBG* (June 25, 1870) (Tweed contract announcements); Moehring, *Public Works,* 256–67, 321 (contracts to Tammany insiders, volume of street projects); New York City, Department of Public Works, *Communication . . . of Streets and Parts of Streets and Avenues, Opened . . . North of Fifty-ninth Street,* Board of Aldermen Document No. 6 (April 3, 1874) (volume of uptown street openings); *RERBG* (June 11, 1870) and report of the Committee of Seventy by Samuel B. Ruggles, Henry Nicoll, and James M. Brown, reprinted in New York *Times* (February 12, 1872) (uptown park and boulevard improvements and monetary awards); *RERBG* (April 15, 1871) (Riverside Park commissioners of estimate); ibid. (January 28, 1871) (Tweed foreclosure).

44. Moehring, *Public Works,* 320–21 (Tammany real-estate activity); *RERBG* (July 1, 1871) (East Side operations of politicians); McCullough, *Great Bridge,* 122–40 (Tweed ring investments in Brooklyn Bridge); *RERBG* (June 3, 1871) (Viaduct railway).

45. New York *Times* (April 8, 1870); *RERBG* (June 11 and June 18, 1870). For commercial and reform support of the home-rule charter, see Callow, *Tweed Ring,* 227 and *Memorial of the Citizens' Association of New-York . . . in Favor of the New Charter . . .* (1870). See also Bernstein, *Draft Riots,* 195–219.

46. "Haussmann the Little," New York *Times* (October 24, 1870); "The Imperial Ring," *Harper's Weekly* (February 11, 1871).

47. For an overview of the new commissions, see Mohr, *Radical Republicans;* for the "police war" between the state-appointed Metropolitan Police and Wood's "Municipals," see Spann, 392–93.

48. John F. Butterworth, letter to FLO, *FLOP* III, 229n; CA, *The Constitutional Convention, The Metropolitan Commissions . . .* (1867), 5.

49. On Minturn, Bryant, and other genteel supporters of an uptown park, see Blackmar and Rosenzweig, *Park and the People,* 15–36. For the founding of the Metropolitan Board of Health, see John Duffy, *A History of Public Health in New York City, Volume II: 1866–1966* (New York: Russell Sage Foundation, 1974), 1–47; and Charles Rosenberg, *Cholera Years,* 175–212.

50. FLO, *Public Parks and the Enlargement of Towns,* 25–26; FLO to John Butterworth, *FLOP* III, 228–29. The ideal of the fiduciary basis of social order received its definitive expression in Charles Francis Adams, Jr.'s trenchant account of the Wall Street "Erie wars." See Charles Francis Adams, Jr., and Henry Adams, *Chapters of Erie* (Ithaca, N.Y.: Cornell University Press, 1956), 8: "The theory of representation, whether in politics or in business, is of the essence of modern development. Our whole system rests upon the sanctity of fiduciary relations."

51. For the expansion of the Central Park commission's duties, see AHG, "Communication . . . Relative to the Laying Out of the Island above 155th Street . . . , and Other Subjects," BCCP, *10th Annual Report* (1866), 100–148; "Communication . . . Relative to Westchester County . . . ," BCCP, *13th Annual Report* (1869), 148–63; and "Communication . . . on the Subject of Improvements in Westchester County," BCCP, *14th Annual Report* (1870), 37–56; address of H. B. Bacon,

reprinted in WSA, *Proceedings of Six Public Meetings . . .* (1871), meeting of March 8, 1871, 41–42; Foord, *Life and Public Services*, 204–9.

52. FLO, *Public Parks and the Enlargement of Towns*, 29, 30, 26. Olmsted stressed the importance of study and travel to the profession of landscape design in "The Spoils of the Park" (1882), reprinted in Fein (ed.), *Landscape into Cityscape*, 423–26.

53. FLO, "The Spoils of the Park," 440, 429. Olmsted wrote this pamphlet several years after he had left New York as a manifesto against the politics of patronage.

54. FLO to CLB (December 6, 1860), in *FLOP* III, 286; FLO to Mary Olmsted (July 24, 1877), quoted in Fein (ed.), *Landscape into Cityscape*, 386.

55. FLO to John Olmsted (January 14, 1858), in *FLOP* III, 113; FLO to CLB (December 6, 1860), in Fein (ed.), *Landscape into Cityscape*, 286. For Olmsted's hiring policies, personnel rules, and time management, see "Rights of Men Employed," in ibid., 296–97; and Blackmar and Rosenzweig, *Park and the People*, 172–79.

56. "Instructions to the Keepers of the Central Park" (1872), reprinted in Frederick Law Olmsted, Jr., and Theodora Kimball (eds.), *Forty Years of Landscape Architecture* (Cambridge, Mass.: MIT Press, 1973), 451; FLO, *Public Parks and the Enlargement of Towns*, 34.

57. FLO to CLB (December 1, 1853), in *FLOP* II, 235, 236.

58. [Henry W. Bellows,] "Cities and Parks: With Special Reference to the New York Central Park," *Atlantic Monthly* 7 (April 1861): 421, 422.

59. For Dillon's proposed amendments to the Greensward Plan and Olmsted's response, see FLO to BCCP (May 31, 1858), *FLOP* III, 193–97; and Rosenzweig and Blackmar, *Park and the People*, 142–49.

60. For an overview of the tensions between Olmsted and Green, see Roper, *FLO*, 54–55; introduction to *FLOP* II, 54–56. For Dillon's suggestion of the segregated transportation circuits, see Rosenzweig and Blackmar, 144–45.

61. CV to FLO (June 3, 1865), in *FLOP* III, 387; CV to Clarence Cook, quoted in Schuyler, *New Urban Landscape*, 99; CV to FLO (July 31, 1865), *FLOP* III, 419. For an overview of Olmsted and Vaux's complex relationship, see *FLOP* III, 63–68, and Rosenzweig and Blackmar, 123–26.

62. CV to FLO (July 8, 1865; July 31, 1865; May 22, 1865), in *FLOP* III, 404, 419, 377.

63. New York *World* (1868), quoted in Foord, *Life and Letters*, 36; [Bellows,] "Cities and Parks," 421, 422.

64. Gramsci, "Modern Prince," 132–33.

Chapter 7

1. *RERBG* (December 23, 1883); FLO and J.J.R. Croes, "Preliminary Report of the Landscape Architect and the Civil and Topographical Engineer, upon the Laying Out of the Twenty-third and Twenty-fourth Wards . . ." (1876), reprinted in Albert Fein (ed.), *Landscape into Cityscape: Frederick Law Olmsted's Plans for a Growing New York* (Ithaca, N.Y.: Cornell University Press, 1967), 352.

2. [WRM,] *The Growth of New York* (New York, 1865), 34; FLO and J.J.R. Croes, "Report of the Landscape Architect and the Civil and Topographical Engineer, Accompanying a Plan for Laying Out That Part of the Twenty-fourth Ward Lying West of the Riverdale Road" (1876), reprinted in Fein (ed.) *Landscape into Cityscape*, 366; [WRM], *Growth of New York*, 34; FLO and Croes, "Preliminary Report," in Fein (ed.), *Landscape into Cityscape*, 353.

3. Restrictive covenants quoted in Morgan Dix and Charles Bridgman, *A History of the Parish of Trinity Church* (New York: Putnam, 1898), V, 66 (St. John's Park); Elizabeth Blackmar, "Housing and Property Relations in New York City, 1785–1850" (Ph.D. dissertation, Harvard, 1981), 426; *Adrian H. Muller, Auctioneer. Executor's Sale of Valuable Property on the Grand Boulevard . . . on Tuesday, October* 14, 1873; "An Act to Open and Widen Portions of Sackett, Douglass, and President Streets," reprinted in *The Eastern Parkway and Boulevard, in the City of Brooklyn* (New York: n.p., 1873), 25.

4. Blackmar, "Housing and Property Relations," 333–34; *Superintendent Reports* (1867), 279.

5. John F. Dillon, *Commentaries on the Law of Municipal Corporations,* 5th ed. (Boston: Little, Brown, 1911), II, 94; John Duffy, *A History of Public Health in New York City,* Volume I: *1625–1866* (New York: Russell Sage Foundation, 1968), 383. For the legal history behind the nineteenth-century redefinition of cities as creatures of the sovereign state, see Gerald E. Frug, "The City as a Legal Concept," *Harvard Law Review* 93 (1980), especially 1095–1120; and Hendrik Hartog, *Public Property and Private Power: The Corporation of the City of New York in American Law, 1730–1870* (Chapel Hill: University of North Carolina Press, 1983).

6. For the history of building law in New York, see John P. Comer, *New York City Building Controls, 1800–1941* (New York: Columbia University Press, 1942), 8–22. On the modernization of fire fighting, see Eugene Moehring, *Public Works and the Patterns of Urban Real Estate Growth In Manhattan, 1835–1894* (New York: Arno, 1981), 164–76; and Richard Calhoun, "New York City Fire Department Reorganization, 1865–1870," *New-York Historical Society Quarterly* 60 (1976): 6–34.

7. Dillon, *Treatise on the Law of Municipal Corporations* (Chicago, 1890), 503, 520; U.S. Senate, Select Committee on Relations Between Labor and Capital, *Report . . .* (Washington, D.C.: U.S. Government Printing Office, 1885), I, 781, testimony of Thomas McGuire. For glimpses of the campaign to regulate street activity, see *Harper's Weekly* (January 30, 1869); "The Sidewalk Trade," New York *Times* (August 25, 1867); "Sidewalk Nuisances and Obstructions," ibid. (March 31, 1869); and "Street Obstructions," ibid. (August 10, 1998). See also the discussion of street life in Chapter 5.

8. For the genesis and activities of the Metropolitan Board of Health, see *RERBG* (October 30, 1869); Duffy, *Public Health,* I, 540–71, and *Public Health,* II (New York: Russell Sage Foundation, 1974), 1–47, 58, 128–32, 220–29; and Charles E. Rosenberg, *The Cholera Years: The United States in 1832, 1849, and 1866* (Chicago: University of Chicago Press, 1962), 175–212.

9. *Harper's Weekly* (February 24, 1872). For the role of volunteer fire companies in antebellum politics, see Amy Bridges, *A City in the Republic: Antebellum New York and the Origins of Machine Politics* (New York: Cambridge University Press, 1984), 73–76; and Sean Wilentz, *Chants Democratic: New York City and the Rise of the American Working Class, 1788–1850* (New York: Oxford University Press, 1984), 259–63.

10. Dr. Ezra Pulling, "Report of the Fourth Sanitary Inspection District," in CA, *Report . . . upon the Sanitary Conditions of the City* (New York: D. Appleton, 1865), 64–65. Such epidemiological rhetoric runs throughout Victorian urban reform; see, for instance, CLB, *The Dangerous Classes of New York, and Twenty Years' Work among Them* (New York: Wynkoop and Hallenbeck, 1872), 26: "The abolishing of one of these centres of poverty and crime [through slum clearance] is somewhat like withdrawing the virus from [a] diseased limb."

For scholarly accounts of reform activity leading up to the tenement law of 1867, see Roy Lubove, *The Progressives and the Slums: Tenement House Reform in New York City, 1890–1917* (Pittsburgh, Pa.: University of Pittsburgh Press, 1962), 1–23; James Ford, *Slums and Housing, with Special Reference to New York City* (Cambridge, Mass.: Harvard University Press, 1936), I, 72–149; Richard Plunz, *A History of Housing in New York City: Dwelling Type and Social Change in the American Metropolis* (New York: Columbia University Press, 1990), 1–21.

11. The provisions of the law and the health board's enforcement efforts are discussed in Lawrence Veiller, "Tenement House Reform in New York, 1834–1900," in Robert W. DeForest and Lawrence Veiller (eds.), *The Tenement House Problem* (New York: Macmillan, 1903), 94–97; Ford, *Slums and Housing*, I, 154–55; Lubove, *Progressives and the Slums*, 25–28; and Duffy, *Public Health*, II, 221–25.

12. U.S. Senate, Select Committee on Relations Between Labor and Capital, *Report*, I, 848 (testimony of Robert Blissert); Joseph Haight, President of the Real Estate Owners' Association, quoted in *RERBG* (January 14, 1871), 17. On the weakness of the 1867 act, see Lubove, *Progressives and the Slums*, 26–27; Ford, *Slums and Housing*, II, 155; and Duffy, *Public Health*, II, 27 and, more generally, 48–90.

13. New York *Times* (February 11, 1868) ("demagoguery"); *Commercial and Financial Chronicle* (July 14, 1877); John A. Dix, quoted in Charles Z. Lincoln, *Messages of the Governors of New York State* (Albany: J. B. Lyon, 1909), VI, 689. More than fifty proposals for development franchises were presented to the Dock Department in its 1870 hearings; see *Public Meetings of the Department of Docks to Hear Persons Interested in Improving the River Front* (New York: n.p., 1870). For the franchise of the Vanderbilt-allied New York Warehouse and Railway Company, see *RERBG* (February 22, 1873); and "The Belt Line Question," *Commercial and Financial Chronicle* (May 17, 1873).

14. *Report of the Committee on Wharves and Piers, Appointed at a Public Meeting of Merchants . . .* (New York: n.p., 1868) details the waterfront commission proposed by the association and other mercantile groups.

15. New York *Times* (February 16, 1868). On the creation and powers of the Department of Docks, see ibid. (February 11 and 21, April 14 and 22, 1870); New York *Evening Post*, "The Department of Docks," quoted in *Address of the Citizens' Association of New York to the Public* (New York: Citizens' Association, 1871), 23–25; R.A.C. Smith, *The Commerce and Other Business of the Waterways of . . . New York . . .* (New York: n.p., 1912), 56; Alexander B. Callow, Jr., *The Tweed Ring* (New York: Oxford University Press, 1965), 225–28; Seymour Mandelbaum, *Boss Tweed's New York* (New York: J. Wiley, 1965), 63–64, 71–72.

16. On the policies of the Dock Board, see *Public Meetings of the Department of Docks*; New York *Times* (July 5 and November 21, 1871); Moehring, *Public Works*, 102–4.

17. Mayor William Havemeyer, "Annual Message . . . to the Common Council," *Documents of the Board of Aldermen of the City of New York* (New York: The Board, 1874), I, 18; William Nelson Black, *Storage and Transportation in the Port of New York* (New York: G. P. Putnam's Sons, 1884), 11–12. On the halting progress of waterfront improvements, see the *Annual Reports* of the Department of Docks (1874–80), as well as Mandelbaum, *Boss Tweed's New York*, 101, 102.

18. Andrew Jackson Downing, "The New-York Park," *The Horticulturalist* 8 (August 1851): 348–49; see also ibid., 3 (October 1848): 153–58. For an overview of Downing's architectural theories and influence, see David Schuyler, *Apostle of Taste: Andrew Jackson Downing, 1815–1852* (Baltimore: Johns Hopkins University Press, 1996). For the early agitation on behalf of a New York park, see Schuyler, *The New Urban Landscape: The Redefinition of City Form in Nineteenth-Century America* (Baltimore: Johns Hopkins University Press, 1986), 59–76; and Roy Rosenzweig and Elizabeth Blackmar, *The Park and the People: A History of Central Park* (Ithaca, N.Y.: Cornell University Press, 1992), 15–36.

19. For the role of Olmsted's social and literary connections in winning the superintendent's post, see *FLOP* III, 1–2, 85–88, 93n; and Laura Wood Roper, *FLO: A Biography of Frederick Law Olmsted* (Baltimore: Johns Hopkins University Press, 1973), 124–29. For the meeting of Olmsted and Vaux at Downing's house, see *FLOP* III, 65.

20. The political infighting over the location and control of the New York park is masterfully reconstructed in Rosenzweig and Blackmar, *Park and the People*, 37–58. See also *FLOP* III, 13–14, 83–84, 90n–92n; and Roper, *FLO*, 126–28.

21. For biographical sketches of the eleven commissioners, see *FLOP* III, 81n, 103n; and Rosenzweig and Blackmar, *Park and the People*, 97–99.

22. On the minority's effort to defeat the Greensward Plan, see BCCP, *Minutes of Proceedings . . . for the Year Ending April 30, 1858* (1858), 187–93; on Dillon's effort to amend the plan, see FLO to BCCP (May 31, 1858), in *FLOP* III, 193–96, and Rosenzweig and Blackmar, *Park and the People*, 142–49; for conflict over contract bidding, see ibid., 154–58; for the state legislative investigation, see ibid., 189.

23. On Green's legal, political, and administrative career, see John Foord, *The Life and Public Services of Andrew Haswell Green* (Garden City, N.Y.: Doubleday, Page, 1913), 26–35; David Hammack, "Comprehensive Planning Before the Comprehensive Plan: A New Look at the Nineteenth Century American City," in Daniel Schaffer (ed.), *Two Centuries of American Planning* (Baltimore: Johns Hopkins University Press, 1988); Hammack, *Power and Society: Greater New York at the Turn of the Century* (New York: Russell Sage Foundation, 1982), 189–91; and *FLOP* III, 55–56. On Green's vexed relationship with Olmsted and Vaux, see ibid., 30–31, 34–35, 37–38, 46n, 56–59; and Roper, *FLO*, 145–46, 154–55. On Green's support for Olmsted's appointment and the Greensward Plan, see *FLOP* III, 26–27, 55, 80; on his budgetary conflicts with Olmsted, see ibid., 284–85, 293–94, 145–46.

24. See Rosenzweig and Blackmar, *Park and the People*, 95–120; BCCP, *Minutes of Proceedings* (1858), 187–93.

25. Olmsted and Vaux, "A Review of Recent Changes . . . in the Plans of the Central Park," BDPP, *Second Annual Report* (1872), reprinted in Frederick Law Olmsted, Jr., and Theodora Kimball (eds.), *Forty Years of Landscape Architecture: Central Park* (Cambridge, Mass.: MIT Press, 1973), 249; Frederick Law Olmsted, *Public Parks and the Enlargement of Towns* (Boston: American Social Science Association, 1870), 31. For scholarship on the design and ideology of Central Park, see especially Schuyler, *New Urban Landscape*, 59–146; Geoffrey Blodgett, "Frederick Law Olmsted: Landscape Architecture as Conservative Reform," *Journal of American History* 62 (March 1976) 869–89; and Rosenzweig and Blackmar, *Park and the People*, 121–49.

26. FLO, *Public Parks*, 4, 10, 14–15.

27. Ibid., 11.

28. Olmsted and Vaux, "A Review of Recent Changes," 249; BCCP, *Tenth Annual Report* (1867), 31; BCPP, *Ninth Annual Report* (1869), 261. The notion of public parks as the "lungs of the city" runs throughout nineteenth-century park and sanitary reform; see, for instance, "The Lungs of London," *Blackwood's Magazine* (August 1839), 212–18. For Walter Benjamin's concept of "shock" as the definitive, daily experience of modern social life, see his essay "On Some Motifs in Baudelaire," in *Illuminations* (New York: Schocken Books, 1970), 157–202.

29, Olmsted and Vaux, "A Review of Recent Changes," 249, 250; Olmsted, "Applications for Appropriations of Park Ground," BDPP Document No. 58 (1874), reprinted in Olmsted, Jr., and Kimball (eds.), *Forty Years*, 426.

30. Olmsted and Vaux, "A Review of Recent Changes," 252.

31. BCCP, *Seventh Annual Report* (1864), 37. For the designers' efforts to suppress rival forms of recreation, see "Ordinances Applicable to the Ordinary Use of the Central Park" (1873), "Applications for Appropriations of Park Ground" (1874), and "Reasons Against Speeding Track in Central Park" (1890), in Olmsted, Jr., and Kimball (eds.), *Forty Years*, 464–65, 421–23, 524–29.

32. Olmsted and Vaux, "Report of the Landscape Architects," in BCPP, *Sixth Annual Report* (1866), 94. For Olmsted's contrast of "receptive" and "exertive" recreation, see *Public Parks and the Enlargement of Towns*, 17–24.

33. Olmsted and Vaux, "A Review of Recent Changes," 258.

34. "Greensward," in *FLOP* III, 122.

35. Ibid., 126. On the importance of promenading to both bourgeois public culture and Central Park, see David Scobey, "Anatomy of the Promenade: The Politics of Bourgeois Sociability in Nineteenth-Century New York," *Social History* 17 (May 1992), especially 208–14; and Rosenzweig and Blackmar, *Park and the People*, 211–25.

36. George Templeton Strong, *The Diary of George Templeton Strong*, ed. Allan Nevins and Milton Halsey Thomas (New York: Macmillan, 1952), III, 567 (March 21, 1865); Junius Henri Browne, *The Great Metropolis* (Hartford, Conn.: American Publishing, 1869), 124. Strong notes accidentally meeting his wife on her way to the Park in *Diary*, III, 106 (March 4, 1861). For the daily volume of carriages, see *The New York Coach-Maker's Magazine* 11 (September 1869): 63.

37. AHG, "Notes on the Educational Department of the Park," in BCCP, *Eleventh Annual Report* (1868), 125. For Green's role in founding the Zoo and other tutelary institutions, see Foord, *Life and Public Services*, 203–17. Although Olmsted and Vaux objected to the erection of educational and scientific institutions within the park grounds, they supported the notion of a park's educative function and advocated siting public educational and cultural institutions along the bordering avenues; see, for instance, their 1866 "Preliminary Report" to the BCPP, in Fein (ed.), *Landscape into Cityscape*, 123–26.

38. Olmsted, *Public Parks*, 18, 21; *RERBG* (August 22, 1868). On the "Children's District" in the lower park, see Olmsted and Vaux, "A Review of Recent Changes," 242–45.

39. Olmsted, *Public Parks*, 18.

40. FLO to BCCP, May 31, 1858, in *FLOP* III, 193–96; on wealthy carriage users at the Saturday afternoon band concerts, see Rosenzweig and Blackmar, *Park and the People*, 228–29.

41. For Olmsted's evaluation of his role as superintendent, see FLO to CV, November 26, 1863, in *FLOP* IV, 144–55. (It was this letter differentiating each partner's contribution to the success of Central Park—and privileging Olmsted's administration of public use—that lay behind Vaux's bitter jibe at "Frederick the Great, Prince of the Park Police," which I discuss in Chapters 1 and 6.) For rules of demeanor and use in Central Park, see the sources cited in note 31, as well as "Regulations for the Use of Central Park," in *FLOP* III, 279.

42. FLO, "Report . . . Relative to the Police Force," BDPP Document No. 41 (1872), 9. On the management of the Park Keepers, see "Rules and Conditions of Service of the Central Park Keepers" (March 12, 1859), in *FLOP* III, 219–21; "Notice Posted in Keepers' Room, Central Park," in ibid., 279; "Letter as to the Policing of the Park" (1860), in Olmsted, Jr., and Kimball, *Forty Years*, 439–41; "Instructions to the Keepers of the Central Park," in ibid., 444–65; and "Report on Recent Changes in Management of the Keepers' Force," in ibid., 466–71.

43. Lawrence Levine, *Highbrow Lowbrow: The Emergence of Cultural Hierarchy in America* (Cambridge, Mass.: Harvard University Press, 1988), 183, 186, 202–3, similarly views Central Park as a key site for the emergence of cultural hierarchy and the assertion of bourgeois cultural authority.

44. BCPP, *First Annual Report* (1861), 9–10. For another instance of this pecuniary valuation of the park, see BCPP, *Seventh Annual Report*, 124.

45. My understanding of the shift from park making to urban design has been enriched by Schuyler, *New Urban Landscape*; Fein, introduction to *Landscape into Cityscape*, 1–42; and Robert Foglesong, *Planning the Capitalist City: The Colonial Era to the 1920s* (Princeton, N.J.: Princeton University Press, 1986), 99–123.

46. Olmsted and Vaux, "Preliminary Report," in Fein (ed.), *Landscape into Cityscape*, 122–27.

47. The "parkway neighborhood" is described and theorized in Olmsted and Vaux, "Report of the Landscape Architects," in ibid., 129–64; quotations are from 132, 160, 159, 155, 163, 150, 157. See also *The Eastern Parkway* and David Schuyler, *New Urban Landscape*, 126–46.

48. BCPP, *Ninth Annual Report* (1869), 272; Olmsted and Vaux, "Report of the Landscape Architects," in Fein (ed.), *Landscape into Cityscape*, 154–55.

49. See Olmsted and Vaux, "Report of the Landscape Architects," especially 149–53, 157–62.

50. For the powers granted to the Prospect Park commission, see "An Act to Open and Widen Portions of Sackett, Douglass, and President Streets . . . ," reprinted in *The Eastern Parkway*, 24–27.

51. For the expansion of the Central Park board's duties, see BCCP, *Ninth Annual Report* (1866), 52–60, 115–18; AHG, "Communication . . . Relative to the Laying Out of the Island Above 155th Street . . . , and Other Subjects," BCCP, *Tenth Annual Report* (1866), 100–148; AHG, "Communication . . . Relative to Westchester County . . . ," BCCP, *Thirteenth Annual Report* (1869), 148–63; AHG, "Communication . . . on the Subject of Improvements in Westchester County," BCCP, *Fourteenth Annual Report* (1870), 37–56; address of H. B. Bacon, reprinted in WSA, *Proceedings of Six Public Meetings . . .* (1871), meeting of March 8, 1871, 41–42; and Foord, *Life and Public Services*, 204–9.

52. *RERBG* (January 8, 1870). The Central Park commission never did gain control of Staten Island's development, but a few months after this column, the state legislature appointed an "improvement commission" to guide the residential, transit, and sanitary development of the island. Among the commissioners were the noted architect Henry Hobson Richardson, sanitarian Elisha Harris, and Olmsted; for their report, see note 58.

53. AHG, "Communication . . . Relative to the Laying Out of the Island," 126–27, and "Communication . . . Relative to Westchester County," 160. For a useful overview of Green's ideas as a planner, see Hammack, "Comprehensive Planning."

54. Green, "Communication . . . Relative to the Laying Out of the Island," 148, 126, 142, 147.

55. *RERBG* (February 20, 1869, and December 19, 1868). For uptown landowners' support for the extension of the Central Park board's powers, see ibid. (May 4 and October 31, 1868), as well as Olmsted, *Public Parks*, 35–36.

56. For the Department of Public Parks' activism on the uptown periphery, see the New York *Times* (February 12, 1872); and AHG, *Public Improvements in the City of New York* (New York: n.p., 1874), 7–14.

57. On Olmsted and Vaux's marginalization by both the Green-led Board of Commissioners of Central Park and the Sweeney-led Department of Public Parks, see *FLOP* VI, 38–39, 560n; and Rosenzweig and Blackmar, *Park and the People*, 269–73. On Riverside, Illinois, see Olmsted, Vaux and Co., "Preliminary Report upon the Proposed Suburban Village at Riverside, Near Chicago" (1869), reprinted in *FLOP* VI, 273–90; Roper, *FLO*, 322–24; and Schuyler, *New Urban Landscape*, 162–67. For other planned suburbs designed by the partners, see "Prospectus of the New Suburban District of Tarrytown Heights," in *FLOP* VI, 503–19.

58. FLO et al., *Report to the Staten Island Improvement Commission of a Preliminary Scheme of Improvement* (1871), reprinted in Fein (ed.), *Landscape into Cityscape*, 183, 205, 197.

59. On Olmsted's return to Central Park and the dissolution of the partnership with Vaux, see Roper, *FLO*, 341–43; *FLOP* VI, 37–45. On the design for Riverside Drive, see "Report of the Landscape Architect on Riverside Park and Avenue," in ibid., 596–99.

60. Strong, *Diary*, IV, 361; "Rapid Transit and Working Men," New York *Times* (April 2, 1873).

61. E. B. Freeland, "The Great Riot," *Continental Monthly* 4 (1863): 308; CA, *Sanitary Conditions*, lxxiv; [Godkin,] "The Future of Great Cities," *The Nation* (February 22, 1879); CLB, *The Dangerous Classes of New York, and Twenty Years' Work among Them* (New York: Wynkoop and Hallenbeck, 1872) 25, 29.

62. "Overcrowding," New York *Times* (April 17, 1875).

63. FLO, *Public Parks*, 21.

64. FLO to Edward Everett Hale (October 21, 1869), quoted in Robert Fishman, *Bourgeois Utopias: The Rise and Fall of Suburbia* (New York: Basic Books, 1987), 129; CLB, *Dangerous Classes*, 58–59; *RERBG* 1 (April 11, 1868); Charles O'Conor, open letter to a public meeting in support of transit improvements (June 5, 1877), quoted in *Rapid Transit Meeting* (1877), 20–21.

65. FLO to Henry H. Elliott (August 27, 1860), in *FLOP* III, 264, 265; FLO et al., *Report to the Staten Island . . .* , in Fein (ed.), *Landscape into Cityscape*, 204, 243; Olmsted and Vaux, *Report . . . to the President of . . . Prospect Park . . .* (1868), in ibid., 161; "An Act to Open and Widen Portions of Sackett, Douglass, and President Streets. . . . ," reprinted in *The Eastern Parkway*, 25.

Chapter 8

1. Franklin Sanborn, *Journal of Social Science* 8 (May 1876): 23, quoted in Thomas L. Haskell, *The Emergence of Professional Social Science: The American Social Science Association and the Nineteenth Century Crisis of Authority* (Urbana: University of Illinois Press, 1977), 132. See also Morton Keller, *Affairs of State: Public Life in Late Nineteenth Century America* (Cambridge, Mass.: Harvard University Press, 1977); and Stephen Skowronek, *Building a New American State: The Expansion of National Administrative Capacities, 1877–1920* (New York: Cambridge University Press, 1982).

2. WRM, "The Financial Resources of New York," *North American Review* 127 (1878): 432, 430.

3. See Eric Foner, *Reconstruction: America's Unfinished Revolution, 1863–1877* (New York: Harper and Row, 1988), 461–88.

4. On Olmsted's involvement with the Sea Islands emancipation initiatives, see Laura Wood Roper, *FLO: A Biography of Frederick Law Olmsted* (Baltimore: Johns Hopkins University Press, 1973), 178–89; and *FLOP* IV, 20–26. On his support for the Freedmen's Bureau, see Roper, *FLO*, 298.

5. For the eruption of labor and racial violence in South Carolina, see Foner, *Reconstruction*, 570–75, and Foner, *Nothing but Freedom: Emancipation and Its Legacy* (Baton Rouge: Louisiana State University Press, 1983), 74–110.

6. George Templeton Strong, *The Diary of George Templeton Strong*, ed. Allan Nevins and Milton Halsey Thomas (New York: Macmillan, 1952), IV, 538 (September 16, 1874). For the evolution of Thomas Nast's treatment of African Americans, see Morton Keller, *The Art and Politics of Thomas Nast* (New York: Oxford University Press, 1968). For changes in the intellectual cli-

mate among northern elites that contributed to growing disillusionment with Southern Reconstruction and racial equality, see Foner, *Reconstruction*, 488–534; George M. Fredrickson, *The Inner Civil War: Northern Intellectuals and the Crisis of the Union* (New York: Harper and Row, 1965), 183–216; and John G. Sproat, *"The Best Men": Liberal Reformers in the Gilded Age* (New York: Oxford University Press, 1982).

7. Strong, *Diary*, IV, 411 (February 3, 1872). For Green's career as city comptroller, see Seymour Mandelbaum, *Boss Tweed's New York* (New York: J. Wiley, 1965), 87–113; John Foord, *The Life and Public Services of Andrew Haswell Green* (New York: Doubleday, Page, 1913), 114–61.

8. See David Schuyler, *The New Urban Landscape: The Redefinition of City Form in Nineteenth-Century America* (Baltimore: Johns Hopkins University Press, 1986); Norman T. Newton, *Design on the Land: The Development of Landscape Architecture* (Cambridge, Mass.: Harvard University Press, 1971).

9. See Chapter 7, notes 50 and 51 for citations of these planning documents.

10. See, for instance, Mel Scott, *American City Planning* (Berkeley: University of California Press, 1969); Anthony Sutcliffe, *Towards the Planned City: Germany, Britain, the United States, and France, 1780–1914* (New York: St. Martin's Press, 1981); and Roy Lubove, *The Progressives and the Slums: Tenement House Reform in New York City, 1890–1917* (Pittsburgh, Pa.: University of Pittsburgh Press, 1962).

11. This historiographical shift is discussed and documented in the Introduction.

12. On the fate of the Staten Island plan, see Roper, *FLO*, 324–26; and Schuyler, *New Urban Landscape*, 177–79. For Olmsted's and Vaux's discontents with the planning and financing process for Brooklyn, see ibid., 127–28.

13. FLO letter to Junius Henri Browne, quoted in Roper, *FLO*, 351; Frederick Law Olmsted, "The Spoils of the Park," in Albert Fein (ed.), *Landscape into Cityscape: Frederick Law Olmsted's Plans for a Greater New York* (Ithaca, N.Y.: Cornell University Press, 1967), 392. For problems on Riverside Drive, see Roper, *FLO*, 356.

14. For narrative and analytical overviews of the fall of Tweed, see Alexander B. Callow, Jr., *The Tweed Ring* (New York: Oxford University Press, 1965), 258–78; Mandelbaum, *Boss Tweed's New York*, 76–86; and Iver Bernstein, *The New York City Draft Riots: Their Significance for American Society and Politics in the Age of the Civil War* (New York: Oxford University Press, 1990), 195–236.

15. "The Growth of New York," New York *Times* (January 27, 1877). On the gentry's turn away from public improvements, see "How to Keep Down the City Debt," ibid. (March 23, 1875); and Mandelbaum, *Boss Tweed's New York*, 87–130.

16. AHG, *Public Improvements in the City of New York* (New York: n.p., 1874), 10, 27–28. See also Foord, *Life and Public Services*, 117–25; and Roper, *FLO*, 352–53.

17. Real Estate Record Association, *A History of Real Estate, Building, and Architecture in New York City during the Last Quarter of a Century* (New York: Record and Guide, 1898), 75; Edward Dana Durand, *The Finances of New York* (New York: Macmillan, 1898) 376, 383.

18. *Commercial and Financial Chronicle* (March 31, 1877), 284–85; George H. Andrews, *Twelve Letters on the Future of New York* (1877). For an overview of legal and political movements for debt limitation in the late nineteenth century, see Keller, *Affairs of State*, 110–21; and John F. Dillon, *Commentaries on the Law of Municipal Corporations*, 1st ed. (Boston: Little, Brown, 1872), which codified debt restriction as the juridical norm for urban fiscal policy.

19. Annual message, Mayor William Havemeyer, *Documents of the Board of Aldermen of the City of New York* (New York: The Board, 1873), Part I; Strong, *Diary*, IV, 419.

20. On the Charter of 1873, see Mandelbaum, *Boss Tweed's New York*, 105–7; on Tilden's role in the anti-Tweed crusade, see Callow, *Tweed Ring*, 254; on the Tilden Commission, see Mandelbaum, *Boss Tweed's New York*, 169–73.

21. *Commercial and Financial Chronicle* (March 31, 1877), 284–85. See also ibid. (April 14, 1877), 332–33. E. L. Godkin played an especially influential role on the commission; for his views on municipal governance, see "The Bottom of the Great City Difficulty," *The Nation* (September 7, 1871), 157–59; and "Municipal Government," ibid. (September 7, 1871), 188–89.

22. The best accounts of these political and fiscal changes are David C. Hammack, *Power and Society: Greater New York at the Turn of the Century* (New York: Russell Sage Foundation, 1982), 131–39, and Mandelbaum, *Boss Tweed's New York*, 87–140.

23. Henry Bellows, public speech against aid to sectarian schools, quoted in Michael Gordon, "Studies in Irish and Irish-American Thought and Behavior in Gilded Age New York City" (Ph.D. dissertation, University of Rochester, 1977), 411–12. For the larger story of elite retrenchment in Gilded Age politics, see Sproat, *"The Best Men"*; Keller, *Affairs of State;* and Fredrickson, *Inner Civil War.*

24. *RERBG* Supplement (June 19, 1875), 1.

25. For an overview of this episode, see Roper, *FLO*, 344–62.

26. For Green's battle with Martin over public workers' wages, see Mandelbaum, *Boss Tweed's New York*, 126–27. Martin resisted Comptroller Green's efforts to cut pay rates by 20 percent. Seeking to enlist New York labor in his progrowth agenda, the parks commissioner called for rescission of the pay cut and urged City Hall to ameliorate the hard times by *exceeding* the market rate for day laborers. In response, a group of elite petitioners obtained a hearing to have Martin and Joseph O'Donohue, his ally on the board, impeached for official turpitude.

27. For Green's attack on Olmsted, see Roper, *FLO*, 352. Olmsted ultimately won a lawsuit against the comptroller securing his position with the Parks Department and collecting a small amount of unpaid salary from the city government.

28. The reports are: FLO and J.J.R. Croes, "Preliminary Report of the Landscape Architect and the Civil and Topographical Engineer, upon the Laying Out of the Twenty-third and Twenty-fourth Wards," in Fein (ed.), *Landscape into Cityscape*; "Report . . . Accompanying a Plan for Laying Out That Part of the Twenty-fourth Ward Lying West of the Riverdale Road," in ibid.; "Communication . . . in Relation to the Proposed Plan for Laying Out the Central District . . . ," Document No. 76, BDPP, *Documents*; and "Report . . . Accompanying a Plan for Local Steam Transit Routes . . . ," in Fein (ed.), *Landscape into Cityscape*.

29. FLO and Croes, "Preliminary Report," 352; "Report . . . West of the Riverdale Road," 366.

30. Schuyler, *New Urban Landscape*, 179; FLO and Croes, "Report . . . West of the Riverdale Road," 362.

31. For Olmsted's relationship with Howard Martin, see *FLOP* III, 39; *FLOP* V, 14–15, 141, 142. For an overview of Olmsted's personal and political conflicts with Green, see Roper, *FLO*, 145–46, 154–55, 352–56; *FLOP* III, 55–58.

32. WRM, "Report . . . upon the Subject of Laying Out the Twenty-third and Twenty-fourth Wards," Document No. 73, BDPP, *Documents*, 25; FLO and Croes, "Preliminary Report," 352.

33. New York *Times* (February 25, 1877); Roper, *FLO*, 356.

34. See Roper, *FLO*, 360–62.

35. For the petition and public agitation on Olmsted's behalf, see "MR. FRED. LAW OLMSTED/A PUBLIC PROTEST . . . ," reprinted in Frederick Law Olmsted, Jr., and Theodora Kimball

(eds.), *Forty Years of Landscape Architecture: Central Park* (Boston: MIT Press, 1973), 113; and Roper, *FLO*, 360–61.

36. For Olmsted's relocation to the Boston area, see Roper, *FLO*, 363–405. For his landscape work in that city, see especially Cynthia Zaitzevsky, *Frederick Law Olmsted and the Boston Park System* (Cambridge, Mass.: Harvard University Press, 1992).

37. Assessed property values increased 48.3 percent during the 1880s and 27.0 percent in the 1870s; see New York City Committee on Plan and Survey, *The Finances and Financial Administration of New York City* (New York: Columbia University Press, 1928), 33. For annual rates of new buildings, see Real Estate Record Association, *History of Real Estate*, 159. For the development of the upper West Side, see "The Great Building Movement on the West Side," *RERBG* (August 29, 1885); Real Estate Record Association, *History of Real Estate*, 56; and M. Christine Boyer, *Manhattan Manners: Architecture and Style, 1850–1900* (New York: Rizzoli, 1985), 193–221.

38. For the growth of rapid transit in New York, see Charles W. Cheape, *Moving the Masses: Urban Public Transit in New York, Boston, and Philadelphia, 1880–1912* (Cambridge, Mass.: Harvard University Press, 1980); and James Blaine Walker, *Fifty Years of Rapid Transit, 1864–1917* (New York: Law Printing, 1918). For the completion of Morningside and Riverside parks, see Boyer, *Manhattan Manners*, 18–21. On the development of Morningside Heights as an educational and civic acropolis, see Robert A.M. Stern, Gregory Gilmartin, and John Massengale, *New York 1900: Metropolitan Architecture and Urbanism, 1890–1915* (New York: Rizzoli, 1983), 396–419.

39. Hammack, *Power and Society*, 185–229, offers an illuminating analysis of the consolidation of Greater New York. For Green's leadership, see also Foord, *Life and Public Services*, 174–202.

40. William Dean Howells, *A Hazard of New Fortunes*, 47. This and subsequent page citations are from the Signet paperback edition.

41. Howells, *Hazard*, 58, 67. For the rise of apartment living in New York and its effect on cultural attitudes toward urban domesticity, see Elizabeth Cromley, *Alone Together: A History of New York's Early Apartments* (Ithaca, N.Y.: Cornell University Press, 1990); as well as Elizabeth Hawes, *New York, New York: How the Apartment House Transformed the Life of the City, 1869–1930* (New York: Knopf, 1993).

42. Jacob A. Riis, *How the Other Half Lives: Studies among the Tenements of New York* (1890); the quotation is from page 1 of the Dover edition. For new currents in social reform and urban oversight, see Paul Boyer, *Urban Masses and Moral Order in America, 1820–1920* (Cambridge, Mass.: Harvard University Press, 1978); and Maren Stange, *Symbols of Ideal Life: Social Documentary Photography in America, 1890–1950* (New York: Cambridge University Press, 1989).

43. See Lubove, *The Progressives and the Slums*; James Ford, *Slums and Housing, with Special Reference to New York City* (Cambridge, Mass.: Harvard University Press, 1936); John Duffy, *A History of Public Health in New York City*, Volume II (New York: Russell Sage Foundation, 1974); and Dominick Cavallo, *Muscles and Morals: Organized Playgrounds and Urban Reform, 1880–1920* (Philadelphia: Temple University Press, 1981).

Index

Page numbers in italics refer to illustrations; page numbers in boldface refer to the appendix tables.